THE
FIRST
BLACK ACTORS
ON THE
GREAT WHITE WAY

THE
FIRST
BLACK ACTORS
ON THE
GREAT WHITE
WAY

SUSAN CURTIS

University of Missouri Press • COLUMBIA AND LONDON

Copyright © 1998 by
The Curators of the University of Missouri
University of Missouri Press, Columbia, Missouri 65201
Printed and bound in the United States of America
All rights reserved
5 4 3 2 1   02 01 00 99 98

Library of Congress Cataloging-in-Publication Data

Curtis, Susan, 1956–
   The first Black actors on the great white way / Susan Curtis.
    p. cm.
   Includes bibliographical references and index.
   ISBN 0-8262-1195-X (alk. paper)
   1. Afro-American theater—New York (State)—New York—
History—20th century.   2. Afro-American actors—United States—
Biography.   I. Title.
PN2270.A35C87   1998
792'.028'089607471—dc21   98-27203
                                                   CIP

Designer: Mindy Shouse
Typesetter: Bookcomp, Inc.
Printer and Binder: Edwards Brothers, Inc.
Typefaces: Minion and Copperplate Gothic

For Charlotte and Don

CONTENTS

PREFACE

ONE OF THE MORE interesting—and troubling—aspects of writing this book has been the response from family and friends to my working on such a project. Upon hearing me describe the story of the first black actors on Broadway, the listener invariably asked, with some hesitation, whether it was my place to write about the experiences of African Americans: "Do you think black people will object to a white woman writing their history?" The first time I was confronted with this question, I was taken aback. I had thought I was telling an inclusive story about "our" American cultural life in the twentieth century, not relating a moment in "their" history. I was tempted to chalk up the misgivings of my family and friends to a lack of familiarity with scholarly endeavor until I began to hear a related response from colleagues in history and American studies. They expressed surprise at my decision to follow up a book on turn-of-the-century Protestant thought and American culture with first a biography of Scott Joplin and now a study of black actors: "Oh, I didn't realize you had switched to African American history."

I allude to these comments not to disparage the people who made them but to present them as attitudes that deserve serious engagement. Implicit in both responses is a recognition that the color line persists as *the* problem of the twentieth century even as the twenty-first century is about to dawn. The question fundamentally asks who can or should narrate the experiences of particular groups in America, and it reflects a deepening skepticism about the possibility of understanding ever developing across the racial, ethnic, class, and gender lines that fracture this diverse population into competing social and political groups. The comment admits that it is possible for historians of one race to study and to write about the experiences of another, but it suggests that taking up African American history necessarily means abandoning the more general field of American cultural history. Both responses partake of an end-of-the-century concern with the problem of representation, and they raise important questions about what it means to be "American," how we as a nation talk to ourselves about ourselves, and the politics of historical writing.

As I hope this book will show, these concerns are not new. A century ago, men and women in the United States wrestled vigorously with the same matters of national identity. At a time not unlike our own, when immigrants arrived in record numbers at U.S. ports of entry, when violence and tension marked the relations between races, and when technological and economic change transformed daily lives at a dizzying pace, intellectuals, artists, social observers, and cultural commentators looked anxiously to the world of the arts and letters for some sign of a cultural expression that captured the meaning of being American. Many bemoaned the lack of a national school of music, the inferiority of American letters, as compared with European fiction, poetry, and drama, and the country's relative youth, which, they believed, delayed the emergence of an essential national character. As one after another aspiring artist took up the challenge of expressing the United States on canvas, in print, with steel and brick, or on stage, each encountered repeatedly the problem of representation. Whose voice best expressed the vision and concerns of a polyglot people? Which values, whose religion, what ideals defined the standard for American respectability, morality, and behavior? Was it possible to locate an American essence that transcended region and condition? *E pluribus unum* makes a nice motto for the national currency, but the quest for cultural unity has proven arduous and frustrating.

The First Black Actors on the Great White Way is the result of my interest in this important turn-of-the-century moment and of my desire to explore the nature and significance of the quest for representative American culture. Like many scholars in recent years, I was both inspired and challenged by the urgent call that went out in the 1980s from people like Thomas Bender and Linda Kerber to reconsider how we historians and American studies scholars imagine America. In 1986 Bender identified the need for a "new synthesis," which he saw as a project to craft narratives that explored relationships between particular communities and a national "public culture." He urged historians to tackle the immense task of making sense of the vast scholarship of the "new social history" by rewriting the narratives of national experience that would show how these differences affected the unfolding of American history. A couple of years later Kerber put the same point in a slightly different way, encouraging American studies scholars to make "diversity" the centerpiece of interdisciplinary research that would reenergize that field. These two pieces fired my imagination. To take part in this major rethinking of the narratives of American history demanded fresh approaches to the study of this nation's past, new questions, and untouched sources, and it promised to speak to issues of immediate social and political concern. My first effort along these lines was a combined biography of Scott Joplin and cultural history of ragtime, *Dancing to a Black Man's Tune.*

In the course of researching the life of the "King of Ragtime," I became intrigued by the writings of Lester A. Walton. As the drama editor of the *New York Age* for the years Joplin resided in New York, Walton provided important bits of information about the musician's activities and accomplishments, and he published a rare interview with the composer. But as I mined Walton's drama page for details of Joplin's life, I began to realize that Walton himself was an interesting figure. By studying his life, I could probe more deeply into the question of representation in multicultural America. He wrote explicitly about black entertainers' efforts to present black life on stage, and he commented occasionally on the "Americanness" of their performances. I wondered how his representation of America compared with that of other drama critics of the day. I decided to pursue a project I tentatively called "Representing America in Black and White."

That project evolved into this one the day I read Walton's lengthy comment on the production of Ridgely Torrence's three playlets, *The Rider of Dreams, Granny Maumee,* and *Simon, the Cyrenian.* Walton hailed the actors who performed these plays as the first black actors to appear on Broadway in serious dramas about black life. On a whim, I set aside the *New York Age* to see how—or if—the *New York Times* reviewed the plays. The *Times* had, indeed, run a review of the opening night's performance, but the plot summaries differed so dramatically from the ones provided by Walton that I scurried from one review to another and then to the works themselves to try to understand what the plays had been about. I quickly realized that I had stumbled upon a more focused way to approach the problem of representation. Here was a rich story of black and white artistic collaboration with multiple layers of meaning. My determination to peel back the layers has provided the driving force of this book.

A few facts had to be established at the outset. Who were Ridgely Torrence, the playwright; Robert Edmond Jones, the director; and Emilie Hapgood, the producer; and what prompted them to sponsor controversial dramas that imagined African American life as a serious subject for the American stage? Who were the actors? What experience had they gotten before appearing on Broadway, and why would they want to perform in this production? Where was the production staged, how long did it run, and who attended? Finally, I wanted to establish the history of these plays. Who had written about them in the years after 1917, and what did the writers say? Obtaining answers to these questions provided the stuff of the story. The greatest challenge came from deciding what the story means.

The story has proven to be several interlocking stories: one explains how a privileged white boy from Ohio decided to write dramas about black life; another traces the steps of African American actors from one side of the color line to the other; and a third recounts the struggle to "democratize" and "Americanize" theatrical productions in the United States, a struggle that pitted commercial interests against an artistic avant garde and forever transformed stage entertainment in America.

Two elements of this drama, however, presented particularly difficult challenges in the telling—the tale of those who reported and forgot this landmark theatrical event in 1917 and the significance of cross-race collaboration. At the same time, both matters strike at the heart of the meaning of this episode for Americans at the time and for those who read about it more than eight decades later. The first of these demanded a look at a part of the process of culture that should be self-evident but that frequently is given short shrift—namely, the way ideas and values implied by Torrence's dramas were received, reworked, and partially incorporated into popular thinking about race, America, and citizenship. By examining both the plot summaries and the evaluations of the actors' performances written by theater critics and other individuals in the audience, we have a chance to see what viewers made of the production before them. The playwright, actors, and director clearly made some statements about black life and race relations in the United States. Audience members absorbed the performances and then made other statements and crafted new narratives that emphasized some points over others, excluded details, and included comments extraneous to the action on stage. I became convinced as I sifted through these secondary narratives that they, in conjunction with the script, laid bare the process by which the boundary between the thinkable and the unimaginable is contested and by which the boundary is either reinforced or redrawn.

Although I do not consider myself a disciple of Victor Turner, I can see how my presentation of this aspect of the event falls rather neatly into Turner's categories for a "social drama." Black actors on a white stage representing their lives as quintessentially American represented a "breach" of theatrical and national conventions. The reviews of and editorials on the plays as well as the growing national self-consciousness in the discussion of the country's war aims defined the "crisis." In the "redressive" stage, various actions restored a sense of equilibrium—purposeful evasion, violent repression of African Americans, and a loud chorus claiming the right to define America in ways that ignored people of color—but these actions left room for some change, too. In the years immediately following the historic production of Torrence's plays, the once all-white theaters slowly opened their doors to black thespians and served as hosts to a small, but growing, number of race dramas in the 1920s and beyond.

In one sense the story is simple: the first black cast cracked the door for future black performers to gain entry to the American stage. In another sense, however, the story is complicated by the silence, evasion, and amnesia that eventually set in. Critics who raved about the production in April had forgotten about it by the time they recapped the season in August. Honors bestowed by George Jean Nathan on Inez Clough and Opal Cooper for their splendid performances had slipped the minds of Drama League members by 1920, when they honored Charles Gilpin as the first black actor to make his mark on Broadway. Except for studies of African Americans' contributions to American theater, most histories of the American stage fail to include the episode as a landmark event. Silence followed the initial clamor; short-term memory loss deepened into cultural amnesia. Both the silence and the forgetting demanded explanations.

Historians are not particularly well prepared to study such phenomena. Typically, we analyze articulation and memory rather than what was not said or not remembered. Thanks to semipermeable disciplinary boundaries in the 1990s, however, we can learn from psychologists and literary scholars who have ways of deciphering these lapses. I particularly benefited from Priscilla Wald's *Constituting Americans,* which combines the insights of Freud and Lacan with the methodology of literary scholarship to offer a model for reading between the lines of text, within the syntax, and against a broader cultural backdrop to explain gaps.

Armed with these insights, I reread the published comments of theater critics and examined the way they framed their narratives. When did they hesitate, breaking sentences with excessive dashes or qualifying their praise with hedging adjectives? When did they rely on the passive voice to avoid assigning responsibility? What did they include and what did they omit from their plot summaries? At what points did they express discomfort with the action on stage? I used the clues I found in their work to explain the silence and amnesia of the majority of white New York critics. As I show in chapter 5, all of this linguistic evidence points to some critics' difficulty affirming African Americans as American citizens and their unease with the implicit critique of American society contained in the plays.

A second strategy involved listening to the African American writers who *did* record their memories after 1917. They blamed the U.S. decision to enter

World War I for the demise of the plays. If they believed the coming of war had ended the run as well as the discussion of this production, then I assumed that the broader discourse on American war aims and the assembling of an army of citizens would help explain the inability or unwillingness on the part of white critics to remember the race dramas and the black actors. This research strategy resulted in a chapter on war in a book about theater, and I hope that reading these two conversations against one another reveals the ways a moment of heightened national self-consciousness produced a heightened racial self-consciousness. The resulting white national self-image proscribed all discussions of American culture.

The second matter—the meaning of cultural hybridity—also posed challenges. Acknowledging cross-race collaboration in the production of Torrence's dramas seemed essential. As recent scholarship has demonstrated, it is nearly impossible to discuss American culture without acknowledging the racial hybridity it represents. In a sense, this insistent scholarship offers an antidote to cultural amnesia. Susan Gubar's provocative *Racechanges* and Ann Douglas's *Terrible Honesty* stand out as excellent sources for seeing the ways American artists reached across various color lines to fashion works of art and literature that depended on a multiracial aesthetic for their form, nature, and, to a large degree, their success and appeal. Viewing American culture as a collaborative project strikes me as absolutely necessary and a perspective that should inform new research in the field. The kind of writing done by Gubar, Douglas, and others offers a way to answer the persistent call to fashion a new synthesis in American history that recognizes multicultural difference as well as the struggle to define the contours of national public culture.

While I agree that American culture, in general, and *Three Plays for a Negro Theater,* in particular, must be viewed as hybrid products, I think it is imperative to point out that cultural hybridity has not erased the color line, it has not led to social equality, and it has coexisted with appalling social, political, and economic injustice. As Michael Rogin has shown, for example, "racial masquerade" in twentieth-century films bought social inclusion for some at the expense of more profound marginalization for others. Likewise, as Eric Lott demonstrated, white Americans' appropriation of blackface minstrelsy and African American music must be seen as a form of "theft" as well as "love." However desirable cultural hybridity might be, it does not obviate the need for determined political action for social change, and it does not lead naturally to equality.

But the challenge goes deeper than one's optimism or pessimism about collaborative culture. No doubt those who celebrate the cultural elisions across racial lines would agree that this kind of cultural production has not resulted in equality. The difficulty for me was checking the urge to simplify these productions for the sake of analytical clarity. That is, if one insists upon a view of cross-race collaboration that is filled with contradictions and crosscurrents as well as some shared hopes, then hybrid cultural expressions cannot be reduced to a single message that audiences considered, embraced, rejected, or partially approved. That is why I maintain a distinction between the production and the responses to it. The fact that many white critics tended to understand the dramas in terms of familiar stereotypes and pervasive preconceptions of black life and art does not mean that that was the meaning of the plays, the intention of the collaborators, or the message that the show conveyed. Cultural expression and cultural consumption are not flip sides of a coin; rather they are two sites of the cultural production of meaning.

As I prepared these prefatory remarks, I reread the opening pages of *Towards the Abolition of Whiteness* by my friend Dave Roediger, and I was struck by his observation that "race may be more easily demystified on paper than disarmed in everyday life." The vast and rich scholarship on race in recent years, critics note, has not translated into greater understanding or improved race relations in the United States. Critiques from within the academy and from without, therefore, condemn as "irrelevant" efforts to understand and explain cleavages along race, class, and gender lines and to explore the constructedness of these categories. Speaking for myself, the disparity between scholarly discourse on race and persistent racial conflict signals the need for redoubled efforts in the classroom, in public forums, and in print—not retreating in despair or, worse, reinscribing the white experience in America as natural.

Moreover, I think the comments with which I opened this preface indicate that the scholarship of recent decades on race and its counterpart in the public arena—identity politics—has begun to bear fruit. The comments contain hints of what might well be called "double-consciousness," the term coined by W. E. B. Du Bois at the beginning of this century for the "sense of always looking at one's self through the eyes of others, of measuring one's soul by the tape of a world that looks on in amused contempt and pity." Recognizing that African American experience and history deserve respect and that whites may not do them justice points to an awareness of white consciousness having become doubled—white and American—instead of being the universal against which all others are judged. While that is not the same thing as viewing race as a social and cultural construct, it is an important step away from assuming white experience to be the norm, the mainstream, and the only experience worth chronicling. Perhaps the spreading of a more fully articulated consciousness of subject positions is the necessary and painful next step toward a world in which human consciousness transcends racial difference.

ACKNOWLEDGMENTS

THIS BOOK OWES its existence in large measure to support and assistance I received from people affiliated with Purdue University, where I teach U.S. History and American Studies. Although I have been working on the project on and off since 1994, the bulk of the research and writing took place in 1996 and 1997, thanks to a sabbatical granted by Purdue. Excused from the demands of classroom teaching and committee responsibilities, I traveled to Chicago, Washington, D. C., New York, Princeton, and Xenia, Ohio, in the summer and fall of 1996 and looked at a rich body of printed and archival material related to the plays, the American Stage, African American performance, and the First World War. A Faculty Incentive Grant awarded by the Purdue Research Foundation helped defray some of the expenses incurred in my research-related travel. In the spring and summer of 1997, I wrote the first draft of this book.

Long before I set out in earnest to research and write, I benefited greatly from friends and colleagues in the History Department and American Studies Program who listened to my ideas and who commented on various proposals and prospecti in which I began to formulate this project. I am particularly grateful to John Contreni, Nancy Gabin, Whitney Walton, Charles Cutter, and Harold Woodman, who offered insightful advice that sharpened the focus of this study. I also would like to acknowledge my indebtedness to Nancy Peterson in the English Department with whom I team-taught a course called "Contemporary Issues in American Studies" and from whom I learned a great deal. As we were preparing the syllabus, Nancy directed my attention to a number of scholarly works that deeply affected my thinking about interdisciplinarity, American history, and the writing of narratives about a multiracial, multicultural nation.

Graduate students in both History and American Studies played a part in this project of which they may be only dimly aware. Their own research projects, probing questions in and out of the classroom, and discussions of work in the field set a high standard of engagement that sent me back to the drawing board on more than one occasion. I especially want to thank the following students, with whom I have worked closely in the past few years and from whom I have learned so much: Anne Boyd, Tom Pendergast, Jake Jones, Rebecca Saulsbury, Robert Cousins, Dan Clark, Chris Elzey, Kelly Phillips, Scott Hoffman, Kevin Scott, and John Stauffer. Of these students, Anne Boyd and John Stauffer (who earned an M.A. at Purdue but completed the Ph.D. at Yale) took time away from their dissertation work and generously agreed to read a draft of this study. Their comments helped me tremendously.

As this project neared completion, Hal Woodman kindly agreed to read and comment on a draft of the manuscript. I thank him not only for posing pointed questions and offering a penetrating critique of my argument, which forced me to rethink some parts of the book, but also for being a great role model—a scholar, a colleague, and a friend. Thanks also to participants in the department's Cultural History Workshop who read and commented on the preface and chapter 1.

I received much-needed assistance, for which I am deeply grateful, from librarians and archivists at the institutions where I conducted research: the Schomburg Center for Research in Black Culture in New York, the newspaper reading room at Columbia University's Butler Library, the New York Public Library, the National Archives, the Moorland-Spingarn Research Center at Howard University, the Manuscript Division of the Library of Congress, the Chicago Historical Society, the Manuscript Division of Firestone Library at Princeton University, and the Greene County Room of the Public Library in Xenia, Ohio. I extend particular thanks to Diana Lachatanere at the Schomburg, who helped make my work there both enjoyable and productive, and to John Taylor at the National Archives, who helped me pinpoint the location of files pertinent to this study in the massive Record Group 165 on World War I.

I am delighted to work again with the University of Missouri Press. Beverly Jarrett is an author's dream editor, ever encouraging and supportive, and Sara Davis is in a class by herself as a copyeditor. The entire staff of the Press makes the final stages of bookmaking a rewarding and pleasant process rather than an ordeal to be endured. I also would like to thank the two anonymous readers whose suggestions and comments were most helpful.

I have incurred large professional debts in the course of working on this book, but without the love and support of my family I would not have been able to complete either the research or the writing. My husband, Charles Cutter, makes life and work adventures to be savored and shared. He held down the fort while I hit the dusty research trail, and he endured with grace and interest my excited reports on research findings and "dramatic readings" from the manuscript as it took shape. He arranged for us to spend six months in Spain, where I wrote without interruption while he continued work on a project on the eighteenth-century Spanish colonial world. Chuck not only read and commented on the entire manuscript, offering insightful observations and excellent stylistic suggestions, but he also helped me survive more than one computer-related disaster. But most of all, I thank Chuck for giving me each day the gift of himself—his intelligence, warmth, sense of humor, and obsession with making sense of the past. I have lost track of the boundaries between colleague, friend, and husband.

I want to thank other family members, too. One of Chuck's sisters, Carmen Cutter, and one of his brothers, Alex Cutter, shared their home in Arlington, Virginia, with me when I worked at the National Archives and at the Moorland- Spingarn Research Center. I thank them both for making my stay in the capital so pleasant and productive. I also want to thank my mother, Lieselotte Curtis, who offers moral support and unconditional love to all her children. This book is about remembering, so I would like to indulge in a few memories of my own. My father, George William Curtis, passed away nine years ago, but I will never forget what a terrific example of integrity he set for everyone who knew him. I miss his presence, but my memories of him sustain me with each passing year. My parents set high standards for their children, for which I am more grateful now, I suppose, than I was growing up. But as I look back on my childhood, I realize that they never expected more of my sister, brother, and me than they did of themselves.

One of the oldest shticks on stage, screen, and television is the comedy revolving around in-laws. It is my great fortune to have parents-in-law who bear no resemblance to the meddlesome, critical figures of that genre. Donald Cutter and Charlotte Lazear Cutter generously shared their apartment in Madrid with their son and me, and for several weeks we discussed current events, enjoyed one another's company, and feasted on strawberries! Don let me use his portable typewriter to pound out the first draft of this book, and both accepted with good humor the unsightly piles of notecards and the frequent disarray in the little bedroom I used for an office. As a small gesture of thanks for their constant, loving support, and with deep affection and great respect, I dedicate this book to them.

THE
FIRST
BLACK ACTORS
ON THE
GREAT WHITE WAY

OPENING NIGHT AND
THE MORNING AFTER

"This was a '*first night*' . . . and the few ifs and a good many buts to the contrary
notwithstanding, it was a great night, a history making night at the play."

Merlin J. Clusium, April 5, 1917

IN MANY RESPECTS the opening of *Three Plays for a Negro Theater* at
the Garden Theatre on April 5, 1917, was like any other. Avid first-nighters
arrived at the Madison Square Complex in New York City, their appetites
whetted for the latest Broadway show. Celebrities like William Faversham and
Billie Burke, veterans of the stage, came to see fellow thespians perform and
to be seen. Wealthy patrons of the arts, among them Otto Kahn, Mrs. George
Gould, and Miss Constance Collier, decked out in their finest theater garb,
made their way into the capacious Garden, lending an air of elegance and
glamour to the usual excitement of a first-night production. And, of course,
sprinkled throughout the audience were the influential critics of New York
City's many daily newspapers and magazines, their pencils and critical eyes
sharp and ready to judge the histrionic display. The flamboyant Alexander
Woollcott of the *New York Times* undoubtedly swept into the theater wearing
his trademark top hat and cape, already mentally composing a stylish phrase
to open his review. Likely already milling about in the lobby would have been
Louis De Foe of the *World*, George Jean Nathan of *Smart Set*, Heywood Broun
of the *New York Tribune*, the sarcastic James Metcalfe, who wrote reviews for
Life, and the affable Charles Darnton, who puffed plays for the *Evening World*.
An opening night on Broadway promised glitter and light, eager anticipation
and affected ennui, a new show and an old crowd.[1]

Perhaps the assembling audience displayed a bit more anticipation and a bit less ennui because of the people involved in the production. One reason critics, socialites, and celebrities flocked to the Garden was to witness the directorial debut of Robert Edmond Jones, who in recent months had sent shock waves along Broadway with his radical new set and costume designs.[2] How would he set the stage for *Three Plays for a Negro Theater*, they may well have wondered. Would his skills as a director match or even complement his fame as a stage artist? Emilie Hapgood, the producer, and Ridgely Torrence, the playwright, no doubt attracted a large number of friends, fans, and well-wishers, too. Hapgood, the wealthy and beautiful ex-wife of Norman Hapgood, was well connected in the city's theater circles. A patroness of the arts and the influential former president of the New York Stage Society, she rapidly was gaining a reputation for producing daring, innovative shows, like her most recent staging of G. K. Chesterton's *Magic* at the Maxine Elliott Theatre.[3] Ridgely Torrence, the author of the three plays, had become an intimate of many of the younger poets, dramatists, and writers who populated the literary and artistic scene in the city and who would have trekked to the Garden Theatre to show support for one of their darlings.[4] Curiosity about a new show and the celebrated people connected with it, as well as friendly professional interest, no doubt intensified the atmosphere surrounding this first night.

But the elements that distinguished this opening night from others were the subject of the plays—African American life—and the players—an all-black cast. If the title of the production did not alert the public to the novel performance they were about to witness, the number of prominent African Americans in the crowd, like W. E. B. Du Bois, James Weldon Johnson, and Lester A. Walton, and advance notices in the newspapers undoubtedly had. As the *Evening Post* had reported two days before the big event, "A dramatic incident of more than common interest will occur in the Garden Theatre on Thursday night," when "for the first time in this city, a series of plays will be performed by a company of colored performers."[5] The crowd that gathered in the Garden Theatre came to witness a landmark event in the history of the American Stage: the first black actors were performing on the Great White Way.

Regardless of the quality of the plays, the abilities of the actors, and the critical reception of the production, this opening night was history in the making. The all–African American cast was the first to appear on a Broadway stage in dramas that portrayed African American life seriously and sympathetically. To be sure, these performers were not the first to entertain a Broadway audience. Indeed, observant first-nighters might have recognized Alexander Rogers, Jesse Shipp, and Lottie Grady as veterans of the popular black musical comedy companies of the early 1900s that performed shows written by Bob Cole and

J. Rosamond Johnson or Bert Williams and George Walker. But unlike those earlier productions, which featured singing, dancing, outrageous comedy, and familiar black stereotypes, the one-act plays that made up *Three Plays for a Negro Theater* featured a variety of African American types and proposed that the drama of black-white relations and of this folk culture constituted an important foundation for a distinctive American Theater.[6] The plays and the players laid claim to central roles in the creation of a modern American dramatic tradition.

If anticipation and curiosity rippled through the orchestra section, private boxes, and galleries of the Garden Theatre, uncertainty mixed with fear reigned backstage. Torrence recalled years later that as opening night approached, the cast developed a severe case of collective stage fright. As he reported to a would-be biographer in 1936, "They believed that Negroes trying to be serious before an audience of white people who had never known them on the stage except as clowns, would be jeered and hooted off the boards. Few of the cast would allow members of their families to attend the performance for fear of the shame of the certain boos, bad eggs and catcalls."[7] But many of the actors were experienced performers, and they knew theater tradition: the show must go on. The members of the company summoned their courage, donned their costumes and makeup, and took their places before the footlights.

THREE PLAYS FOR A NEGRO THEATER

When the curtain rose for the first play, a comedy called *The Rider of Dreams,* on stage were Blanche Deas as Lucy Sparrow and Joseph Burt as her son, Booker. From the opening scene, the play must have startled the audience, for neither character sang or danced, and the stage was set to suggest a humble dwelling of black working people. Little Joseph Burt won the audience over with his impish portrayal of the lovable but pert Booker as well as by his mere presence on stage—black musical comedies from the previous decade typically did not include child characters. The good-natured banter between mother and son amid Lucy Sparrow's preparation of the evening meal set the tone for an inside view of black family life.

When Opal Cooper entered the scene as Lucy's husband, Madison, carrying a guitar that he obviously could not have afforded to buy, it became clear very quickly that the play would examine competing American dreams within black families. The drama revolves around their savings account, to which Lucy has been faithfully contributing for twelve years. Unbeknownst to his wife, Madison has just withdrawn all the money from the bank. A white confidence

" Raisin's inspiration

man, Wilson Byrd, has forged Lucy's signature to complete the transaction and then stolen a guitar as a token of the wealth he and Madison will make.[8] Lucy's dream is to own their home; Madison's dream is to invest the money in a get-rich-quick scheme so they can live in luxury without having to endure the drudgery of work. The Sparrows offered the audience a study in contrasts: Lucy's steady, pious, long-suffering embrace of deferred gratification versus Madison's poetic desire for independence and wealth and his rich, cajoling laughter that bespoke his zest for immediate satisfaction. As he explains to his wife that he must go out early the next morning to do some business, but hiding from her the nature of that business, Madison discovers to his horror that the money he has withdrawn from the bank is gone.

What follows are a frantic confession, shattering dreams, and the shared recognition that they have no money to pay the rent due that day, let alone buy the house or launch an enterprise. In the middle of their panic, the landlord, Dr. Williams, played by Alexander Rogers, arrives to collect the rent. He alone knows what has happened to the thick stack of bills, because he found it lying on the ground after Sparrow and his partner in crime hastily parted company to avoid being seen together. He caught the white forger and thief and wrested a written confession from him. With this knowledge the good doctor decides to extract from Madison the promise to mend his irresponsible ways. In the end, Williams accepts the money as payment for the Sparrows' home and hires Madison to teach his children how to play the guitar. Beholden and shamed, Madison Sparrow resigns himself to the disappointment of steady labor, but he wails one final lament about his longing to make his own music, which in this play, unlike in lighthearted comedies, must remain unfulfilled.

As the curtain descended, the audience thundered its approval. The Sparrows had come alive, thanks to the talents of Deas, Burt, and Cooper. Their efforts along with Alexander Rogers's offered the audience four distinct types of African American characters, whose pathos and obvious affection for one another struck a human chord that transcended race. After several curtain calls, the actors left the stage, Deas scurrying off to change costumes for her part in the next play. As the stage hands, led by a black carpenter named John Ahearn, arranged the set for *Granny Maumee,* the Clef Club Orchestra, under the direction of J. Rosamond Johnson, assembled in front of the curtain and dazzled the waiting audience with instrumental and vocal arrangements of popular black music.[9]

The second play was much darker than the first. Marie Jackson-Stuart starred in the title role as an old, blind woman preparing her simple country cabin for the arrival of her great-granddaughter Sapphie (Deas) and her great-great-grandson, the only male heir of her "royal black" line. The opening dialogue between Granny and her other great-granddaughter, Pearl, played by Fannie Tarkington, reveals the tragedy that has set this drama in motion. Years earlier, Granny had lost her eyesight trying to rescue her son from a white lynch mob who burned him alive for a crime he did not commit. Her son died, and in the two generations that followed, there were no boys to replace him. Granny has a burning desire to see one male heir before she dies and a hatred of the white murderers that makes her cling ever more tenaciously to her pure African descent. Granny disapproves of Sapphie's decision to leave the farm to work for a white family in the city, but she eagerly awaits the chance to hold the girl's baby in her arms and to know that her family's racial purity will continue for another generation.

Sapphie's arrival with her child—a mulatto—sets up the bizarre events of the second half of the play. Barely greeting her great-granddaughter, Granny snatches the baby from his basket and clutches him to her breast. The ecstasy she experiences miraculously restores her eyesight. Horror-struck and betrayed at the sight of the pale infant, Granny flies into a rage, madly plotting the demise of the white father, who is expected later in the evening. To compound the old woman's fury, the father turns out to be a descendant of one of the men who killed her son. Granny begins frantically to assemble the relics from that long-ago fatal day—two charred posts and a link of chain that had bound her son to his fate—as well as bunches of herbs that when burned create poisonous smoke. She uses the smoke first to incapacitate Sapphie and Pearl; she hopes it eventually will help her destroy the white man who has "tainted" her black family's blood. Now sighted, but blind in her anger, Granny resorts to voodoo to avenge the death of her son and the violation of her royal black line.

Hovering somewhere between an evil spirit world she is trying to conjure up and this world of pain and tragedy, Granny is addressing her dead son when the white man knocks at the door. Struggling mightily with her desire to wreak vengeance, she believes she hears her dead son pleading with her to forgive the white man so mother and son can be reunited in heaven. Suddenly, a power stronger than her hatred overwhelms her. Granny shrieks her forgiveness to the unseen man at the door and collapses in a heap. The two girls see that Granny Maumee is dead and flee from the room, leaving the crumpled figure in the center of the stage. As the full force of the play hit the audience, the curtain slowly descended.

As before, the first-night crowd clapped excitedly, more than once calling Deas, Tarkington, and Jackson-Stuart to the curtain to accept their hearty approval. The Clef Club again provided *entr'acte* entertainment while the stage was changed for the next play. In this set, the orchestra played their instruments, sang, and featured a novelty number with a trombonist dancing while he played the blues. When the curtain rose for the third time, the audience observed the kind of staging and costuming for which Robert Edmond Jones had become famous. A few simple props and striking, boldly colored costumes evoked ancient Jerusalem on the night Jesus of Nazareth was arrested, scourged, and eventually crucified. In minutes, the previous set had been transformed and the audience transported to the world of *Simon, the Cyrenian,* far removed from the backwoods cabin of Granny Maumee.

As the title suggests, the third play of the trilogy was built on a brief passage in three of the gospel accounts of the crucifixion of Jesus that tells how the soldiers enlisted Simon, a man of Cyrene, to carry the cross to the place of execution when its weight became too much for Jesus to bear.[10] In Torrence's play, Simon, played by John T. Butler, was no mere bystander, plucked at random from the crowd by Roman soldiers. Rather he was a bold African rebel whose leadership of the downtrodden posed a potentially serious military threat to the Roman Empire. As the play begins, Inez Clough, as Procula, the wife of Pilate, recreates another moment in the crucifixion drama reported in Matthew. Procula warns her husband to have nothing to do with the Nazarene, because, according to the gospel account, Jesus had given her frightful dreams.[11] In *Simon, the Cyrenian,* Torrence imagines that she sends for the African rebel to urge him to incite a disturbance if Jesus is sentenced to die. The rest of the play shows Simon's struggle to remain true to his cause and his people even as he recognizes the revolutionary message of the condemned carpenter's son. Simon, it turns out, happened to be in the garden of Gethsemane when the soldiers arrested Jesus; their eyes met, and Simon reports to Acte, an Egyptian princess, "I have seen the whole world's sorrow in one man's eyes."[12] Simon is determined to save both his own people and this champion of the oppressed.

Acte, played by Lottie Grady, and Barrabas, played by Jesse Shipp, both fear Jesus and urge Simon to leave. Simon, however, unable to abandon this strangely powerful man, remains in Jerusalem and eventually falls into the hands of the Roman soldiers. No actor portraying Jesus appears on stage, but a voice backstage recites familiar sayings attributed to Him at crucial moments when Simon prepares to use violence to make his escape and to free the Judean. At last, mocked and scorned himself, the mighty Simon bears the cross of Jesus, humbly dons a crown of thorns, and closes the drama with the words, "I will wear this, I will bear this till he comes into his own."[13]

The audience in the Garden Theatre on Maundy Thursday, 1917, no doubt was particularly susceptible to the emotional force of the last play.[14] Simon's violence was transmuted into Christ-like humility, and love, not revolutionary armies, promising to transform the world—pertinent ideals to Americans as they contemplated with dread the coming of war. Still applauding the performances in *Simon, the Cyrenian,* the audience remained seated for one final appearance by the Clef Club Orchestra. But when the last echo of the music faded away, the audience finally departed. The critics had to compose the reviews that would appear the next day in dailies throughout the city. Friends and supporters searched backstage for Torrence, Hapgood, and Jones to heap on them their praise and delight. Celebrities and theater regulars completed the first-night ritual with gay parties or late suppers at the fashionable gathering places along the Great White Way. The actors, still unsure of their reception in spite of the enthusiastic applause, shed their costumes and face paint and headed home to await the reviews that would determine their future.

One man in the crowd, Merlin J. Clusium, anticipating the flood of praise that would cover theater pages the following day, could not retire for the night until he had dashed off congratulatory letters to two of the actresses and to Torrence. After making his way from Madison Square Garden to his apartment on West 131st Street, Clusium wrote, "It is 12 o' the night but without writing you, Marie Jackson [*sic*] and Inez Clough, this uncrowned King of the Lion Tribe of Judah could not go to rest. This was a '*first night*' (for 18 years I was a New York First-nighter) and the few ifs and a good many buts to the contrary notwithstanding, it was a great night, a history making night at the play." This African American first-nighter saw in Torrence, "the first son of Japheth . . . who has been able to write of his brother's greatest sin in North America, without stigmatizing Negro womanhood." The night for Clusium had been marked by a "[g]ood crowd—good plays well played and everything pleasingly fine to the minutest detail," and he reveled in having witnessed "a new form of literature." By the time Torrence received this hastily written note, it was but one voice in a loud chorus of praise for his *Three Plays for a Negro Theater.*[15]

THE MORNING AFTER

The next morning, as newspapers began to appear on newsstands throughout the city, the audience, actors, playwright, producer, and director, as well as those who had not attended the opening of *Three Plays for a Negro Theater,* all learned what the critics thought about the plays. J. R. Crowe for the *New York Sun* declared the opening at the Garden Theatre, "epochal for negro plays and players, as it represented their emancipation from the inertia and prejudice which has heretofore kept them from a general hearing and gave them their first unspecialized and catholic audience." Broun, writing for the *New York Tribune,* called the performances "a triumph for the actors, for

Mrs. Hapgood, the producer, and for Robert E. Jones, director and designer of sets and costumes." The *World*'s De Foe described the production as "extremely novel in design and quite the most interesting of the numerous experiments in the theatre . . . this season." Of the early responses, only Woollcott's in the *New York Times* cast aspersions on the production. Conceding "the sympathetic quality" of Torrence's "unusual and deeply interesting texts," the "gracious spirit" of Mrs. Hapgood, and "the unerring eye of the director," Woollcott nevertheless blasted the cast for "a disturbingly and needlessly inadequate performance."[16]

When critics for the evening papers weighed in, it was clear that few had been persuaded by Woollcott's cranky review. The *New York Evening Post* reported that the plays offered "singular, novel, and possibly significant entertainment," and that the "performance was remarkable in many ways." Stephen Rathbun in the *New York Evening Sun* called *The Rider of Dreams* "a little gem of a comedy," and Burns Mantle entitled his review in the *New York Evening Mail* "Negro Actors Present Unique Programme of Negro Plays at Garden Theatre," which conveyed his generally positive appraisal of the production.[17] The decision was nearly unanimous—*Three Plays for a Negro Theater* was a hit on Broadway.

In the days that followed, the commentary generated by Torrence's plays snowballed into an enthusiastic consensus. Cards and letters from delighted audience members poured into the theater.[18] Advertisements placed in the city's daily and weekly newspapers contained the most enthusiastic and flattering comments from New York's most influential critics, which added to the general perception that something quite remarkable had happened on April 5, 1917, at the Garden. Before long, articles in journals like *Theatre Magazine,* the *New Republic,* and *Theatre Arts Magazine* added to the critical acclaim. When he drew up his list of the ten best actors and ten best actresses for the season, George Jean Nathan included Opal Cooper and Inez Clough from the cast of the three plays at the Garden.

African American response to the plays was overwhelmingly positive. The first response from a black publication was a front-page story in the weekly *New York Age* written by its drama editor, Lester A. Walton. As a member of the first-night crowd, Walton described the production as "a notable occasion, exciting more curiosity and commanding more general attention than any of this season's large crop of dramatic presentations." From his perspective, "the launching of this bold dramatic endeavor was an unqualified success."[19] Other African Americans echoed Walton's sentiments. James Weldon Johnson felt the plays marked "an epoch for the Negro on the stage"; W. E. B. Du Bois also believed the show was "epoch making"; and the *Southern Workman* saw the production as "a remarkable dramatic experiment."[20]

According to Ridgely Torrence, after the actors read the first wave of reviews, they gained courage and confidence, their performances, which had been good from the start, steadily improved, and the audiences grew a bit each night. After a successful short run at the Garden, Mrs. Hapgood arranged with Lee Shubert to have the plays moved to the house he managed, the Garrick Theatre, and there they remained until late April, when the show closed permanently. The sponsors openly admitted that the plays did not yield a cent, but even their financial losses did not dampen their hearty support for the plays or the players.

The same cannot be said for the fickle critical community. As the days melted into weeks after opening night, the critics seemed to have forgotten their initial fervent applause. Arthur Hornblow, author of the regular column "Mr. Hornblow Goes to the Play" in *Theatre Magazine,* suffered from the most dramatic case of critical amnesia. In the May issue, he had called the plays "the first noteworthy achievement of the kind on an elevated plane and worth considering."[21] The next month, the influential theater periodical had followed up Mr. Hornblow's review with a lengthy story on the production and had included photographs of Opal Cooper and Ridgely Torrence. The piece ended: "The presentation commends itself to respectful attention because of the sincerity of the purpose and the dramatic and literary value of the plays."[22] By July, however, Mr. Hornblow seemed to have no memory of the "noteworthy achievement" he had hailed just weeks before. He sarcastically summed up the past season: "I think I may safely say that the season just passed, like all former theatrical seasons, is one of the most significant we have known. As to what it is significant of, I am less positive. Possibly that theatrical managers, authors and actors like the idea of riding in limousines, dining now and then on terrapin stew and seeing their names in the papers. If the season signifies anything more significant, just at this minute I can't think what it is." When he published *A History of the Theatre in America: From Its Beginnings to the Present Time* in 1919, Hornblow not only had completely forgotten *Three Plays for a Negro Theater,* he also had excluded all other contributions made by African Americans to the American Stage.[23]

Hornblow, however, was not alone. James Metcalfe's review in *Life* in mid-April concluded that "judging by some bits in the performance of the colored players at the Garden Theatre, there seems to be no reason why in the not remote future our fellow citizens of negro blood should be ineligible to dramatic honors." Two weeks later, *Life*'s "Confidential Guide" called the plays "novel and interesting." But at the end of May, Metcalfe summed up the 1917 season by complaining that he had seen "no new accomplishments of great originality in any direction," and that "our native authors . . . have given us little of novelty or value."[24] A disappointed Louis De Foe confirmed the fact that the critics' "conclusions were practically unanimous that [the season] did not afford even one work of distinguished dramatic or literary quality which understandingly dealt with the problems of contemporary life." He reported that the committee chosen to award a Pulitzer Prize for the best American drama had found none worthy. Augustus Thomas, Richard Burton, and Hamlin Garland, the committee members, decided that none of the seventy American plays that had appeared on Broadway deserved recognition as "the original American play performed in New York which shall best represent the educational value and power of the stage in raising the standard of good morals, good taste and good manners."[25] So, quickly forgotten, *Three Plays for a Negro Theater* drifted from collective memory as dramatically as it had fired the imagination of the audience on opening night.

Historians of the nation's stage have done little in the intervening eight decades to jog the American memory of this notable, pathbreaking production. Contemporary chroniclers and academic drama critics of the 1910s and 1920s—notably, Arthur Hornblow, Margaret G. Mayorga, Mary Caroline Crawford, and Brander Matthews—relying on end-of-the-season summaries, their own first-night notes and commentaries, and periodic retrospectives on the theater, reconstructed a history of dramatic performance that looked forward, wistfully, to a time when the nation would produce the native-born equivalents of Denmark's Henrik Ibsen and Ireland's John Millington Synge. As a reviewer wrote of Crawford's *Romance of the American Theatre*, "The work of our 'social-minded young playwrights' . . . , the author believes, will presently bring about a state of affairs wherein 'there will be done for America what the Irish players' (and, presumably, dramatists) 'are now doing for Ireland.' "[26] They generally concurred that the 1890s had yielded works on the American West, some of which succeeded in capturing and representing on stage that elusive "American character" that must be the foundation for a national theatrical tradition. They typically identified stock figures in our national drama—the Yankee backwoodsman, the Western wit, the wily Irishman, the city slicker, and the stage Negro—but they were less precise in naming the thematic elements fundamental to a distinctive American school of drama and almost completely blind to the contributions made by African American performers. Thus, these early-twentieth-century histories of the American Stage, touted as comprehensive, made the mainstream white achievements in play writing and acting the whole story.[27]

In later decades, two developments provided for both the continued for-getting of the first black actors on the Great White Way and the promise for recovering our collective memory. Interest in establishing a canon for dramatic literature prompted scholars to return to the standard histories of the stage to see what, if any, works had displayed sufficient staying power to warrant inclusion in the distinguished plays of the American theater. Their efforts necessarily drew them to histories whose claims for comprehensiveness belied the limitations of their investigations. Based on histories of the stage that appeared between the 1920s and 1940s, these studies marked the arrival of African American themes and actors on Broadway and elsewhere with the staging of Eugene O'Neill's plays in the 1920s and thus perpetuated the ignoring of *Three Plays for a Negro Theater*.[28]

At the same time, efforts by black scholars and intellectuals to preserve the history of their race's achievements—scholarly endeavor that reflected the profound racial segregation in the United States—resulted in a number of books that kept alive the memory of events not typically included in general surveys. Studies on Negro dramas, actors, theater circuits, stock companies, and entertainment venues appeared, making no claims for a comprehensive treatment of the American Stage and consequently seldom serving as sources for later generalists. Works by W. E. B. Du Bois, James Weldon Johnson, Edith J. R. Isaacs, and Frederick Bond thus represented the tip of the nation's tongue, a site of not-quite-remembered information.[29]

The failure to include *Three Plays for a Negro Theater* in histories of the American theater may not seem at first glance to be egregious—many individual productions have escaped notice, and in spite of frequent performances of the three plays in the next three decades, they were never revived on Broadway. But what *is* startling and perplexing—and ultimately very revealing—is the glaring inconsistency between the rave reviews that hailed the daring experiment as a possible first step toward a distinctive national theater and the utter critical silence that set in within months of the debut. Why was a nation, so fascinated with "firsts" and obsessed with innovation, able to forget these first black Broadway actors in a trend-setting production so quickly and so nearly completely? To answer this question is one of the central tasks of this book.

Over the years two explanations for the demise of *Three Plays for a Negro Theater* have been offered by writers reflecting on African American theater history. The first and most persistent of these noted a fatal coincidence: The plays opened on April 5, 1917, and the next day, the United States entered the Great War in Europe. James Weldon Johnson, for example, argued that "the increasing stress of war was too great, even for stronger enterprises in the theatre, and it crushed them out."[30] Like others who blamed the short run of the plays on the coming of war, Johnson implied that a frivolous diversion on the stage could not compete with the weighty matter of war.

The playwright himself offered the second explanation for his plays' lack of success. He believed that the actors he selected to interpret his plays simply lacked the talent to put the plays over. Had they been more experienced, better trained, or more familiar with working behind the footlights, they might have been able to breathe life into their roles and help audiences and critics see the artistic merit of these unusual dramas. Sadly, however, he had been unable to find any actors with stage training and experience, so he had been forced to make do with the men and women who came forward during auditions. The production, he believed, could not overcome their weak performances.

The United States' declaration of war on the day after the three plays opened at the Garden no doubt did have an effect on the production and its place in American theater history, but not for the reasons writers like Johnson offered. A brief look at other forms of entertainment during the war shows that the war did not dampen American enthusiasm for popular diversions. The budding film industry, for instance, blossomed between 1914 and 1918, enjoying increases in both the number and quality of films.[31] Actors like Douglas Fairbanks, Mary Pickford, and Charlie Chaplin gained respect and prestige as entertainers who supported the war effort by appearing at patriotic rallies and by selling Liberty Bonds. The war scarcely dampened public enthusiasm for jazz and dancing, two popular diversions of the 1910s.[32] And in spite of early concerns that the war would spell doom for American theaters, theater managers staged new productions, and the world of make-believe carried on as American casualty counts mounted.[33]

The war did not upstage Torrence's dramas, or the all-black cast, any more than these other forms of entertainment, but it did contribute to their early closing. The war inspired a kind of national self-consciousness about American character and citizenship that provided the backdrop against which the plays were viewed and evaluated. The theatrical experiment, its initial triumph, and the eventual critical silence in a nation at war suggest that the themes explored in Torrence's plays, the author's perspective, and the black performances could not be faced squarely by a country at war. As cultural and political leaders crafted a national campaign dedicated to "making the world safe for democracy," writers like Lawrence Southerland argued that "the time is ripe for a big patriotic play voicing the sentiments of our people. The native dramatist never had a more splendid opportunity."[34] Torrence's plays apparently articulated "sentiments" that made people uncomfortable; after all, it is difficult to reconcile racial injustice with the ideal of equality, a hallmark of the American way.

Writers and critics *did* talk about the plays, even as they talked about war. What they said about what they saw in the Garden and Garrick Theatres, I argue, betrays deep doubts that blacks qualified as citizens and provides important insights into the role of culture in defining citizenship in a way that bolstered the reality of social inequality in the theaters of New York as well as in the theater of war.

Torrence's explanation, while not particularly persuasive, reveals the ways racism works. Contrary to Torrence's belief that none of the actors had training or experience, the cast represented an extraordinarily seasoned and talented cross-section of the black acting fraternity in the 1910s. Torrence's disparagement of the performances of his cast members points to the racial dimension of the term *Great White Way.* Torrence and many of the men and women who paid to see performances of his three plays knew absolutely nothing about the people, institutions, training opportunities, and drama criticism that dominated black stages in Harlem, Chicago, Washington, D. C., and national theater circuits. Their ignorance of past performances by the actors, their ungrounded assumptions about the absence of professionalism in African American theaters, and their *invidious comparisons with white actors all demonstrate their immersion in white theater and their insistence that white theater and American theater were synonymous.

The very weakness of Torrence's explanation for the failure of his three plays to remain on Broadway for more than a few weeks points to an even more persuasive approach to the plays. His ignorance of black theater and actors as well as his implicitly white assumptions about what qualified as talent, training, and experience force us to see this production and its fate as a revealing episode in the shaping of American culture by a racially diverse society. Perhaps without intending to do so, the dramas, by advancing Negro themes as essentially American themes, posed a number of questions. How does a diverse people express itself culturally? Who decides what is an accurate reflection when a people collectively stands before the looking glass of culture? What happens when this mirror contains dead spots that refuse to reflect the visages of some, or when they look into the mirror expecting to see one image and find instead an unfamiliar or unattractive face looking back?[35]

The story of the first black actors on Broadway forces us to consider these matters quite seriously. For the Great White Way, having gotten its name from the thousands of brilliant lights that illuminated streets and marquees in New York's famed theater district, was white in the more important racial sense and consequently reflected only a portion of the people who made up the body politic in the early twentieth century. The arrival of the first black actors in this province of white playwrights, managers, actors, and plays represented the first major confrontation of racialized assumptions about art and nationality in the twentieth-century American theater. The first African American actors to take their places before the footlights of a Broadway stage did more than interpret their parts and speak their lines. They were engaged in a race drama

* discriminatory

that sounded their desire to become legitimate participants in the making of American culture—to find their reflections in the looking glass of culture. Thus, attempting to solve the mystery surrounding their debut promises to shed light on the ways Americans dealt with the desire for biracial cultural collaboration.

These two episodes—the debut of African Americans on Broadway and the United States' entry into the First World War—viewed together promise to reveal a great deal about the painful birth pangs of modern "Aframerican" culture in the 1920s, the subject of Ann Douglas's fascinating book, *Terrible Honesty*. I believe that the 1917 debut of black performers in serious drama on Broadway paved the way for this later, more pervasive interracial cultural development. At the same time, because this study is more narrowly focused on the participants in and events surrounding a single, history-making production, and because it pays as much attention to cultural reception as to cultural expression, I offer a less optimistic assessment of cross-race cultural collaboration. One can point to any number of artistic achievements that represent the combined efforts of blacks and whites, but joint efforts do not necessarily mean that all contributors will receive the same recognition for their parts in the whole. One advantage of a pointed examination such as this one is that the crosscurrents, inequality, and ambiguity of cultural hybrids emerge as clearly as the beautiful image of black and white artists joining hands across the color line.

Shining the spotlight on this single event offers another advantage as well—one can chart with some thoroughness the extent to which the messages of the dramas resonated in one of the nation's important cultural centers. What critics and other witnesses wrote about the plays indicates what they saw and what they agreed or disagreed with, what they liked or disliked, and what made them reconsider or staunchly uphold cherished beliefs. Beyond these individual responses to and reflections on the content of the plays, critics fashioned their own narratives as they summarized the basic plots for their readers. These summaries reveal what parts of the dramas mattered to the witnesses, what parts they ignored, and how they transformed the playwright's, director's, and actors' aims by adding their own descriptive flourishes and behind-the-hand commentary.

Buried in these eyewitness accounts lie important clues to the mystery of the shifting fortunes of the dramas of Negro life in a land preparing for war. Expression and reception both contribute to the process by which people define their bedrock values and the ground rules for social interaction by which they agree to abide. In April 1917, the dramatist, stage decorator, and cast expressed a desire to present race dramas as fundamentally American plays. At the same time, those who reported on their efforts found language that not only reinforced stereotypical views of African Americans but also cast doubt on the black claim to citizenship. Under ordinary circumstances the claims and counterclaims would have made for lively debate and open cultural conflict. In a nation on the eve of assembling an army of citizen soldiers, these differences, I argue, helped account for the averted eyes and eventual cultural amnesia. Closing ranks to make the world safe for democracy demanded that a national self-image that could be construed as negative or antidemocratic be denounced, ignored, or forgotten.

The Theater and National Culture

One of the claims of this study is that the theater offers more than diversion and can be studied as one site where national culture is made, a claim that requires some explanation. The first matter to consider is the relationship between the theater in general and a nation's culture. There are, of course, many ways that a people can consider its core values—in speeches by statesmen, sermons, national historical narratives, fiction, and advice literature, to name but a few. As a public venue in which action and dialogue combine to tell a story, the theater also represents a setting in which ideas and ideals are presented, observed, and, in due time, embraced, ignored, or rejected. As such, theaters are potentially important sites for the shaping of public culture.

More difficult to sort out, however, is *when* and *how* the theater shapes national culture. Do theaters shape culture by presenting plays their managers believe reflect views already widely held? Does the appearance of a controversial play automatically upset the applecart of culture? Do all theaters in all places have an equal impact on the national conversation about national values and character? In recent years, scholars of national theater have suggested that the best way of gauging the role of a theater in the process of culture is to take into account its location and influence and to place its productions in the context of more generalized discussion.[36]

While theaters dotted the landscape of the United States in the early 1900s— even most small towns boasted a lyceum, community theater, opera house, or popular auditorium—relatively few of these venues presented shows that elicited commentary by critics, scholars, and entertainers writing for publications with a national readership. Without diminishing the importance of small town theaters in advancing or curbing certain themes on the stage for their respective communities, it is safe to say that national trends were set in America's cities, and the most important theater district in the United

States, which in the early 1900s lacked a national theater, was Broadway in New York. Broadway represented the pinnacle of theatrical achievement in the early twentieth century, and discussions about the long-sought-after American drama focused on productions that appeared in theaters on the Great White Way. Drama pages in newspapers and many theater periodicals took the nation's theatrical pulse on this artery of entertainment in New York City. Indeed, it was the appearance of black actors specifically on a *Broadway* stage that excited curiosity and interest, for most of the performers in the three plays had appeared before the public on other stages from Chicago to New York to Washington, D. C., and in many towns in between. Their performances elsewhere had gone unheeded; their performance on Broadway made headlines.

To understand what a particular Broadway production might mean requires contextualization. Any given production is little more than a contribution to an ongoing conversation—a point of view, a judgment, an idea. It is not just the substance of that view, however, that commands attention; the range of alternatives to it must be understood as well. Any given drama, therefore, succeeds in advancing an idea and seeking widespread acceptance among those who hear it, write or read about it, or choose to repeat it in another cultural forum. The theater, then, functions as a public venue in which positions vie for—but may or may not achieve—cultural legitimacy. Studying the presentation of ideas and responses to them becomes the study of a more general process by which a society determines what is legitimate, acceptable, representative, and what belongs beyond the pale.[37]

In the early twentieth century, virtually any play written by an American and performed on Broadway became subject to particularly close scrutiny—especially when it claimed to be an "American" drama. Since the turn of the century, artists in many fields of endeavor had sought ways to express the essence of American life, and they had worried aloud in speeches, articles, and books that the United States continued to look in all the wrong places for inspiration and that the great American drama, novel, poem, architectural style, or composition had yet to be created.[38] As the country increasingly became involved in important international relations, cultural commentators yearned for native arts that matched the nation's rising status in world affairs. The suggestion, made by critics like Robert Benchley and Lester A. Walton, that *Three Plays for a Negro Theater* might well be a pioneering work of American drama placed the production—and the discussion that surrounded it—squarely in the middle of this ongoing debate.[39]

The linking of the three plays and an American dramatic tradition, not surprisingly, brought to light the unspoken racial assumptions that had underlain the quest for a great American drama for more than two decades, and it revealed the racist assumptions made about African Americans in society and on stage. These two strands, suddenly exposed, were subtly intertwined with and dependent upon one another, for the "whiteness" of the American Stage was more often than not taken for granted rather than explained and became apparent only through comparison with "blackness."[40] Themes and characters in the most celebrated American plays of the turn of the century provided some markers of race. Melodramas set in the frontier typically featured homesteaders, miners, claim-jumpers, and bankers, all fashioned from stock white figures. Detectives and crooks matched wits in popular mysteries that required nearly equal characters. And social dramas that explored such themes as loveless marriage, female desire for independence, or love without marriage focused on middle-class men and women. These markers—the frontier, the law, and the parlor—were not inherently white, but they did not easily or automatically conjure up nonwhite mental images.[41]

When writers described the representative American drama, however, they inched a bit closer to race-specific language. In discussing the great themes for American drama, for example, a writer for *Theatre Magazine* in 1908 argued that "the American has sentiment, plenty of it, the sentiment of the conqueror," and that the insurgent plays of Eugene Walter—the subject of the piece—captured the American as "a creature of mighty impulse and tremendous achievement, the whole-souled, big-brained man who is a pioneer." He believed that themes for American plays abounded if derived from the people: "We are a big, powerful people with work to do. We are proud of our work and anxious to do it. That is what it is to be an American."[42] Two years later, Randolph Hartley provided a composite of the new American dramatist whose work had begun to catch the essence of American life. "Nationality, American; Age, 30 years; Height, 5 feet 10 inches; Weight, 165 pounds; Features, regular, clean shaven . . . . Said citizen is noticeably quiet in demeanor and dress, and has the general appearance of a prosperous professional man," he wrote. Drawn as a composite of such dramatists as W. J. Hurlbut, Edward Sheldon, A. E. Thomas, and P. E. Brown, the American playwright was "clear of head, clean of speech, serious of purpose, well-educated, totally devoid of pose."[43]

"Conqueror," "pioneer," "proud of work," an "active" people, and "serious of purpose"—these terms take on a white cast when juxtaposed against the terms reserved for African Americans. Consider, for example, the opening passage of Burns Mantle's review of *Three Plays for a Negro Theater:* "The American negro is to the American white man, essentially a comic figure" who "represents to the children of the men who freed him from slavery the irresponsible child of nature who accepts his small world as a playground and life as much of a frolic as he can make it."[44] According to common wisdom, Americans were responsible, hardworking, conquering men; here, African Americans were irresponsible, playful, formerly enslaved children. The contrast between the two sets of traits could not be sharper. Louis Sherwin made the same point more obliquely when he wrote that none of Torrence's characters stole chickens or brandished a razor blade, "so naturally New York audiences did not recognize these characters as negroes."[45] From comments such as these, which were repeated many times over, the contrast between the generic American and the African American betrays the essential whiteness of the former.

The incongruity between Torrence's three plays and the preconceived ideal of the great American drama sparked a good deal of the ambivalence about the production and calls to our attention the challenge this biracial collaborative expression posed for American identity. Could a national dramatic tradition rest securely on a foundation anchored in the experience of African Americans? Then, as now, the question begged for an answer, and it forced the more thoughtful to consider how a nation like the United States, with its diverse population, could and should express itself.

The responses to that question will recur as a leitmotif in this study, for whether direct, evasive, or obdurate, those responses constituted a critical contest over the shape and substance of American culture. As the progressive cultural amnesia of 1917 attests, Americans then were unprepared to face the issue squarely. The flowering of "Aframerican" culture in the following decade suggests that eventually Americans found ways to exploit their differences in the creation of distinctive national art.

An important example of successful cross-racial cultural production can be seen in the stunning popularity of African American musical forms like ragtime and jazz. In spite of considerable resistance from so-called "serious" musicians, Americans in the first two decades of the twentieth century hailed ragtime as their quintessential national music, even as they acknowledged its roots in African American culture.[46] As ragtime gave ground to jazz in the late 1910s and early 1920s, no one argued with its essential Americanness or with its ties to black life. Not only did African American rhythms, improvisational style, and melodic riffs leaven American popular music, but also African American artists increasingly performed in prominent places, shared the stage with white artists, and became visible as American celebrities.[47]

Without aiming to diminish the significance and the promise of cross-racial music like jazz or ragtime, I think it is imperative to recognize crucial differences between music and drama as art forms expressive of national culture, for the desire to create a unique hybrid culture should not divert attention from ongoing social exclusion and economic exploitation nor should scholars naively underestimate the difficulty of creating such a hybrid. In my recent biography of Scott Joplin, the "King of Ragtime" in the early 1900s, I argued that ragtime achieved enormous popularity nationwide among white and black listeners because it spoke to various communities in different ways. To African Americans it captured familiar sounds and beats that had reverberated in their communities for decades. To whites, frustrated with the unfulfilling strictures of Victorianism, it beckoned toward a culture of expressiveness and exuberance and dovetailed with a more general transformation of cultural values. From all listeners it called forth movement—swaying, toe-tapping, knee-slapping, and hand-clapping—and gaiety.[48]

Both the form and the experience of the music contributed to a subdued awareness of the racial conflict that was in a sense overcome in the music. Because composers like Joplin established set patterns for writing this music and, indeed, wrote it using conventional notation, key indicator, time, and meter, ragtime became a musical genre that any composer, regardless of race, could write. The quality of compositions varied, but the essential sound and form required the blending of African American and European melodies, harmonies, and rhythms, which gave ragtime its distinctive flavor. Hearing or reproducing this American music did not force either the audience or the performer to contemplate the plantation setting that nurtured its constituent parts. In fact, contrary to the harsh reality of slavery that helped forge two musical traditions into one distinctly New World music, ragtime music evoked immediate pleasure rather than dark reveries on man's inhumanity to man. The cakewalks, two-steps, and slow drags inspired by ragtime music featured up-tempo movements and frivolity. And even writers like Carl Van Vechten, who happily acknowledged ragtime as "a hybrid product" of black and white musical influences, could downplay the black by identifying such white ragtime musicians as Irving Berlin and Louis Hirsch as the chief creators of America's only national music.[49]

Race dramas contrasted sharply with race music. Like ragtime, they grew out of experiences on the old plantations. But seeing the dark faces of the actors and the crude settings that represented their homes made it impossible to ignore the matter of race. Characters in race dramas were not always good-natured and fun-loving; they portrayed emotions other than irrepressible joy. And the tragedies of their lives arose from their positions in and treatment by white American society. The evil forces arrayed against African American protagonists included race prejudice and white characters disposed to act on it. Of course, evil characters locked horns with good characters in more typical American plays—crooks, claim-jumpers, and cheating husbands all failed in some way to live up to American ideals. But the difference between those stock bad guys and the antagonists in race dramas lay in the source of their evil. The former erred as individuals, the latter as products of a system based on inequality, exploitation, racial oppression, and violence. Race dramas—unlike race music—forced Americans to confront slavery as a blot on the nation's past that marred their desired self-image.

The distinction between music and drama was vividly borne out in response to Torrence's three plays. Without exception, critics loved the Clef Club performances between plays, finding nothing politically or aesthetically upsetting in their music. The *New York Sun,* for instance, sang the praises of the black musician who "loves to strum his banjo, to sing his ragtime melody and shuffle his syncopated rhythm all at the same time," and asserted that the Clef Club Orchestra played music that reflected "the very spirit of the Sunny South."[50] Even Alexander Woollcott, who disliked the plays, noted at the end of his review that the audience "enjoyed greatly" the African American orchestra, which, he observed, "had the whole audience swaying to the great strains of 'Go Down Moses.'"[51]

The dramas themselves, however, presented more of a problem, on which African American critics, most sensitive to the challenge they represented, commented. W. E. B. Du Bois put it most poetically when he wrote, "The American world is not a white world in tint of flesh, but white shading into every beautiful color from cream to dark brown. Yet the painter has not dared in most cases to paint the scene before him save in white . . . . Of the beauty and variety which Negro blood has given to millions of American faces almost nothing appears except startling caricatures." Torrence's plays, he believed, were a major break with that tradition because they featured the undistorted stories of dark-skinned people.[52] Lester A. Walton of the *New York Age* recognized the challenge of the plays even more directly. He wondered aloud how white playgoers would respond to seeing members of their race as forgers, thieves, murderers, and rapists. "[M]aybe our pale-faced brethren will not be as thin-skinned after all," he concluded hopefully.[53]

Part of the burden of this book will be to explore with care the challenge posed by an African American perspective to American theatrical expectations and to recognize the obstacles to as well as the desirability of cultural hybridity. Cross-race cultural collaboration coexisted with racial inequality, and what I hope to show is that the former did not necessarily work against the latter. Other scholars have demonstrated the myriad ways that American culture has drawn life from collaboration across the color lines. Susan Gubar's *Racechanges: White Skin, Black Face in American Culture* and Ann Douglas's *Terrible Honesty: Mongrel Manhattan in the 1920s* provide a mountain of evidence to support the view that America's distinctive cultural productions depended upon the desire to blur the line between races, to slide from one racial position to another, and to blend multiple perspectives into unique new world artistic expression.[54] Before we rush to congratulate ourselves for overcoming profound racial divisions through cultural collaboration, however, we would do well to remember that cultural victories ring hollow when they are not accompanied by social and economic improvement. As the commentaries about these remarkable black actors in 1917 will show, even the most enthusiastic critics found ways of praising their performances without fundamentally challenging racist stereotypes or providing new ways to think about African Americans as American citizens and coworkers in the kingdom of culture.

THE POLITICS OF CULTURAL COLLABORATION

Two final matters deserve attention before we return to the story of the first black actors on the Great White Way. In one way or another, both involve the political implications of cultural production in the United States in the twentieth century. The first has to do with culture itself. This elusive subject has captured the imagination of a generation of historians at the end of the twentieth century who are obsessed with the gap between the ideal of democracy and the reality of unequal voices in political decision making in the United States. In recent years scholars have explored the role of culture in shaping the structure and assertion of power in modern America. Culture, they have shown, encompasses a wide range of beliefs, values, practices, artistic expressions, and ideals that constitute an intangible matrix within which people live their lives and regard their actions and relationships with others as meaningful. At the same time, they see that culture has the power to limit choices and the exercise of power. Because the contents of any given culture are malleable, being constructed and reconstructed by the words and actions of those best positioned—by birth, wealth, intellect, or inclination—to articulate and enforce their ideals, most scholars agree that culture is intimately bound up in a process of social change even as it influences the nature and direction of that change.[55]

The question of how a culture is formed, however, is much more difficult to address, the extent of its reach equally difficult to measure. Add to those issues the fact of profound racial inequality and segregation in the United States, and the matter of pinpointing "American" culture seems nearly hopeless. At least two options have attracted scholars in recent years. One is to discuss the culture of a particular group or community; the other is to explore those expressions that achieve some semblance of national influence and study them as dominant. The drawbacks of each are apparent immediately. The proliferation of studies of particular social groups, while informative and essential to a greater understanding of American life, has postponed the equally daunting task of distilling from these varied stories a synthetic narrative of our collective experience. At the same time, the focus on the "dominant" has forced us to think backward. We have to presume to know what was, in fact, dominant and seek reasons for its occupying a place of importance in the national consciousness.

Of course, no matter how neat we want these categories of analysis to be, they have a way of blending, blurring, and interpenetrating one another, so that we have come to recognize that neither specific subcultures nor national culture could exist as they do without the presence and influence of the other. As Shelley Fisher Fishkin recently summarized the matter: "We are now and have always been a culture in which a vast range of voices and traditions have constantly shaped each other in profound ways. Our teaching and our scholarship must take into account our increasingly complex understanding of what our common culture is and how it evolved. Doing so will force us to examine how an unequal distribution not of talent but of power allowed a patently false monocultural myth to mask and distort a multicultural reality."[56]

Three Plays for a Negro Theater offers a valuable glimpse into one episode in this masking of "multicultural reality" that can help make concrete some of the abstract speculations on culture, hybridity, and power in twentieth-century America. Opening night on April 5, 1917, could not have taken place without the joint efforts of blacks and whites, performers and witnesses, and the status quo and the avant garde, nor without a lived past and an artistic representation of that past. Theatrical performances are, by their very nature, social enterprises that combine the literary expression of a playwright, the connections and financial resources of a producer, the mind's eye of a stage designer, the labor of stage hands to give that vision physical form, the overarching vision of the director, and the varying interpretive skills of the actors. Authorship necessarily must be shared.

In the case of *The Rider of Dreams, Granny Maumee,* and *Simon, the Cyrenian,* the social dimension is further complicated and enriched by the interplay between different races. Ridgely Torrence imagined and wrote the dramas, but he based them on African American types he remembered from his childhood in Xenia, Ohio, in a sense cribbing his stories from the pages of history. African American actors spoke Torrence's lines and interpreted their roles based on what they thought would make such characters believable, but they did so in costumes and on sets designed by Robert Edmond Jones, a Harvard- and European-trained exponent of the New Movement in the Theater. To categorize them as either black plays or white plays threatens to minimize the interdependence of both races' contribution to the production.

Acknowledging the many strands of experience, vision, and expression that were woven into this single production only begins to explain the relationship of the plays to American culture. The performances evoked immediate responses from audiences, later reflections by some, and a body of critical commentary, all of which represented engagement with the plays as embodiments of ideas and perspectives potentially to be incorporated into a widely shared cultural worldview. In other words, what people chose to say about the plays offers important evidence of the process of cultural production at work. The responses can tell us much more than the published script or photographs of the players ever can about the way a given artistic event may have modified how people thought about their national heritage and essential values. Moreover, the failure by the public and the critics to remember the production as the United States deepened its involvement in war helped to mask this cultural hybrid in favor of a monocultural myth of American democracy.

A second related matter has to do with the agents of cultural change. In the United States, groups or individuals who identify themselves with progressive causes typically are credited with being forces for change. Being in the vanguard of change implies blazing trails in hitherto unexplored regions and necessarily leaving behind, willingly, the way things always have been done. In the early twentieth century, progressives in the world of theater worked to redefine the way theaters conveyed drama. Historians of turn-of-the-century theater refer to their efforts as a "revolution"—a complete transformation of all aspects of the play, from contents to staging to acting technique to the size of the playhouse itself. Those who pushed for this revolution—whether they advocated subsidized art, the "little theater" movement, a shift away from realism to imagination, or the exploration of social issues once thought inappropriate for the stage—came to be identified with the New Movement in the Theater; they were, for their day, the artistic avant garde.

The principal white theater people involved in *Three Plays for a Negro Theater*, Torrence, Hapgood, and Jones, all considered themselves advocates of the New Movement in the Theater, and as such prompt a slightly unusual inquiry into this particular progressive movement. There is no question that the new movement shook up important aspects of the theater in the early years of this century. But less certain is the role the movement's proponents played in shaking up race-based assumptions about American drama. Even though they promoted or supported dramas about Negro life, Torrence, Hapgood, and Jones, in particular, as well as others in the movement, in general, did not necessarily want to chart a new course for race relations in the United States. At the same time, their identification with this controversial movement offered critics an easy target for dismissing their work without having to address directly the racial inequality demonstrated by the plays. Like their progressive political counterparts, the theatrical avant garde occupied an extremely ambiguous position on the matter of racial equality and the need for social justice for *all* Americans, regardless of the color of their skin. Their beliefs coexisted uneasily with those of their African American collaborators, who far more forcefully saw the production as a medium for redressing the second-class citizenship of American Negroes.

These ambiguities should jolt us into an awareness of the tremendous crosscurrents at work in cultural collaboration. Coworkers in the kingdom of culture bring to the realm the freight of past experience, unexamined and often unspoken assumptions, deeply ingrained habits of mind, and a wide range of hopes and aims that do not necessarily complement one another and may even work at cross purposes. As we shall see, the people who made *Three Plays for a Negro Theater* frequently sought different paths even as they tried to pull the same wagon.

On April 5, 1917, the cast, the playwright, the director, and the producer could only guess at the long-term significance of the plays about to be performed. They had lived with the difficulty of working together across the color line, but few gave voice to the pain and frustration involved. They knew that the plays' themes were "unusual" if not openly challenging to what most people thought about the "race question" in America. In short, they hoped that the plays would blaze a new trail for the American theater, but they could see only dimly where that trail might lead. What the cast, at least, *did* know on that historic evening, was whence they had come and how hard they had struggled for this chance to shine on Broadway. Their story was the least known of the various stories that made up this dramatic event, and with their experience we shall begin the journey on the road to Broadway.

2

The Road to Broadway

"It is a difficult task to produce native plays and wholly leave out the colored American, and when portrayed the character should be the real thing and not a cheap imitation."

Lester A. Walton, New York Age, *February 12, 1914*

ACCORDING TO RIDGELY TORRENCE, the greatest challenge he and Robert Edmond Jones faced in staging *Three Plays for a Negro Theater* was finding good black actors. "[A]t the very outset," he wrote Jean Cavinee in 1936, "we were confronted with . . . the difficulty of finding actors among the race capable of taking serious parts. There had been no serious racial drama; there were no actors with experience of it. The men and women who had had professional training had only been in minstrel or 'pick' (pickaninny) shows or they had 'Tommed' (been with an *Uncle Tom's Cabin* troupe)." Torrence admitted that he had begun working on the project with the assumption that "Negroes were, racially, actors, that almost any Negro could act." But after he had "combed the Negro population of New York, Baltimore, Washington and Philadelphia" and had come up empty-handed, he decided to select the best men and women from among those who auditioned and "to train the actors fundamentally." He remained convinced that the actors' inexperience had hampered the plays and that his singular efforts on behalf of African American actors set them on the path that eventually led to later Broadway successes.[1]

While Torrence saw his production as a new beginning, those whose talents he disparaged knew that it represented but one more step on a road they had been traversing for years. No one rightfully could accuse the black actors of either lack of desire, lack of experience, or lack of preparation. The path had not always been direct or free from obstacles, but the destination always had been clear. For more than two decades African American entertainers had set their sights on the bright lights and the coveted recognition that came with performing on a Broadway stage.

More was at stake, however, than a place in the spotlight for the talented few who would make it to the Great White Way. The stage offered diversion and lighthearted amusement to audiences, to be sure, but as many black performers knew, it also provided black people a chance to present themselves, their culture, and their artistry to fellow Americans from whom they lived fairly separately. To make it on Broadway meant to win favor, recognition, and, perhaps, wealth as individual entertainers, but always at work was the knowledge that African Americans on stage were trespassing on the other side of the color line, making visible those lives that all too often remained hidden. Individual success on Broadway coupled with the striving of an outcast race prompted African Americans to claim full citizenship and the right to shape their nation's theatrical tradition. The two impulses—personal success and the advancement of the race—however, produced enormous tension, for the requirements of one did not necessarily coincide with the interests of the other. As one critic put it, the stage promised to place "the Negro before the public in his true and proper light," but "being ridiculed before the footlights" had been more typical of the experience of black actors who got the chance to portray African American characters on stage.[2] Working through the tension between individual opportunity and collective uplift, more than any other factor, colored the experience of African Americans in American show business, and it is crucial to understanding what *Three Plays for a Negro Theater* meant to blacks in Harlem and around the country.

DARK STARS IN THE FIRMAMENT

Of the dozens of letters that poured into the Garden and Garrick Theatres to congratulate Ridgely Torrence on the stunning success of his three one-act plays, a handful stand out for the common question they contained. "I want to thank you for what you have done for the Negro concerning the theatre," began Miss Bryant's undated letter from 1917. "If you should ever need an extra girl," she continued, "please let me know." Kathryn Hunt, writing near the end of the run, asked directly, "Have you understudies for the parts of the Colored Players now at the Garrick? If you have may I apply for a position?" Philip M. Brisbane, from Massachusetts, had read of the production in the *Crisis* and offered the following information: "I have a little experience of stage work as I have been playing in Musical Dramas only, such as 'Joseph' the Shepherd, Jeptho and his Daughter . . . . If you [are] selecting your help and think you will have an opening for such I will gladly accept." Hallie E. Queen, a graduate of Cornell University, cut right to the chase in her letter dated April 14, 1917, "Will you give me an opportunity to take part in the plays you are presenting? . . . I could come to New York at any weekend for a tryout."[3] All written by African Americans apparently overlooked in Torrence's efforts to find actors for his plays, Bryant's, Hunt's, Brisbane's, and Queen's letters testify eloquently to the desire of black actors to work in the field of dramatic acting.

These young hopefuls, however, were not the first black actors to aspire to careers on Broadway. They were simply the latest generation to seek a place among the dark stars in the firmament of America's galaxy of entertainment. Like those who had gone before them and those who now appeared on stages on Broadway and elsewhere, Bryant, Hunt, Brisbane, Queen, and dozens more were learning the hard lessons of darkness—the frustrating invisibility and the inevitable and invidious comparisons with the bright white stars who claimed the attention of the nation. Torrence's inability to find black stars resulted from the general lack of awareness that an African American star system existed, not from an actual absence of performers. Indeed, whether he realized it or not, Torrence selected some of the most popular and talented African American entertainers who had been working in the theater since the turn of the century.

Turn-of-the-century black actors, of course, were not the first such professionals in the United States. The history of black performance includes numerous episodes and incidents from earlier in the nineteenth century. But like so much of the story of African American culture, the development of the dramatic arts lacks continuity. For example, most chroniclers of the black experience in American theater begin their accounts with Ira Aldridge and the African Company in New York in the 1820s. But Aldridge, a celebrated tragedian best known for his portrayal of Othello and Oroonoko, actually performed very little on the American stage, making a name for himself instead in Great Britain and continental Europe. Similarly, while the African Company performed *Othello, Richard III*, and other such classic plays between 1821 and 1823, it, too, eventually shut down before establishing a secure foundation on which a later generation of dramatic actors could build a tradition of fine acting.[4]

Other precursors to the generation of actors who came of age in the 1890s— minstrel performers—also developed sporadically. Hardly "professional" in the strict sense, early minstrels were slaves called upon by their masters to sing, dance, and clown for family and guests. By the 1830s, white performers had appropriated the black forms, exaggerated the features and movements of black entertainers, and established traveling shows that, until after the Civil War, largely excluded African American performers. When blacks did take part in minstrel shows in the later nineteenth century, they performed vocal and instrumental pieces, danced, and told jokes more or less in keeping with the conventions of the genre developed by white minstrels. But their use of burnt cork to blacken their dark skin complicated the entertainment—maintaining the caricature of African American features for white audiences and creating a humorous parody of white minstrelsy for black audiences.[5]

The 1890s brought a number of "firsts" in the field of African American entertainment that eventually produced an array of popular modern black stars. In 1892, for example, Sam T. Jack organized the Creole Company, which not only legitimized the appearance of Negro women on stage but also introduced songs, costumes, and themes that reflected urban rather than plantation settings. Within a couple of years, John W. Isham's *The Octoroons* and *Oriental America* produced shows that set a course toward musical comedy, a path followed by such teams as Bert Williams and George Walker and Bob Cole and the Johnson Brothers. By the end of the 1890s, Ernest Hogan, known as the "Unbleached American," the doleful Bert Williams, dandy George Walker, Jesse Shipp, Alex Rogers, Bob Cole, and Inez Clough had become household names in the black world of entertainment.[6]

Of these black celebrities, Bert Williams enjoyed the greatest renown and at the same time revealed the enduring power of the color line to hinder widespread respect and recognition for African American actors. Williams's life story contrasted rather sharply with the characters he brought to life in the 1890s and early 1900s. Born in the West Indies in 1874 and spending most of his adolescence in Riverside, California, where his family moved in the mid-1880s, Williams's roots were not sunk into the plantation experience of blacks in the American South. A high school graduate and a student at Stanford University, he did not try his hand at entertaining until he was nearly twenty years old and in need of funds to continue his college studies. He met up with George Walker in 1893 in San Francisco, and by the time they made their way to New York, Walker had assumed the comedic roles against Williams's straight lines and ballad singing. Before starring in 1899 in *The Policy Players,* which was one of the first ambitious black shows of the decade to feature a plot rather than an olio of song, dance, and gags, the pair appeared in Victor Herbert's *Gold Bug* (1896), Will Marion Cook's *Clorindy* (1898), and Hurtig and Seamon's *A Lucky Coon* (1898). Two years after arriving in New York, the team was engaged at Koster and Bial's on Broadway for a forty-week run, during which they catapulted the cakewalk into a popular, fashionable craze.[7]

Beginning in 1900, Williams and Walker set the pace for black musical comedy with such shows as *The Sons of Ham* (1900), *In Dahomey* (1902), *Abyssinia* (1906), and *Bandanna Land* (1907).

After Walker collapsed on stage during a performance of *Bandanna Land* in 1909, Williams tried to go it alone. In 1909, he starred in *Mr. Lode of Koal*, which toured the country in the late summer. Lester A. Walton, drama critic of the *New York Age*, saw the show in St. Louis in mid-September and predicted, inaccurately, a "long and successful life" on Broadway and praised Williams for living up "to his reputation of being one of the funniest in America." Two weeks later, however, the misadventures of Williams's company in Davenport, Iowa, supplied material for a Walton editorial on the color line and the stage. No one had bothered to make hotel reservations for the *Mr. Lode of Koal* company in the small river city, and most of the city's hotels refused to accommodate the black performers. As a result, the would-be Broadway stars spent most of the day dragging suitcases, costumes, and props through the streets of the town until they could find a place to stay. Such treatment, Walton observed, was making actors out of comedians, for they had to appear lighthearted on stage in spite of their troubles.[8] After a disappointing 1909 season, Williams took to the vaudeville stage, appearing at the Hammersteins' Victoria Theatre billed as "the greatest and most original comedian in the world."[9] A few months later, he joined Florenz Ziegfeld's Follies of 1910.

As a performer in the Follies, Williams was extremely successful and howlingly funny. Carl Van Vechten considered Williams one of the finest actors in the early twentieth century. "Bert Williams shuffled along in his hopeless way; always penniless, always the butt of fortune, and always human," he wrote.

> He reblackened his face, enlarged his mouth, wore shoes which extended beyond the limits of even extraordinary feet, but he never transcended the precise lines of characterization. He was as definite as Mansfield, as subtle as Coquelin. Duse saw him on one of her American tours and promptly decided he was America's finest actor.[10]

A writer for *Theatre Magazine* in 1903 agreed. "Bert Williams," the author noted, "has long enjoyed the reputation of being a vastly funnier man than any white comedian now on the American stage. He is spontaneously and genuinely humorous, he is not only a funny man, he can act. Those who know what Williams can do are convinced that in a part combining comedy and pathos, this colored thespian would score a great triumph."[11]

Years later Heywood Broun would argue that only Eddie Cantor and Al Jolson came close to Williams's level of humor in Ziegfeld's shows, but neither possessed "the subtlety, which belonged to Williams at his best."[12] Although

Williams's name appeared inconspicuously at the bottom of the program, critics agreed with the *New York Tribune* in 1910 that he was the "real star." The *New York World* argued that the black comedian had "more real talent than all the rest of the cast combined," and the *New York Times* asserted that "there is no more clever low comedian on our stage today."[13] At different times, prominent theater people like George M. Cohan and David Belasco sought Williams's services for plays they hoped to produce, but the black merrymaker remained loyal to Ziegfeld and Erlanger because they had been the "first to give a Negro actor a featured place in a white company."[14]

Success and acclaim, however, did not protect Williams against the unthinking racism of the theater or society in general. In spite of Williams's being the hit of the vaudeville program at the Victoria Theatre, for instance, the Hammersteins caved in to pressure from a white vaudevillian organization—the "White Rats"—and refused to give the black star top billing. The "headliner" was a lesser known white comedienne, Maude Raymond.[15] Similarly, when he joined the Follies, Williams agreed never to appear on stage at the same time as any of the white women performers so as to avoid rousing outrage among white theatre patrons.[16] A popular attraction, Williams could not socialize familiarly with whites in the audience; after the curtain descended, the "star" was just another black man unwelcome on the other side of the color line. Articles on American comedians in mainstream periodicals never included the artistry of Bert Williams, even though critics typically gushed with enthusiasm whenever they witnessed one of his performances. His trademark song, "Nobody," must not have seemed so amusing when in daily life Bert Williams disappeared as one more dark face in an ebony crowd, segregated from white society. By the early 1950s, little more than two decades after his untimely death and less than a decade after the publication of two important studies on black theater in America, would-be biographers still knew little about him, and the author of a Broadway "Hall of Fame" did not even think to include Williams until he contacted an aging Lester A. Walton, who insisted that "the inimitable comedian of yesteryear" deserved to be so honored.[17]

If the "funniest man in America" could be so easily marginalized in the theater world and forgotten so quickly in spite of the encomiums published in the immediate aftermath of his death, no wonder equally talented but lesser-known black artists escaped the notice of white theater people. And no wonder Torrence maintained that the men and women who portrayed the characters in his three plays were untrained and inexperienced. For what Torrence did not realize was that many of the actors who played prominent roles in *Three Plays for a Negro Theater* had been on stage for years and were well known to black theatergoers in New York.

Blanche Deas, for example, who played Lucy Sparrow in *The Rider of Dreams* and Sapphie in *Granny Maumee,* had nearly a decade of experience in various shows. She sang and danced as part of the chorus in Cole and Johnson's Red Moon Company in 1909, where she studied acting with Elizabeth Williams, who had organized a dramatic class for women connected with the show. The following year she joined S. H. Dudley's Smart Set Company, which opened at the Howard Theatre in Washington, D. C., in early September. By the following spring she was back with Cole and Johnson, this time as a soloist, who, according to reviews, had become "the vocal hit of the act," and in the summer of 1912, she had stepped into vaudeville, doing a "single turn which is full of merit" at the Crescent Theatre in New York. From late December 1912 until her appearance in *Three Plays for a Negro Theater,* Deas pursued more acting opportunities. She starred in a two-act musical farce, *Who Wins?,* at the New Star Casino, earned a spot on the program at Young's Casino to honor old-timer Sam Lucas in 1913, joined the Lafayette Players later that year, and starred in *The Real Estate Agent* at the Lafayette Theatre in 1914. Indeed, Torrence had first become aware of Deas in early 1914, when he asked James Reese Europe for a list of African American actresses who might be suitable for the Stage Society's production of *Granny Maumee.* Europe recommended Deas along with Abbie Mitchell, Mrs. Samuel Knight, and Grace Lee Cook. When Deas returned to the vaudeville stage in the summer of 1916, the *New York Age* reported that she was "effusively received," her "bright future in the ranks of professional actors" having become, among African American audiences at least, a reality.[18]

Torrence's search for an actress to portray Acte, an Egyptian princess in *Simon, the Cyrenian,* ended with the selection of another veteran performer, Lottie Grady. With about two weeks to go before opening night, Torrence and Jones were still holding auditions to fill the part. Lester A. Walton reported in the *New York Age* that "applicant after applicant has appeared at the Park Theatre . . . and signified a desire to play the part of the Egyptian princess." Some amateurs, some professionals, and even "young women prominent in the social life of Greater New York" sought the coveted role. In the end, Lottie Grady walked away with the part.[19] But Grady, like Deas, was no ingenue and certainly no stranger to Broadway; she had considerable acting experience and training behind her. Like many African American actresses of the period, Grady started her career as a singer and dancer with a large traveling show. In 1899, she began a western tour with Charles T. Trux's Black 400s. By the early 1900s, she had settled in Chicago and had begun working at the Pekin Theatre, which was run by African Americans devoted to black shows. She appeared as one of the "featured players" in such productions as *In Zululand* (1907),

Doctor Dope (1907), and *The Merry Widower* (1908) and starred as "the Belle of San Domingo" in *The Grafters* (1907). When the Pekin changed hands in 1909 and the new manager, Robert Mott, reorganized the stock company, Grady became one of the theater's leading actresses. That year she starred as Ada Norton in *The Chambermaid,* as the wife in *The Husband,* as Nora Smith in *The Man Upstairs,* and as Mrs. Helen Harding in *The Idlers,* with Charles Gilpin as her costar in the last two shows.[20]

Grady grabbed attention in New York in 1909 with her part in *Mr. Lode of Koal,* a part she landed when George Walker's illness made it impossible for his wife, Aida Overton Walker, to continue with the show. When Sylvester Russell of the *Indianapolis Freeman* saw the show in the Great Northern Theatre in Chicago, he reported that although Grady had but an incidental part, she "made much out of a small scene with Mr. Williams," and when the company played in New York later that year, he called Grady a "finished artist" who had "captured Broadway."[21] Although known in Chicago for her "enviable reputation at the Pekin Theatre as an actress, a dancer, and a mimic," she was a newcomer to New York theater circles, but Williams and Walker believed "she [would] make good if given an opportunity."[22]

Make good she did in the next several years. After the Williams and Walker show closed, she won a part in S. H. Dudley's production of *His Honor, the Barber* in 1910 and opened with a solo act at the Monogram Theatre in Chicago when the Smart Set's show had closed for the summer. Earning the "largest salary ever paid a single [black] performer" in Chicago—one hundred dollars a week—Grady drew large crowds. The *Chicago Evening American* reported that the manager of the Monogram Theatre boasted that with Grady on stage, "his house is S. R. O. at every performance."[23] For the next couple of years she divided her time between acting in the Pekin Stock Company in Chicago, traveling the Western Vaudeville Circuit as a solo artist, and working with S. H. Dudley's Smart Set, starring, for example, in *Dr. Beans from Boston* in 1913.[24] When Will Foster organized a motion picture company "dealing exclusively with Negro life," in 1913, he selected Lottie Grady to star in one of the first films, *The Pullman Porter.*[25] After a brief, well-earned vacation in the posh resort in West Baden, Indiana, in April 1916, Grady returned to the road, joining up with the Irwin C. Miller company to perform in Jacksonville, Florida.[26] Thus, landing the role of Acte was something less than a major triumph for an actress whose career had grown up with the new century.

Appearing with Grady in *Simon, the Cyrenian* as Procula, Inez Clough may well have viewed their parts in *Three Plays for a Negro Theater* as something of a reunion. Clough had worked with Grady in *Mr. Lode of Koal* eight years earlier and, like Grady, had been working in show business since the 1890s. She sang in John W. Isham's *Oriental America,* a daring venture in operatic performance that broke away from the traditional cakewalk dancing and burlesque comedy of earlier African American shows and that played at Palmer's Theatre and Wallack's instead of at burlesque houses. When the troupe toured England, Clough decided to remain in London. For five years she worked in the British Isles, as a soloist, in the pantomimes, and in musicals.[27] In the halcyon days of the big touring colored shows of the early twentieth century, Clough found work in Cole and Johnson's *Shoo Fly Regiment* (1906) and Williams and Walker's *Bandanna Land* (1907) as well as in *Mr. Lode of Koal.* When the companies disbanded in 1910 and 1911 in the wake of George Walker's, Bob Cole's, and Ernest Hogan's deaths and the flight of Bert Williams to Ziegfeld's Follies, Clough turned to the vaudeville stage before joining the new stock company in New York's Lafayette Theatre in 1913.[28]

Remembered at her death in 1933 as "one of the 10 great actresses of America" whose "unusual talent," "sterling character," and "keen intellect" made her "a lady to the manner [*sic*] born," Inez Clough played a wide range of characters in the course of her career. "Her splendid acting in *Earth*," wrote Robert J. Douglass in 1933, "opened Broadway for the Negro of today." She played the Queen in *Salome,* Mrs. Mabel Jamison, a widow, in *The Hebrew,* and rose "to unsuspected heights as Mme. Catherine Lockwood" in *The Lure.* As a member of the stock company at the Lafayette Theatre in Harlem, Clough also appeared in *The Deep Purple* and in Clyde Fitch's *The City* in 1916, just months before the opening of *Three Plays for a Negro Theater.*[29] When George Jean Nathan included Clough on his list of the ten best actresses for the 1916–1917 season, he was honoring a black star, "thoroughly educated in the technique of interpretation, acting and stagecraft," whose talents "so thrilled her audiences that repeated curtain calls and ovations were thrust upon her."[30]

Two other actors with prominent roles in *Three Plays for a Negro Theater* were, like Deas, Grady, and Clough, no strangers to the world of make-believe. Indeed, Jesse Shipp was on the verge of retirement when he auditioned for the part of Barrabas in *Simon, the Cyrenian.* At the age of forty-eight, Shipp knew all aspects of the theater from writing scripts for musical comedy to working as a stage director to performing before the footlights. Before joining his first minstrel show at the age of nineteen, he had performed as a singer and had toured with an *Uncle Tom's Cabin* troupe. In 1896, Shipp left the Primrose and West Minstrels—famous for their combination of forty white and thirty black performers—to join John W. Isham's Oriental American company, where he met Inez Clough for the first time. They would work together again when Clough appeared in Williams and Walker's *Bandanna Land,* for which Shipp wrote the book. By then, he had worked with the great comedy team for nearly a decade and had written the books for *The Policy Players, The Sons of Ham, In Dahomey,* and *Abyssinia.* He also had gained experience as a stage manager, director, and actor in the various Williams and Walker shows. Shipp played "Hustling Charley" in *In Dahomey* at the New York Theatre on Broadway and in the Shaftesbury Theatre in London, and he later played the part of "Mose Blackstone" in *Bandanna Land.* By 1906, Joseph W. Reed included Shipp among the new notable Negro actors who no longer used "a loud voice, a knowledge of a few coon songs . . . a few stale and time worn jokes, [and] an inexhaustible supply of slang phrases and vulgar language."[31]

Actually, Shipp came to Williams and Walker as a seasoned theater man. According to a eulogist in the *New York Age,* "by the time Williams and Walker came along with their shows, Mr. Shipp had made quite a name for himself as a writer of dialogue and dancing teacher, as well as an end man in the minstrels of those days." And when the team was broken up by Walker's illness and eventual death, Shipp had no trouble finding work. By 1909, at the ripe old age of forty, Shipp had earned a reputation as an "actor, playwright and school master of actors," who already had "done a great deal to emancipate the Negro actor from minstrelsy."[32] He went to the Pekin Theatre in Chicago in 1910 at the invitation of Robert Mott to produce stock shows for about thirty weeks. When he returned to New York, he was hailed as "a representative [man] of the colored theatrical profession" and praised as "the race's most prominent stage director." Indeed, Shipp staged and directed the two-act farce *Who Wins?* at the New Star Casino in 1912, and later became the director of the newly founded stock company, the Lafayette Players, in 1913.[33]

One of Shipp's long-time associates, Alexander Rogers, appeared in *The Rider of Dreams* as Dr. Williams. From the first Williams and Walker show, *The Policy Players* (1899), to the last, *Bandanna Land* (1907), Shipp and Rogers had collaborated to make the team's shows popular and successful. While Shipp wrote the book for most of these productions, Rogers penned lyrics to such songs as *I'm a Jonah Man,* one of Bert Williams's most popular hits; *Nobody,* Williams's signature tune; and *On Broadway in Dahomey Bye and Bye.* Like Shipp, Rogers got his start in show business as an eighteen-year-old minstrel performer, but in the 1890s he left minstrelsy for the African American shows then organizing. With a grammar school education and a passion for reading, he began writing lyrics as a young man, and he wrote more than one thousand songs in his lifetime. Williams and Walker's chief composer, Will Marion Cook, remembered that "nobody since Paul Laurence Dunbar was as good as Alex Rogers at writing Negro dialect and capturing the spirit of his race in his work." Because of his talents as a writer, Rogers was commissioned in 1909 by

N. Smith Clark of the Tuskegee Institute to write a short history of the life and work of Williams and Walker.[34]

Rogers continued with Bert Williams, writing the lyrics for songs used in *Mr. Lode of Koal* (1909). The next year, he wrote lyrics for a show called *A Trip to Africa,* and in 1911, he joined forces with J. Rosamond Johnson when Johnson's partner, Bob Cole, fell ill. Later in the year Rogers reunited with Shipp and Cook to create a headlining act at the Grand Theatre, which the *New York Age* reported was "the hit of the show."[35] But in between writing jobs, Rogers gained a great deal of experience as an actor. He portrayed "George Reeder," when *In Dahomey* appeared in London in 1903 at the Shaftesbury Theatre and "Amos Simmons" in *Bandanna Land* at the Majestic Theatre in 1908. By 1913, Rogers was billed as "America's Greatest Colored Character Actor, 'The Negro David Warfield' " in an advertisement for *The Old Man's Boy,* in which he starred.[36]

One of the co-stars in *The Old Man's Boy,* Andrew Bishop, also appeared in *Three Plays for a Negro Theater* in 1917, as Drusus in *Simon, the Cyrenian.* More typical of the younger generation of black actors, Bishop had begun his career in stock companies. One of the players in *Who Wins?,* Bishop was, according to Lester A. Walton, "perfectly natural in his part," and in *The Old Man's Boy,* he also received praise. When the Anita Bush Stock Company formed, Bishop performed in *Over the Footlights* (1915) and in *The Octoroon, The Gambler's Sweetheart, The Deep Purple, The Lure,* and *The City* (1916). Walton wrote of the young actor, "Should Mr. Bishop take the stage seriously and conclude to make it his life's work he could easily do so. He has everything in his favor, even to joining the ranks of those who today are 'passing' and enjoying big reputations." In *The Lure,* Walton wrote that Bishop had been given an "opportunity to do some strong and effective work," and a month later, in Clyde Fitch's *The City,* Bishop "gave evidence of newly developed power."[37]

Others in the cast of *Three Plays for a Negro Theater* had less experience. John T. Butler, who played the title role in *Simon, the Cyrenian,* had developed his talents largely as an amateur. According to James Weldon Johnson, Butler worked for the post office but had gained some "experience in amateur and semi-professional theatricals." Five years before appearing as Simon, Butler had come to the attention of Lester A. Walton when he performed in an annual pre-Lenten recital in New York. Butler "was the hit of the evening," according to the critic. "His enunciation is good and although he does not pose as a singer he gives evidence of being able to creditably render vocal selections if ambitious in that direction." A few months later, Butler participated in the Soap Box Minstrels' Show as one of the "leading colored reciters." This time Walton called him a "talented reader" with "much histrionic ability."[38] Similarly, Marie Jackson-Stuart, the star of *Granny Maumee,* was known principally as a dramatic reader rather than as an actress, and Jervis Wilson, who had a non-speaking part as one of the soldiers in *Simon, the Cyrenian,* may not have acted much in New York since 1910. Then, as a member of the Mignonette Coterie Club, "Jervey" Wilson had a bit part in a one-act musical comedy called "Flora's Birthday."[39]

Opal Cooper, celebrated almost universally for his portrayal of Madison Sparrow in *The Rider of Dreams,* had built his career largely as a cabaret entertainer. After 1912, opportunities to work in clubs and at hotel-restaurants like Sherry's, Delmonico's, the Waldorf-Astoria, and the Ritz-Carlton attracted a large number of actors and vaudevillians because of the relative paucity of opportunities on stage. As Walton explained in the *New York Age,* when these actors-turned-cabaret-artists "are approached about returning to the stage, they begin to think of their trooping days with the one-nighters and the call notifying them to be at the railroad platform in 'Squeedunk' to catch the 6:30 train in the morning." Most, he argued, preferred "the bright lights of Broadway, where . . . a more intimate and profitable an acquaintance is had with the dimes and quarters." If Cooper's experience was at all typical, then it is safe to assume that when acting opportunities *did* arise in New York, cabaret artists eagerly grabbed them. Although Cooper was known primarily as a cabaret singer whose rich voice pleased the club crowds and later the audiences at the Garden and Garrick Theatres, he did appear in at least two shows at the Lafayette Theatre—*Darkydom* and *The Deep Purple*—where he was heralded as "a promising tenor" with "all the requisites to success."[40] His eighth-place appearance on George Jean Nathan's list of the top ten actors in 1916–1917, perhaps only confirmed those earlier predictions of success.

Grady, Clough, Deas, Shipp, Rogers, Bishop, Jackson-Stuart, Butler, and Cooper must be seen as seasoned performers with a world of experience and striving in the theater who landed roles in Torrence's historic production. It is important to remember, however, that they were not the only and perhaps not even the most talented African American thespians in the 1910s. These brief sketches show clearly that as they used their natural talents in the venues available, they participated in an effort to develop a tradition of fine acting by studying, reading, watching others, and forming institutions to build up the profession. While Ridgely Torrence may have believed that they were unschooled in the histrionic arts, the actors themselves knew better. Since the turn of the century, they had been struggling mightily with limited capital and limited time to create schools, societies, and companies where they could learn to act naturally.

LEARNING TO ACT NATURALLY

In an undated autobiographical statement probably written in the 1930s, Ridgely Torrence reflected on the "pioneer work" he had done in trying to establish a Negro Theatre in America. In this statement, as elsewhere, he reiterated that a cast had been "gathered with great difficulty" and that he and Jones had been "obliged to train their actors from the beginning" because they had had no training for serious drama. One of Torrence's friends, however, told a slightly different story shortly after opening night. In her review of the plays for *Theatre Arts Magazine,* Zona Gale noted that the cast had been "selected from colored people all over New York, a few acting in stock companies." During the course of rehearsals, she wrote, "the players came . . . to be themselves. Intonation, business [*sic*], interpretation, were never given to the players first—merely modified as the work progressed." Robert Benchley, a drama critic for the *New York Tribune* who had been invited to a morning rehearsal a few days before opening night, agreed with Gale. "Many of those chosen have had experience in elocution and dramatic reading or in vaudeville, where their natural talents have been developed," he wrote. Moreover, he noticed that "the director and author have not tried to direct in the sense that a company of white actors have to be directed. The producers are trying to give the players as free rein as possible, hoping that they will play the parts as they feel they ought to be played." And, according to Benchley, the approach seemed to be working. "I saw one lithe youth, who was rehearsing the part of an Egyptian slave, make an obeisance before the king (who was not there)," he reported. "It was a move which, if it were being rehearsed by an average actor, would have to be done over, at a conservative estimate, twenty-five times, and then probably abandoned as impossible. At the first attempt this colored boy, out of his own intuitive sense of what was right, made as perfect and complete a gesture as could have been drawn with a pair of compasses and with infinitely more animation." Left more or less to their own devices, Benchley implied, African American performers were natural actors.[41]

In these brief passages quoted from longer comments by Torrence, Gale, and Benchley, much more is at work—and at stake—than accurate reporting. By this I do not mean to imply that they wrote dishonestly or with the aim of dissembling. They no doubt reported what they had observed or remembered. But their telling the story of these pioneering actors revealed their biases as well as their sympathies and demonstrated a profound lack of awareness of African American experience in the theater. Writing sometime in the second decade after his grand venture, Torrence may well have been seeking some explanation for its limited impact on the development of African American actors and themes on the American stage. While in some respects Gale and Benchley qualified Torrence's claim for having trained inexperienced performers by noting the relatively free rein Jones and the author gave the actors, neither gave African Americans credit for efforts they had made prior to 1917 to professionalize the African American Stage. They emphasized the natural instincts of the actors over their experience. Indeed, Benchley noted that few had been chosen from stock companies "for it was found that long association with melodrama and comedy written for white actors had made them less natural in their speech, more stagy in their gestures and not so well adapted to the expression of the pure African or those who have not imitated themselves away from it." Gale similarly discounted the importance of work in stock companies by noting that the members of the cast who had experience in such groups had been largely "untouched by the crudities of the burlesque written for them."[42] Perhaps Benchley simply was unaware that nine of the fourteen major speaking parts in the three plays were performed by actors attached to repertory theater. Perhaps Gale believed that the former stock players had been "untouched by the crudities" of black shows because the actors simply were not crude. But can one assume that others *were* coarsened by association with African American stock companies?

At the bottom of these particular comments—and, as we shall see, in many white commentaries on the black acting—lay a powerful tension between white observers' preconceived ideas about black performance and the actual performances they witnessed. Recognizing that African American performers did not associate with or study under respected white actors and were barred from noted acting classes, they still could not resist comparisons with histrionic standards set by white performers, whose names and styles were widely known. The black actors, according to Benchley and Gale at least, were "natural," but the two writers rued the fact that they were not trained professionals. Indeed, Benchley looked forward to a time when a "National Negro Theatre" would feature plays "written by colored playwrights" and "dealing with the many problems of negro life." Perhaps, too, one would find "colored players who devote their whole time to the performance of this service to their race."[43] Many members of the black acting fraternity, including several in the cast of the three plays, may have been surprised by this observation, undoubtedly believing they were so devoted.

Whether because of prejudice or ignorance, these writers wanted to believe that the African American "Adams" of the stage had been created in the image of the benevolent theater people who prepared the stage for their arrival on Broadway. But the idea of professionalism in the African American theater was not born with the production of *Three Plays for a Negro Theater,* nor did it spring, fully formed, from the heads of Torrence, Jones, and Hapgood. Ever since the big musical comedies of the 1890s and early 1900s, African American performers had sought access to schools to develop their creativity and expression; they had created venues and opportunities to perform when white stage doors were closed to them; and they had cultivated the artistic community in New York by organizing clubs and associations designed to advance the interests of and to establish standards for black entertainers. Ironically, they, too, were torn between a desire to gain acceptance by white critics for their work in white plays and to present themselves as representatives of a race apart. For they wanted the training that seemed to give white actors an edge, but they also hoped to act naturally and thereby express on stage distinctive racial characteristics too often obscured in black characters interpreted by whites.

An education in the performing arts took many forms for African Americans at the turn of the century, and for some, education came through fairly traditional means. Inez Clough, for example, born and raised in Worcester, Massachusetts, attended schools in her hometown and in Boston, specializing in voice and piano. When she remained in London after the *Oriental America* company departed, she received voice lessons in England, and later she traveled to Austria to take lessons there.[44] Similarly, Leigh Whipper, a character actor in the early 1900s who in the 1930s achieved national fame in *Porgy and Bess,* attended public schools in Washington, D. C., took courses at Howard University, and finished his education at St. Paul's in Newcastle under Lyme in England.[45] Several of the popular composers of music for African American shows were graduates of respected music schools in the United States. Will Marion Cook studied music at the Oberlin Conservatory and the National Conservatory of Music in the United States and obtained additional advanced instruction in Germany. Bob Cole was a graduate of Atlanta University, and his partner, J. Rosamond Johnson, studied at the New England Conservatory.[46] All of these examples, of course, demonstrate the high level of musical training achieved by black performers in these years, and such training is not the same as learning the art of dramatic expression. Professional musical instruction, however, does promote poise, stage presence, and virtuosity, all of which are basic ingredients of effective acting.

Those who had been formally educated in the United States and abroad built on that schooling when they prepared for the stage. In a *New York Age* editorial urging black performers to take their professional preparation more seriously, Lester A. Walton noted that successful African American performers had learned that "it is just as necessary that you be a close student in the theatrical profession as it is for those ambitious to shine in other professions." He noted that Harry Fiddler studied others to try to improve his act, that George Walker practiced his strutting dance steps in front of the mirror, and that his wife, Aida Overton Walker, had studied dance.[47] Howard-educated Leigh Whipper learned acting "by observing the techniques" of famous white actors such as Richard Mansfield, Julia Marlowe, Nat Goodwin, Edward H. Sothern, and David Warfield.[48] And, as mentioned above, Elizabeth Williams of the Red Moon Company in 1909 organized a dramatic class for women in the show. "Mme. Williams is very proud of the class," the *New York Age* reported, "and says that the time is not far distant when there will be six new character artists in the profession"—Blanche Deas, Lula Coleman, Leona Marshall, Mamie Butler, Bessie Tribble, and Bessie O. Brown.[49]

As valuable as these forms of study could be to hopefuls, nothing could substitute for experience, and here the color line made itself felt most dramatically. Access to white venues remained relatively constricted for black performers through most of the early twentieth century. Even when plays called for African American characters, managers on Broadway and elsewhere in first-class theaters typically employed white actors wearing burnt cork. When the Stage Society produced Torrence's *Granny Maumee* in 1914, for example, Dorothy Donnelly appeared in the title role, in spite of the playwright's request that the producers use black actors.[50] Such plays as Thomas Dixon's *The Clansman,* produced at the Amsterdam Theatre in 1905, Edward Sheldon's *The Nigger,* which opened at the New Theatre late in 1909, Robert Hilliard's *Pride of Race,* which played at the Maxine Elliott Theatre in early 1916, and a comedy by Laurence Eyre called *Sazus Matazus,* which was given a "preliminary hearing" at the Apollo Theatre in Atlantic City in June 1916, all included African American characters, but they were performed by all-white casts (though one wonders what self-respecting African American actor would have *wanted* to appear in *The Clansman*).[51] With a few exceptions—perhaps the most notable being Bert Williams in Ziegfeld's Follies and a spectacle at the New York Hippodrome in 1911 called *Marching through Georgia* that used a fairly large number of African Americans as "extras" in a plantation scene—until *Three Plays for a Negro Theater,* the white theatrical community stubbornly persisted in casting blackface white performers in African American parts even after the advent of successful all-black shows.[52]

Of course, some light-skinned African Americans did work in white productions, but there is no way of knowing how many did so, for "passing" usually demanded a fairly complete break with family and friends behind the veil. When Charlie Case died in November 1916, for example, the *New York Age* obituary noted that he had "been passing so as to advance himself in the white world of theater." "Coming to New York and finding the numerous handicaps which the ambitious must face, and soon learning that the path trod by the colored performer is far more rocky than that of the white performer," the eulogist wrote, "many have buried their true racial identity and secured work as Caucasians."[53] A 1916 production of *The Octoroon* by the Anita Bush Stock Company at the Lafayette Theatre also elicited comment by the *New York Age* on the issue of passing. This timely presentation, the critic observed, coincided with white America's "awakening to the fact that there are thousands of colored people throughout the country of Negro origin who are living in their respective communities as white people."[54] But working on the stage or living among whites necessarily demanded that such people suppress any indication that they were African American, so their presence, while perhaps beneficial to themselves, did nothing to increase the awareness of black life, culture, or expression on the American stage. So officially and openly, black actors remained barred from the so-called legitimate theaters.

Given that reality, African American theater people created their own venues whenever possible and developed themselves professionally in stock companies of their own devising. One of the earliest of these stock companies, the Pekin Players, formed in Chicago in 1906. The impulse for the group came earlier, when young black entertainers, frustrated by the limitations of vaudeville and musical comedy, began gathering in the evenings to read serious plays aloud. Some invited friends, and the group grew to nearly thirty black men and women. Eleven of these people succeeded in persuading the manager of the Pekin Theatre to let them present plays, and, accordingly, they took the name Pekin Players. According to James Haskins, the Pekin Players principally presented "refined white comedies," some appearing in "white-face" to play the parts. Others, however, reported more variety in the productions. The author of the *Colored Actors' Union Theatrical Guide,* for instance, recorded *The Mayor of Dixie* as the company's first show and noted that the cast included Lottie Grady, Charles Gilpin, and Lena Marshall.[55]

More than a year after the founding of the Pekin Players, Lucie France Pierce prepared an article on the group for *Theatre Magazine.* She noted that everyone involved—"on the stage, in the pit, in the office"—was black. Celebrating its success, she noted that "it was founded by a negro for his own race, and yet so excellent and so simple and refreshing is the performance on the stage that the thirty boxes set apart for white men are filled every night." Pierce reported that Joe Jordan and Will Marion Cook composed most of the music for the shows, and twenty-year-old Harrison Stewart performed as the "chief comedian." Pearl Brown, a "singing comedienne," and J. Ed. Green, stage manager and the satirical author of the books and lyrics, were the only other participants she mentioned by name. Pierce *did* discuss the "peculiarly original" shows, which she described as filled with self-deprecating humor. Each week, Green selected "some foible of the negro to turn to ridicule," Pierce wrote. "His childishness in a bargain, his love of games of chance, his vanity in dress, his adoration of tinsel and titles, all these are turned to gentle absurdity before the negro's eyes."[56] Whether the mainstays of the Pekin Players were original plays about Negro life or recycled white plays, this Chicago institution provided opportunities for black actors to gain experience in a variety of roles on a regular basis.

Stock companies like the Pekin did not form in New York until 1913, when Henry Creamer, Alex Rogers, and Will Marion Cook formed the Negro Players. The purpose of the company, clearly articulated by Cook, was "to aid in the development and perfection" of black musical and dramatic talent—to further professionalize the African American Stage. Moreover, Cook explained, the company intended to produce plays that provided "real pictures of Negro life both of city and plantation," an aim that encouraged the development of black playwrights as well as black actors.[57] Lester A. Walton hailed the effort as an "advancement of the colored theatrical profession" and as an important shift in the style of representing African Americans on stage "from slap-stick and a ridiculing of the race—to dramatic work, minus the crudities of method, acting full of human interest, wherein the Negro is shown as a man among men, possessing a heart and finer feelings the same as others."[58] The Negro Players, though relatively short-lived, paved the way for other such efforts.

Within two years of the founding of the Negro Players, a young actress, Anita Bush, established her own company for the Lincoln Theatre in Harlem, and she, too, envisioned both more opportunities for black actors and the cultivation of dramatic talent. A decade later, Bart Kennett credited her with "driving the first wedge into a field in which her people had hitherto been considered as jokes," and noted significantly that "before her there had been no 'Rider of Dreams,' 'Simon the Cyrenian,' 'Granny Maumee,' no operatic Faust. All of these wonderful dramatic accomplishments of Negro artists came after her."[59] In late December 1915, Bush's stock company moved from the Lincoln Theatre to the Lafayette Theatre and became known as the Lafayette Stock Company. They presented a new play each week, including popular plays like *Dr. Jekyll and Mr. Hyde* and *The Count of Monte Cristo* as well as classics like *Othello,* which the company performed in 1916 during the Tercentenary of William Shakespeare.[60] The variety of shows presented by these companies in New York demanded versatility from the actors and provided tremendous experience on the stage.

The Lafayette Theatre and Lincoln Theatre themselves became important venues for the professionalizing of the African American Stage. Built originally in 1912 as a theater for white plays, white actors, and white audiences, the Lafayette Theatre on the corner of Seventh Avenue and 131st Street quickly found itself surrounded by a fast-growing African American community hostile to its unpopular segregated seating policy. Within a couple of years, the original managers sold out to a black/white team, Lester A. Walton and C. W. Morganstern. The Lafayette Theatre in many respects symbolized the enormous obstacles that stood in the way of professional development of black performers. While Walton, the day-to-day manager of the theatre, saw it as "an artistic arena" for black acts, his partner saw it as a financial investment and demanded entertainment that would generate a big return. Without sufficient capital to buy or lease the theater outright, African American theatre people continued to form partnerships with white investors whose demands for profits limited the artistic experimentalism of the producers. Walton did succeed in bringing the Anita Bush Stock Company to the Lafayette before he and Morganstern gave up the lease to the theater in 1916. Three years later, when the Lafayette had been purchased by the Elite Amusement Corporation, Walton returned to manage the theater and to organize traveling shows for the parent company. This time, after the First World War, the Lafayette Theatre became a showcase for talented black actors and writers.[61]

At the same time that Walton and Morganstern sought to make the Lafayette into a theater for black dramatic actors, the Lincoln Theatre was in the process of converting itself from a movie house into a legitimate playhouse. Each week, the Lincoln put on a four-act play as well as vaudeville acts and photoplays. In 1915, the Lincoln produced Scott Joplin's ill-fated opera, *Treemonisha*, without proper costumes, props, or orchestral accompaniment. Nevertheless, the desire to produce a Negro opera suggests the level of commitment to high-quality entertainment featuring African American performers to which the Lincoln Theatre aspired. A stock company, directed initially by Billie Burke, prepared the players well to present a new play each week, and many of the actors built on their previous vaudeville experience. Although relatively short-lived, the stock company at the Lincoln Theatre and the theater itself contributed to the general development of black talent in New York.[62]

The Elite Amusement Corporation was not the first to organize tours for black shows. Obviously, the various companies—Williams and Walker, Cole and Johnson, and Ernest Hogan—had made tours decades before this effort. Perhaps the most successful, however, to establish a regular circuit for colored shows, was S. H. Dudley, known affectionately as "Uncle Dud." Organized in 1911, S. H. Dudley's Theatrical Enterprise operated out of an office in the nation's capital, and the circuit included theaters in Richmond,

Norfolk, Newport News, and Roanoke, all in Virginia, Louisville, Kentucky, and Philadelphia. Dudley also helped establish the Theater Owners' Booking Association, a well-known circuit of performance venues mostly in the South that ultimately included houses in the western states Texas and Oklahoma and in several northern cities.[63]

Dudley's Smart Set Company, which developed numerous talented performers, and his establishment of the circuits represented important efforts to create opportunities in a theater world divided by the color line. Dudley also helped form the Colored Actors' Union, another example of African Americans seeking to help themselves as professional entertainers.[64] Two other organizations predated the union, both of which advanced the interests of black actors. In the summer of 1908, a number of "the leading actors of the race" met at the home of George Walker to form an organization called "The Frogs." The purpose of the group was to promote "social intercourse between the representative members of the Negro theatrical profession and to those connected directly or indirectly with art, literature, music, scientific, and liberal professions and the patrons of the arts." The Frogs hoped to maintain a library devoted especially to the history, folklore, music, and literature of African Americans and to keep a record of "all worthy achievements" by members of the race. The first officers included George Walker, J. Rosamond Johnson, Jesse Shipp, Bob Cole, and Alex Rogers.[65]

Even the simple act of forming a society like The Frogs exposed the barriers to black performance and association in early-twentieth-century America. A few weeks after the first Frogs met, they drew up the appropriate papers to incorporate themselves in the state of New York. The first judge to examine the petition refused to grant the black artists the right to incorporate. "Art" and "frogs," Judge Goff argued, did not jibe. Within days of the decision, editorials denouncing Judge Goff's decision appeared in the *New York Tribune, New York World, New York Sun, Brooklyn Eagle,* and *New Haven Register*—all reminding the hapless justice of Aristophanes. Lester A. Walton of the *New York Age,* one of the group's charter members, left it to his white fellow journalists to "question the knowledge of Justice Goff on Grecian history," but he identified a more pointed issue. "It could be possible that it was not the combination of art and frogs that appeared so incongruous to the learned Judge as it was the combination of the Negro and art."[66] The judge continued to refuse to approve the charter for incorporation and ordered his secretary to fire off a heated rebuttal to Walton's accusation of racism. Indeed, it was not until August 18, 1908, when Justice Henry Bischoff heard the case on appeal, that The Frogs won recognition in the state of New York as a legitimate association for black performers.[67]

In the next few years after their legal victory, The Frogs emerged as an important social organization that attracted the leading black stars in the city. Each year they organized a "Frolic of the Frogs," an evening of entertainment put on by members, accompanied by music, food, and dancing. Its offices became, in a way, the focal point for the black stars in New York's world of entertainment, and until the hard times of the 1930s depression, the club stood as a reminder of the race's efforts to promote excellence in entertainment.

Similarly, the Colored Vaudeville Benevolent Association, or C.V.B.A., which formed about a year after The Frogs, was intended to be both a social organization and a collective effort to establish and maintain high standards for black acts performing on various vaudeville circuits. The men and women who joined the C.V.B.A. did not perceive it as a union to make demands for better wages and working conditions, but rather as a voluntary association by which "the colored performer" could "elevate himself in the profession" by adhering to "a higher standard artistically, morally, and financially."[68] Like The Frogs, the C.V.B.A. held socials, dinners, and evenings of entertainment for members and established club rooms where members could meet informally and share information about opportunities, managers, and acts.[69]

Thus, well before 1917, African American actors had taken numerous steps to professionalize the stage. From schools to stock companies, from theatrical venues to interstate theater circuits, and from impromptu acting classes to professional associations, black artists learned from one another the demanding art of dramatic expression. They worked tirelessly on several fronts to create opportunities where they could gain valuable experience believed necessary to overcome the color line in the American theater, and they looked to leading black performers—and regular critical commentary— for cues on representing African Americans on stage with subtlety, accuracy, and sympathy.

In spite of decades of activity, a host of experienced and talented black stars, and regular performances by black companies in New York and around the country, white theater people—even those purported to be interested in establishing a national Negro theater—could still claim in 1917 that no competent actors could be secured for a Broadway drama, a claim that reveals more than anything else a profound lack of awareness of the theatrical profession as it existed in the African American community of the early twentieth century. The writer Ralph Ellison captured beautifully and poignantly four decades later this painful reality of "invisibility" that black performers in the 1910s knew all too well. Black actors found themselves caught in a double bind— for to become "visible," they had to be seen in theaters prominent enough to merit comment in the influential daily newspapers and magazines that shaped national (white) perceptions of the race. But in order to land roles in such productions (when auditions by blacks were even entertained) they had to overcome prejudice against black performers, about whom, it turns out, most white theater people were amazingly ignorant.

For one man, Lester A. Walton, the problems encountered by African American performers in the 1910s ran much deeper than mere lack of knowledge. As a drama critic, lyricist and songwriter, theater manager, and, ultimately, a civil rights activist, Walton believed the essential question of the stage boiled down to one of *citizenship*. On stage and in the audiences, a drama far more vital than anything imagined by the country's leading playwrights was underway—the drama of a nation remaking itself in the aftermath of civil war. The theater, he believed, was a crucial battlefield on which the struggle for a broader definition of American citizenship would be waged. If the battle was over citizenship, then Walton was a war correspondent whose eyewitness accounts offer important insights into the political implications of art in a racially divided nation.

Walton's criticism deserves attention in the story of the first black actors on the Great White Way because, as a writer on an influential black weekly, he helped establish critical standards by which African American performers came to judge themselves. Moreover, Walton provided readers not connected to the stage a way of thinking about music and drama in their community that transcended mere momentary diversion. In a sense, all of his columns in the years leading up to the Broadway debut of African American actors represented important chapters of a master narrative about race, drama, and nation in the twentieth century. Through his criticism—his encouragement of good performers, his insistence on race consciousness, and his willingness to chide those who fell below his standard of excellence—and through his activism on behalf of black performers, Walton played a central role in charting the course toward Broadway. The rocky road to this destination was worth it, Walton believed, because with the applause and the attention would come visibility and first-class citizenship.

LESTER A. WALTON, THE TENTH CITIZEN

Sometime in the early 1950s, Lester A. Walton wrote a script for a documentary film called "Tenth Citizen, U.S.A.," which he envisioned as one segment in a series of programs devoted to the achievements and lives of American Negroes. As Walton saw it, every tenth citizen in the United States had some African blood coursing through his veins, but the other nine citizens had little knowledge of the lives of these fellow Americans. In March 1953, Walton invited executives of the Pepsi Cola Company to consider sponsoring his show as a television series, thus gaining "a valuable advertising medium" and promoting "better interracial relations."[70] A few months later, Walton wrote to Stockton Hellfrich of the National Broadcasting Company about a similar idea for the radio. "It is most unfortunate that millions of white Americans know so little about the nation's one-tenth," he wrote, "and entertain preconceived, erroneous ideas so often uncomplimentary." Walton saw NBC's radio broadcasts as a "medium through which a campaign of education could be effectively and successfully conducted, designed to give the public a larger opportunity to know more about the remarkable advancement the Negro is achieving, due to vision, initiative and enterprise, also cooperation and integration."[71] No one understood better than this veteran journalist the power of the mass media in shaping popular consciousness, and in 1953, as a decorated former diplomat, respected journalist, and civil rights activist, Walton pushed harder than ever to use the media in the black struggle for social equality.

Throughout his long career, beginning in the early 1900s and ending in the mid-1960s, Walton recognized the political implications of black performance, and no history of African American actors' striving would be complete without an examination of this man's efforts to clear the path to Broadway and to equality of obstacles like prejudice, misunderstanding, and ignorance. As one of the first black critics to offer guidance to young performers, as a charter member of both The Frogs and the C.V.B.A., and as a theater manager, Walton dedicated much of his early career to enhancing the profession of acting in the African American theater world. But perhaps most important, as a fearless editorialist and sometimes agitator, Walton articulated the politics of art. For he recognized that if people of color in a predominantly white world wanted to take part in the shaping of national culture, they first had to be acknowledged as fellow citizens.

The man who devoted many years to the *New York Age* as drama editor and, for a time, managing editor, began his career in St. Louis, the city of his birth. The oldest son of a head bellman and a schoolteacher, Benjamin and Ollie Walton, Lester A. Walton was born in 1882, grew up in a middle-class household, and enjoyed the benefits of an excellent education at Sumner High School. In 1902, after completing a privately taught course in business, Walton joined the staff of the *St. Louis Globe-Democrat* as a general reporter, a position he held until 1906. In that year he worked for both the *St. Louis Post-Dispatch* and *St. Louis Star Sayings*. As a young black writer on big city white dailies, Walton learned firsthand the perniciousness of race prejudice, but he refused—even then, at the height of "Jim Crow" and violence against African Americans—to succumb to it. Years later he recalled arriving at a hotel, where he had an assignment to interview a famous musician, and being directed to the freight elevator. "I refused to take the freight elevator as directed and informed the city desk of my implacable stand," he wrote. "It was not until after a heated argument ensued over the telephone between one of the editors and hotel clerks that I was permitted to ride on a passenger elevator."[72]

Although the outcome of this unpleasant encounter with Jim Crow is in some ways rather surprising, the assignment that sent Walton to the hotel is not. St. Louis in the early years of the twentieth century had become an important center of popular music, and Walton had become friends with some of the leading musicians and entertainers in the city, many of whom had reached the pinnacle of their fame as innovative ragtime composers and performers. He counted among his friends Charlie Turpin, Louis Chauvin, and Sam Patterson, and he may well have known their friend Scott Joplin, who still lived in St. Louis.[73] Walton's combination of performance and journalism attracted the attention of two influential figures, who enticed him to leave St. Louis for New York. When Ernest Hogan heard a song that Walton and Sam Patterson had written, he invited the young writer to write lyrics for his new show, *Rufus Rastus.* Similarly, an article Walton wrote for the *Colored American Magazine* in 1903 made him the top candidate for the position of drama editor when Fred R. Moore purchased the *New York Age* in 1906. Between working with Hogan and fashioning a new drama section on one of the most influential black weeklies in the country, Walton immersed himself in the world of performance.[74]

For his premiere article in the *New York Age,* Walton prepared a full-scale review of *Bandanna Land,* then playing at the Majestic Theatre. The review set the tone for Walton's column for the next several years, for it discussed in detail various elements of the performance rather than just offering information about its location and stars, and the show provided material for editorial comment as well. After opening with enthusiastic praise for the Williams and Walker extravaganza, Walton went on to confess that he had attended the musical comedy with the intention of "tear[ing] it to pieces" in his column, but "the energy and personal magnetism" of the company were so intense that he "forgot" he was on hand as a "critic" and enjoyed the show as much as others in the audience. Although he did not offer negative critiques of the entertainers, Walton subjected the show to a critical appraisal by comparing the Walkers' dance number with the current "Merry Widow" waltz craze, which began on Broadway. He praised the actors for having introduced "some little character-bits that bring out strictly Negro traits and customs of which the race should feel justly proud." And he praised the music of Will Marion Cook, whom he dubbed "the greatest Afro-American composer" of the day.[75]

Walton's review segued into editorial at a couple of points. First, he saw the efforts of the Williams and Walker Company as a source of inspiration. "If all the colored patrons were inspired as was the writer after seeing Williams and Walker's new show," he wrote, "they will strive the harder to succeed in their particular avenue of endeavor." The implication that stage performance represented not just an evening's diversion but rather part of the struggle for the advancement of the race became a leitmotif in Walton's criticism. Here, he argued that the success of black actors in musical comedy on Broadway should alert all blacks that diligence and initiative undergirded individual achievement. Elsewhere, he emphasized the importance of the stage for presenting truer pictures of black character and culture than those promoted in stereotypical blackface caricature. In addition to pointing out the example of hard work and merit set by Williams and Walker, Walton also used his review as an opportunity to socialize fellow African Americans in the mores of first-class theaters. He chided "the fellow members of [his] race" for "making their presence known as well as themselves obnoxious to those seated near them by their unsuppressed laughter and merriment." Enthusiasm and pleasure were fine, but decorum, Walton believed, would earn the respect that African Americans deserved as American citizens.[76] Walton's scolding words, of course, betrayed his own class biases and exposed divisions within the black community; the critic hoped to enforce a genteel urban, middle-class code of conduct and attitude toward the performing arts, a code not necessarily in force among those who viewed the show business as a purveyor of fun.

Before the week was out, Walton received a letter from Sylvester Russell, a drama reviewer for the *Chicago Defender,* complaining about an unflattering headline on Walton's page. In responding to Russell, Walton spelled out his critical aims. "*The Age* decided to publish a dramatic page in the interest of the colored artist," he explained, "but it does not believe that the printing of only the good that is said about him is the method that will ultimately do him the most good. A true friend is not one who always tells you how great you are; but one who sees your faults and tells you about them. In the columns of *The Age* the policy of the writer will be to show the performer (to the best of his ability) his faults as well as his virtues."[77] In the months that followed, Walton proved to be as good as his word. In April 1908, Walton gave S. H. Dudley's play *The Black Politician* a generally positive review but urged "the Negro actor to consider more seriously the meaning of character work." He thought women actors especially needed to work on this aspect of acting instead of just looking pretty on stage. A few months later, he analyzed Aida Overton Walker's interpretation of the "Salome" dance, which just then had taken Broadway by storm and which her husband decided to introduce into *Bandanna Land*. Walton disliked her version mainly because it was imitative rather than original, and he reminded her that the cakewalk, which she and others had introduced at the turn of the century, had won acclaim on two continents and expressed something essentially black and distinctively beautiful. In 1909, Walton urged the popular team, Brown and Nevarro, to change their opening number from a "rather tame" song to one that would instantly grab the audience's attention. Three years after establishing the drama page, Walton criticized his old friend, J. Leubrie Hill, for including such devices as "gun plays, dice games, . . . gin, razors and watermelon" in *My Friend from Dixie,* material that "may have 'pulled' laughs years ago, but not now." The bottom line, Walton believed, was to produce shows that showed the race in the best possible light and that did not reinforce mindless stereotypes "which do the race no good."[78]

By writing such columns, Walton sought to instruct and improve the performance of black actors, and he hoped to establish critical standards necessary for the development and professionalization of the African American Stage. But Walton also recognized that black actors worked deeply in the shadow of the "Stage Negro," the caricature of African Americans advanced by white playwrights and blackface performers, and in the first decade of the twentieth century, he still believed that this unflattering image of African Americans could be overridden if black actors portrayed a variety of black types with honesty and sympathy. In an article on Bob Cole's and J. Rosamond Johnson's return to vaudeville in 1910, for example, he wrote, "Being a Negro and knowing his characteristics, his ways and mannerisms, not from study and observation, but by eating, sleeping, and coming in contact with him daily, I seldom relish the stage types so frequently presented by our white artists." White entertainers "in cork," he believed, had "taught the white audience to appreciate imitations and regard with disdain many types of the Negro race true to life."[79] About a year before, Walton had witnessed a performance by McIntyre and Heath, a white comedy team in blackface, and had objected to such terms as "nigger," "coon," and "wench" used in the show, had noted that most songs had "chickens" as their theme, and had concluded that this insensitive portrayal of Negroes betrayed their ignorance of Negro life.[80]

The ignorance against which Walton spoke out in the McIntyre and Heath act had profound consequences for African Americans. In an editorial that appeared on Christmas Eve 1908, Walton articulated the serious political results of continued white misunderstanding of blacks. "If you want to learn how grossly ignorant the white man is, in general of Negro home life, of Negro mannerisms, of Negro ideals and what not," he began, "attend a theatrical performance where a Negro character is being depicted." Whites, he argued, typically portrayed "the happy-go-lucky stage type," and consequently, "some of our white citizens have formed an idea that such is the Negro in general," and they "underrate the Negro's true status in this body politic and fail to give him the respectful consideration which he deserves." To counter that misperception, black performers could offer a more accurate portrait of the race on stage by emphasizing "the correct way we talk, dress, sing and carry ourselves generally." But always, in the end, was the issue of citizenship. The refusal of Judge Goff to allow The Frogs to incorporate in 1908 elicited from Walton an impassioned editorial. "In the effete East," he observed, "do we look to the powers that be to assist the race in all endeavors that tend to elevate and instruct, for education and culture make us better citizens, and to be a good citizen—regardless of color—means that much more to this country, for the higher the development of citizenship the higher is the status of the United States." And in case the point was not clear enough, Walton noted that African Americans "are counted in the list of Americans compiled by the Census Commissioner," that "the Negro is evidently in America to stay," and that any improvement made by Negroes would redound to the benefit of all Americans.[81]

When Cole and Johnson's *The Red Moon* appeared on Broadway in 1909, Walton found yet another opportunity to underscore the larger, political significance of black performance and to rail in frustration at the tension between white expectations and black self-perception. Walton delighted in reporting to readers of the *Age* that white critics called the show "a hit," but he also included a passage from a white review that gave him pause. The white critic liked the show but rued the fact that the members of the chorus were "as near white as paint and talcum" could make them. "Their voices," the critic wrote, "nearly all had the correct English accent and intonation. Only two or three stuck to the tradition of the real Negro." Well, "what is the real Negro from a white man's standpoint?" Walton fumed. The absence of "dis" and "dat" should "speak well for the various public schools throughout the country," he argued, and urged white critics to "wake up . . . to the fact that colored people are talking just like white people." That, of course, was the problem. If black performers like J. Rosamond Johnson dressed well, spoke correctly, and sang and danced with elegance, they were "too refined" to be black, as if dark skin tone and refinement were mutually exclusive traits. And again, Walton identified the issue as a matter of citizenship. "The Negro in this country is an American and not an African," he reminded white critics. "Stop regarding him as an alien, for he is an American first, last, and all the time and does not know how to be anything else."[82]

Walton soon believed that in spite of the positive reviews and the accuracy of portrayals by the African American performers, *The Red Moon* was doomed.

He learned from people in the show that the publicity agent at the theater—whom Walton caustically dubbed "A. Toxen Worm"—refused to promote the show because it "did not contain enough 'niggerism' to suit his fancy." He accused white critics like Frederic McKay of the *New York Evening Mail* and Ashton Stevens of the *New York Evening Journal* of conspiring through their published comments and their refusal to publish pictures of black actors in their newspapers to kill *The Red Moon*. Although this "conspiracy" apparently failed—*The Red Moon* continued through the summer of 1909—Walton recognized that the comments made by such critics undermined the positive work of the black performers by giving their readers an unflattering way of thinking about the production.[83]

As the years passed, Walton's frustration grew more intense. At times he chided black performers for failing to act responsibly and professionally in their theater dealings. At other times, he railed at their unpolished performances, which he believed lay at the root of the racial tension. But Walton could not ignore the fact that white Americans' prejudice against black Americans continued to thrive in spite of the best efforts of talented performers like George Walker and Bob Cole to "exhibit on the stage the real life of the progressive, cultured Negro of today."[84] In 1914, Walton reviewed a spectacular production called *America* staged by the Shuberts at the New York Hippodrome, and he stormed at the glaring inconsistency between the producers' claim for "attention to detail" and the depiction of "Negro life with white people—*something that cannot be done* with any degree of success."

> With many theatrical managers allowing their conscious and unconscious prejudices to blind them to such an extent that they are blocking the progress of dramatic art, it seems that the American stage is likely to suffer dire consequences until they have been emancipated from their absurd notions with respect to one-ninth of the entire population of the United States—a people who have been on this soil for hundreds of years and whose life is one of the chief fabrics of our American civilization. It is a difficult task to produce native plays and wholly leave out the colored American, and when portrayed the character should be the real thing and not a cheap imitation.[85]

In editorials like this one, Walton insisted that African American expression and the presence of Negro people were essential to a truly representative national stage. Neither the nation nor the rights of an oppressed people could be made whole without the other.

By the time this piece appeared in the *Age,* Walton had already waged a couple of protracted campaigns against the barriers to full citizenship for black Americans. One involved the practice of discrimination against black theatergoers. If a theater sold tickets to African American patrons, they typically were in the balcony rather than on the main floor; some theaters, of course, refused to admit any black people. Walton became incensed in 1909, when James S. Metcalfe argued in the pages of *Life* that "practically the Negro has more rights with respect to the theatres under the laws of the State of New York than the white man has." The civil rights laws of the state made it difficult to ask a black patron to leave a theater unless the manager could demonstrate "pretty conclusively" that the exclusion stemmed from some reason other than skin color. By contrast, he argued, whites could be excluded for no reason at all. Walton responded angrily to Metcalfe's essay, because he saw it as the foundation for "an organized effort" to exclude blacks from theaters—"to deprive us of rights and privileges to which we are justly entitled by law." What he found "particularly galling" was the "thought that we who are native-born American citizens are discriminated solely on account of color," and that when blacks sought simply to protect their rights as citizens, they were accused of "being radical." And above all, Walton well knew that theater managers had virtually no trouble finding ways to remove or to segregate Negro patrons in their theaters.[86]

In the months that followed, Walton began to document cases of discrimination against African American theatergoers. In March of 1910, he reported a story about two black women who had paid a dollar apiece to see a matinee performance of *The Jolly Bachelors* at the Broadway Theatre and who were refused the first-balcony seats. The women were given a refund, but Walton warned that theater employees may soon "find themselves principals in a number of damage suits, where they would have to answer the difficult question: 'Why did you discriminate [against] and mistreat the plaintiff?' "[87] In another case at about the same time, A. M. Barrow of Brooklyn told of having sent a messenger to buy tickets in the orchestra section for a performance of *Mr. Lode of Koal* at the Court Square Theatre. When he arrived at the theater, the tickets—clearly stamped for Friday—were seized as Thursday night tickets, and Mr. Barrows was forced to sit in the back of the theater, which obviously had been set aside for African American theatergoers.[88]

Neither of these instances of discrimination resulted in a lawsuit, but one involving James J. Davis did, and Walton followed the case closely. Davis, mistaken for a white man, purchased two expensive tickets (three dollars each) to a show at Hammerstein's Victoria Theatre, but when he and his wife, a dark-skinned woman, arrived for the performance, ushers refused to seat the couple. When Mr. Davis refused to exchange his seats for less desirable ones, the ushers literally threw him out of the theater. Davis sued the Victoria Theatre for five hundred dollars in damages for denying his civil rights and two thousands dollars for the assault on his person. Both Davis and Walton viewed the suit as a test of the Malby Act, which had been passed in 1895 to guarantee "the full and equal accommodations, advantages, facilities and privileges" of public institutions including "theatres," "music halls," and "all places of . . . amusement." Davis vowed to take the case to a higher court if the Municipal Court found against him. While the case was pending, Walton noted that its accompanying publicity had resulted in better treatment of African American theatergoers in the city.[89]

Walton believed that such demands for fair treatment were essential to black citizenship. He reported joyfully when Mrs. Clarissa Evans of Troy, New York, won a case against Proctor's Theatre in that city. He saw Evans's victory as one more blow against "Demon Color Prejudice in its present campaign throughout New York State, known for unfairness, un-Americanness and inconsistency," and which had been "inaugurated in the City of New York."[90] Walton agitated against the Lafayette Theatre for months because of its Jim Crow practices. Shortly after the theater opened its doors, Walton reported that "a number of the most prominent Negroes of the city have been refused accommodation at this house since it was opened last week, and great indignation has been aroused." By February 1913 the theater had dropped the discriminatory seating practices, thanks partly to Walton's relentless newspaper campaign. When the managers, Martinson and Nibur, finally gave up their lease on the theater in 1914, Walton and a white partner, C. W. Morganstern, took over and maintained an open seating policy.[91]

Walton never completely abandoned the world of entertainment, as the story of his "Tenth Citizen, U.S.A." and his idea for a radio program attest. Indeed, amidst his editing of the Age's drama page, he managed and produced shows at the Lafayette Theatre and for a theater circuit with houses around the country. When the United States entered the Great War in Europe, Walton helped organize entertainment for the troops stationed in camps stateside as well as those abroad. And over the years, he continued to write songs, one of which, entitled "Jim Crow Must Go," was featured in a playlet presented in the 1950s as part of an NAACP rally. In virtually every instance, Walton used entertainment to serve the larger end of advancing the interests and rights of people of color. Eventually, however, he turned his attention more completely to the arena of politics, working in the 1920s and 1930s to encourage fellow African Americans to switch from the Party of Lincoln to the Democratic Party and serving in the 1930s and 1940s as the American Minister to Liberia. Upon his return to the United States in 1946, after nearly eleven years in Monrovia, Walton, then in his sixties, became active in the Negro Actors' Guild, New

York City's Commission on Intergroup Relations, and eventually, the City Commission on Human Rights.[92]

In 1917, as the first black actors made their debut on the Great White Way in serious drama, Walton identified for readers of the *Age* what he believed was the larger significance of this bold, dramatic experiment, and typical of his point of view, he saw it in political terms. "The mission of the stage is twofold—to furnish wholesome entertainment and to instruct," he insisted, "and the Negro play can play a most important part in the solving of one of America's most vexatious problems, made so in large measure because of the average white American's misconstruction of and indifference to what the Negro is really thinking and doing. 'Getting the Negro right' without 'Getting the Caucasian right' will never bring about the desired racial amity in this country." Most important about this passage—and in some ways, in all of Walton's writing—is the emphasis on collective benefits for the race rather than acclaim and stardom for individual performers. Walton wanted individual black artists to reap the rewards they richly deserved—fair remuneration for their performances, decent accommodations on the road, notice in black and white periodicals, and the affection of an adoring public. But Walton encouraged African American entertainers to continue struggling along the rocky road to Broadway because he believed it would help the cause of full citizenship and social equality for Negro Americans and the fulfillment of America's egalitarianism for all. As he put it in 1917, "The drama, America and the Negro will greatly profit by this daring and unique move in the interest of 'Art for art's sake.'"[93]

IN THE SHADOW OF THE STAGE NEGRO

With decades of experience behind them—studying their art; perfecting their performances on the vaudeville stage, theater circuits, and in venues of their own creation; organizing professional associations; and establishing critical standards for African American expression—what did the first black actors hope to accomplish on Broadway in 1917? Perhaps, most of all, they hoped to emerge from the shadow cast by the century-old "Stage Negro." Maybe the time had now come for the convergence of realistic portrayals of black characters with the quest for a distinctive American drama, a convergence that would offer a clearer picture of both the nation and one-tenth of its people. In 1917 several members of the cast already had performed on Broadway in musical comedies, so the novelty of the Great White Way alone surely did not excite their imaginations. Indeed, appearing on Broadway did not obviate the need to accept gigs elsewhere if a paying job could be had. One of Torrence's friends was astonished to see five of the musicians in the Clef Club Orchestra performing at a "big birthday party, at midnight," on the same night that he had seen them perform between the three plays.[94] *Three Plays for a Negro Theater,* with the backing of three prominent white theater people, however, offered hope that this time the bright lights of Broadway would expose the Stage Negro for the caricature it was and illuminate the variety of characters in the African American community.

The Stage Negro, of course, did not represent a single type, but rather a cluster of images, none of which was particularly accurate or flattering. Black characters in American plays typically fell into one of four categories: a buffoon introduced for comic relief but not essential to the drama, the faithful old gray-haired servant, the tragic mulatto "cursed" with a "taint" of black blood, or a monstrous, savage beast wreaking vengeance on innocent white victims. The types persisted in one way or another into the early twentieth century. The humor of the buffoon depended on a peculiar way of speaking English, exaggerated physical movements, and a kind of childlike simplicity that obviously stood in marked contrast to the sober, responsible white characters, whose actions and words advanced the theme of the drama. Likewise, the faithful servant typically did little to advance the plot, except to vouch for the character—either positively or negatively—of the main white protagonists. Both clown and servant happily remained subservient to and dependent on whites. Because the tragic mulatto operated mostly in a white world and only found out "the truth" from a trusted family friend or through the birth of a dark-skinned child, the character did not explore Negro life as such. Instead, the story of the tragic mulatto served as a cautionary tale against racial mixing and underscored the inherent "taint" of African blood. Finally, the savage beast—usually either a bloodthirsty slave or a monstrous rapist—represented the Negro as a creature of instincts, irrational and out of control. This character helped to justify the diminution of rights and opportunities for blacks after the Civil War. With a few notable exceptions these characters usually were played by white actors.[95]

Since black performers in the 1890s and early 1900s had gained much of their early experience in minstrel shows, the stage type with which they were most familiar and on which they embroidered their own patterns was the buffoon. Dancing, singing, telling jokes, and speaking in dialect, the latter-day black comedians gained recognition and opportunities by remaining fairly true to the antics of this comic type. The chief difference in the big African American musical comedies, of course, was that these humorous figures supplied the motive, action, and the high jinks that set the farce in motion and drew it to its hilarious conclusion. And by the early 1900s, modern dress and up-to-date fashion replaced ill-fitting clothes, and dialect occasionally gave way to standard spoken English. The themes of the comedies explored issues basic to the black experience in America and offered their own comic critiques.

Challenge the stereotypes as they might, however, African American entertainers found themselves caught in a vicious cycle that had so far proven impossible to break. If they wanted opportunities to perform—especially if they wanted to play before white audiences and in prominent venues—they dared not stray too far from the conventions of the Stage Negro. Like black musicians in the 1890s who wrote songs in the "coon song" tradition, actors who developed comedy acts had made a choice between work and advancement, on the one hand, and unemployment and no recognition, on the other. Ernest Hogan regretted having written *All Coons Look Alike to Me,* he told Walton before his death, but he defended himself on the grounds that without songs like these, he never would have been able to attempt anything more serious, and the American Stage would have remained as white as ever.[96]

Others found that when they abandoned some of the traditional elements of black expression that whites had come to expect in a Negro show, they drew sharp criticism. When Williams and Walker hired singers for the chorus on the basis of their vocal quality and without regard for hair type and skin tone, for example, a critic for the *Dramatic Mirror* wondered why the manager "permitted" them to wear straight hair. "The types would be very much closer to natural," he insisted, "if it were not for this point." In a rejoinder, Walton exploded that "like most white critics, in fact white people in general, the [*Dramatic Mirror* critic] has certain set ideas as to just how colored people should look, and when they appear other than what he has in mind he charges that the members of the chorus wear wigs and are not strictly Negro types."[97] Bob Cole and J. Rosamond Johnson likewise were dismissed by white critics as too refined to be Negroes.[98]

In light of this bind, the formation of stock companies in Chicago, New York, and Washington takes on even greater significance. For in these repertory theaters, black actors and black producers sought ways to break out from under the burden of racial stereotype to which they had unintentionally contributed. If they played characters drawn by white playwrights for white actors, and even if they played them in whiteface, at least they expanded the variety of roles in which they might feel comfortable. They need not be clowns and servants forever. Scholars and critics who have taken these stock companies to task for staging white plays fail to recognize that in the hands of black actors, white drama could be transformed and other meanings derived from it. Consider, for example, Walton's review of Cleveland Moffatt's *Battle* performed at the Lafayette Theatre by a Negro cast. After summarizing the play's story, which involves a conflict between a callous millionaire slumlord and his bastard son, who lives in the world of poverty created and sustained by his father, Walton noted that the chief motive of the play was to advocate equality. No doubt it was—Moffatt, by setting the play in the slums, engaged a highly charged issue of class inequality and the possibility of class warfare that threatened to pit father against son. Walton, however, read the performance as a metaphor for the greater struggle for racial equality. With black performers playing to a black audience, Moffatt's play became a race drama.[99]

Struggling to free themselves of the limitations of the Stage Negro, African American actors must have recognized the bold departure Torrence's characters made from the usual black types. In the story of *Granny Maumee*, for example, Torrence reverses the meaning of the tragic mulatto—in his drama, the tragedy is that white lust has "tainted" Granny's "Royal Black" line. Indeed, the mulatto child is the product of a forced sexual union between the black servant and her white employer. As Sapphie explains herself to her sister, Pearl, "He des would have his way."[100] In *The Rider of Dreams*, Madison Sparrow's comic antics are contained and overturned by the hard work and determination of both Lucy Sparrow and Dr. Williams, neither of whom fits *any* of the usual stage types. Simon, as a revolutionary African leader seeking to overthrow the tyrants of Rome, avoids being typecast as the savage beast by virtue of his embrace of Christian love. Nowhere to be found in these plays were examples of the faithful servant. If Granny Maumee had, at some point in the past, been somebody's slave, she had long since dropped any hint of Mammy-like love and nurture for the "master race." And the role of the Egyptian princess, landed by Lottie Grady, may well have been so coveted because it demanded proud, regal bearing and attractive, exotic costuming—both of which transported black women from the kinds of roles in which they usually were seen.

Thus, as the cast prepared for their debut on Broadway, they relished the roles they were to play, and if they experienced stage fright, it was not from lack of experience on stage but from concern over white reaction to the complete lack of fidelity to the Stage Negro these characters displayed. And perhaps their enthusiasm for the production as well as their eleventh-hour jitters arose from the idea that at last they shared in the shaping of the nation's dramatic tradition. For as journalists alerted the public to the coming production, they frequently linked it to the quest for an American drama. Being a part of American culture—rather than invisible in a segregated Negro America—appealed to many in the African American theater world. Indeed, nearly a decade earlier, the subject of Negro themes as fundamental to the development of American drama had been raised by James Metcalfe. He thought that the "racial problem" could easily replace "the exhausted social perplexities" in dramas imported from Europe. At the request of Lester A. Walton, Bob Cole penned a response to Metcalfe's suggestion—a response that summarizes well the hopes and aims of the black actors who crossed the color line in April 1917. "Why our dramatists have failed to touch this question is obvious," he began.

> They lack the ethical and aesthetical courage; they have the technical ability, but they fear they will offend. We know that the drama must regard prejudice but do we not also know that the great American spirit of right is the guiding star of this great commonwealth? Are they not fortified with the knowledge that right must prevail? Do they not know that the great American spirit of right is with them in handling this theme?
>
> The drama is that the Negro is in your midst, the comedy is that he survives, the tragedy is that he is black.
>
> For no such fertile field exists anywhere in the civilized world as does here for dramatic material, and a dramatic poet should want for no more a divine inspiration than the spectacle of the great American spirit of right, born and cradled by the founders of this great republic, in its God-made armor of Christianity and education, battling with the bloodstained witch-tradition, armed with prejudice and ignorance, for the bleeding hearts of 10,000,000 of black Americans.[101]

African Americans could only hope that in Ridgely Torrence they had found the "dramatic poet" driven by the "great American spirit of right" whose work would weave the thread of black experience into the fabric of America's dramatic literature.

3

WHITE ARTISTS
BEHIND THE SCENES

"It was not until Mrs. Hapgood read these three plays and Robert Edmond Jones became enthusiastic over the prospect of producing them with Negro actors that they came within sight of a Broadway run."

New York Times, *April 15, 1917*

OF THE DOZENS OF commentaries on *Three Plays for a Negro Theater* that appeared before, during, and after the historic production in April 1917, one stands out for its recognition of the collaborative nature of the dramatic venture. Two days after the opening performance, several friends and supporters of Torrence, Hapgood, and Jones prepared a flyer to be distributed to members of the Drama League, encouraging them to support the show. In the flyer, Percy MacKaye noted—in red letters—that the production was "indeed an historic happening," because "for the first time, in any comparable degree, both races are here brought together upon a plane utterly devoid of all racial antagonism, a plane in which audience and actor a[re] happily peers, mutually cordial to each other's gifts of appreciation and interpretation."[1] With these words, MacKaye represented *Three Plays for a Negro Theater* as a genuinely cooperative effort in which both black and white Americans had a hand, and in which the creators, the interpreters, and the audience all played a part.

More typically, people who wrote about the plays discussed the merits of Torrence's, Hapgood's, and Jones's interest in and work on behalf of African Americans. These three people, it was widely believed, were going "to do for the negro theatrically what has been done for the Irish by the Irish Theatre movement," in the words of Zona Gale.[2] Although the distinction is subtle, working *with* is not the same as working *for*. The latter, in this context, implies altruism, if not condescension. The implied inequality of the participants in this theatrical experiment does not diminish its importance, but it should alert us to a problem that exists inherently in collaborative, hybrid cultural projects such as *Three Plays for a Negro Theater*. To be sure, the three plays would not have been the same had any of the collaborators not taken part, but their cooperation in envisioning, staging, and interpreting the plays did not mean that their aims necessarily coincided.

Three Plays for a Negro Theater as seen on Broadway undeniably represented a cultural event marked by racial hybridity and interracial cooperation. But in some ways, the African American contribution came relatively late. For long before a casting call went out, signaling to black actors the opportunity to perform on the Great White Way, a playwright wrote three plays, a producer found the financial backing to stage them, and an up-and-coming set designer agreed to direct the plays and to design the sets and costumes. These three white people, who literally set the stage for the black actors' debut, undertook the project for very particular reasons and with clear preconceptions about race relations and American drama in the early twentieth century. Without understanding the creative impulses and marshaling of resources that propelled Torrence, Hapgood, and Jones into the world of Negro theatre, we can only partially understand what these race dramas meant in 1917 and beyond.

The three white artists behind the scenes joined forces to present these plays about Negro life in America, but they did so for reasons that arose from their own careers and experiences. Promoting black citizenship and social equality played a much smaller part in their venture than did the desire for fame for a novel production, a place in the annals of Broadway lore, altruism for a downtrodden people, and enthusiasm for experimentation. They hoped and expected to be evaluated on the merits of their contributions to the production in spite of the limitations their African American co-laborers brought to the stage. Moreover, because Torrence, Hapgood, and Jones enjoyed reputations within white theater and literary circles before *Three Plays for a Negro Theater*—unlike the black actors who interpreted the plays—their parts in the production could be placed in relation to their earlier accomplishments, shifting the focus away from the themes of the dramas and toward the careers of the playwright, impresario, and designer. In fact the very collaboration between the black actors and the white producers reflects much of the drama of race relations in the early twentieth century. For whether they liked or disliked the plays, approved or disapproved of the actors' performances, critics never doubted the legitimacy of white theater people to envision a Negro Theatre and certainly never questioned their credentials as

Americans—issues that came to the forefront in the discussion of the black participants.

RIDGELY TORRENCE:
ENVISIONING A NATIONAL NEGRO THEATRE

Perhaps the most perceptive comment on the author of *The Rider of Dreams, Granny Maumee,* and *Simon, the Cyrenian* appeared in the *New York Times* a week and a half after the plays opened in the Garden Theatre. "When Ridgely Torrence left his native town of Xenia, Ohio, to make his career as a poet, he had no idea that he would ever have plays about negro life played by negro actors in a New York Theatre. What interest he felt in the American negro was primarily aesthetic. It was the example of the Irish Players which suggested to him the possibility of American negro plays." So began an article entitled "Mr. Torrence's Story," which sought to familiarize the *Times*'s readers with the latest Broadway phenom. The unidentified author of the piece went on to reconstruct Torrence's life—from his birth in Xenia in 1875 through his college years in Oxford, Ohio, and Princeton to his arrival in New York in the late 1890s, where he worked as a librarian (and later, as an associate editor) by day and a poet/dramatist by night. To underscore the dramatic departure *Three Plays for a Negro Theater* represented in Torrence's career, the author took pains to establish the playwright's connections to the cultural mainstream by noting, in addition to his respectable education, his serving as secretary to a visiting diplomat, working on the editorial staff of *Cosmopolitan Magazine,* and authoring such poetic dramas as *El Dorado, A Tragedy* (1903) and *Abelard and Heloise* (1907). Nothing in his professional resume predicted that Ridgely Torrence would be featured in the *New York Times* as the author of three plays about American Negro life, and as the writer correctly observed, he certainly had not left Xenia to champion the cause of African Americans in the world of letters.[3]

Another section of that same edition of the *New York Times* contained an interview with Torrence. The author of this piece noted that the playwright lived in a Greenwich Village apartment occupied at different times by William Vaughn Moody, Percy MacKaye, Vachel Lindsay, and Edwin Arlington Robinson. These writers, friends of the playwright, constituted an important circle of poets and dramatists with whom Torrence wanted to be identified. After arriving in New York, he had sought out Edmund Clarence Stedman, whose work he admired and respected. Torrence impressed the older man as a poet of great promise. Indeed, Stedman included one of Torrence's poems in *An American Anthology: 1787–1900* published in 1900. Through Stedman, Torrence began to meet others in the world of literature and eventually became close friends with Moody, MacKaye, and Robinson. Torrence and Robinson frequently took long walks together, talking about poetry, and then joined MacKaye at local watering holes, where they continued their impassioned conversations well into the night. According to one of Robinson's biographers, they became "convinced that the time for a great forward movement in the American drama had come, and that all that was needed to start it on its way was a group of playwrights with imagination and something to say."[4] They determined that they might well be such poet dramatists and sought in the early 1900s to set a new course for America's dramatic literature.[5]

In the first decade of the twentieth century, these writers produced a number of works that seemed for a time to promise what Percy MacKaye later called "a nucleus of dramatic literature." MacKaye himself contributed *The Canterbury Pilgrims* (1903), *A Garland to Sylvia* (1910), and *Fenris, the Wolf* (1904); Moody published two verse dramas, *The Masque of Judgment* (1900) and *The Fire-Bringer* (1904), as well as two prose plays, *The Great Divide* (1906) and *The Faith-Healer* (1908), before his shocking and untimely death in 1910; and Torrence had brought out *El Dorado* and *Abelard and Heloise*, both admired primarily for their poetry rather than their potential as works for the stage. Robinson alone struggled with play writing. In 1913, recognizing that his plays were disasters, he returned to poetry, confessing to a friend, "It isn't that I can't write a play, so far as the technique goes, but I cannot hit the popular chord, and for the simple reason that there is no immediately popular impulse in *me*."[6] In some ways, however, Robinson simply was more honest than the others in the group, for most of the plays they wrote met with limited success. Indeed, when Moody introduced one of Robinson's plays to Charles Frohman, he ended up by presenting it as an example of the work by this circle of young dramatists, all of whom labored diligently in the name of the future American drama. A few days later, Frohman returned the play with a brief comment: "Not available for stage."[7]

One reason for the tepid response to these poets' plays may well have been the themes they chose to explore. While large and ambitious, most of the plays were on subjects that had little to do with America. Stedman explained to Torrence that while he and his friends constituted "a school which I have looked for," their work did not show sufficient "evidence in it of the spirit of the New World. . . . You only show your own limitations when you profess to show yourselves unable to find American atmosphere and themes for American dramas," he lectured.[8] They wanted to revitalize American drama—"to run Clyde Fitch off the boards," as Torrence put it to his family in a 1906 letter—but they struggled to find subjects that spoke to the American public.[9] Another reason may have been the very insularity of their experience. Moody and MacKaye, both graduates of Harvard University and students of George Pierce Baker, and Torrence, another Ivy Leaguer, spent countless hours with each other, talking, drinking, reading each other's work, introducing one another to others like themselves, and entertaining themselves in their rooms at the Judson Hotel or when they met up in travels abroad. The circle of literary and cultural friends became rather extensive, but it was not particularly diverse, and individuals in the group rarely moved outside its orbit to witness and experience life more familiar to those who attended the theater and were eager to hail the long awaited great American play.

Although clearly a favorite among this group of creative writers and de-scribed affectionately by Hermann Hagedorn as a "sprightly mischievous being," the "incarnation of youth, so individual, yet so free of pose, so fluid, so witty, so imaginative, yet so honest, and so loyal," and "the sunlit piece of original creation," Torrence did not fit the same profile as the others. While Percy MacKaye's father, Steele MacKaye, had gained a solid reputation as an American dramatist in the late nineteenth century, Torrence's father earned his living in Xenia, Ohio, as a merchant. While William Vaughn Moody, as a freshman, had impressed fellow Harvard man, Norman Hapgood, as a poet "above our average standard," Torrence eventually gained some recognition at Princeton, only to be asked to leave the institution after an illness his classmates feared was a venereal disease.[10] In spite of the cosmopolitan crowd in which he mixed socially and artistically, and in spite of his own later sophistication, Torrence was a child of small town America, and this background eventually provided the inspiration for the three plays that brought him fame in 1917.

In some ways, it was almost as unlikely that Torrence would become a poet as it was that as a poet he would write sympathetically about African American life. Torrence grew up comfortably in a small town in Ohio, the oldest son of Mary Ridgely and Findley Torrence, whose roots ran deep in the Buckeye state. Findley Torrence's grandfather had moved west in the late eighteenth century and helped plan the town of Lexington, Kentucky, where he had been given a large grant of land in exchange for service during the War for American Independence. In 1804, he sold the land in Kentucky and moved to Xenia, Ohio, where by the dawn of the century three more generations of Torrences were to live and prosper.[11] Findley Torrence, a solid citizen of the region from his birth in 1842 to his death in 1916, appeared as the subject of a biographical sketch in an 1881 history of Greene County, Ohio, which noted his family's ties to the area, his courageous service during the Civil War, the success of his business, his "estimable wife" and their two children, Fred and Mary, as well as his membership in the United Presbyterian Church.[12] Throughout Ridgely Torrence's life, his father owned and ran a lumber store, with "everything in their line necessary for builders," on North Detroit Street, which was described locally as "one of the principal business streets of the City."[13] The family no doubt expected that when he came of age, Torrence would follow in his father's footsteps and carry on the family business.

Although he did not remain in the town of his birth, Torrence could never quite erase the deep imprint the region had made on his life and imagination. He had learned to love poetry in the public schools of Xenia, where he excelled in all subjects except arithmetic. He spent his first two college years at Miami University in Oxford, Ohio, until boredom and the recommendation of a favorite professor propelled him to Princeton. And often, when overcome by nervous exhaustion or illness, he returned to the family hearth, where he was nursed back to health. Perhaps most significantly, however, when Torrence began to respond to Stedman's critique of the young poets' ineffectual efforts to rejuvenate American drama, he turned to his native Ohio for original material.

In late 1906, Torrence began working feverishly on a play he would call *The Madstone*. Completed in about one month, in early 1907, *The Madstone* drew on local Ohio folklore and in fact was set in Greene County. According to local legend, if one possessed a genuine madstone, one could draw poison out of wounds and magically cure illnesses. While the play featured a stone, which various characters hoped to put to their own uses, it also used the madstone as a metaphor for innocent womanhood and traditional marriage. Like the magical stone, women, innocent and untainted, become the objects of desire of men of the world who hope that they can draw off the poison of their past with the presence of a pure influence. As the unhappily married protagonist of the play recognizes, however, the madstone does its job by absorbing the poison or infection or madness it is called upon to cure and when full, it "drops off." So, too, did tainted women lose their capacity to love and heal—they became filled with men's poison and "dropped off." Torrence's friend, William Vaughn Moody, thoroughly approved of the play, telling his beloved Harriet that if Torrence's play succeeded, "one could begin to think the American drama, [the] so long awaited and devoutly prayed for babe, really about to be born."[14] Moody passed the play along to Henry Miller, an influential Broadway producer, always on the lookout for dramas suitable for the current stars of the stage. Torrence had cannily dedicated the play to Madame Nazimova, one of the great tragic actresses of the turn of the century, who he hoped could be interested in interpreting his work on the Great White Way. Both Miller and Nazimova liked the play and planned to introduce it at the beginning of the 1907–1908 season. Over the summer of 1907, however, the great actress lost interest in appearing in *The Madstone,* and that caused Henry Miller to abandon the project as well.[15]

While still believing that Nazimova would play the lead in *The Madstone* in the summer of 1907, Torrence began working on a second play that drew on a legend from his Ohio childhood. *The Thunderpool,* like *The Madstone,* used a folk belief as a metaphor for a woman's nature. In the second play, the thunderpool was believed to be a body of water that attracted lightning, absorbed its energy and power, and, seething with turbulence, erupted unexpectedly and violently. The female "thunderpool" quietly resists the pressures of her society, falls in love and in a burst of pent-up power and passion saves her lover from a wild lynch mob, then spends a night of passion with him without the benefit of marriage vows. The play ends with the couple marrying and the heroine having chosen her life's path without being driven by the dictates of society. Torrence found no one who was interested in staging this play, but he believed he had struck a valuable vein of material by tapping the sources of his youth. While making ends meet in New York with various jobs, a few published poems, and the generous assistance of more successful friends, Torrence kept searching for the subject that would be "American," novel, and successfully adaptable to the stage.[16]

Torrence certainly kept in touch with his family in Xenia, and he frequently returned to his hometown in times of trouble, perhaps feeling a sense of belonging that eluded him in New York. But these early plays that revolved around the folklore of his youth should not be mistaken for the works of a devoted regionalist seeking to acquaint the rest of the country with the treasures of a hidden, beautiful people. Instead, it appears that the lore served as a lure—a novel, earthy, folk motif that he could link to contemporary social issues. In other words, the Ohio themes were like aesthetic curiosities that Torrence hoped might interest theatergoers in the great metropolis who sought the unusual and the quaint—in somewhat the same way Torrence had interested the people who became his friends as a curiosity from the Midwest. When Torrence turned his attention to the African Americans of Xenia, the same might well be said for the plays that resulted.

Torrence's decision to write about African Americans in the early 1900s, however, requires some explanation. Although the "race question" consumed countless pages in widely read journals and newspapers and uncounted angry words and actions in the United States among people seeking to resolve it by reason or by force, the African American as a sympathetic subject for art was not widely accepted. In an age of lynch mobs, Jim Crow, race riots, disfranchisement, *The Clansman,* and profound racial discrimination, what possessed Ridgely Torrence to seek in African American life a novel theme for the Great American Drama and a way to advance his shaky career? The answer lies partly in the trajectory of his career to that time. He had moved from the grand, romantic subjects and settings to realistic social commentary grounded in native folklore between 1903 and 1907. Although *El Dorado, Abelard and Heloise, The Madstone,* and *The Thunderpool* all explored, in one way or another, the meaning of true love, the latter two did so in modern America rather than in the Spanish colonial Southwest or Medieval Europe. The decision to style American art from folklore suggests Torrence's desire to appeal to an audience interested in their own world and time and fascinated by indigenous myths and legends that promised a distinctly American art. The problem with the last two plays was that the characters lacked the folksy qualities and speech patterns necessary to bring folklore to life. The strong female leads in the two Ohio plays displayed the wide-awake consciousness of the "New Woman" rather than the marks of tradition associated with rural tales, and this character trait weakened Torrence's claim to having fashioned high art from folk art.

Another explanation for his decision lies in the group to which he belonged. The men and women who were his friends were sowing the seeds for great changes in the theater that would bear fruit in the late 1910s and 1920s. Torrence's generation set in motion a number of processes and institutions essential for that dramatic harvest. In the 1900s and 1910s as they struggled to express matters of importance to their cohort, they began experimenting with new, daring themes for plays, and they understood the potential of social drama to which European playwrights and performing companies introduced them. Torrence's circle pushed for new venues for artistic performance, and their efforts succeeded in breaking the twenty-year hold of the Theatre Syndicate on dramatic entertainment across the nation. From university courses and little theaters to new stagecraft and stock companies, theater people in the 1910s prepared the way for a new way of thinking about the stage in America. This circle of experimentalists—earnest, whimsical, daring, and clearly un-comfortable with the prevailing conventions—created the climate in which people like Torrence could think about the theater an as appropriate venue for confronting social problems like the race question rather than escaping into a world of make-believe.[17]

At about the time Torrence became interested in material to be derived from the state of his birth, he fell under the influence of a dynamic movement in Ireland to portray the language, customs, beliefs, and lives of the Irish folk. In interviews, articles, and later reminiscences, Torrence admitted that "the example of the Irish Players" had "suggested to him the possibility of American negro plays."[18] He told students at Rockford College in Illinois that he had been inspired by the plays of John Millington Synge and Padraic Colum, who "awakened in Ireland a whole race of Irish dramatists who voiced their own people," and he believed that the United States had "an even more dramatic peasantry in the negroes."[19] Journalists picked up on these statements and frequently dubbed Torrence the John Millington Synge of the United States and Emilie Hapgood as the Lady Gregory of America, for both worked to initiate a folk theater in this country like the Abbey Players and the Dublin Theatre in Ireland.[20] In his autobiographical statement from the 1930s, Torrence conceded that early in the century he had become disillusioned with "all present day attempts (including his own) to write verse for the stage," and, influenced by the work Synge had crafted from the lives and speech of "the Irish of the Aran Islands," set out to do the same "with one of our national groups—the American negro."[21]

Having decided that folklore lay closer to the heart of America than the conquistadors of the sixteenth century or lovers in the Middle Ages, what Torrence needed was "the folk." Being a friend of Daniel Gregory Mason and living near the center of much cultural criticism, Torrence must have been aware of an ongoing discussion about the sources of native American music. Although many—including Mason—denied its validity, a powerful argument made by numerous music critics held that the only "folk" on which serious composers could draw for native, folk, American themes were Indians and African Americans. These two groups, by virtue of their simplicity, their grounding in the land and nature, their exotic beliefs and superstitions, and their supposed lack of acquaintance with European culture, it was believed, made them the closest American equivalent of the folk that had inspired the pathbreaking serious compositions and literature in modern Russia, Germany, Scandinavia, and elsewhere. Given his background and the resources on which he could draw in his native Ohio, Torrence reasonably—and perhaps calculatingly—turned his attention to African American life.

The story that circulated about the playwright in the immediate aftermath of the triumphant opening of *Three Plays for a Negro Theater* is that Torrence had come to know Negro life in his childhood in the Buckeye state. The *New York Times*'s account of Torrence, for example, asserted boldly that in Xenia, "Mr. Torrence really came to know the soul of the Negro."[22] *Theatre Magazine* echoed the story a month after the three plays closed, noting that "in his boyhood," Torrence "knew well the negro quarter of his Ohio town, and acquired a sympathetic knowledge of the negro."[23] And Lester Walton put his own spin on this bit of information by noting that the *New York Times* interviewer who revealed Torrence's firsthand knowledge of African Americans in his childhood should not have been surprised that a northerner could know blacks as well as a southerner. As Walton saw it, few southerners in the twentieth century saw the Negro as he is instead of how he was as a slave.[24]

Torrence did little to contradict this story—indeed, he may have supplied some of the necessary details in his interview after the plays—and over the years, he added a few flourishes of his own. In an unpublished autobiographical statement written sometime in the 1930s, Torrence remembered that as a boy he had seen "a great deal of my colored townsmen," whom he found to be "entertaining playmates." In another passage, he recalled taking pigs to market with his father, brother, and four African American men—Zachariah Letts, Milo Alexander, Carl Hatcher, and Alec Morgan—the only black Xenians, incidentally, that he reported by name. He took the opportunity here to reproduce their dialect and stories of "their owners past and present."[25] But the story served a kind of mythic function by bestowing on Torrence a familiarity and kinship with his Negro neighbors that he did not altogether deserve. In August 1907, for example, having finished *The Madstone* and *The Thunderpool* and eager to start a new play, Torrence wrote to Moody, "I have been here in Xenia nearly all summer, I go as much as possible among the darkies and country people and have picked up some folklore material. It is mostly useful— what I've found lately—for comedy and I believe it would make a cow laugh."[26] This letter, written as Torrence began to contemplate writing what eventually became the three one-act plays, suggests a much more self-conscious and selective search for African American life and traits than a simple, lifelong acquaintance with and sympathy for Xenians of color.

Whether derived from memories stored since childhood or from active searching as an adult, the Xenia Torrence depicted in his plays was a good deal less interesting than the actual Xenia of his youth. The small Ohio city, located about fifteen miles east of Dayton and halfway between Cincinnati and Columbus, had been marked by strong abolitionist sentiment before the Civil War, had established itself as an important station on the Underground Railroad by the time the war came, and after the war had become one of the few centers for higher learning for African Americans, when the Methodist Episcopal Church decided to found Wilberforce University just outside of town.[27] Although in many other respects a typical midwestern town, bustling with small businesses, eager to establish ties with an outside world with railroads and communications networks, and organized around church, club, and political activities, Xenia stood out for a couple of reasons. First, because of its history of struggle against slavery and its location on the Underground Railroad, many white Xenians prided themselves on their personal racial tolerance and on the city's open-mindedness on racial issues, a pride that manifested itself in the generally benign language used to report the lives and activities of African Americans in local newspapers. Second, because of the presence of Wilberforce and the city's reputation for racial tolerance, African Americans in Ohio and elsewhere around the country viewed Xenia as an attractive city to which to migrate. By 1900, Xenia had a larger proportion of African Americans than any other place with twenty-five hundred inhabitants or more in the entire country—more than 20 percent—and nearly half of the people of color had been born in Ohio.[28]

Perhaps because of the presence of black public schools and Wilberforce University, many of whose graduates staffed the local schools, the African American population of Xenia enjoyed literacy rates well above the national average for the race and just below the average for whites nationwide.[29] Moreover, although the majority of Greene County residents farmed, very few African Americans did so, and of those who did farm, nearly half worked lands of which they were either owners or part-owners.[30] A few black Xenians worked as farm laborers, but the vast majority labored in the cordage factory, artisanal workshops, building trades, on the railroad, and as small-businessmen in the town of Xenia.[31] Black Xenians contributed to the bustle of the town through their enterprise, their social clubs, church life, entertainments, and engagement in politics. Students at Wilberforce organized such groups as the Philomathean Society, Payne and Dodds Literary Society, and the So-dalian Society, which published a monthly journal, as well as the Wilberforce Harmonic Association—"to cultivate higher music"—and the African Choir and Glee Club.[32] Blacks in town held church suppers and organized societies like the United Brethren of Friendship among themselves, and such Negro performers as the Big Six Band ("a musical organization of leading colored men"), the Wilberforce Grand Concert Company, and Miss Hallie Q. Brown ("the wonderful elocutionist") appeared frequently at the Opera House before black and white audiences.[33] And during Torrence's youth in the 1880s, local entertainment was bolstered by traveling black acts, such as the Hyer Sisters' production of *Out of Bondage* and the Haverly Minstrels in 1881, and a performance by the Fisk Jubilee Singers two years later.[34]

From this vibrant community emerged a number of prominent African American citizens who gained the respect of their white neighbors. Campbell L. Maxwell, for example, a Wilberforce graduate admitted to the state bar in 1872, served as the city clerk in 1879 and 1880. Joseph Shorter, likewise a graduate of Wilberforce, returned to the institution as a professor of mathematics and later led the university through the difficult years at the end of the century. Lewis Sides, a respected stonemason and carriage maker, had been born a slave but had made his way to Xenia and established a flourishing business.[35] Wilber-force contributed a large number of well-prepared professionals—teachers, ministers, lawyers, doctors, and businessmen—many of whom remained in Xenia. College presidents, college professors, "two well-known lawyers," and two physicians of note got their undergraduate training from the famous institution, and whether they left Ohio or remained near their alma mater, they furnished examples of culture and refinement to the permanent residents—both black and white—of the town.[36]

Two figures stand out for their remarkable influence in both the black and white communities of Xenia. B. W. Arnett, prominent in local Republican politics, ran for state representative in the mid-1880s. After defeating a white opponent, John Allen, in the primary, he garnered Allen's support for the race against a white Democrat. Allen urged fellow Republicans to support "our candidate" in spite of his race. "He is a worthy gentleman fitted for the position for which he stands as the Republican nominee," Allen insisted, and he pledged to support Arnett.[37] Arnett won the seat, and as state representative, he began immediately to eliminate the remaining "black laws" from the books and urged state-mandated desegregation of the public schools. He succeeded in securing state support for Wilberforce, which stabilized the struggling institution and set it on a course of growth and development in the next several decades.[38]

Hallie Q. Brown, also connected with Wilberforce, attained considerable fame as a professor and an elocutionist in the last two decades of the century. Her father, Thomas A. Brown, had been born into slavery in 1814 and escaped to Canada in 1861, where he remained until 1871, when he decided to move to Xenia "for the purpose of educating his children."[39] After completing her bachelor's degree in 1873, Hallie Q. Brown remained in the area, serving as a principal in one of Dayton's public schools until 1875. After a one-year stint as principal of public schools in Yazoo, Mississippi, Brown returned to Ohio and built a reputation as an accomplished speaker and elocutionist. A report on a Wilberforce concert in 1885 in which Brown performed noted that she had been "cheered to the echo" for the excellence of "her character delineations and varied modulations of tone." The reporter noted as well that "[n]early all our ministers and a large number of leading citizens were in attendance and all came away greatly delighted."[40] When she left the city in 1885, it was to assume a deanship at Allen University in Columbia, South Carolina, a position she held until 1887. In 1892, she went to work for the Tuskegee Institute, and she also lectured at the London Polytechnical Institute before returning in 1912 to join the faculty of Wilberforce.[41]

Yet for all of these achievements and these remarkable figures, Xenia in the late nineteenth century was a profoundly segregated town. More than 90 percent of the African Americans who resided there lived in a neighborhood known as the "East End," where they endured crowded and squalid living conditions. While many African Americans viewed Xenia as a mecca for educational and employment opportunities and as an escape from the violence and poverty of the South, even in the town where whites congratulated themselves for their progressive views on race relations, blacks could not escape the color line. Other than the faculty of Wilberforce, who lived near the school, the handful of blacks who lived in other parts of the city were predominantly the live-in servants of Xenia's wealthy white families. In spite of Arnett's efforts in the state legislature in the 1880s, schools remained segregated, and as a new wave of migrating African Americans from the South arrived in the 1890s, literacy levels among the adult black population began to decline. The idea of African American blood as a "taint" emerged as a theme when social investigators set out to identify and study Xenia's African American population in the late 1890s. Anyone who was "reported upon reliable authority" to be either "black, or brown, or light" was counted as "black." Moreover, eight "white women, wives of colored men," and one "white child adopted into a Negro family" were considered "for the purpose of this study" to be "Negroes."[42]

As the 1890s began, black citizens in Xenia became involved in organizations to counter the discrimination. Some attended the Afro-American Convention held in Columbus in 1890, the purpose of which was "to create a healthy, progressive public sentiment in favor of right treatment to every American citizen, no matter what the color or condition may be," and they succeeded in making Xenia the site for the convention's meeting the following year.[43] At the local level, they organized the Greene County Equal Rights League to devise ways to avoid inadvertently "keeping up the color line." They decided to "discourage all organizations among our people that are not conducive to the best interest of both races" in the belief that as "a part of the whole people" they should "act accordingly."[44] But even these efforts did little to end segregation or to alter racist ideas held by their white neighbors.

For all of his commendable determination to write dramas sympathetic to the lives of African Americans, Ridgely Torrence could not entirely escape the prevailing ideas of white Xenians absorbed in his youth and early adulthood. Growing up in the town's first ward, Torrence lived in the whitest section of the biracial community. There, where 92 percent of the inhabitants were white and lived comfortably in roomy houses with spacious, well-kept yards, the only African Americans were servants, probably not well educated and in many ways cut off from other members of their race. Torrence's memories of Xenia's African Americans differed little from those of Helen Hooven Santmyer, whose *Ohio Town* (1956) pictured a black presence that was folksy, quaint, southern, and unrefined set against the culture of the dominant white majority.[45] The contact Torrence may have had with people of color—while driving hogs to market, in his father's lumberyard, or as playmates—did not change the fact that the playwright viewed his subjects as an outsider and that his family's experience and preconceptions shaped his own.

Torrence's mother's family had come from Maryland and had owned slaves before the Civil War. As a boy, Torrence traveled with his mother to visit family in Maryland who, as he recalled, "lived on a generous scale, served by a retinue of former slaves." At the age of six, Torrence may not have witnessed firsthand the outbursts of his relatives, but the oft-repeated stories formed the nucleus of his "memory" of relationships between masters and slaves. The Ridgely clan believed that white mistresses—not African Americans—had been enslaved in the antebellum period. "It is like having a whole lot of helpless and imbecile little children," they wailed. "It is nurse, mother and sew from morning to night to make clothes to cover their nakedness and we cannot teach these butter-fingered field girls to make a decent garment."[46] Given his close ties to a slaveholding past, Torrence not surprisingly frequently referred to his Negro neighbors as "darkies" and to his dramas as the "darky plays."[47] In a 1916 letter to his mother, Torrence spoke offhandedly about the African American woman ("our girl") who cooked and cleaned for him and his wife. For $2.50 a week, she cooked midday meals, mopped the floors, and stretched their meager income to cover expenses, and Torrence believed that she would happily cook evening meals for fifty cents more a week. "All we have to do," he explained, "is see that she gets a pork chop or some fish every day or two at noon. Like most darkies she can't resist pork and fish."[48]

The African Americans of Torrence's memory—and perhaps of his experience—were not the B. W. Arnetts and Hallie Q. Browns or the club women and leading musical men or the successful graduates of Wilberforce. For Torrence, the image of the Negro that sparked his imagination assumed the features and inflections of the rural southern migrants who arrived in Xenia in fairly large numbers at the end of the century. Although he claimed that the ways of his Negro "playmates" became "as familiar to me as the ways of my own relatives," Torrence at some level recognized the gap. "Their speech, their voices, their laughter, evoked an unconscious but perfectly sympathetic mimicry," he later recalled, "so that Negro dialect became the only language not my own that I have ever learned to speak with facility and I believe with pretty complete accuracy."[49] Torrence also confessed that "the Negro has been a race apart and usually a race in subjection. . . . Its life under slavery with its intense but seemingly hopeless longing for liberty produced in it a certain epic spirit unconscious of course. . . . In modern life, the negro comes face to face with many tragedies unknown to the Anglo-Saxon."[50] Separated by skin color, customs, and a different language and experience, Torrence's Negroes remained a people apart—a people whose peculiarities he sought to express dramatically in the hope of becoming America's answer to Ireland's John Millington Synge but whose hopes, aspirations, concerns, and struggles were not his own.

Thus when Torrence set out in 1914 to stage *Granny Maumee* and developed the laudable but ill-formed idea that the play should be performed by African Americans, he hardly knew where to begin to search for suitable actors. Apparently his main contact with black people—even in New York—had been with individuals working as servants. A letter from the famous Clef Club Orchestra leader, James Reese Europe, dated March 4, 1914, suggests that Torrence had asked Europe for some names of actresses who might be interested in the play. But the response from Europe (and perhaps the request from Torrence, as well) came too late for the Stage Society or the playwright to act on his recommendations. The play was scheduled to open in March, so the Stage Society opted to present Dorothy Donnelly, made up in blackface, as the title character.[51]

Although he later reported that he regretted the Stage Society's unwillingness to use black actresses for the performance, Torrence apparently did little in the next three years to familiarize himself with performers on the African American Stage. When Emilie Hapgood and Robert Edmond Jones eagerly supported the idea of assembling an all-black cast for the 1917 production of *Granny Maumee* and the other two short plays, Torrence set out once again on a frantic search for black performers. In late February 1917, Torrence and Jones decided to go to Harlem "to attend a performance of colored people so that we may look over the ground," he told his family, and in early March, just a month before opening night, he was still complaining to his mother: "We have lots of discouragement in trying to assemble a company of colored people. We have the plays and Mrs. Hapgood has the money and readiness to hire a theatre and pay all the expenses and Jones has his costumes and scenery designed but we are blocked so far by not being able to find the proper people available for casts."[52] Late in March, with part of a cast assembled, Torrence traveled to Baltimore to see Bert Williams perform then went on to Washington "to look for actors for our company."[53] Apparently it never occurred to him to consult members of The Frogs, the C.V.B.A., or black drama critics like Lester Walton, who could have suggested numerous actors for the parts. It also did not occur to him to discuss the matter with Hallie Q. Brown at Wilberforce on one of his many trips home, for he received a letter from the famous elocutionist dated April 27, 1917, saying she had read about the plays in a Cincinnati paper and offering to "help you in some way—Be one of your characters or direct or train others."[54]

Thus, Torrence's contact with African American actors and his familiarity with their performances remained fairly limited. His idea of presenting sympathetic black characters betrayed his rather narrow view of black life. Still, the slice of African American experience he sought out in Xenia and expressed in two of the three plays struck a chord with black theatergoers and black critics. Algernon Brashear Jackson, a black physician in Philadelphia, traveled to New York to see *Three Plays for a Negro Theater* and wrote Torrence to say that as he reflected on the "fine plays" his "enthusiasm [had] increased with each telling of them to [his] friends."[55] James Weldon Johnson praised Torrence for having created in Madison Sparrow of *The Rider of Dreams* "a real human being and a real Negro"—"the type of colored man that may be found in every Negro community."[56] Similarly, the *Crisis* asserted that "no white man has written of colored people more sympathetically than Ridgely Torrence," whose plays had given black actors "their first chance at self-expression in dignified and beautiful drama."[57] And Lester Walton, though disappointed that Torrence resorted to the usual "dialect" instead of exploring black "idiom," nevertheless gave the white playwright credit for having created Negro plays "void of exaggeration" and filled with "spontaneity and naturalness that make a serious appeal."[58]

Moreover, as the years passed, African American professional and amateur companies continued to request permission to stage the plays even though they were never revived on Broadway. In 1921, for example, the Howard University Players presented a special performance of *Simon, the Cyrenian* for delegates to a Conference on the Limitation of Armaments being held in the nation's capital, and the play was attended by dozens of dignitaries from around the globe.[59] The following year, Walter White urged the Howard Players' sponsor, Thomas M. Gregory, to get permission to stage *Simon, the Cyrenian* in New York, where, he believed, the Players "could fill Town Hall," but for unspecified reasons, Torrence refused to grant permission for the venture.[60] By 1934, a review of *Stevedore* that appeared in the *Crisis* indicated that in the seventeen years since its premiere, *The Rider of Dreams* had become a staple of African American dramatic clubs, and in that year the Virginia Union Players performed *Granny Maumee* in the annual Negro Intercollegiate Dramatic Association tournament and won second prize.[61] In the late 1940s, the famous Karamu Players in Cleveland televised a production of *The Rider of Dreams*, a broadcast that received "a number of favorable comments."[62]

In an interview during the plays' run on Broadway, Torrence responded to a question about his intentions to continue writing Negro plays. "I don't know— perhaps," he began. "At least I have this off my mind. I have done something for those people who have been so greatly misjudged and ignored. Now I am free to do other things."[63] To Ridgely Torrence's credit, his interest in African American art and drama did not evaporate after the three plays passed into Broadway memory. The poet wrote *Danse Calinda*, a pantomime that featured

African American music, dance, and drama, shortly after the plays closed, and it was performed by the Howard Players and featured in *Theatre Arts Magazine*. Thomas M. Gregory wrote Torrence in 1922 that African Americans involved in drama had become "conscious of our indebtedness to you . . . for the pioneer work which you have done" in trying to launch a National Negro Theatre.[64] Friends also kept Torrence apprised of new folklore material they encountered; in 1918, Robert Edmond Jones told Torrence about a "kind of aboriginal Passion Play opera sung every year by Negroes in the Louisiana bayous."[65] In the 1930s, having reestablished himself as a poet and longing to be named poet laureate of Ohio (an honor he never received), Torrence began jotting down notes on and reminiscences about the Negro Theatre he had tried to initiate in the 1910s, and he also wrote a touchingly poetic biography of an African American educator named John Hope. Torrence accepted a commission in the late 1930s from the Rockefeller Foundation to conduct a thorough survey of the dramas, players, and theaters of the black communities across the country, a task that required long hours of traveling, interviewing, auditing, and reading and to which Torrence devoted immense energy even though he was approaching retirement age. He kept detailed notes on every play he read and on companies he watched and submitted a report on his findings in 1939.[66]

But in 1917, Ridgely Torrence had presented three plays that bore the marks of a struggling writer seeking fame with a fondness for a type of African American and an unfamiliarity with the complexity and variety of African American life in the United States. Insofar as he hoped to present portraits of real people with dark skin and a life different from that of white Americans, Torrence's aims blended with the African American cast that had been struggling for decades to use the theater as a way to advance their race in America. But Torrence was not completely in synch with his cast; he was less concerned than they with racial equality and first-class citizenship, and he insisted on telling stories only about working-class and rural blacks. And the limits of Torrence's vision placed boundaries on the impact of this dramatic experiment, for the parts of the black world he chose to see, was able to remember, or self-consciously sought were parts not vastly different from those with which most Americans already were familiar.

EMILIE HAPGOOD:
THE WOMAN OF FASHION AND THE STAGE

Although unquestionably the least artistic of the three white people who worked behind the scenes of *Three Plays for a Negro Theater*, Emilie Hapgood often received credit for artistic daring and for being the driving force behind the black actors' debut on Broadway. Oft-quoted was her comment to an interviewer for the *Crisis* that her objective in the project was "to give a numerous and somewhat neglected race its first real chance in dramatic art."[67] At least two New York dailies implicitly gave her credit for the shows in headlines, the *New York Evening Post* hailing "Mrs. Hapgood's Colored Players" the morning after opening night, and the *New York Herald* exploring "Mrs. Emilie Hapgood's Theatrical Negro Novelty" later on during the run.[68] African Americans in particular praised her. Mary Burrill wrote in a flyer to promote the plays among members of the Drama League, "I believe that Mrs. Hapgood's object is to show that there is something beautiful, something truly artistic in this neglected life of the Negro. In that she has succeeded gloriously."[69] And Lester Walton proclaimed simply that "Mrs. Emilie Hapgood has endeared herself to colored Americans for having the temerity to do something no other theatrical manager of standing would ever think of attempting. She is entitled to a Carnegie medal for bravery," and though the three plays "may not prove as big a financial success as 'Magic' and other enterprises in which Mrs. Hapgood is interested," he argued, "they will win for her more enduring fame."[70]

Emilie Hapgood did not write the plays; she did not design the sets or costumes; no account suggests that she coached the actors or took an active role in the rehearsals; but the writers who praised "her" colored players recognized that without her efforts, the plays would not have premiered. Hapgood brought to the enterprise attributes that eluded many people on the African American Stage—money, connections with influential Broadway managers, and social status that made her a force few wanted to offend. Hapgood symbolized the network of whiteness and wealth that could open or close the doors of opportunity on the American Stage and without which sensitive subjects like race dramas remained beyond the pale. Elizabeth Hiatt Gregory's sketch of Hapgood for *Theatre Magazine* in 1917 recognized that "the stage and the woman of fashion are assuming more intimate relations" and that women like Hapgood, with money, "brains and talent," helped bridge the gap separating "the polite world from the footlights."[71] As a representative of the "polite world," Hapgood enjoyed the authority to say that the time had come for people of her class and race to consider seriously the drama of race relations in the United States.

In 1917, Hapgood's interest in the theater extended back at least two decades. Raised in Chicago, Emilie Bigelow met and fell in love with a young reporter for the *Chicago Evening Post*, Norman Hapgood, and the two married in 1896. In the following year, the newlyweds moved to New York, where Norman

Hapgood had accepted a position as a drama critic and editorial writer for Lincoln Steffens's *New York Commercial-Advertiser.* Surrounded by such rising literary stars as Abraham Cahan, Philip Littell, Finley Peter Dunne, Steffens, and Norman's brother Hutchins, Hapgood succeeded in building a solid reputation for the newspaper's treatment of political and cultural issues.[72] As part of his work, Hapgood attended the theater regularly, and he usually took his wife with him. Within five years, he felt sufficiently steeped in the world of the theater to prepare a book entitled *The Stage in America, 1897–1900,* which consisted of numerous articles on the drama, actors, and the role of the stage he had published in prominent journals.[73] With the help of his brother Hutchins, who had become fascinated with New York's ethnic theaters and who had agreed to give his brother material for the column on German, Yiddish, and Italian plays, Hapgood earned the reputation of being a reliable critic with wide-ranging interests.[74] Hutchins later recalled that on the nights he covered ethnic plays, Norman was "free to take his wife to the plays she wanted to see."[75] Thus, for the first few years of their marriage, at least, the Hapgoods spent a great deal of time together in New York's theaters.

Emilie Bigelow's marriage to Norman Hapgood undoubtedly shaped her views on and experience of the theater in America. Certainly, some of his ideas are reflected in her involvement in *Three Plays for a Negro Theater.* While Norman enjoyed the works of many dramatists and appreciated them primarily as literature, he gave special notice to native writers struggling to give America dramatic expression. Part of his interest in the work of this rising generation of American dramatists may have sprung from his acquaintance with students from George Pierce Baker's classes in dramatic writing at Harvard. He became friends with Baker and one of his students, William Vaughn Moody, and undoubtedly knew both Edward Sheldon and Percy MacKaye, who were also Baker students and Harvard graduates.[76] Influenced as they all were by Professor Baker, Hapgood and these playwrights shared a view that American dramatists needed above all to be liberated from the demands of the commercial theater, which was loath to take risks on anything that lacked melodrama and mass appeal. Through newspaper columns, muckraking articles in leading journals of the day, and in a good portion of *The Stage in America,* Hapgood hammered away at the necessity for creating alternative venues for artistic productions and subsidization by either the state or wealthy patrons of the arts for high quality plays that might not be lucrative commercial ventures. The kind of plays Hapgood envisioned appearing in the new theaters were dramas that were good literature and that appealed to the imagination. He despised the elaborate "realistic" sets designed for the middle class who went to "the theatre to see cartloads of scenery and acres of heather, and real horses," and who cared little that the play being performed had little or nothing of importance to say.[77] Judging from her sponsoring of *Three Plays for a Negro Theater* in 1917, Emilie Hapgood shared her husband's support for American dramatists, his devotion to theatrical art for art's sake, and his conviction that the theater should appeal to the imagination.

The drama critic offered his wife more than a way of thinking about the theater; he also provided both the means to enjoy it regularly and a style of life that made her a "woman of fashion." In 1902, Hapgood had resigned from the *Commercial-Advertiser* to accept the position of editor of *Collier's Weekly.* Robert Collier, the son of the magazine's founder, had set out in the early twentieth century to attract the best writers, artists, and illustrators in the country, and he paid them well. Collier sought Hapgood's talents to enhance the editorial page and to give the magazine a distinctive tone. Shortly after accepting the new job at *Collier's Weekly,* Norman purchased a home on East 73rd Street in New York and hired an architect to completely redecorate it—a remodeling job ultimately featured in the *Architectural Record.*[78] Surrounded by marble floors, stone walls, Italian mantle pieces, and luscious tapestries, the Hapgoods could—and did—entertain the most elite of New York's high society.

Emilie Hapgood's social climbing combined with her interest in the theater is conveyed in her brother-in-law's rather unflattering portrait of her in his autobiography: "A striking-looking woman, in her dark way beautiful, with languid language and concentrated personality, and a constant and insatiable wordly ambition, she was the object about which Norman's life revolved," wrote Hutchins Hapgood. "She had always been a self-conscious invalid, able only to be active in her personal pleasures and ambitions; at other times she would be lying in a chaise lounge looking picturesque and impressive; in this effective posture, she would often receive her visitors, among whom more and more of the rich and successful appeared."[79] She viewed him, Hutchins, as "useful to Norman," he wrote, because the material he wrote on ethnic plays "added a good deal to his column." After 1912, when Norman left *Collier's Weekly* to become the editor of *Harper's Weekly,* his wife began more openly to display her ambitions and her interest in the workings of the theater. She became involved in the New York Stage Society, serving as its president in 1914 and 1915.[80] In that capacity, she came to know actors and their agents, playwrights, patrons of the stage, and other artists involved in the theater. In 1914, for example, she used the editorial page of the *New York Times* to promote the Stage Society's show on Fifth Avenue of the new stagecraft, which featured work by Maxfield Parrish, Sam Hume, and Robert Edmond Jones.

"The present exhibition is the first attempt to gather together the representative work of American stage artists," she wrote. "Because of the wide-spreading character of American life, as well as the American geography, few people could have realized what a quantity of original and stimulating work has been done here in the new staging." Her letter to the editor planted the idea that she and other members of the Stage Society had actually assembled the materials for the show, when, in fact, the exhibition had originated in Cambridge, Massachusetts, and had been transported to New York when the society made suitable arrangements for the show.[81] Regardless of her precise role in introducing New York to the new artists designing sets and costumes for the American stage, Hapgood nevertheless came to know the most influential designers of the 1910s.

Hapgood's involvement with the Stage Society also gave her experience with producing plays. In 1914, the Stage Society presented two plays—the feature was Thomas Heywood's *A Woman Killed with Kindness* and the second was Ridgely Torrence's *Granny Maumee*. Carl Van Vechten exclaimed that Torrence's drama was "as real, as fresh, as the beginning of the Irish theatre movement must have been in Dublin."[82] The Stage Society could offer any playwright only two shows, but it attempted as much as possible to give struggling American dramatists a place to introduce their work, which too often was rejected by Broadway managers who wanted sure hits from veteran playwrights.[83] As Hapgood explained it to Torrence when she decided to promote his work, "If the Stage Society does not exist to help the American dramatist, I shall certainly not have much interest in trying to make it the real power that it is to-day in England." Under her leadership, the group had decided to seek out "wonderful American plays" and to put them on the stage "in *the* most beautiful way possible" and then try to arrange for commercial runs.[84] Indeed, she promised Torrence to "help toward getting [Sarah] Bernhardt to do the play." Later she urged Torrence to write a different Negro tragedy "with a part as fresh as Granny Maumee," and she would try to get Bernhardt to play it in America. Bernhardt's "manager is a friend of mine," she noted.[85]

In the two years following the stunning success of *Granny Maumee* in March 1914, Hapgood not only pushed Torrence toward the historic production at the Garden Theatre, but also pursued other offers to produce daring pieces. Within two months of *Granny Maumee*'s maiden performance, Hapgood wrote Torrence that she wanted copies of the play to show Granville Barker (a famous playwright), Gordon Craig (one of the most influential stage artists of the day), and Constantin Stanislavsky (of the Moscow Art Theatre), and she urged him to write new material. Could he prepare "a wordless play—a pantomime" that would appeal to Stanislavsky? Would he consider creating a Negro comedy to go along with the tragedy? Was it possible to rewrite *Granny Maumee* in Creole dialect, more suited to the talents of the great Bernhardt? And she also wanted to buy the rights to the play so she would have greater control over staging, casting, and presenting it.[86] While Torrence worked on additional plays, Hapgood bought the rights to John Galsworthy's *The Little Man* and produced G. K. Chesterton's *Magic* in the 1916–1917 theater season. According to *Theatre Magazine*, O. P. Heggie, who owned the American rights to *Magic*, had "searched in vain for someone with the temerity to put on this comedy of the superhuman before he found Mrs. Hapgood." She worked tirelessly, overseeing the casting and attending rehearsals, to ensure the drama's success, and at the last moment, "she stepped in and did the unexpected by designing the scenery as Robert Edmond Jones could not undertake the task."[87]

By the time Hapgood undertook the production of *Magic* and *Three Plays for a Negro Theater,* another reason for urgency and enterprise had arisen. After nineteen years of marriage, the Hapgoods divorced in the spring of 1915. Norman had nothing to say about the unpleasant matter in his 1930 autobiography, but judging from his brother's comments, the Hapgood family placed most of the blame on Emilie. Her utter devotion to the theater came at the expense of their only daughter, Ruth, Hutchins Hapgood insisted, and what he regarded as her feigned inability to perform the traditional roles of wife and mother made Emilie responsible in his eyes for the break-up. When the couple took separate residences, however, Ruth lived with her mother.[88] Without Hapgood's steady income and constant support, the fledgling producer may well have felt a special pressure to succeed in the theater. Indeed, in the midst of arranging for *Granny Maumee* "to be done as you would like it," she asked Torrence if she could buy the rights, but explained, "As I have not much money at present . . . would you be willing I should have the ordinary play agent's percentage in case I arrange anything?"[89]

Hapgood's commitment to the plays, however, is unquestionable. Torrence reported to his family three weeks before the plays opened that "Mrs. Hapgood is pouring out money on the production, thousands of dollars and we hope the thing will be a success."[90] His wife noted as well that Mrs. Hapgood "is so deeply interested [in the production] that she has been to every performance but two and doesn't miss a single speech."[91] When the plays brought less of a return than had been hoped at the Garden Theatre, she approached Lee Shubert, one of the most powerful New York theater owners, to see if *Three Plays for a Negro Theater* could be moved to one of his theaters. Although "at first unwilling that Negro actors should come to his theater," after Shubert saw a performance, he promptly agreed to have them moved to his Garrick Theatre, which was closer to the heart of the Great White Way than was the Garden.[92] Moreover, Hapgood had persuaded Robert Edmond Jones, the brightest star in a constellation of daring new stage designers, to become involved in the production. So regardless of how anxious Hapgood may have been about the need to succeed for personal reasons, she spared no expense and drew on her contacts with important people in the theater to pave the way for the three plays to enjoy a long and successful run on Broadway.

As for her devotion to the African Americans whose lives were expressed in the dramas, the case is far less clear. As a woman of means, traveling comfortably through Europe and living in a posh home on East 73rd Street, Hapgood likely encountered African Americans only rarely and probably often as employees. Her husband, not known as a sympathizer with Negroes on the race question, believed that Radical Reconstruction had been a terrible mistake, hoped that the Fourteenth and Fifteenth Amendments were ignored, and in the 1904 presidential race, threatened to withdraw his support from Theodore Roosevelt, who had invited Booker T. Washington to the White House.[93] Given her enthusiasm for casting black actors in Torrence's plays, and later presiding over the Circle for Negro War Relief, a private relief effort for African Americans in uniform during World War I, Hapgood did not share her ex-husband's utter disdain for American citizens of color. Indeed, the *Crisis* hailed her as an exemplar of the "new philanthropy" in 1918 for her efforts on behalf of Negro performers and soldiers.[94] In November 1917, she helped arrange a benefit concert that featured African American performers such as Harry T. Burleigh and the United Colored Choir under the direction of J. Rosamond Johnson. A few months later, she tried to book Enrico Caruso at the Manhattan Casino for a benefit to raise money to buy an ambulance. The concert, however, fell through when the great tenor could not make the engagement.[95] In September 1917, Olivia Torrence reported to her husband that Hapgood "had been talking with Dr. Dubois [*sic*]" about sponsoring a pageant he had written and which would be of interest to the African American community. But her reason for passing along this information to Torrence was to push him to get his pantomime to the producer "as soon as possible." Olivia Torrence believed that Hapgood "must be crazy to get some showy sort of display" and that it would matter little to her if the piece were written by Du Bois, Torrence, or someone else.[96] These efforts on behalf of African Americans do not necessarily mean that Hapgood counted herself among the ranks struggling for equality between the races.

In 1914, Hapgood claimed that advancing the American dramatist interested her above all else—"As you know American plays are *the* thing in my mind," she wrote Torrence—but she did not abandon practicality because of her belief. Recognizing that Constantin Stanislavsky probably would not attempt an American play unless it was a pantomime, she urged Torrence to write something that the foreign director would like. Similarly, the idea of rewriting *Granny Maumee* in Creole dialect, however much it may have attracted Bernhardt, betrays a weak understanding of the central idea of Torrence's drama. Would a Creole display the same fierce protectiveness of her "royal black" ancestry as the black-skinned Granny Maumee?[97] Hapgood may well have enjoyed the comparisons some journalists made between her promotion of the African American Theater and Lady Gregory's efforts on behalf of the Irish Theater, but this claim to fame did not chart a new course for her in African American productions after 1917.

Emilie Hapgood's role in *Three Plays for a Negro Theater* was both indispensable and problematic. With her connections, her ability to shake the money tree, and her status as a woman of high society, Hapgood had at her disposal the necessary means and cultural authority to give three plays about Negro life a hearing on an important stage in America. Her efforts made *Three Plays for a Negro Theater* the talk of the town because she saw to it that it employed a prominent designer and appeared in a venue that critics could not afford to ignore. But her personal reasons for sponsoring the plays and her relatively lukewarm interest in the advancement of an African American agenda for social equality diluted the aims of the black actors who appeared in the cast and the black critics who hailed the experiment. Her willingness to sponsor black actors forced some progressive journalists to examine their own credentials for racial toleration, but it often elicited more of a sense of noblesse oblige than camaraderie. Emilie Hapgood, a "woman of fashion," carried the drama of race across the bridge she helped build to the Stage, but it was always clear that Hapgood could at any moment return safely to the haven of "polite society," unaware and perhaps uncaring of the color line that prevented her cast and the people whose lives they interpreted from following freely along.

ROBERT EDMOND JONES: IMAGINATION AND RACE

During one of the rehearsals for *Three Plays for a Negro Theater* in the final week before opening night, Robert Edmond Jones, the director, stood offstage to watch the black actors perform. Standing next to him was a black stagehand who turned to Jones to say the dancers were not moving properly. Their movements were "too studied," he explained to the director, "a dance should be natural," whereupon the African American onlooker "demonstrated what he meant." The journalist who told this story, Robert Benchley, added with some surprise, "Oddly enough, Jones didn't laugh. These artists have a queer sense of humor." Those who knew Jones well, however, would not have been astonished by his listening to a stagehand or finding in his impromptu dance "natural grace and freedom of movement."[98] The famed scenic artist believed that the aim of the theater should be to provide harmony between music, light, dialogue, movement, and scenery, and that aim could be reached only through cooperation between all people involved in the production—"even . . . the stagehands."[99]

Of the three white artists working behind the scenes of *Three Plays for a Negro Theater,* Jones brought to the project the most clearly articulated ideas about collaboration and the greatest degree of "color blindness" on the issue of race. As he wrote during the run of the three plays, "My idea of the correct production of a play is to start from the author's original idea and make it something truly alive, organic." The animation of a written drama could be accomplished, he believed, only when everyone involved discussed the drama and shared ideas for bringing it to life. He urged producers to "call a conference of the people that will make the play live on the stage so that in a body they may work up the idea. Can't you imagine the effect it would have on a play if the producer, the playwright, the painter of the scenes, and the leading actors were to talk over the idea as it was to be worked out?"[100] What witnesses to the rehearsals for the plays interpreted as an absence of "directing," was perhaps more accurately a case of Jones trying to put these ideas into practice. By letting the actors create the scene, decide on the proper inflections and gestures, and move about the stage in ways they considered natural, Jones recognized that there was no single "right" way to do a scene. His job, then, as director consisted of harmonizing the various views of a play or scene to create an aesthetically pleasing experience for the theatergoer. Moreover, as far as Jones was concerned, it mattered not that the actors or stagehands with whom he collaborated were African American. His enthusiasm for the all-black cast arose not because he wanted to do something for a downtrodden people, but because he believed that the best way—the most believable way—to stage plays about African American life required actors who knew the experience of American Negroes firsthand.

Perhaps as important as Jones's collaborative ideal of the theater and his color blindness, however, was the fact that he did not stake his career and future good fortune on this production. Although his first effort at directing, Jones worked with confidence and disinterestedness that sought only the most effective presentation of people, scenes, and ideas to spark the imagination of audiences for whom their Negro neighbors remained shrouded in mystery and stereotype. Considerably younger than Hapgood, Torrence, and many of the veteran performers in the cast, Jones nevertheless had the least—personally speaking—at stake in the show. His reputation as a scenic artist of distinction was firmly established. After only two years at his craft in the United States, he was eagerly sought by playwrights and managers for their shows. Indeed, in the three years after *Three Plays for a Negro Theater,* Jones would work on fourteen different productions, including several major community masque-dramas involving casts of thousands, one opera-ballet, and many traditional stage plays.[101]

For good or ill, Jones's presence as the director and scenic artist on the production staff also ensured that the three plays would be viewed as part of the New Movement in the Theater, an important effort to redefine dramatic expression and the focus of much heated controversy in the 1910s. Jones's fame and the generally high regard that critics had for his work guaranteed that if for no other reasons, influential cultural commentators would witness and write about the Negro plays, making them a topic of fairly general conversation in artistic circles. Like Hapgood, Jones had become a significant figure in the world of make-believe—a figure critics and managers could not afford to ignore. Thus, the artist's following meant that this highly experimental production would receive the full attention of cultural critics in the mainstream, and that for this one moment, the white theater world would consider seriously the race issues raised by the plays. At the same time, however, the plays being viewed as part of the New Movement also meant that their fate depended to some extent on critics' attitudes toward this dramatic movement and that matters of taste and artistic politics could push race relations to the side.

In some respects, Robert Edmond Jones's youth and experience up to 1917 made him an unlikely candidate to volunteer for work on three plays about African American life, or even to be a force to be reckoned with on Broadway. Born in 1887 in Milton, New Hampshire, Jones grew up in a fairly homogeneous, white environment. One of his earliest biographers attributed to him a "New England quality of vision" and saw him as exemplary of the pioneering spirit of "our Mayflower race."[102] Immediately upon completing his education in the Milton public schools, Jones entered Harvard in 1906 to study art, and he remained there after earning a bachelor's degree in 1910, working as a graduate instructor in the fine arts department. One of his contemporaries at Harvard, Hiram K. Moderwell, remembered his work at the august institution as "feeble and sloppy." His classmates and, later, his students "loved Bobbie Jones" but they could "never find anything to take seriously in his work." Typical of Jones's lack of seriousness, he had only to finish one portrait to satisfy the department's requirement for retaining his instructorship, but after six months of ineffectual daubing, the portrait remained unfinished, and Jones was invited to leave the program in 1912.[103] Surrounded by people from backgrounds similar to his own in a bastion of educational privilege, Jones had little contact with African Americans, and his work as an artist seemingly lacked focus, craftsmanship, and direction.

Jones's devotion to theater art remained strong, but he lacked the discipline to make an impression on potential employers. Friends helped him find work in New York designing costumes for Comstock and Gest and for Gertrude Hoffman, who was appearing at the Manhattan Opera House. But instead of focusing on the work at hand, Jones spent countless hours drawing sketches of "smashing" scenery designs for plays that existed only in his imagination, attending extravagant Broadway shows, and offering his imaginative sketches to theater managers, who made a few practical changes and used them without crediting the unknown artist. Before leaving the great metropolis, Jones did execute some bold posters for a pageant in Madison Square Garden arranged by striking silk workers from Paterson, New Jersey. But before the year was out, Jones had decided to travel to Europe with no definite plans.[104]

Jones's sojourn in Europe began in Italy, where he witnessed several marvelous spectacles that fired his imagination, but it ended in Germany in the Deutsches Theater with Max Reinhardt, a revolutionary stage artist. As early as 1911, Reinhardt had begun to stake a claim for a more artistic theater experience by avoiding both nineteenth-century "literary dramas" and twentieth-century "problem dramas" and seeking instead dramas cloaked in beautiful sets, that gave "pleasure and joy" and that made audiences "feel at peace" with themselves. In other words, Reinhardt's ideal theater placed "infinitely more value" on the art of presentation than it did on the substantive matter being explored in the play.[105] Jones had read work by Gordon Craig, who had been influenced by Reinhardt's aesthetic vision, so when an acquaintance in Florence invited the young artist to accompany him to Berlin to meet Reinhardt, Jones eagerly accepted. Some later biographers tried to present Jones as an official student or apprentice of the great master of the new stagecraft, but the relationship between the two men had no official institutional standing. The German simply permitted Jones access to the backstage and studio of the Deutsches Theater so he could watch and learn as he pleased, and only much later did he promise to let Jones design scenery and costumes for a production in Budapest.[106]

Although clearly influenced by the German pioneer, Jones left the Deutsches Theater having formulated his own view of the place and nature of stage art. From the Germans, Jones came to appreciate not only the imagining of beautiful sets and costumes, but also the executing of the designs. He admired the artists' firsthand knowledge of carpentry, sewing, and electricity, all of which went into the creation of an aesthetically pleasing set. He also immersed himself in the German theater scene, which, both behind and in front of the footlights, thrived on discussion, debate, and engagement with the virtues and drawbacks of the art. Jones also picked up on the German use of clean simple lines and bold colors, which in the audience created a far more powerful impression than overly decorated costumes with fine prints. But he eschewed both Reinhardt's flashy showmanship—in the belief that the most effective set is the one that does not upstage the drama itself—and his unwillingness to concern himself with "problem plays." As a mature artist, with skills and experience in making as well as designing scenery and costumes, Jones returned to the United States when war broke out in Central Europe in 1914, determined to put his hard-won skills and vision at the service of the American Stage.[107]

Upon his return to the United States, Jones found himself one of a small, but rapidly growing, group of stage artists bent on revolutionizing the American Theater. Shortly after his arrival, he hooked up with Sam Hume, Maxfield Parrish, Howard Cushing, Helen Dryden, and others whose designs went on display in various cities in early 1915 as representative of the new stagecraft.[108] Like Jones, these artists hoped to dethrone the reigning realism of the David Belascos on Broadway, whose elaborate sets left nothing to the imagination of the audience. Whereas Belasco tried to please his audiences with "dramatic illusion" and truck loads of props, Jones and his friends in the New Movement sought to inspire the imagination of theatergoers with "allusions" to the world being represented. As Percy MacKaye observed, the new stage artists of the 1910s hoped to "project in the theatre the world reflected in the dramatist's mind—not the actual world which caused that magic reflection" and in that way explore its "reality."[109] So instead of trying to recreate a middle-class drawing room or a Medieval fortress or a humble African American's cabin, the new artists wanted to evoke them and to capture what it felt to inhabit those places rather than to reproduce, imperfectly, how they might have looked. Thus, for example, Jones created a forest scene on stage, not by cluttering the stage with dozens of potted trees or artificial replicas, but by "hanging clumps of dark canvas in heavy folds" to create "the sense of a forest."[110]

Shortly after the exhibition of the new stage art appeared in New York, offers for work came pouring in to Jones. His first show, Anatole France's *The Man Who Married a Dumb Wife,* staged by Granville Barker and the New York Stage Society, can be best described as a stunning triumph. Moderwell remembered two years later that the "first night of this play was breathless. It was the first trial of the 'new stagecraft' on Broadway," and the critical community "had its hatchet out for fads."[111] Alexander Woollcott of the *New York Times* began his review by commenting not on the play, but on the perfect set. "It happens to be a pretty good example . . . of what is loosely termed the new art of the theatre," he wrote, and after extolling the backgrounds, the props, and the costumes, he concluded that "Robert E. Jones, the young American disciple of the 'new school' who did the decorations is to be congratulated."[112] A week later the *Times* noted, with astonishment, that Jones had designed the scenery and had painted it, had designed the costumes, headdresses, and sandals worn by the cast, and had made them; in fact, "Mr. Jones really made the decoration with his own hands."[113] Critics elsewhere agreed with the *Times* writers. As Moderwell put it, "The beauty of the scene literally took everyone's breath. The thing—startling and novel as it was—was so utterly right that criticism had no place." From that day forward, he wrote, "It became lodged in the minds of reviewers that whatever Robert Edmond Jones did was right."[114]

Indeed, a year and a half later, when Jones designed the scenes for *The Happy Ending*, critics panned the play but hailed Jones as a creative *wunderkind*. *Theatre Magazine*'s Arthur Hornblow called the play "a singular combination of long-winded banality, crude modernity, and allegorical futility," but he lauded Jones's stage settings as "something truly beautiful in design and execution." Similarly, James Metcalfe of *Life* reported that Jones had "provided delightful settings" for the dramatic episodes contained in *The Happy Ending*, but that the "authors [had] done little in the way of poetry, sentiment, logic or language," to deserve them.[115]

In the year preceding *Three Plays for a Negro Theater*, Jones undertook some of the costume designs for Percy MacKaye's *Caliban*, which drew on themes and characters from *The Tempest* to honor the three-hundredth anniversary of Shakespeare's death. *Caliban*, dubbed a community masque, involved thousands of people in the cast and required a multitude of costumes. Moreover, at the last minute, when another of the designers fell ill, Jones designed and supervised the execution of three hundred additional costumes for fifteen hundred people in the space of about six weeks. The results were "splendid" and "a new revelation to most Americans, of the potency of pure color on a large scale," and some considered them "the most successful element of the giant spectacle."[116] According to Frank Cheney Hersey, who saw *Caliban* when it was revived in Boston in 1917, "It was gratifying to see again the brilliant costumes which in color and pattern Mr. Jones devised to carry a long distance."[117] He also designed the set and costumes for *Til Eulenspiegel*, an opera ballet staged by the Russian Ballet. Relying more on a German than a Russian aesthetic, Jones convinced Vaslav Nijinsky, the head of the company, that his art complemented the story line, and when the staging won widespread critical acclaim, Jones not only avoided an impassioned temper tantrum from the director, but also succeeded in making a sharp deviation from typical

Russian Ballet scenery.[118] In addition to the masque and the ballet, Jones designed the scenery for *A Successful Calamity* and *Good Gracious Annabelle,* the first act of which he found more satisfying "than any piece of work I have ever done."[119]

By early 1917, when Jones began working in earnest on the three plays by Torrence, the stage artist had earned the respect of most people associated with the theater, and the effect of his work on theatrical conventions had been enormous. Sheldon Cheney, writing in *Theatre Arts Magazine* in February 1917, noted that Joseph Urban and Jones "seemed to be fast convincing the managers that the newer forms of stage decoration are the best," contributing to the emergence of New York as "the liveliest dramatic studio in God's slowly bettering world."[120] But while Urban, an Austrian, and Bakst, a Russian, had shocked Broadway with their "highly colored and weird decorative effects," an American was "surpassing them all." Robert Edmond Jones, *Theatre Magazine* argued, was a "native artist" who brought "originality of design and color to the theatre."[121] In early 1917, Jones turned his original vision to the race question. Jones had known Torrence and Hapgood since 1915, shortly after his return to the United States, and in February 1917, he and the playwright discussed the dramas and worked together to assemble a cast. Long before the final cast had been selected, Jones had designed the costumes and sets, and he began rehearsals sometime in March. His ideal of collaboration, best demonstrated by his directorial style, and his designs would add "distinction to the inspired plays for a Negro Theatre" that opened at the Garden Theatre in April.[122]

Catching the spirit of Torrence's plays, Jones set out to create the proper mood for each drama and to clothe the stage and the actors in raiment that he thought would help audiences imagine the experience of an embittered former slave and her citified great-granddaughter, of a struggling working-class couple, and of the powerful, conflicted African rebel in the presence of transcendent love. In *The Rider of Dreams,* for example, Madison Sparrow's modest suit and unshined shoes befit his station as a laborer, but the clothes were neither too big, too small, nor patched with garish, mismatched fabric, and the colorful kerchief tied around his neck subtly conveyed to the audience his desire—in spite of limited means—to enjoy the finer things in life. Similarly, *Granny Maumee*'s title character wore modest clothes and a turban in keeping with her rural existence, but she did not appear in tatters. Her pride showed through in her attention to the household which she readied to greet the next generation in her royal black line, and in her effort to present herself well. By contrast, Sapphie, fresh from her job in the city, sports more up-to-date clothing, from the ready-made cape she drapes over her shoulder and her baby, to the high-button boots that peek out from under her ankle-length skirt. Neither the humor of the first play nor the tragedy of the second depended on sartorial cues. Implicitly, Jones invited audiences to imagine African Americans dressing according to their means, taste, locale, and personal proclivities, and through that vision he reinforced one of the basic impulses shared by the actors and the playwright—the desire to humanize and individualize Negro Americans. Given the lack of commentary on the props and wardrobe for the first two plays, suggesting that they harmonized so well with the dramatic literature and action on stage that they served only as background, Jones succeeded stunningly in these modern race dramas.

Critics who commented on his contribution to the production believed that he did his best work in *Simon, the Cyrenian*. Certainly, the costumes he created to evoke Jerusalem on the eve of the crucifixion of Jesus of Nazareth resembled in style the work in *Caliban* and *Til Eulenspiegel*, which had brought him fame. Bold colors, broad contrasting stripes, and simple, elegant lines sprang more from his imagination than from the pages of history, but they helped transport the audience to a distant past where Egyptian princesses wore high, regal headdresses; slaves, bare-chested and muscular, padded around palaces without shoes; and servant girls wore turbans and straight shifts without any other adornment. To add to the drama of Simon's "conversion" to Christ-like pacifism and love, Jones designed a kind of partial tunic that exposed the actor's powerful shoulders and arms. A leather strap across the front secured his weapons. Clad in this costume, John Butler looked the part of a man who could, indeed, fight for and lead his people to freedom, as Simon, the African rebel from Cyrene.

Jones had risen to the challenge of Torrence's plays and had succeeded in all three to harmonize the art of the stage with the message and mood he believed was conveyed by the dialogue and movement of the actors. In the days and weeks that followed the grand opening night, however, Jones had relatively little to say about the plays or his role in them. Except for designing the set of Marc Connelly's Pulitzer Prize–winning play *The Green Pastures* in 1930, he pursued no other opportunities to participate in the staging of race dramas.[123] In the early 1920s, when Thomas M. Gregory asked if he would be willing to serve as a member of the advisory council for the Howard Players in Washington, D. C., he happily agreed to do so. But in answer to Gregory's request for the sketches he had made for the plays, he replied, "Unfortunately, the designs for Torrence's plays are no longer in existence."[124] Jones would not be counted among those who struggled politically or artistically on behalf of African American rights, although the *Crisis* considered him one of the "philanthropists of the new order" in 1918.[125] And while he liked the idea of a

Negro Theater, he did not devote his career to its founding and flowering. But in spite of this apparent lack of interest, Jones represented an ideal for creating hybrid cultural expression. For he listened to, watched, consulted, and worked *with* his collaborators—from the playwright to the actors to the stagehands. His own indomitable personality, brilliant imagination, and craftsmanship did shine through, but not at the expense of the main messages of the plays and always in tune with the contributions made by others. Although he had to imagine the experience of American Negroes—a race apart—Jones worked with the black actors to make these race dramas a reality on Broadway.

BECOMING CULTURE IN AMERICA

The lives of Torrence, Hapgood, and Jones and their contributions to the three plays illustrate the role of money, fame, authority, and race in the shaping of cultural conversation in America. Even within the limits of theater, the writing or staging of a play did not necessarily mean that the subject expressed in the drama would become part of the cultural debate. Perhaps this point would be clearer if Torrence's three plays were compared to those of another playwright. In 1913, the *Crisis* noted briefly in one of its columns on art that W. P. Saunders of Nashville, Tennessee, had produced his second play, a play presumably about African American life. Neither play, it has turned out, became part of a more generalized discussion of how best to express American life before the footlights. One might track down extant manuscripts of Saunders's work and subject them to rigorous cultural criticism—what were the themes, how were they structured, do the plays take a position on key issues like education, opportunities, work, and the franchise that would help one locate them within a broader discussion, and so on—but after that, what precisely can one say about their relationship to American culture? They might be viewed as an example of a "voice" stifled by race prejudice, the recovery of which might provide important insights into the ways African Americans spoke to one another about the meaning of their experience. The lack of engagement by a wider public, however, forces one to take note of the limited extent to which plays by W. P. Saunders became a part of the national culture.[126]

I offer the example of Saunders, not to cast aspersions, but to invite a comparison with the three Negro plays of 1917. What I think Torrence, Hapgood, and Jones show is that the three plays were engaged by a wide variety of commentators and individual theatergoers because of issues that have nothing to do with the subjects of the plays. The plays by Torrence came to be a subject of excited conversation in 1917 because of Hapgood's money and cultural authority, Jones's fame as the *wunderkind* of scenic art, and Torrence's network of influential friends, who introduced him to the "right" people. Torrence's plays were not culture when they existed merely as strings of words written or printed on stacks of paper. They became a cultural issue as the result of a process, a process in which not all Americans can effectively take part.

Perhaps it is stating the obvious, but one of the most important barriers to participating in this process in the 1910s was race. Some African Americans in the professional and middle classes had money, and some like Lester Walton, for example, willingly used their money to invest in theaters. But lacking the social stature to influence the managers of the leading playhouses on Broadway, their money, by itself, could not open doors to opportunities to participate in ongoing discussions about the appropriate content for a distinctly American culture. Similarly, other African Americans had connections of sorts—they had performed in musical comedies and in the Follies on some important venues on the Great White Way. But none, including Bert Williams, Bob Cole, J. Rosamond Johnson, George Walker, and Ernest Hogan, succeeded in then using their stage triumphs as leverage to gain the support of theater managers for a wider variety of artistic expression and race-specific performance. In the case of the three Negro plays, Lee Shubert's knee-jerk response to the idea of the plays being moved to the Garrick Theatre was complete opposition solely on the grounds of race—he did not want to let black actors onto his stage. Why did he change his mind? Likely, it was not because Lottie Grady or Inez Clough or Alexander Rogers persuaded him; rather, Emilie Hapgood invited him to see a performance and afterward, not wishing to make an enemy of this "lady of society" or hoping at some future date to employ the great Robert Edmond Jones, he relented. Monetary self-interest probably figured very little in his decision. For although he got rent for the theater from Hapgood, the shows did not make a cent beyond that. In terms of rational calculation, Shubert's decision to lease the theater to Hapgood was not a particularly sound investment or use of a physical asset, but in cultural terms it promised huge dividends.

In addition to race, cultural authority—or lack thereof—also presented obstacles to free engagement in the culture process. Of course, both whiteness and wealth underlay this authority, but something more also played a part. Scholars in various disciplines over the past three decades have named and described the process by which a "ruling class" or "social elite" is formed. While they might disagree on specifics, most would concur that having the power to define the standards of taste, morality, and significance gives an edge to those who write and publish ideas for public consideration. In the early twentieth century, many of the people best positioned to establish the parameters of "good taste" in the theater and whose opinions gained wide currency shared common experiences, common acquaintances, and similar backgrounds—Ivy League associations, familiarity with the work and students of Harvard's George Pierce Baker, and knowledge—sometimes intimate— of each other. Thus, not surprisingly, Robert Edmond Jones's two earliest "biographers," Percy MacKaye and Hiram K. Moderwell, knew "Bobbie" from their Harvard days. Their celebratory writings helped confirm the spreading idea that America had found in Jones an artist of exceptional merit. MacKaye also edited the letters written by William Vaughn Moody to his wife, Harriet, after the poet's sudden death in 1910, and in the lengthy introduction he asserted the existence of a budding school of "American" drama that revolved around Moody, MacKaye, Torrence, and Edwin Arlington Robinson, all part of the crowd that gathered in the Judson Hotel in Greenwich Village. Similarly Kenneth Macgowan, who helped organize the exhibit of the new stagecraft in 1915, penned an article about the show without mentioning his role in its establishment. Assuming a reportorial tone, Macgowan made "news" of, and assigned importance to, an event in which he was hardly a neutral observer. Multiplied many times over, these bits of information, positive appraisals, and serious commentary presented by people who knew each other snowballed into a consensus, somewhat artificial because of the closed circle in which it was produced.

In some ways quite remarkably, three insiders in this process—Torrence, Hapgood, and Jones—decided to veer off the beaten path of mainstream drama in 1917 and to collaborate with black actors on plays that took black life seriously. But as we have seen, even this decision sprang as much from personal concerns about career (Torrence), independence (Hapgood), and friendship (Jones) as it did from a commitment to using the theater as a forum for social justice and racial equality. Moreover, each of these white artists brought baggage that cluttered the field of collaboration. Torrence brought acute powers of observation, skillful writing, and a desire to present a sympathetic view of Negro life, as well as the tunnel vision and racism of a white boy from the first ward of Xenia, Ohio. Hapgood packed up her noblesse oblige inside her bulging purse, along with considerable stores of ignorance and misunderstanding. Finally, Jones, in some regards the most efficient traveler, carried a versatile wardrobe of imagination, ingenuity, and a genuinely cooperative spirit, with only a few excess bags of reputation and ties to the New Movement that could weight the importance of the production away from race. The black actors came culturally laden, too, with hopes for freer access to the stage and to social equality, an aesthetic developed from past performance, and a vision of collective improvement for the race. In the midst of all this freight, black and white artists created a cultural product that reflected the hybridity as well as the contradictions of their joint efforts. Thus, in the process of working together, Opal Cooper, Alex Rogers, John Butler, Blanche Deas, and the other cast members, along with the playwright, producer, and director produced a statement—or really a collection of statements—that launched a serious discussion in the journals and spheres where culture was r.egotiated. The consideration these statements received was as important to the process of becoming culture as was the statement itself. For in the process of assessing the merits and messages of the three plays, cultural commentators revealed where the boundaries of race relations existed, where they might expand or contract, and what of the artistic messages made a difference in American thoughts and beliefs on race.

The commentary generated in response to the productions in the Garden and Garrick Theatres also reveals one of the most critical issues faced by the United States in the twentieth century—the nature of democratic art. In the course of engaging the plays, players' performances, the sets and scenes, and the combined aspirations of those involved in the production, witnesses to the production invariably segued into such issues as the best representation of America in the world of make-believe, the manner in which art in a democracy is deemed democratic, and the extent to which African Americans or the artistic avant garde could be considered legitimate bearers of American or democratic art.

All three principals on the production staff identified to some degree with the New Movement in the Theater. Hardly a unified movement, the theatrical avant garde nevertheless shared strong convictions about democracy and culture. But none of the people associated with these radical artists were African American. Three representatives of the New Movement made the debut of black actors on the Great White Way a reality in 1917, but it would be a mistake to assume that the African American view of art in a democracy coincided with that of their benefactors. As we shall see, while the New Movement helped clear the way to Broadway, its old prejudices limited the impact of the *Three Plays for a Negro Theater* on the nation's conversation about just race relations.

Bert Williams in *Bandanna Land*, *Theatre Magazine*, April 1908.

Bob Cole as Slim Brown (left) and Rosamond Johnson as Plunk Green (right) in *The Red Moon, Theatre Magazine,* June 1909.

Aida Overton Walker and George Walker in *Bandanna Land, Theatre Magazine,* April 1908.

Marie Jackson-Stuart as title character in *Granny Maumee, Current Opinion,* May 1917.

Blanche Deas as Sapphie in *Granny Maumee,*
Current Opinion, May 1917.

Opal Cooper as Madison Sparrow in *The Rider of Dreams, Theatre Magazine,* June 1917.

Blanche Deas in costume for *Simon, the Cyrenian, Vanity Fair*, June 1917.

Lottie Grady as Acte, an Egyptian princess, in *Simon, the Cyrenian, Vanity Fair,* June 1917.

Inez Clough as Procula, and extras (left and right), in *Simon, the Cyrenian, Vanity Fair,* June 1917.

Emilie Hapgood, *Theatre Magazine,* June 1917.

Robert Edmond Jones, *Theatre Magazine*, October 1916.

Entrance hallway of the Norman and Emilie Hapgood home in New York, *Architectural Record*, 1905.

Costume sketches for *Simon, the Cyrenian* by Robert Edmond Jones, *Theatre Magazine,* May 1917.

THE MEN WHO ROAST THE PLAYS—NE

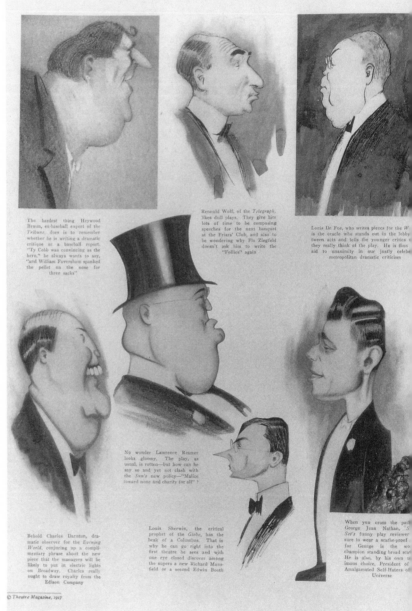

The hardest thing Heywood Broun, ex-baseball expert of the *Tribune*, does is to remember whether he is writing a dramatic critique or a baseball report. "Ty Cobb was convincing as the hero," he always wants to say, "and William Faversham spanked the pellet on the nose for three sacks"

Rennold Wolf, of the *Telegraph*, likes dull plays. They give him lots of time to be composing speeches for the next banquet at the Friars' Club, and also to be wondering why Flo Ziegfeld doesn't ask him to write the "Follies" again

Louis De Foe, who writes pieces for the *W* is the oracle who stands out in the lobby tween acts and tells the younger critics they really think of the play. He is thus aid to unanimity in our justly celebr metropolitan dramatic criticism

No wonder Lawrence Reamer looks gloomy. The play, as usual, is rotten—but how can he say so and yet not clash with the *Sun's* new policy—"Malice toward none and charity for all"?

Behold Charles Darnton, dramatic observer for the *Evening World*, conjuring up a complimentary phrase about the new piece that the managers will be likely to put in electric lights on Broadway. Charles really ought to draw royalty from the Edison Company

Louis Sherwin, the critical prophet of the *Globe*, has the beak of a Columbus. That is why he can go right into the first theatre he sees and with one eye closed discover among the supers a new Richard Mansfield or a second Edwin Booth

When you cross the path George Jean Nathan, *S Set's* funny play reviewer sure to wear a scathe-proof for George is the wo champion standing broad sca He is also, by his own te imous choice, President of Amalgamated Self-Haters of Universe

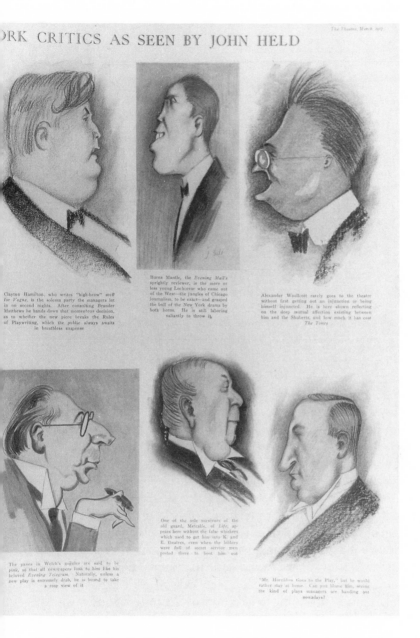

The Theatre, March 1917

Clayton Hamilton, who writes "high-brow" stuff for *Vogue*, is the solemn party the managers let in on second nights. After consulting Brander Matthews he hands down that momentous decision, as to whether the new piece breaks the Rules of Playwriting, which the public always awaits in breathless suspense

Burns Mantle, the *Evening Mail's* sprightly reviewer, is the more or less young Lochinvar who came out of the West—the jungles of Chicago journalism, to be exact—and grasped the bull of the New York drama by both horns. He is still laboring valiantly to throw it

Alexander Woollcott rarely goes to the theatre without first getting out an injunction or being himself injuncted. He is here shown reflecting on the deep mutual affection existing between him and the Shuberts, and how much it has cost *The Times*

The panes in Welch's goggles are said to be pink, so that all newspapers look to him like his beloved *Evening Telegram*. Naturally, unless a new play is extremely drab, he is bound to take a rosy view of it

One of the sole survivors of the old guard, Metcalfe, of *Life*, appears here without the false whiskers which used to get him into K. and E. theatres, even when the lobbies were full of secret service men posted there to boot him out

"Mr. Hornblow Goes to the Play," but he would rather stay at home. Can you blame him, seeing the kind of plays managers are handing out nowadays?

Caricatures of New York's white theater critics, *Theatre Magazine*, March 1917.

4

New Movement,
Old Prejudices

"Had not the Little Theatre Movement fostered the new, the original, the unusual
things of drama it is very possible New York never would have seen the
Negro Players, and a stimulating controversy would have been lost."

Constance D'Arcy Mackay, 1917

I N 1917, Constance D'Arcy Mackay introduced American readers to
the history and development of the Little Theater Movement, an important element of a more generalized "revolution" in American theater in
the first two decades of the twentieth century. She called the Little Theater the
"newest and most vital note in the art of the United States" and the "arch-foe
of commercialism." Little Theaters had arisen, she explained, "from love of
drama, not from love of gain. Their workers are all drawn together by the
same impulse—they are *artists,* or *potential artists* in the craft of acting, of
playwrighting, of stage decoration or stage management." Those involved in
the Little Theaters that had sprung up all across the country were engaged in
an endeavor to define an American dramatic tradition and to do so without
the limitations imposed by the box office. They were an avant garde interested
in experimentation and unwilling to be bound by the conventions of the late-
nineteenth-century stage.[1]

Mackay's book offered as complete an analysis and chronology of the Little
Theaters in the United States and abroad as possible, and it even included
a brief discussion of the three plays that had run on Broadway in April of
that year—"the first time that Negroes had ever appeared in plays interpretive
of their own race." Mackay made essentially two points in her treatment of
Three Plays for a Negro Theater. First, she argued that had it not been for the

Little Theater movement, which "fostered the new, the original, the unusual things of drama," New Yorkers might never have seen the Negro Players, a name the cast adopted after the opening performance. She implied that the avant garde in the New Movement, because of their broad-mindedness and willingness to entertain subjects that might not be commercially popular, deserved credit for bringing serious race drama to the New York Stage. They had, in a sense, championed the cause of African Americans in the world of dramatic expression. The second point in the discussion involved the impact Torrence's plays had on the audience. She saw the production as "a storm center for critics and drama enthusiasts" and argued that "such storms made people think about the theatre in terms more creative and constructive than is their wont." The plays, she believed, had shaken up the audiences' thinking about American drama, the theater in general, and race relations in particular.[2]

While both these assertions need to be carefully scrutinized, Mackay's inclusion of the three plays on Negro life in her study of the Little Theater movement makes hers an exceptional work. Most popular and scholarly books on Little Theaters and the New Movement in the Theater did not consider race as an important issue. But virtually any historical treatment of the American Stage that covered the first two decades of the twentieth century without exception took note of the artistic ferment generated by the new stagecraft, experimental play writing, and acting styles. At the same time, none of the studies on African Americans and the theater indicate a connection between the African American Stage and the New Movement until the 1920s, when Eugene O'Neill, Charles Gilpin, and others emerged and began to explore race issues on small but influential stages. This difference suggests above all else a deep division in American cultural production along race lines, but it also suggests the essential "whiteness" of the New Movement that rarely attracts attention. While the transformations of the drama in the United States have been likened to a cultural revolution, this implicit racial division helps us identify the limits of its horizons. For while sexual mores, gender relations, class conflicts, the need for imagination, and the whole question of the role of the marketplace in the promulgation of culture all came to the fore with this experimental movement, "the problem of the twentieth century—the color line," in the words of W. E. B. Du Bois, almost escaped the notice of progressive artists.

As Mackay's book shows, however, the race issue did not entirely elude those in the New Movement. Indeed, as the sketches of Torrence, Hapgood, and Jones demonstrated, the three white principals in the production of the 1917 Negro plays all had ties to the theatrical avant garde and all saw their involvement in the shows as part of their radical vision. And because of their involvement, the three plays would be judged, in part, in the terms of that movement. Thus, in spite of the absence of black participation in the general development of new trends in the theater, the meaning of the all-black show depended in large measure on the New Movement.

More significant, perhaps, the place of race issues in American art can be better understood by a close examination of the New Movement and this one production, for much more than the fate of one production of three one-act plays was at stake. If the New Movement represented a vanguard in the politics of theatrical expression, then their ideas about what constituted "American" drama, who should or could represent the nation on stage, and what subjects deserved to be explored before the footlights determined in large part the role they believed African Americans could play in the development of theater in the United States. And the long-term significance of Torrence's plays as well as the issue of cultural hybridity in the making of a distinctive American aesthetic can be gauged more precisely. Despite the good intentions of people like Torrence, Hapgood, and Jones, who placed the race question in dramatic fashion before an influential, critical audience, the movement as a whole bore the marks of persistent race prejudice that cannot be ignored, and it evoked from some of its critics a dismissive attitude toward racial equality of which the proponents of change were seen as bearers.

A new movement and old prejudices—both played a part in the serious attempts to fashion culture in the American century. Mackay rightly credited the New Movement with bringing to the stage a critical component of American life—the experience of Negro Americans portrayed by those who knew it firsthand—but she may have overestimated its effect on the thinking of even progressives on the matter of race. For the "Terrible Honesty" of "Mongrel Manhattan," with its affirmation of "Aframerican" culture in the 1920s, displayed both the willingness to examine attitudes toward racial difference, up to then either scorned or ignored, and the limitations placed on that examination. The New Movement, no less than the mainstream against which it rebelled, betrayed its doubts about the legitimacy of African Americans as citizens of the nation and as bearers of its culture.

THE NEW MOVEMENT AND THE AMERICAN STAGE

The New Movement arose in the waning years of the nineteenth century from many different corners of the world of theater—it was not a single, unified effort. Those interested in dramatic literature, for example, longed for a departure from the melodramatic tendencies of the late-nineteenth-century stage and sought to develop more intellectually challenging themes in serious plays. They hoped as well to introduce to the American theatergoing public subjects that up to then had not been considered the stuff of art, appropriate for open examination. Stage artists, troubled by the prevalent realistic clutter found in many productions, began experimenting in the dawn of the twentieth century with sets that evoked a place rather than tried to reproduce it. They employed various lighting effects, painted backdrops, and cloth props that were inexpensive, easily transportable, and harmonious accompaniments to the dramatic action unfolding on stage. Producers and playwrights pushed for new venues—from little theaters that created greater intimacy between the actors and audience and that broke with the view of the stage as a three-sided room into which an audience voyeuristically peered; to community pageants that involved casts of thousands and that played in open-air theaters. And some critics promoted such ideas as repertory theater and state-supported theaters to cultivate both better acting and experimental drama. So although these individual impulses remained in many cases unconnected to one another, taken altogether, they eventually worked a major transformation of the American Theater.[3]

The movement took shape sporadically, though in some respects fairly quickly, in the early twentieth century because of the lack of any unified theatrical center and supporting institutions outside of the stages devoted to providing commercially profitable entertainment. As Percy MacKaye later remembered, "no organized dramatic movement" existed in America because "no little theatre, no drama league, no university theatre, no university course in modern drama (except one, at Harvard, just beginning), no civic or municipal theatre, no poetry society, no anthology or critical summation of American poetry since Stedman's, no poetry journal, or college course in contemporary poetry and drama" had been formed that could foster the changes in American theater imagined by his generation. Indeed, he believed that their aim "was to create" such institutions, and by the time he penned these words in 1935, he recognized that "some of us helped to attain them."[4]

Although largely independent of each other, these various "reformers"—or "revolutionaries," as some scholars have seen them—shared a common cause: the initiation of theater with a distinctly American flavor, befitting a nation that was already known worldwide for its industrial prowess and was gaining importance as a force in international affairs. The quest for an "American Theater"—like similar quests for national music, art, architectural style, and character—sprang in part from pride in the country's great accomplishments and from the desire to gain greater cultural independence from Europe. But other forces, darker and more uncertain, also fired the search for distinctly

American forms of artistic expression. Although the urge to define the essence of America had surfaced periodically over the century since the first thirteen colonies won independence from England—from Crevecoeur's famous essay to Emerson's call for a national literature and through the grave identity crisis sparked by sectionalism and civil war—the desire to craft American cultural forms became particularly acute at the end of the nineteenth century for a number of reasons. Masses of immigrants from around the globe swelled the population and raised fears about the ability of the native-born majority to assimilate so many different traditions and people. Ongoing battles within and between sections over the status and treatment of former slaves and their children kept alive fundamental questions about citizenship and race. Even the large-scale industrial development, which was the envy of many nations, produced enormous dislocations that prompted concern. As the economic crisis of the late 1880s and early 1890s deepened into a nationwide depression, affecting those in the countryside as well as those in industrial centers and raising the spectre of class warfare, even long-held beliefs in such matters as the work ethic, Victorian propriety, and individual self-control appeared shaken if not altogether false. In a context filled with tension and seriously in flux the question of establishing an American identity begged for solutions that did not come easily.[5]

Deciding what was essentially "American" raised all kinds of related concerns that have continued to plague American society in the century that has followed. Who decides what is American? By what means is American culture to be determined? Who constitutes the people? Had there ever existed a single national "flavor" into which diverse people and customs could be "blended"? Did questions about the country's character persist because it was always in the process of being formed by the individuals and groups who made the United States their home? In 1914, writers like Alfred Kuttner added a few queries of their own. Kuttner noted that when "the Great American Dramatist" came to redeem the nation, Americans assumed that he would "express our true ideals." But "what he is to represent," he asserted, "and how we are to recognize him is not imparted by his prophets. His possible coming raises the whole question of the social function of art in a democratic civilization such as ours. Can any art be finer or nobler than the people that are its spiritual soil? Have we attained the national maturity and the underlying unity without which a national art cannot flourish? How can a democracy which is still as inchoate as ours hope to find artistic expression? Such questions," he concluded, "force us to searching interrogations."[6]

In the field of music, many were persuaded by Antonin Dvorak's pronouncement in the 1890s that African American melodies and rhythms provided the best foundation for a unique national school of music; others quailed at the prospect of the expression of a despised people speaking for the whole. Even as ragtime music—a hybrid of European and African American elements—took the country by storm in the late 1890s and early 1900s, writers in popular and serious periodicals continued to wring their hands in despair and to debate the possibilities of any American music ever taking shape.[7]

In the world of theater, the questions were no more easily addressed. By the 1890s, Laurence Hutton could discuss at length the various forms the "Stage American" had taken. Among them were the typical Yankee, which he described as a "shrewd old man from New England, with a soul which soared no higher than the financial value of a bar'l of apple-sass," and the Politician, "vulgar to an impossible degree, personally offensive, and yet entirely delightful to meet." Such types were widely known, but they represented a relatively narrow slice of American life.[8] The humble backwoodsman, popular in the early nineteenth century, had given way in later decades to Westerners—miners, bankers, and claim-jumpers—all of whom were white and native-born. The Stage Englishman, a pompous buffoon, the Stage Irishman, a rustic lout, and the Stage German, a comic mangler of the English language, all represented stock figures who livened up many American plays, if in rather predictable ways. The Stage Negro, of course, appeared as well, usually in the guise of an inept, childlike lackey who provided little more than comic relief or as a dangerous, libidinous force armed with a razor and a larcenous mind. These stock figures, however, did not add up to a dramatic tradition, and the plays in which they appeared had done little to elevate the reputation of the American Theater either at home or abroad. As John Corbin put it, writing in 1902, "It is no secret that the drama in America is in a parlous state."[9]

Those who eventually crowded under the umbrella of the New Movement believed that the keys to improving this "parlous state" lay in the land and its people and in devotion to experiment. As early as 1890, Hamlin Garland had insisted that "if America ever produces an indigenous and therefore enduring drama it will be by delineating the common life of our day, being sympathetic, and above all true."[10] Similarly Edmund Clarence Stedman had insisted to the small group of Ivy League playwrights—Torrence, Moody, MacKaye, and Robinson—that they had to seek and capture the spirit of the New World and explore American themes.[11] Thus Moody's trip to the Rocky Mountains and the western states beyond yielded *The Great Divide,* considered by many to be a seminal work of American drama because it explored this country and its people. After seeing Moody's drama, Torrence turned immediately to his childhood home in Ohio for inspiration—inspiration that resulted in *The Madstone, The Thunderpool,* and the three Negro plays.[12] Robert Edmond

Jones, though having learned his craft in Germany, nevertheless proclaimed proudly in 1917, "I am distinctly pro-American, and I believe that in a few years we will lead the world in stagecraft. America does not have to go to Europe for plays, actors, and actresses, nor for producers or artists." The energy of this nation and its citizens would drive the new theater.[13]

Even as these artists searched the land for suitable material for the stage, however, they tried to look at it as if for the first time. They wanted to avoid the stock figures and well-worn themes and present instead the America of the early twentieth century in all its grandeur as well as with all its warts. As the first issue of *Theatre Arts Magazine* declared, "We stand for the creation of a new theatre in America," and to that end "we stand for the encouragement of all experimental groups." If the strands of the avant garde were separate in the early years of the century, by 1917, they had begun to grow together, for as the editors of this signal periodical saw it, the new theater in America required "a new point of view" in play writing, acting, stage decorating, and "a new race of artist-directors."[14]

By the end of the 1910s, the playwrights of the New Movement had already begun to leave their mark on the American stage. In *The Romance of the American Theatre* (1913), Mary Caroline Crawford noted that less than a decade earlier *The Dial* had denounced drama in America as " 'little more than a low form of stagecraft,' " but if the article were to be rewritten in 1913, the works of Edward Sheldon, Edward Knoblauch, William Vaughn Moody, Elizabeth Robins, Rachel Crothers, Josephine Peabody, and Percy MacKaye would seriously revise that gloomy assessment. All of these writers, Crawford believed, "write seriously" and "deal . . . earnestly with important aspects of human life and human thought." They had produced "problem plays" on critical issues in modern America—class conflict, women's rights, race prejudice, and the "problems of the plain people"—and in the process helped their audiences "to see clearly the things we have been puzzled about." She concluded that the "prospects of the American Theatre were never so encouraging as now; for besides being the heir of all the ages in the realm of dramatic expression, it presents to knight-errants of every race and of every Cause an open door of opportunity."[15]

This "open door of opportunity," however, was a bit deceptive. Gatekeepers in the form of critics, professors of dramatic literature and play writing, sympathetic patrons of the arts, and the theater artists themselves guarded the door against interlopers from commercial theaters, from low comedy houses, and from other entertainment realms that threatened to storm the citadel of high art with vulgarity. Indeed, the avant garde of the theater found themselves engaged in pitched battles over the nature, production, and dissemination of art in the United States, and all the combatants believed that they knew best how the nation's democratic ethos should be expressed. Since the late eighteenth century, the desire for cultural independence from Europe had been driven in large part by republican ideology, which touted the virtue of a free people against the decadence and corruption of the tired, despotic monarchies of the Old World. In the late nineteenth century, as evidence of corruption and extravagance began to appear in the New World in the political scandals that came to light at all levels of government, in the conspicuous consumption of the robber barons, in the ominous rise of a leisure class, and in the utter dependence of a growing underclass, republican ideals, invoked and revised by populist politicians and progressives of various stripes, fueled the fire of the cultural crucible. As a writer for *Theatre Magazine* put it in 1908, "Themes for American plays are plentiful enough and big enough. They are just coming into their own. We don't need European ideas or European art for our dramas. We want none of their 'My Lords' or 'My Ladies' here; we have progressed beyond that. We are just plain Joe or Jim or Bill."[16] The sovereign people of America must have art that reflected their democratic society—on this point, all agreed. But the firestorm raged over another question: What makes art "democratic"?

In one camp were those who answered the question by insisting that the people essentially had the right to "vote"—they would determine the nature of democratic theater in America by buying or refusing to buy tickets to the programs presented by theater managers. Franklin Fyles, a critic speaking for the theater managers in 1900, noted that thousands of theaters across the country, all on "the routes of the traveling dramatic companies," attracted at least a million and a half theatergoers every week during a typical eight-month theater season. The plays, he argued, were "widely and thoroughly discussed, and the average of taste and judgment concerning plays and setting" was "intelligent." Because of this kind of support, theater managers had accumulated sufficient capital to invest in new playhouses made of steel and spacious enough to accommodate ever growing audiences, and they decorated their stages with the "real things" one expected to find in any given setting. Moreover, the managers themselves had become "trustworthy and responsible" friends of the drama, seeking only the plays that would satisfy the taste of their clientele. As for the budding New Movement, Fyles asserted that America did not need it. "We are getting along very well under the prevailing conditions."[17] A few years earlier, before the great contest over democratic culture had begun raging in earnest, T. R. Sullivan had noted, with a bit less partisanship, that the typical theater manager in the United States bore the marks of "a shrewd business man, seeking personal profit, demanding from his authors novelty," and a man who "serves the time."

Without intending to influence prospective clients or their taste, the man of the theater watched "foreign markets closely," selected what he believed—based on past experience—American audiences would like, and put those shows on the stage.[18] So although many of the theaters featured European plays, rather than those written by Americans, the theater represented "democratic" art because it appealed to the American democracy.

This argument, with its faith in ordinary people to decide what they found interesting and entertaining, was hard to refute without damning the people for whose interests critics claimed to speak. And those in the "reform" camp, did at times, express regret for the poor taste of the American public. Norman Hapgood, for example, ascribed the "degeneration of the drama" to the "deterioration of the audience." Ordinary people with enough money to go to the theaters—"ignorant spectators," as he saw them—"formerly followed the lead of the educated," but now they "read, have opinions and enforce them." As a result, "Caliban is in power and sits in judgment at the theatre."[19] Winthrop Ames agreed with Hapgood. The great promise of social mobility, which he thought had been kept in America, gave lower classes the means to attend the theater, but the masses, he believed, "were innocent of dramatic standards and of culture. To them a play was just a 'show.' They cared nothing for such things as character delineation or psychological analysis, or subtleties of dialogue." The trouble with American theater, he concluded, was that "it is dominated by a great, new, eager, childlike, tasteless, honest, crude, general public."[20] Others, like Maurice Campbell, put the matter even more bluntly. "To-day the American audience hangs like a millstone about the neck of the theater," he wrote. "Progress is made in spite of it."[21]

Still, in their own way, advocates of the New Movement offered "democratic" solutions to the problems they saw. The problem, they believed, rested fundamentally in the commercial aims of most theaters and managers. Because they viewed their endeavors principally as business ventures, most such managers chose not to take many risks, opting for action-oriented plays and melodramas. Were other venues open, where a greater variety of dramas could be presented, American audiences would have the chance to develop a liking for better productions and would learn to distinguish the good from the bad. In 1910, for example, W. S. Lockwood reported on a production of Shakespeare's *Romeo and Juliet* in a working-class theater on Halstead Street in Chicago. Determined "to risk crowds, fights, odors, and who shall say what else, to witness the experiment," Lockwood attended the play and rejoiced at the reception of this classic work by the audience. Although this crowd knew little about the bard of Avon—Lockwood claimed to have heard some in the crowd hollering to friends to learn whether they had ever seen any of Shakespeare's "shows"—and although they had seen only "wretched plays" up to the time of the Shakespearean production, they were moved by its excellence. *Romeo and Juliet* "touched the heart, . . . stirred the emotions," and "raised us to awe, as the supreme drama ever does, by opening the door of the human soul."[22]

As advocates of the New Movement saw it, the chief enemies of democratic art in America were commercial theaters and showmen who valued spectacle over drama. In the spirit of progressive reform, they exposed the evil ways of both and proposed a variety of alternatives that they believed would lead the people to the light of true art. They focused their muckraking efforts on the practices of a group of theater owners and managers, who in the 1890s had gained a stranglehold on most of the first-class theaters in New York and across the country by forming a syndicate and agreeing to limit head-to-head competition between major performers and popular shows. Those who fought it called it a "theatrical trust," and in the spirit of "trust-busting," set out to destroy it in the name of the people. The syndicate, like other combinations in constraint of trade, consisted of several major management companies that conspired to gain control of their industry. The two most important firms in the theatrical trust were Klaw & Erlanger and Hayman & Frohman of New York. In 1895 they reached an agreement among themselves not to book shows in the same cities on the same dates so as to avoid needless competition and financial losses. They sought the services of the best and most popular performers and playwrights and signed them to exclusive contracts. Those who refused to sign were, of course, free to work elsewhere, but in reality, they found themselves working in the least desirable venues if they could find work at all. Moreover, theaters that agreed to show only syndicate productions had a guarantee of thirty weeks of attractions. Reducing the risk of idleness and lost revenue drew even more theaters into the syndicate's network.

Between 1895 and 1897, the theater trust succeeded in signing all the most attractive (white) actors but three—Francis Wilson, Mrs. Fiske, and Richard Mansfield. Using highly inflammatory language, Wilson characterized the trust as an "enemy" determined to "harass and squeeze out the life and soul and all ambitions of players." "Who loves fair play more than an American," he asked, "and what choicer subject could one select upon which to address an American public than that of independence?" Likewise, Mansfield called the syndicate an "octopus" out to strangle the theater and to force actors, playwrights, and audiences into submission and dependence. Both men eventually reached an agreement with their "enemy." Mrs. Fiske, alone, held out. By 1899, the syndicate's method of organizing theater circuits, controlling the offerings available, and using stars and resources efficiently had prevailed.

As a result, popular shows at popular prices appeared in theaters across the United States, but the chances of staging experimental works remained slim.[23]

The reformers, however, did not completely give in. Conceding with Norman Hapgood that the fascination with money that made the syndicate's rise so rapid and so complete simply reflected "one of the gloomy qualities of American life," they nevertheless continued to battle the commercial foundation of the theater.[24] Recognizing that state support for a "national theater" likely would not materialize, they worked in other ways to establish alternative venues for artistic production. One of the earliest such ventures was New York City's New Theatre established in 1908 with the support of such friends of the arts as the Vanderbilts, Astors, Schiffs, Goulds, and Belmonts. Winthrop Ames, a student of George Pierce Baker at Harvard, served as the first director and in the first season, 1909–1910, staged mostly avant garde plays, only one of which was written by an American. The first season's bill kept alive the widespread suspicion that the New Theatre existed "only for the 'High Brows.' "[25] By the end of the next season, having remodeled the original theater in the hope of improving the play-going experience but also having continued with the same line-up of programs, the New Theatre had fared little better to attract large audiences. At a banquet at the Waldorf Astoria in February 1911, at which Judge Gary of U.S. Steel served as toastmaster before guests that included J. P. Morgan and Otto Kahn as well as critics and playwrights sympathetic to the experiment, Ames defended the theater. "We have been called the millionaire's theatre. We have been called the fashionable theatre," he began. "I shall not reply to those criticisms. But our purpose was truly altruistic, and I see about me the men who can help us to realize our ideals—representatives of educational institutions, magazines, authors and critics, as well as the managers of the commercial houses." The purpose for Ames remained clear—and democratic—"to develop the American drama and thus benefit the American people."[26]

As the New Theatre foundered, other alternatives moved forward. Inspired by small experimental theaters in Europe, Little Theaters opened, and within five years more than fifty were in operation. Indeed, Ames gave up the position of manager at the New Theatre to run a Little Theater on Forty-fourth Street.[27] "Insurgent Theaters" in Wisconsin arose as part of a grassroots effort to install artistic productions among people removed from the large centers of cultural activity.[28] Companies like the Washington Square Players, Provincetown Players, and East-West Players, founded in 1915 and 1916, performed exclusively works by playwrights in the United States and abroad who explored controversial subjects or adopted experimental forms.[29] Others like Percy MacKaye initiated efforts to stage community pageants involving thousands of amateurs as well as noted professional actors in spectacular outdoor shows designed to foster participation in the making of democratic art.[30] In 1916, the *New York Times* reported that a New Play Society had organized "for the presentation of plays which under ordinary circumstances would not be produced on the commercial stage." Composed entirely of women, the New Play Society promised to "specialize in plays of an educational or sociological character, particularly those of American authorship."[31] Although they clearly did not displace the attractions of the Lee Shuberts, David Belascos, and Klaw & Erlangers of Broadway, these efforts amounted to an important challenge to the dominance of commercial theaters, and with the aid of magazines, playwrights, educators, and wealthy patrons—like those who had gathered at the Waldorf Astoria in 1911—the New Movement made significant inroads among the American public.

With the new venues came new stagecraft, and no one felt the sting of the challenge more keenly than David Belasco. The name "Belasco" had become synonymous with extravagant "realistic" stage decoration; the famous director spared no expense to reproduce in minute detail interiors from the past and the present as well as outside scenes that required flora, fauna, and elaborate machinery. With the arrival of the new stagecraft of Maxfield Parrish, Sam Hume, Gordon Craig, and Robert Edmond Jones, Belasco—frequently singled out as the representative of the art they wanted to replace—reacted defensively, even as he recognized the merits of these younger men's work. Striving always to "keep a little ahead of his audience," Belasco believed that he presented shows that people wanted to see. Moreover, by going to great lengths to dress the stage in keeping with the setting of the play, he tried to fulfill Shakespeare's charge to players " 'to hold, as 't were, the mirror up to nature.' " For this "old arter," pleasing "the public" was the "principal object."[32] By contrast, "new arters" like Jones sought not to imitate nature but to inspire the imagination. His use of sparse, evocative sets encouraged individuals in the audience to participate in the drama by entering into the mood of the play, by imagining how it felt to be in the circumstance represented, and by empathizing with the characters, thereby developing a kind of "group consciousness" and "sense of common humanity."[33] As the differences between the "old arters" and the "new arters" indicate, the struggle between the two camps involved the best means by which to please the American public; both sides claimed vehemently to purvey democratic art.

The conflict in the United States between commercial theaters and these avant garde forms of dramatic expression epitomizes an even larger conflict at work in the nation over the outlines and content of American culture—a conflict felt both privately and publicly. In a letter to Ridgely Torrence in 1915, for example, the poet Edgar Lee Masters wrote, "I see a renascence now all over the country. The economico-political agitation, the sex furore [sic] in plays etc. and other things have fertilized the mind. The audience is at hand."[34] About a year later James Metcalfe gave public voice to this sea-change-in-progress in an article about modern dance for *Life*. "Dancing, like everything else," he wrote, "has felt the revolution against law of every kind which is affecting modern life, and in other directions finds its expression in anarchy, feminism, cubism, vers libre, cacophony, go-as-you-please spelling and a valuation of mob rule." Dancers like Maud Allen, who but a few years earlier had been considered quite advanced and daring, in 1916 appeared "almost conservative and Puritanical" compared with the "barbarous sensuality" of modern dancers; and likewise, plays "condemned only fifteen or twenty years ago" now lagged "far behind present freedom from restraint."[35] Masters's "renascence" and Metcalfe's "revolution" both pointed to upheavals in questions of taste and collective values in a society undergoing rapid social change. While Masters continued in his letter to Torrence with the assertion that poets might now "have a say in affairs," Metcalfe, far less optimistic, saw the world rolling "down-hill" and predicted that "rolling it back will be tedious or violent work for those who have to do it."

Whether embraced or rued, the cultural tumult in the 1910s could not be denied, and its importance for social cohesion, public policy, and the definition of widely accepted boundaries between appropriate and inappropriate belief and behavior should not be underestimated. In these years at the dawn of the twentieth century, the cultural conflicts represented serious efforts to reconstitute the rules by which a diverse people would govern itself— socially and legally. And embedded in the struggle over democratic art and the American Stage were even more far-reaching issues fundamental to citizenship, collective action and purpose, and the reality of self-government. For though all those involved in the struggle championed the cause of "the people" of the nation, the people themselves remained ill-defined. Who would have a hand in shaping this mighty cultural moment? Who *were* the people?

RACE AND THE LIMITS OF REVOLUTION

The question—Who were the people?—seems to require a simple, straight-forward response. Surely all citizens, native-born and naturalized, constituted the people. The answer never was so simple, of course, even if in principle writers, politicians, educators, cultural commentators, and orators endorsed it. As Priscilla Wald has recently demonstrated, in ages of anxiety, when crisis and change threaten to overturn the experiment in democracy, Americans betray uncertainty in their written and spoken words—in what they say, how they articulate it, and what is left unsaid—and find ways of eliding over the clear, direct embrace of all citizens as citizens. She likens the responses of these makers of culture to the Freudian experience of the "uncanny," that jarring momentary revulsion the Viennese psychoanalyst noted among some of his patients who encountered Doppelgängers or reflections of themselves in unexpected mirrors. If individuals can be repelled by their own image, which they find to be unattractive or not the picture of themselves they see in their mind's eye, Wald suggests that perhaps this same denial can occur collectively and culturally when a society confronts itself. Marginal social groups typically provoke this recoiling from the American social portrait. "Their" difference and the ugly—undemocratic—response to them from the majority inspire repugnance. If Wald is correct, then this deeply rooted social psychology accounts, at least in part, for the difficulty Americans have found in expressing the essence of American culture.[36]

The early twentieth century was an age of anxiety for Americans. Multitudes from Europe and Asia arrived in coastal ports, bringing with them strange customs, languages, religions, beliefs, and dress, even as they sought the "promised land" of America. Native-born, dark-skinned people—notably former slaves and various tribes of Native Americans—might lay claim to citizenship by birth or by constitutional decree, but their physiognomy and culture somehow did not square with the self-image of the majority. Policies like Jim Crow and laws like the Dawes Act reinforced the status of these people as provisional citizens at best. And even among the native-born whites of Anglo-Saxon stock, changes in the economy and in communities so altered familiar patterns of interaction and life that many could barely recognize themselves in the fast-moving beings who lived in flats, worked for a corporation, listened to ragtime music, or attended naughty plays. How, indeed, could anyone hope to speak for—or even to—this motley assemblage who claimed American citizenship?

The problem was not unique to Americans living in the early twentieth century, nor for that matter, to Americans. Nations like Mexico, Spain, Germany, and the former Soviet Union, just to name a few, have confronted the challenge of creating a single national identity from the various people living in proximity with widely varying languages or dialects, racial heritages, and quotidian traditions and of forming a unified nation state. In the United States, whether "progressive" or "conservative," and in the theater, affiliated with the New Movement or the commercial theaters—"new arters" or "old arters"—Americans had to face these issues of identity as they tried to voice a national culture.

The backgrounds of the people at the forefront of the debate did not reflect the great diversity of the population. Although one might find ethnic variations among the writers and managers vying for dominance in the American Theater, the vast majority were white, and most were native-born. As the recent scholarship on "white ethnics," has shown, there were some advantages for those who, after a generation, could blend into the white mainstream, but in the early twentieth century, those who bore clearly "old country" names remained suspect. In the world of theater their plays, "national characteristics," accents, and stereotypical appearance found some enthusiasts who incorporated them into popular shows and who wrote about their art with approval. Hutchins Hapgood, for example, writing material for his brother's theater column and later collecting material for his *Spirit of the Ghetto* (1902), did perhaps as much as any writer to introduce American audiences to a wide variety of ethnic theaters in New York. He focused principally on the Russian Jewish theater, but he also included sketches on German playhouses and Chinese theaters. In 1900 he praised writers like Jacob Gordin and actors like Jacob Adler for their expressing "the distinctive realism of the intellectual east side." But he also recognized the limits of this ethnic appeal; Adler's "Yiddish dialect," he admitted, stood "between him and the distinction of a wide reputation."[37] More than a decade later, Gregory Mason reminded "Gentiles" that "side by side with the American Stage there exists a Yiddish theatre," a comment that indicates coexistence *and* difference.[38]

The subtle difference between the "American Stage" and the "Yiddish Theatre" noted by Mason points to an essential characteristic of the conversation about Americanness and the theater in the early twentieth century. Such enterprises as the Yiddish theater had a clientele that was not quite American. Mason observed that Jews rapidly became "Americanized" but he believed that "as long as the Semitic stream continues to pour into the United States," a separate theater would exist.[39] Norman Hapgood commented in a similar vein about Germans who attended Irving Place Theatre to see plays by Schiller, Goethe, and Lessing. "The older Germans in New York go home to discuss the play," he wrote. "Their children, already Americanized, demand farce."[40] In American productions in which either Jews or Germans figured, the serious art of the group gave way to stereotype. Until Israel Zangwill's *The Melting Pot*, the typical Jew on the American Stage was a greedy villain, conniving, dishonest, and untrustworthy. And in spite of the art of the famous German romantic playwrights of the early nineteenth century, Germans appeared in American shows as sausage-eating, beer-guzzling, solid citizens. They drew laughs for their caricatures of Germans many had seen in the streets of the city. Edward "Ned" Harrigan, for instance, had created Irish, English, German, Italian, and

Chinese characters in the late nineteenth century. As one early chronicler of the American Stage put it, "These characters are depicted by Harrigan in all of their humorous aspects, and if he was not the first writer to introduce certain of these types to the American stage, he was the first to make the conflicts and novelties inherent in race amalgamation the basis for a dramatic form."[41] So while Richard Burton, a professor of English Literature at the University of Minnesota, could include "the American foreign-derived, in any one of his almost infinite variations," as one of the "types that make up our seething population" in his overview of the "New American Drama," he also insisted that their ethnic flavor distinguished them from the typical American or even Americanized ethnic.[42]

While both commercial theaters and new experimental theaters were open to ethnic variety in the plays they presented, their record on race issues was clearly more mixed. Constance Mackay credited the Little Theaters with giving African Americans their first chance on Broadway, but this is only partially true. The production of *Three Plays for a Negro Theater* did represent a landmark event in which African Americans portrayed black characters in serious drama for the first time, but that breakthrough should not lead to the faulty conclusion that the New Movement was inherently sympathetic to the cause of racial equality. For up to that opening night in 1917, the avant garde had not shown much interest in African American dramatic art at all.

In fact, according to African American theater lore, one of the earliest signs of support for black shows came from Klaw & Erlanger of the infamous syndicate. Theopolis Lewis and Leigh Whipper, in an unpublished essay called "These Are They," remembered that when Bob Cole had been with the Black Patti Troubadours in the 1890s, his treatment at the hands of a white theater manager had prompted him to issue a "colored actor's Declaration of Independence." The Troubadours were performing at Proctor's Fifty-eighth Street Theatre, when Cole and others "left the show flat" because of low pay and poor working conditions. Even after the manager had Cole arrested for breaking an agreement, the black composer/performer refused to budge. Jesse Shipp, Tom Brown, Billy Johnson, Hen Wise, and Loyd Gibbs all stuck by Cole, when the manager convinced others across the country to blacklist those who stood by their demands. Cole wrote and organized a company for *A Trip to Coontown* in 1897 in the midst of this conflict in the hope that a show written and performed by blacks could begin to break white managers' control over black performance. But his show only provoked a more extreme response—a lockout of Cole and company. This action "closed practically every important theatre in the country to Cole and his followers," Lewis and Whipper recalled, "and the show was driven into the woods." The company played in a few theaters in the

United States whose managers were willing to defy the boycott, but eventually they were forced to move on to Canada, where they won enormous success. When news of the smashing success of *A Trip to Coontown* reached New York, Klaw & Erlanger booked the show into Jacob's Third Avenue Theatre in early 1899. Over the next several years, Cole and Johnson, Williams and Walker, and Ernest Hogan produced shows that were highly sought after by Broadway managers.[43]

Klaw & Erlanger's willingness to ignore the boycott, of course, had the beneficial effect of setting African American musical comedy on a decade-long course of great success. Their belief in giving the public shows it wanted to see led to this partial breaking down of racial barriers on the American Stage. And years later, when Marc Klaw was named to the Commission for Training Camp Activities in World War I, he remembered African Americans in the world of entertainment by inviting Lester Walton to serve with him on the commission to organize entertainment for the black soldiers.[44] At the same time, however, the embrace of Cole's *A Trip to Coontown* and its successors in musical comedy also meant that the range of black characters that white audiences found attractive remained relatively narrow. Singing, dancing, and clowning, however double-edged the humor may have been, did little to broaden the white public's awareness of the variety of character types in the African American community.

When the "revolution" of the New Movement began in the early years of the century, it barely touched the world of black theater. None of the institutions affiliated with the avant garde—Harvard and its drama courses; the Drama League; the New Theatre—and none of the new publications included African American participants. When the theatrical vanguard took on the subject of race relations in their plays, they refused to cast Negro actors in the appropriate parts, as in the Stage Society's 1914 production of *Granny Maumee,* which featured Dorothy Donnelly in blackface. Similarly, in 1916, Winthrop Ames produced a pantomime called *Pierrot the Prodigal* at his Little Theater, but according to James Metcalfe, he "cut the acting of the negro servant and the effective music" that accompanied the part, a decision the critic considered "a [great] mystery."[45] Furthermore, the race plays of the new playwrights typically explored the experience of the "tragic Negro"—the man or woman who carried the "taint" of black blood, which was undetectable in the color of his or her skin. Such plays, while examining one dimension of race relations in America, nevertheless did not require the services of African American performers.

One of these plays about the "tragic Negro," Edward Sheldon's *The Nigger,* appeared in the 1909–1910 season as the only American drama staged at the New Theatre. *Theatre Magazine* considered it a "great play" but also noted that it never would have made it on a strictly commercial basis.[46] Having been presented at an experimental theater, which itself had become the focus of much discussion, the play attracted considerable attention and revealing commentary. Perhaps not surprisingly, Walton of the *New York Age* proclaimed in a lengthy review that Sheldon's drama was "truly a great play" that confirmed the black critic's long-held position that "the American Negro will play an important part in the great American drama that is to be written." Walton did not believe *The Nigger* was, in fact, *the* great American drama, because he, like the editor of *Theatre Magazine,* recognized that this "wonderful drama" would not be seen anywhere "outside of the New Theatre, at least for years to come." Still, Walton wished that every African American could see the play because "all would appreciate the many truths that are told of which they are familiar." He also regretted that "every white person cannot witness the production, for it would prove instructive as well as entertaining, and give them an opportunity to study and reflect."[47]

In contrast to Walton's glowing review, a writer for *Theatre Magazine* commented on Sheldon's caveat in the program that *The Nigger*'s " 'purpose is purely to present a dramatic picture—urging no thesis, subserving no faction.' " "Surely this is interesting—here is a play without a purpose on a subject that is full of purpose," the critic noted acidly. After summarizing the plot, the critic concluded that *The Nigger* contained "inane and nauseous nonsense." Still trying to pinpoint a thesis in the play, he decided that Sheldon seemed to argue "for the physical unity of the American people with the negro." But such a proposition "would mean the disappearance of the whites in the black quicksand. . . . The races will be kept apart."[48]

More than a difference of opinion emerges from these two reviews. Where Walton saw "truth," the reviewer for *Theatre Magazine* saw "nonsense." Where Walton saw the American Negro playing a part in the creation of distinctive national art, the other writer made a distinction between "the American people" and "the negro." At another point in his commentary, Walton declared that the play "rings true" by "laying bare the illegitimate relationship that frequently exists between the whites and blacks of the South, and one of the principal issues that has made a Negro problem in this country." The *Theatre Magazine* critic could not imagine a white woman wanting to marry a man with "tainted" blood and recoiled from the idea of amalgamation. These differences reveal two perspectives shaped by separate race-bound experiences in the United States and a hesitation on the part of the white critic to embrace the notion of a biracial society. Given these differences, the two critics chose to emphasize certain parts of the play over others as they summarized the story for their readers—as they made the play a subject for cultural debate.

Consider Walton's summary:

> "Philip Morrow," who is the central character in the piece, is candidate
> for Governor in a Southern State. His campaign manager is Clifton
> Noyes, his cousin and president of the Noyes Distillery Works. Morrow
> is in love with Georgiana Byrd, a Southern woman, and expects to
> marry her at the close of the campaign. The development of the story
> begins immediately. A Negro employed by the candidate has committed
> a crime for which he is pursued by lynchers to Morrow's estate, where
> he secretes himself. To refuse to turn the Negro over to the mob would
> mean the political death of Morrow, but the candidate quickly decides
> that rather than betray his office he will forfeit his political ambition. At
> this moment Noyes delivers the fugitive into the hands of the mob and
> he is lynched. With the election won Morrow is brought face to face with
> another crisis.
>
> A prohibition bill has been passed by the Legislature, and he comes to a
> realizing sense that the measure is a just one and necessary to the welfare
> of the Negroes of the State. He is about to sign the bill when Noyes,
> who would be ruined by such a measure, declares that if the Governor's
> signature is affixed to the statute he will expose him by publishing to the
> public that Morrow has a trace of Negro blood in his veins and proves
> the truth of his statement. Undeterred by these threats, however, Morrow
> signs the bill and releases his fiancee. As the curtain falls, he resigns the
> Governorship to take up his work again bravely for the Negro race.[49]

In this narrative, Walton focuses on issues of paramount importance to
himself and his readers—lynching and politicians who consider the welfare
of their black constituents in policy-making. In order to make Morrow a
sympathetic figure, Walton slides over the point that when Noyes undermines
his principled position to refuse to let a black man—even a guilty black man—
die at the hands of a mob, Morrow does nothing except to remain in the race
and win the election for governor. In this basic summary of the story, Walton
does not dwell on the relationship between Morrow and Georgiana Byrd,
though he does comment later on that he felt "embarrassed for the white
brother" during scenes in which the two protagonists "kissed, hugged, and
fondled each other before the gaze of the public." But for Walton, interracial
liaisons were facts of life—seen daily in the infinite variety of skin tones seen
among African American people. But the main points Walton conveyed to his
readers included Sheldon's recognition of the ferocity and reality of lynching,
his imagining that representing the people of a state should mean *all* the
people, and his exposure of the politicization of race.

Theatre Magazine's summary, somewhat shorter, also demonstrates a different sense of the play and its significance. The story involved

> a white man in the South after he has become Governor of his State
> to be informed by Verita—or One Who Knows—that his mother

was a "beautiful octoroon" and, furthermore, that if he did not veto a prohibition bill the fact would be published on the front page of a newspaper with horrescent headlines, with the result that his taint would disgrace him and deprive him of the woman (free, white and twenty-one) whom he was about to marry. That is the whole story, lacking certain details. In a scene with the girl, realizing that his ruin is at hand and that he must confess to her, preferring that she hear it from his own lips, when she turns with horror from him, he yet declares his love and determines to hold her in his embrace and smother her with kisses for the last time. . . . In the end, just before he resigns office and himself announces publicly his taint, she visits his office and tells him that she has reconsidered and will stick to him and implores him to marry her.[50]

The critic essentially ignores the entire first act containing the lynch mob scene and Morrow's struggle over the right action to take. The central spotlight remained on the "taint," the blackmail, and the unbelievable love scenes between the two protagonists—both of whom were, of course, played by white actors. Not actually witnessing kisses and embraces between two people with obvious racial differences, the reviewer is riveted—and repulsed—by the *idea* of "interracial" love.

A week after Walton's review appeared, the *New York Age* published a letter sent by Edward Sheldon to the black critic. "I should find it difficult to tell you how delighted I was to read such a review of my play by you," he began. "It has made me very happy to feel that you understood so clearly what I was trying to do. I thank you with all my heart."[51] The letter suggests that Walton's summary reflected Sheldon's intentions better than the review in *Theatre Magazine* did. Walton perceived the same issues that the playwright conceived in the drama. Such an endorsement from the author, however, does not negate the importance of reviews that did not see the play in the same way. For the summaries that appeared in other journals were narratives, too, and they conveyed points of view in a debate that interested a large number of people.

At least two conclusions beg to be drawn from this commentary. First, presenting a serious play about race relations in the early twentieth century did not guarantee that everyone who saw it would derive a single meaning, and second, this kind of "race drama" focused on white people with "taints" completely undetectable in their physical appearance. The general revulsion against them indicates something of the "uncanny" to which Priscilla Wald alluded. Regardless of whether critics liked the script, disliked the idea of racial amalgamation, approved of the daring experiment, or used the play as ammunition against the New Movement, the language used to discuss the drama and especially the subject of race relations betrays discomfort with the thought of including Negroes as full-fledged Americans.

Edward Sheldon remained interested in African American themes in the drama. In 1926, for example, his *Lulu Belle* was staged by David Belasco with more than forty black actors appearing in the production and stars like Lenore Ulric, Ruby Lee, and Evelyn Preer in leading roles.[52] But his sympathy for African American culture was not universally shared or appreciated. In fact, as histories of the stage in the early twentieth century began to be written, Sheldon was included as a representative of the younger playwrights but not always explicitly linked to *The Nigger*. Writing in 1913, for instance, Richard Burton called Sheldon "wholesomely American" whose sympathies lay with "the unconventional corner life of social strays." But Burton selected *The High Road* as Sheldon's exemplary work.[53] Montrose Moses dismissed all of Sheldon's plays, noting of *The Nigger* that it was "a little too advanced for the regular theatre to risk at that time," and that in any case it lacked "real moral bravery."[54] Margaret Mayorga similarly dismissed Sheldon and *The Nigger*, because the playwright asked audiences to set aside their rational concern for "future generations" in favor of the improbable love between a black man and a white woman.[55] In his review of Torrence's plays, Francis Hackett dismissed Sheldon's *The Nigger* as a genuine precursor to the three plays at the Garden Theatre. Sheldon, he argued, "like most Americans, . . . had remembered his newspapers too well. The things he associated with the Negro were copy-desk conventional things."[56] Mary Caroline Crawford's *Romance of the American Theatre* (1913) mentions Sheldon without discussing any of his plays, and Arthur Hornblow did not include Sheldon anywhere in *The History of the Theatre in America* (1919). So in contemporary reviews and early histories of the New Movement, Sheldon's contribution of a dramatic treatment of race issues went largely unnoticed and undervalued, thus diminishing the perception of the avant garde's openness to bold discussions of touchy race issues. Years later, Torrence admitted that he had neither seen Sheldon's play nor read the text, but he had "heard enough about his play to perceive that it had nothing" in common with his own endeavors. Sheldon, he believed, accepted "the traditional conception of the Negro."[57]

A few years after Sheldon's *The Nigger*, another play called *Pride of Race* dealt with a "tragic Negro" whose racial heritage is discovered when he and his wife produce a black baby. While Lester Walton called *Pride of Race* a "powerful play" that explored "colorphobia," "the most virulent and contagious of all American diseases," other reviewers expressed far less enthusiasm for it. The *New York Press*, for instance, did not think the play's star, Robert Hilliard, acted "black" enough for one who was one-sixteenth African American. The *New York Sun* shrank from the play because of its "morbid" theme, as did the *New York World*, which called it an "unpleasant discussion" not usually brought to the stage.[58] *Theatre Magazine,* eerily echoing its objection to *The Nigger,* dismissed *Pride of Race* as "purposeless." "If it had an original purpose it has been smothered," the critic insisted. "In every way the play was an unnecessary one and, consequently requires no discussion."[59]

If they themselves were reluctant to write plays on race relations, the New Movement playwrights, and their supportive critics, certainly had no trouble writing critically about black shows that did appear on Broadway. Whether approvingly or not, critics saw most of the big African American musical comedies as forms of "low" entertainment and the African American characters in them as being of a certain type. Heywood Broun, for example, commenting on the breakthrough that Torrence's plays represented, noted that "negro life has meant little to the stage but burnt cork, lumbago and the word 'massa.' "[60] Similarly, *Theatre Magazine* remembered Negro characters as "caricatures" or as "an excuse for offering plantation melodies."[61] Louis Sherwin believed that vaudeville, which employed hundreds of black performers, nevertheless offered only "a bastard form of Negro humor."[62] Even Carl Van Vechten, who praised such shows as J. Leubrie Hill's *My Friend from Kentucky* and the comedies of Bert Williams and George Walker, lauded this form of entertainment because it "did not dilute the essential charm, the primitive appeal of the Negro." What did Van Vechten identify as the "charm" and "appeal" captured in black shows? The "reminiscences of the plantation, reminiscences of the old minstrel days, and capital portraits of the new coon," all made the plays characteristically African American—or in Van Vechten's words, "real nigger stuff."[63] With the exception of Van Vechten, writers sniffed at the stage work of black performers and of black characters depicted by whites in blackface, which suggests that they believed that these shows failed to portray Negroes accurately and fairly.

Their experiences and comments, however, indicate that they privately shared many of the preconceptions about African Americans that they publicly denounced. Daniel Gregory Mason, one of a group of artists who gathered regularly at the Judson Hotel in New York, had publicly decried the rage for African American ragtime music and privately used his version of Negro dialect to amuse his friend Ridgely Torrence. A 1910 letter to "Marse' Torrence," is filled with broken English and incorrect uses of words designed to reflect what he assumed to be African American speech patterns. "The po'try seems like it comes outen you jes' like the despiration comes out'n me this warm weather," he wrote, and ended the letter with "I must now preclude this 'pistle."[64] A few years later, having spent several months in Europe, Mason returned to the United States in need of money. He wrote Torrence that he had put his serious compositions on hold and was trying to write "footless literature" to satisfy "the public" and make a living. He then asked Torrence for "a negro libretto—'that shall be worthy of censorship,' " as part of his scheme to make money by playing down to popular taste.[65] In both cases, Mason viewed African Americans in stereotypical fashion—as objects of ridicule and sources of titillating sexuality—and except for inartistic hack work, African Americans could inspire none of his serious compositions.

Another of Torrence's friends, Zona Gale, who was involved with the "insurgent dramatists" in Wisconsin, told the poet's mother of her visit to Wilberforce University in Xenia in 1914. Although she considered the whole stay in Ohio "delightful," Gale mentioned that two large photographs had been taken of her with about a dozen Negroes associated with the university and had been sent to her by President Scarborough. The photographs, however, would not be on display in the main, downstairs rooms of the house she shared with her mother. "Mother recommends that I keep it [sic] upstairs," she explained, "though she is most sympathetic in their long fight from below the bottom up."[66] Gale's mother sympathized with blacks in their struggle, but she apparently could not imagine displaying a photograph of blacks with whites in her parlor, and her daughter obviously did not offer much resistance.

These public and private comments suggest that the revolution in the theater in the early twentieth century had limits. The radicals *did* imagine new ways of presenting drama to the public, by experimenting with the size of the stage and a variety of unusual props. They also brought to the stage subjects that up to that time had been considered out of place in polite society or as a theme for dramatic entertainment, and as a result, issues like class conflict, inequality of women and men, and the meaning of marriage in modern society all came before the critical gaze of theatergoers. The revolution did bring the race question to the stage but did not completely overturn older ideas on the race question, at least partly because those involved in the movement had little interest in or contact with African American life. In the first two decades of the twentieth century, the changes in theater conventions did not create many opportunities for black performers to interpret black characters in mixed companies before mixed audiences. And when they did, representatives of the New Movement, like their counterparts in the commercial theaters, found ways of discussing such productions in language that betrayed their shared misgivings about black art and black citizenship. But with all its limitations, the theatrical revolution did provide an opening for hybrid cultural production, black performance, and a broader consideration of American culture.

In the 1910s, while the contest over the theater raged between the avant garde and the traditional managers of Broadway, association with the New Movement became an additional burden for productions like *Three Plays for a*

Negro Theater. Shows produced in Little Theaters or by well-known supporters of experimental theater became subject to criticism as examples of the art of "high brows" as well as on their own merits. When critics focused on the creators, they deflected attention from the subject of the plays or reduced the themes to the peculiarities of the playwrights or managers who thought them to be art. At the same time, the theatrical vanguard hoped eventually to dominate the theaters of the nation and to create a "democratic" art in keeping with their vision of American culture for the people. They produced narratives of the American Stage in which the avant garde figured prominently. In the midst of such heated exchanges, it was easy for causes like racial equality to get lost in the shuffle. As each camp circled the wagons, it was clear that the fight over Broadway was a white man's fight.

PERCY MacKAYE
AND THE BURDENS OF THE NEW MOVEMENT

In 1915, Alfred Grunberg prepared a humorous one-act, three-scene play for *Theatre Magazine* that imagined George M. Cohan and Percy MacKaye collaborating on a Broadway production. Cohan, the symbol of the Broadway musical extravaganza, and MacKaye, the representative of the experimental art theater, join forces to create a successful American musical comedy. As Cohan puts it, "You supply the artistic side, and I'll put in the material that will make it a commercial success." The dialogue in the first scene exposes the chasm that separates the showman from the poet—Cohan relies on the tried-and-true crowd pleasers, expects to crank out the book in a few hours, and hopes to make at least one hundred thousand dollars on the venture; MacKaye needs time, inspiration, and a show devoid of symbols like the American flag and Uncle Sam. Cohan finally convinces MacKaye that together they cannot fail—"By the use of your name we will get the highbrows, and by the use of mine we'll please the rest."

As the second scene unfolds, the rift between the two theater men widens. They argue over the "conception of the part" to be played by popular comedienne Marie Dressler. "The part is one that must be played airily and daintily," MacKaye explains to Dressler. "You are supposed to be a woman whose thoughts are about lofty peaks, the ethereal heavens, and the mysticism of Maeterlink. I wish to show that even a fat woman can be idealistic." Cohan, by contrast, wants to "overcome" MacKaye's script by staging a final scene in which the hero hides from the enemy behind Dressler's ample person. "They know he is behind you, but being unable to flank you, they raise their guns to fire. You whip out this American flag from your bosom, place it on your chest, and say, 'Fire at my thin, anemic body if you must, but Gawd help you if one bullet perforates the flag of Uncle Sam!' Then the chorus sings the finale."

While the conflicting ideals of the two men seem to be completely irreconcilable, Grunberg nevertheless imagines a happy ending in the third scene, where in the lobby of the Astor Theatre, "Everyone is praising the play." "Mr. Highbrow" hates that "that Hebrew person, Cohan" had spoiled "MacKaye's poetry," but notes that the "verse we heard between his wretched songs was exquisite. Such metre, such iambic nothingness." "Miss Pretender-Intellectual" thinks the show "soulful," "dreamily gripping," and "inspiring." "Mr. Know-It-All" notes loudly, "Betcher ten t' nine Cohan put in the flag stuff." The playlet concludes with Cohan gloating over the "knockout" play they had co-created and MacKaye still ruing its lack of artistry.[67]

Grunberg's witty reflections on MacKaye and Cohan illustrate the ongoing tensions between the commercial and artistic interests in the American theater. His selection of George M. Cohan to represent the commercial elements coincided with other general assessments that Cohan's shows demonstrated his affinity for popular taste in entertainment, and his identification of Percy MacKaye to stand for the artistic avant garde also made sense given the poet's central role in promoting the interests, institutions, and writers of the New Movement in the Theater. The humor of this little comedy rested on the widely held belief that commerce and art remained incompatible, but the sardonic twist at the end suggested that were the two merged, everybody, from the overeducated highbrow to the ordinary Joe in the street would find something to admire. Although clearly meant to be a humorous piece wedged in between more serious reports on current dramas and popular actors, Grunberg's little script provides insights into the challenges faced by the New Movement as it sought to transform the nature and conventions of the American Stage.

Although Percy MacKaye is largely unknown in the late twentieth century except among specialists in American poetry and literature of the early 1900s, his work and experience represent better than anyone else the vital center of the New Movement. He served as both a symbol of the theatrical avant garde as well as a target for animus against it. His plays and masques bore all the marks of the unusual and the imaginative, and wherever one turned in the experimental theatrical scene, there one probably would encounter Percy MacKaye. The Drama League, the New Theatre, the Poetry Society of America, the Dramatists' Guild of Authors, and the American Drama Year Committee in 1917 all listed him as a member. Through his books, articles, pamphlets, and letters to the editors of influential newspapers, MacKaye kept the New Movement and its key participants before the public, and his work also gave readers reasons for thinking highly of the experimental work, thinking of it as distinctively American, and eventually considering its standards appropriate for dramatic expression.

Perhaps MacKaye served as something of a lightning rod for the movement because of his family background. As the son of James Steele MacKaye, Percy MacKaye appeared to some to be the heir apparent of American drama who was, in the words of Richard Burton, "honorably maintaining the family relation to the drama and the theatre." His father enjoyed critical acclaim in the late nineteenth century as one of a handful of playwrights—William Gillette, Bronson Howard, and Clyde Fitch were the others—who had come nearest to crafting a characteristically American dramatic tradition. And like his son, Steele MacKaye refused to limit himself to writing plays; he acted in some of his works, experimented in stagecraft, as an architect for the Lyceum Theatre and as the inventor of the double stage at the Garden Theatre, and helped found the Sargent School, an academy for the dramatic arts.[68] As Percy MacKaye himself put it in an autobiographical essay for the twenty-fifth anniversary report of Harvard's class of 1897, "Together father and son have contributed to the American drama, in creative continuity, an average of one dramatic work a year for fifty years (1872–1922)."[69]

MacKaye's claim to the mantle of American drama arose from more than being the son of the much-admired Steele MacKaye. Percy MacKaye's family ties stretched back to the earliest years of English settlement in New England. Directly related to William Bradford, he enjoyed a membership in the Society of Mayflower Descendants, and he claimed direct ties to one of America's best-known dissenters, Roger Williams. His grandfather, James Morrison MacKaye, an ardent abolitionist, served during the Civil War as chairman of the Commission to Promote the Emancipation Proclamation. Although born in New York in 1875, MacKaye nevertheless was a scion of New England, and judging from the autobiographical details he chose to include in his report to the class, he considered himself a bearer of that region's traditions. Both degrees he held by the early 1920s came from New England—a bachelor's degree from Harvard in 1897 and an honorary master's from Dartmouth in 1914. Explaining his and his son Robert's absence from the battlefront of the Great War—Percy in 1917 was too old and his son too young—MacKaye told of writing three major community dramas (*The Roll Call, The Evergreen Tree,* and *Washington, The Man Who Made Us*) and of presenting at Harvard his "Lowell Centenary poem, 'The Returning,' in Sanders Theatre, under conditions very similar to those under which Lowell himself read his 'Commemoration Ode' on the return of Harvard men from the Civil War."[70] The son of Steele MacKaye, a child of New England, a graduate of Harvard, a patriotic poet, these strands of his genealogy strengthened his sense of being tied to the development of American dramatic literature.

MacKaye came of age in the late 1890s, an era when the United States sought artistic expressions reflective of the national temper, and in the early twentieth century, he fancied himself one of the poets on whose shoulders the burden of crafting a dramatic tradition would rest. He explained to E. A. Robinson and William Vaughn Moody that if a school of drama were to take shape, it might as well revolve around their circle of poets. He recognized that as a Harvard man he had perhaps a special calling to rise to the occasion. He noted, for example, in his introduction to the letters of William Vaughn Moody that the cluster of budding American poet-dramatists all had emerged from "apprenticeships" at college at about the same time. "At the time of my first meeting with Moody (Harvard, '93)," he wrote, noting matter-of-factly the college and graduation dates of his friends, "he was thirty-five, six months older than Robinson (at Harvard, 1891–93), while Josephine Peabody (at Radcliffe, 1894–96) was thirty, Torrence (Princeton, '97) thirty, and I (Harvard, '97) twenty-nine."[71] He saw these writers as the spark that would ignite an explosion of American dramatic literature, and their constant company, correspondence, and criticism certainly did create a self-conscious community of artists. In the first decade of the new century, MacKaye published eight plays, including *The Canterbury Pilgrims* (1903), which Norman Hapgood gave a two-column review in the *New York Commercial-Advertiser,* and *The Scarecrow* (1908), which attracted considerable attention at home and abroad and which was produced by Rudolf Schildkraut under Max Reinhardt's direction at the Deutsches Theater.[72] In addition to the dramas, MacKaye also published several speculative works about the theater, in which he advanced his ideas for creating democratic art. In *The Playhouse and the Play* (1909), he first introduced the concept of a civic theater, which he developed more fully three years later in *The Civic Theater, in Relation to the Redemption of Leisure* (1912).

Like many of his fellow Ivy League playwrights, MacKaye believed that Little Theaters held the key to a higher standard of art for the democracy. He wrote a poem in honor of the new Bandbox Theatre that opened in late 1914 in which he invited theatergoers to help "christen our little new-born venture." Playing with the unusual name of the theater, MacKaye declared that the Bandbox would "furnish headgear fair enough / To fit your high-bred choice in varied modes adapted to your pleasures," and, tipping his hat to popular favor, he ended the poem with "Your good-will is our garland. Help us win it! / Our Bandbox holds the palm—while YOU are in it."[73]

While others in the New Movement pinned most of their hopes on small, experimental theaters, MacKaye promulgated a different theory of democratic art that set him apart from his peers. "The Civic Theatre idea," he explained, "implies the conscious awakening of a people to self-government in the activities of its leisure." Self-government here referred to participation in as well as making decisions about the kinds of diversions that would be meaningful. Thus, instead of mere "spectatorship," people would help create art in their communities, and rather than making art or drama subject to the vagaries of the marketplace, public support would free groups and individuals to express ideas and values without concern about profit or loss.[74] In practice, the civic theater productions MacKaye wrote were gigantic community spectacles involving hundreds or even thousands of ordinary citizens in cooperative endeavors of great beauty and symbolic importance. From the time this book first appeared until the early 1920s, MacKaye wrote and produced several such works that have been rivaled since only by the pageantry of Olympic ceremonies or Super Bowl halftime extravaganzas.

Two of these pageants—*The New Citizenship* (1915) and *Caliban* (1916)— stand out for the insights they offer into MacKaye's view of America and American citizenship, and the responses to *Caliban,* in particular, demonstrate the ways that racial ideas influenced questions of civilization. *The New Citizenship,* subtitled "A Civic Ritual Devised for Places of Public Meeting in America," appeared a year after the Great War had begun in Central Europe and at a time when thousands of European immigrants arrived at American ports each month. The ritual MacKaye imagined represented something like a crash course in American ideals and traditions for "newly naturalized citizens"— "to symbolize to eye and ear—within brief time-limits—the main historical significance of the living tradition of American liberty," and "to introduce into his historical background the new significance of Americanization to-day."[75] And the purpose was equally clear to MacKaye. Should these new citizens be called to lay down their lives for the nation in the impending war they should know what ideals they were defending.

Not surprisingly, the pageant ritual featured such representative figures as George Washington, Thomas Jefferson, Abraham Lincoln, and then-current president, Woodrow Wilson, whose interpreters recited lines from famous speeches as landmark statements of the American experiment in democracy. Perhaps a bit more surprising was MacKaye's determination to include traditional dances, music, and costumes from the new citizens' old countries, to demonstrate "the multiform meanings of America." Instead of a "national melting pot," which MacKaye believed "reduce[d] all precious heritages to a cold puddle of shapeless ore," the playwright wanted "a national studio to perpetuate them in new creative forms of plastic life."[76] He conceived of the pageant as an opportunity for native-born and naturalized citizens alike to ponder the essential tradition of liberty in the United States and to work together to incorporate the new "folk cultures" into a vibrant, ever-evolving New World culture in America.

MacKaye's community drama included music, singing, dancing, speaking parts, and a stunning moment when "first-voters" took part in the program to affirm their comprehension and appreciation of the democratic process. And while it was quite expansive in its vision of a multicultural society or pluralistic culture, conspicuous by its absence was any reference to people of color in America. Not only did Abraham Lincoln appear on the stage reciting the Gettysburg Address without mentioning slavery or emancipation, but at no other point did the cultural contributions of native-born "folks" appear. Moreover, MacKaye seemed much more interested in the immigrants and especially in the "15,000,000 foreign-born white persons" who were "wholly unnaturalized."[77] Although the question of "whiteness" was itself not always clear in the nineteenth century, MacKaye makes it explicit. Since the ceremony was designed for Columbus Day, the first immigrant spokesman was to be Italian, followed by leaders from other national groups in costume—"e.g. the Russian, Scandinavian, German, Greek, or whichever group may follow next."[78]

Obviously, such a ceremony could be adapted to any group represented, whether or not they stemmed from Europe or had white skin. And MacKaye's *The New Citizenship,* of course, was not the only ritual imagined in these years for making new arrivals into new citizens. The Ford Motor Company built a huge cauldron into which traditionally clad immigrants descended and from which they emerged, transformed, in dress indistinguishable from that of native-born Americans.[79] And with the provisions for Native American citizenship outlined in the Dawes Act, the government devised such rituals as the "Last Arrow" ceremony, whereby Indians would dress up in tribal garb, shoot an arrow into the sky for the last time, then change costumes and emerge as newly minted Americans.[80] MacKaye wrote the ritual for *The New Citizenship* specifically for new citizens in New York City at the request of Frederic C. Howe, Commissioner of Immigration at Ellis Island.[81] It would be hard to say how many times the ceremony actually was carried out or what kinds of people took part in the ritual. But it is significant nevertheless for understanding some of the connections made by a representative of the New Movement between race and citizenship. For MacKaye, given the groups he targeted for the program, citizenship implied whiteness.

The community drama that did place Percy MacKaye in the public eye and made him the subject of lively discussion was *Caliban,* which was written in honor of the three-hundredth anniversary of William Shakespeare's death in 1616. As the title of MacKaye's play suggests, the drama was inspired by Shakespeare's New World drama *The Tempest*. Along with the savage Caliban appeared Prospero, the symbol of civilization and art and bearing a striking resemblance to the great Bard, Miranda, Ariel, Sycorax, and Setebos. Unlike Shakespeare's drama, in which Caliban turns on his master, renounces his learning, and seeks to possess and defile the fair Miranda, MacKaye's play imagined a progressive encounter between the primitive and the civilized, an encounter that results in Caliban's stumbling efforts to understand, appreciate, and master the great works of art from those produced by the ancient Egyptians to those created by the early-seventeenth-century English. To honor Shakespeare, but to speak to Americans of the early twentieth century, MacKaye conceived of the "art of Prospero" as the "many-visioned art of the theatre which, age after age, has come to liberate the imprisoned imagination of mankind from the fetters of brute force and ignorance." Caliban, rather than being the uncivilized "other" to be exploited or enslaved, represented the "child-curious part of us all [whether as individuals or as races], grovelling close to his aboriginal origins, yet groping up and staggering . . . toward that serener plane of pity and love, reason and disciplined will, where Miranda and Prospero commune with Ariel and his Spirits."[82]

MacKaye's community drama—grounded in large measure in his idea of the "civic theatre"—demanded popular participation on an unprecedented scale. More than fifteen hundred ordinary citizens were selected to play roles as extras—spirits, armies, dancing girls, and Greek choruses—to illustrate the dramas of the past to which Caliban is introduced. Famous actors played the main roles—Lionel Braham as Caliban, Howard Kyle as Prospero, Edith Wynne Matthison as Miranda, Gareth Hughes as Ariel, and John Drew as Shakespeare.[83] To accommodate such a large cast, the play required an outdoor venue—usually a stadium or large public park or square—and sets and costumes that could be easily seen from afar. MacKaye engaged Joseph Urban to design most of the main stages, but the task of creating stages for the inner scenes that featured the dramas of the past fell to Robert Edmond Jones. Fresh from Europe and quickly gaining a reputation for striking designs, Jones also made costumes in bright colors that evoked the different periods and cultures represented in the inner scenes. Here on a grand scale, various streams of the New Movement flowed together—poetry in drama, art of the imagination, and the participatory civic ideal. And at a time when Shakespeare's works had come to be seen as the symbol of "highbrow" theater instead of widely known, popular entertainment, MacKaye envisioned democratic art that brought the best of high culture into the orbit of the people, or as MacKaye saw it, "drama *of* and *by* the people, not merely for the people."[84]

The first production of the masque took place in New York City College's Lewisohn Stadium in late May of 1916. Opponents had blocked the use of Central Park, which MacKaye thought would have been the perfect setting for a show of such magnitude.[85] Five hundred carpenters built the grandstands to augment the seating capacity of the stadium, and they helped build three stages. Ten performances attracted more than 130,000 spectators in 1916, and when the show was moved to Boston the following year nearly 225,000 people attended the seventeen performances.[86] After only two performances in New York, the Drama League declared *Caliban* a dramatic success and initiated a movement to make 1917 the "American Drama Year" to "preserve this enthusiasm for the drama" instigated by MacKaye's masque. The head of the Committee for the American Drama Year, Ridgely Torrence, established an information bureau at the Drama League offices in New York, accumulated books on American drama, maintained a list of published plays by American authors, and arranged a series of lectures on the American Stage by such noted theater people as Montrose Moses, Walter P. Eaton, and Samuel M. Tucker. Within a couple of weeks a second organization, the Community Drama Association, had formed to perpetuate the interest in American theater sparked by *Caliban*. MacKaye served on this committee and cooperated with Arthur Hopkins in creating a special performance of "scenes from plays that have been of special significance in the development of the American drama."[87]

Caliban and its author attracted much attention during and after the ten performances in New York. The *Brooklyn Eagle* considered the masque "magnificent" and its creator "a man who cannot be ignored henceforth in recording the evolution of the art of the theater." The *New York Times* called *Caliban* a "notable achievement," and a critic in *The New Republic* concluded, "There is now no longer any question that Mr. MacKaye's conception of community art is established in America."[88] *Theatre Magazine,* a bit less enthusiastic, praised MacKaye's "ambitious" show as "something distinctly original in the history of the drama" and raved about the "rare beauty displayed in the color and light accessories" designed by Robert Edmond Jones. But too much of the verse-dialogue was hard to hear, leading the critic to the conclusion that the public "had a good time" but not necessarily because of the poetry of the play.[89] About a week before the first performance of *Caliban,* the *New York Times* devoted a two-page feature in the Sunday magazine to an interview with MacKaye. Identifying himself directly with the "new movement in the theatre," MacKaye used the *Times* as a forum for clarifying the larger aims of the avant garde. He saw *Caliban* as "part of a movement which shall bring poetry to the service of the community, which shall make poetry democratic, in the best sense of the word, and that the result of this movement will be to create conditions likely to produce out of the soil of America a great renascence of the drama." Furthermore, the huge casts promoted a "message of cooperation" to transform individualistic thinking into collective thinking. He told of the reception of a community masque he had written in 1914 for the city of St. Louis, where the program was presented to "assemblies of ministers, in negro high schools, before clubs of advertising men, at I.W.W. meetings— before men of all conditions of life and shades of opinion." Like the St. Louis masque, *Caliban* was intended to "interpret the people to themselves."[90]

In the first flush of this spectacular production, much of the commentary focused on the lofty ideals expressed by MacKaye. But not all spectators were taken with the neo-Shakespearean poetry or with the prospect of witnessing more such shows, and they used MacKaye as a symbol of the highbrow pretensions of the New Movement. For example, when *Life* assembled a list of the "Follies of 1916," "The Ford peace excursion" appeared at the top and "Doing honor to the genius of Shakespeare by producing plays of Beaumont, Middleton, Chapman and Percy MacKaye," brought up the rear.[91] *The Masses* published a parody of *Caliban,* called "Education: A Community Masque," intended to expose the limitations of MacKaye's art for liberating the people.[92] Perhaps the most interesting was a spoof of the masque, called "Caliban, Jr." organized by students at City College, where the original had premiered. Hundreds of students took part in their own "community masque," which they intended to mirror the spirit of the spectacle in Lewisohn Stadium. In the student version, however, the tale of Caliban, Jr., is conveyed through a minstrel performance, complete with blackface, endmen, an interlocutor, and buck-and-wing dancing. The program "kept [participants] in gales of laughter," reported the *New York Times.* "It was great fun."[93] In all of these instances, MacKaye became the object of ridicule that blunted the impact of the New Movement on popular conceptions of American drama.

These varying responses to MacKaye's ambitious community drama—one of the most widely discussed productions involving the avant garde before *Three Plays for a Negro Theater*—illuminate some of the burdens associated with the New Movement. In spite of the deeply felt democratic aims of MacKaye, Joseph Urban, and Robert Edmond Jones, critics unsympathetic with their art and aspirations could classify *Caliban* as a "highbrow" project, out of touch with popular taste. And in the process of lampooning MacKaye's tribute to Shakespeare, the students at City College could not resist the temptation to couch their critique in racial terms. Why did black minstrelsy seem like an appropriate way to poke fun at the poet's lofty aims? None of the language or costumes in *Caliban* marked the title character as a person of color. Indeed, MacKaye implies a Cartesian view of humanity and seeks in the play to show that it is the life of the mind that distinguishes mankind from the animal kingdom. Caliban is made to utter truncated statements to indicate his lack of cultivation, but his primitive utterances are not even a pale reflection of what passed for Negro dialect on the American Stage. Still, in imagining a spoof of the clash between the civilized and the primitive—between Prospero and Caliban—the students howled with laughter at the prospect of African Americans taking part in the uplift of "Caliban, Jr." Their response betrays a deep-seated perception of African Americans as uncivilized. Thus, those engaged in the creation of culture could dismiss African American artistic expression as unworthy of serious consideration or incorporation into the mainstream of American life.

Without the New Movement, perhaps *Three Plays for a Negro Theater* would not have been produced in 1917. But the New Movement did not, and probably could not, clear the path for an open embrace of the race questions posed in the three plays. The dramatic revolutionaries turned many aspects of the theater upside down, but they did little before 1917 to make race prejudice a target of their critical art. Perhaps just as important, the image of the highbrow poet conjured up by references to dramatists like Percy MacKaye and Ridgely Torrence and their circle of friends redirected attention in the popular press away from the subject of their art to the artists themselves. As MacKaye found out in 1915 and 1916, and as Torrence would learn in 1917, their art was not judged only on the merits of plot, dialogue, performance, stage decoration, and directing, but became in a sense referenda on the objectives of the movement in the theater with which they were associated. So instead of discussing MacKaye's perspective on democratic art as participatory and cooperative, critics measured his masque's popularity and the extent to which *Caliban* lived up to the standards of the new stagecraft. A year later, Torrence's ideas on race would fall in the shadow of discussions of his affiliation with the New Movement as well as his position on the impending war.

Finally, as this discussion of the New Movement in general and of Edward Sheldon and Percy MacKaye in particular shows, regardless of the intentions of the authors, audiences' reception of drama plays an important role in the process of culture—a role as significant as the work of art itself. For what people see determines what they have to say about a production, and no playwright, producer, designer, or actor can control what the audience perceives. The critical, public conversation centered on a work of art is the means by which the main idea is considered to be worthy (or not) of modifying prevailing belief. As we shall see, the critical community made *Three Plays for a Negro Theater* the talk of the town in April 1917, and what they had to say illuminates what they saw.

THE TALK OF THE TOWN

"We heard the echoes of the applause through the press clippings. . . . We were delighted with the criticisms of the opening performance. The varying opinions as to which plays were the more interesting it seems to me will keep the discussion alive. I look for a long run and packed houses."

Findley Torrence, April 10, 1917

THE FIRST REVIEWS OF *Three Plays for a Negro Theater* appeared on Good Friday, April 6, 1917. The cast may well have greeted the day with something of the dread and anticipation appropriate to that Christian celebration—the fear of immediate wrath of the critics mingled with the hope that their sacrifice would lead someday to greater chances for fellow African Americans. Critics on the most influential dailies all commented on the plays, and as he read the reviews one after another, Ridgely Torrence clipped them from the newspapers to send off to his family back in Xenia, none of whom had been able to witness the gala opening night. When Findley Torrence read the stack of first responses, he told his brother that he "heard the echoes of the applause" in them. From afar, the Torrence family was "delighted with the criticisms of the opening performance," which Findley believed signaled "a long run and packed houses." And in a perceptive observation, Torrence's brother wrote, "The varying opinions as to which plays were the more interesting it seems to me will keep the discussion alive."[1]

As it turned out, of course, Findley Torrence was wrong about the long run and the packed houses. Before the month was out, the show had closed, never to be revived on Broadway; the audiences were of respectable size, but neither the Garden Theatre nor the Garrick Theatre had to turn people away for lack of room. But whether he realized it or not, Torrence's brother in Ohio did recognize the significance of the "varying opinions" about and the lively "discussion" of the production to the plays' ultimate place in the annals of American drama. The critics, no less than the playwright, producer, director, and cast, made the three experimental dramas the talk of the town. And what they said about them established the terms within which they would be considered by the public—those who saw the plays as well as those who did not—as legitimate expressions of American culture.

As we have seen, the people who created the race dramas hoped to achieve a variety of particular objectives—a novel American drama, personal fame, vindication for the New Movement, and greater understanding of the lives and values of one-tenth of the American population so long caricatured or ignored. They also wanted to convey specific ideas about race relations in the United States. But as clear as these aims may have been to the performers onstage and to the artists and sponsors behind the scenes, they were not always apparent in the discussion of the plays that took place in the print media. Moreover, the printed commentaries represented a vital part of the process by which the plays became cultural grist. Vision, interpretation, representation, and reception all constitute important raw materials of culture; but it is in the reception that we can see most clearly which of the propositions advanced by the plays were attractive and which were not; which messages were received and which were not; and the kinds of new narratives critics created as they engaged the theatrical expression.

Findley Torrence was also correct when he noted that the reviews generally were positive. Some were less enthusiastic than others, but all agreed that something extraordinary had taken place at the Garden Theatre. Yet, as they summarized the plots of the three plays, critics tended to emphasize different parts of the story, leaving out some details and adding descriptions that revealed their biases and perceptions. They commented on the acting, making inevitable comparisons with the style and technique of white performers with whose work they were most familiar and exposing their preconceived ideas about essential racial characteristics. They rarely mentioned the performers by name, betraying their lack of awareness of the stars and style of the African American Stage. The ways critics structured their praise placed certain limits on the potential challenge posed by the avant garde race dramas.

Perhaps most important, the commentary that flooded the New York dailies, weeklies, popular periodicals, and journals devoted to theater in the days and weeks after opening night represented a sustained conversation about what this theatrical "first" meant for American culture. The criticism provides a chance to hear how a group of influential writers in 1917 talked about the idea of a multiracial culture and society—how their praise for the plays nevertheless could leave nearly untouched the question of African American citizenship and equality. The distinctions white critics made between "they" and "we," "their art" and "American culture" suggest an unwillingness in 1917 to acknowledge the vital contributions of people of color to an evolving national culture. Black critics addressed these issues, too, and they noted differences along racial lines as well. But their "we" typically was more inclusive, demonstrating a desire to alter fundamentally the nature, content, and complexion of a distinctive national art.

The debut of black performers on Broadway in serious race dramas, sponsored by three influential white theater people, forced a significant group of opinion shapers to confront the difficult relationship between race and nationality—to peer into the looking glass of culture and to discover and make sense of the variety of visages reflected back. How did they respond when some of the faces claiming American citizenship were dark or when white-skinned people were villains, or when the "taint" of race was a "white taint"? How did they encourage their readers to deal with the changing complexion of the social portrait? And what did their commentary imply about appropriate national consciousness in 1917? These are not idle questions, for at base they show how a venue of entertainment served as a site for serious discussions fraught with social and political implications. The various narratives about the plays composed in response to these questions helped to shape a cultural consciousness that challenged an all-white national sensibility and at the same time limited the idea of social equality they implicitly espoused.

RACE DRAMAS AND THE DRAMA OF RACE

The plot summaries that appeared in chapter 1 were based on my reading of the scripts published by Macmillan in 1917, but, of course, I did not see the dramas performed. Not having seen the actors' stage movements and facial expressions or the costumes and sets, and not having heard the delivery of the written lines, especially the actors' tones and pronunciation of words, I cannot— and do not—presume to evaluate the accuracy of the eyewitness accounts of the performance in 1917. Those in attendance obviously experienced much more than the lines printed in the published version of the plays, and they reported what they saw and heard. Judging from the range of descriptions and plot summaries that appeared in the newspapers and magazines, the audience at the Garden Theatre saw more than three plays written by Ridgely Torrence. It is clear that not all members saw the same show; their expectations and experiences affected the way they received the dramas and colored the narratives they constructed about them for their columns.

Near the end of his review, Lester Walton of the *New York Age* pondered aloud the differences in perception. He wondered whether "the public at large will take kindly" to the race dramas and admitted that one question "persistently flashed" through his mind as he prepared his column: "How will the bulk of the white theatregoing public take 'Granny Maumee' and 'Simon, the Cyrenian?' " Walton doubted that every white American would be as "liberal minded and big-hearted" as Torrence and Jones, willing to look at the race issue from a point of view sympathetic to African Americans. His experience as a black man in America had made him nervous about confronting white prejudice against blacks. "Each day we are compelled to move about warily," Walton explained, "so fearful are we of offending the white man, thereby raising the race issue, that caution becomes second nature." How would white playgoers respond to seeing themselves as villains—forgers, thieves, rapists, and killers of Jesus of Nazareth. "It must be admitted," he continued, "that the three dramatic offerings treat the white many [*sic*] very much as the Negro is mistreated by the daily press—magnify his faults and suppress his virtues. But maybe our pale-faced brethren will not be as thin-skinned after all."[2]

In these remarks, Walton identified the central meaning he had derived from the three dramas; to him, an African American journalist who had endured and combated discrimination against people of color, the plays reversed the usual roles of "heroes" and "villains." Indeed, this way of seeing the plays was so obvious to him that he prepared himself and his readers for the worst from white critics, who, he believed, were bound to be offended. As it turned out, Walton need not have been quite so concerned, for others in the critical community did not see the dramas as he had, and they wrote reviews that gave their readers ways of thinking about the plays, the actors, and the issues they raised that only obliquely addressed racial prejudice and discrimination in America.

The differences in perspective appeared in various subtle ways, most notably in the descriptions of the characters, in the extent to which reviewers considered the story credible, and in the meaning derived from the plays. In a general sense, white critics found elements in the dramas to praise even as they portrayed characters in unflattering ways. The manner in which they saw and chose to relate the basic plot suggests that many found the plays either hard to believe or difficult to understand. Finally, the basic message of the dramas differed from review to review. Few of the white critics displayed the same certainty as Walton as to what the plays conveyed.

Of the three plays, only *Granny Maumee* had been performed prior to the debut of the united presentation of the three plays in 1917. It had startled the original audience three years earlier, and some of the critics knew the basic story before they saw the Negro Players' version at the Garden Theatre. Because of the seriousness of the issues the play contained and because no touch of humor interrupted the emotionally charged dialogue and action, *Granny Maumee* posed the greatest challenge for critics. But as troubling as it may have been, this tragedy nevertheless lent itself to an analysis that left many of the prevailing attitudes toward black Americans intact.

Torrence provided a few hints about his vision of the title character. As he described the opening scene, Torrence imagined Granny Maumee sitting in a high-backed chair while her great-granddaughter Pearl scampers about the room "straightening chairs and rearranging flowers." Granny is "seen to be blind," he wrote. "She is black and thin, with white hair and a face so seared by burns that it masks her great age." In the first few minutes of the dialogue, Granny orders the young woman to prepare the room for the long-awaited baby boy her other great-granddaughter will be bringing home by laying out her "fine-spun sheets" on the good bed. The burns and the woman's "great age" are explained as Granny remembers how she acquired the one good piece of furniture. Her son, the girls' grandfather, had bought the bed for his mother decades earlier on the day before he was taken away by a white mob who wrongly accused him of murder. They burned him at a hitching post, and Granny had rushed into the flames to rescue her only son. When the lynchers pulled her away, she herself had been badly burned and blinded. In the years that followed she waited in vain for another male descendant, but, as she told her great-granddaughter, "Dee wuz all gals fum dat on, you an' yo sisteh Sapphie an' yo' mammy an' yo' mammy's mammy, all down from my breas': all gals."[3]

Relatively few of the drama critics saw Granny precisely as Torrence imagined her. Typically, they underestimated her age by defining her relationship to Sapphie and Pearl either as mother and daughters, as did the critics for the *New York Evening Post* and the *New York Sun* and Arthur Hornblow in *Theatre Magazine,* or as grandmother and granddaughters, as did Lester Walton in the *New York Age* and Heywood Broun in the *New York Tribune.* Only Alexander Woollcott of the *New York Times* reported the relationship in the same terms as Torrence. But all recognized that she was very old, and some used descriptors that added details extraneous to her age. Arthur Hornblow, for example, referred to Granny as "an old crone, given to voodooism on occasion," who "curses her daughter" when she brings home a mulatto child. Here, the critic for *Theatre Magazine* included a number of pejorative adjectives that made the old woman something less than a sympathetic character. The *New York Sun*'s drama critic described Granny as "one of those ebony mummies of great but uncertain age and blind, who cherishes a bitter hatred of the whites who lynched her only son." The first phrase presents her as a type that serves to blunt the second phrase, which offers the particular details of her life story that have formed her character.[4]

In addition to her age, Granny's struggle between Christian belief and voodoo practice provided opportunities to present the title character as heroic, confused, or unbelievable. Lester Walton mentioned that Granny "practices the black art" and plans to use voodooism to destroy the white father of the newborn, but he hailed the triumph of Christianity in the end. "[S]he and her dead son would show more kindliness toward him than he and his people did toward them," he reported.[5] For the African American writer, Granny served as an example of black endurance in the face of white injustice and of the superior moral character and Christian spirit of oppressed people. The reviewer for the New York Evening Post considered the same tension between Christianity and voodooism "unfortunate" and "confusing." Indeed, instead of seeing a triumph of Christian faith, the critic concluded that Granny "dies of a broken heart after anathematizing and then half-pardoning the father," and he praised Marie Jackson-Stuart for playing the part "in the right vein of intense and purposeful menace."[6] For the white reviewer, the spiritual victory is compromised by a more basic belief in black magic.

It was the presence of voodooism in the play that gave many white reviewers a chance to discuss this tragedy in ways that left their preconceived ideas about Negro Americans unchanged. The New York Evening Sun's critic reported, "The play is lurid and hectic with a touch of real black magic added for good measure."[7] Burns Mantle described the basic plot as "the tale of an ancient voodoo worshiper who had waited for years for a man child to be born to her line and prayed for the right to see it before she died, only to have her prayer answered and then learn the child to be white."[8] The New York Evening Post noted that the play was "very crude" but contained "much that is vivid and striking in its barbaric spirit and coloring," and Rennold Wolf of the New York Morning Telegraph considered Granny Maumee to be "a weird and fascinating study of a primitive type."[9] Alexander Woollcott identified "the strong call of an ancient half-remembered magic" in Granny's life that suggests a primitive spirit bred in the bone, and Louis De Foe pointed to the "latent voodooism in her nature," which wells up in the face of the tragic discovery of white blood in her long-awaited male heir.[10] These writers all used familiar language that made Granny comprehensible. She was the center of a tragedy, but her story was alternately "crude," "lurid and hectic," "barbaric," "weird," "primitive," and marked by "ancient voodoo worship." All of these remarks served to locate the title character somewhere beyond the boundaries of modern American life and belief.

For some writers the fundamental primitivism they perceived in Granny Maumee made the play's denouement unexpected and mystifying. Heywood Broun, for example, acknowledged some "impressive moments" in the drama and Marie Jackson-Stuart's "interesting performance" in the title role, but he argued that the play "rather breaks down at the finish because the dramatist brings it to a conclusion which is by no means inevitable." Broun apparently expected the "horrors" that were promised by Granny's fury and incantations to be carried out in the end. Since he took no note of the ethos of Christian forgiveness and the promise of eternal life to which Granny ultimately succumbed, the triumph of forgiveness over vengeance puzzled him.[11] More critically, Arthur Hornblow decided that "the play is in reality, theatrically and dramatically, untrue," and "less creditable" than *The Rider of Dreams* and *Simon, the Cyrenian*. He offered no explanation for this position other than a brief summary of the plot, the sketchiness of which might reveal why the drama made so little sense to him. "An old crone," he wrote, "given to voodooism on occasion, curses her daughter when, after a long absence, she comes back with a child with white blood in him. The old negress is proud of her race and wants no contamination. She dies in an incantation calling down evil on the white malefactor."[12] No wonder Hornblow believed the play lacked credibility. This narrative about the drama focuses on the fundamental badness of the title character and ignores all background information that might account for it. Hornblow left his readers with the impression that Granny, wicked from the beginning, died in the end without being redeemed. That being the case, the *Theatre Magazine* critic could see neither the drama, the tragedy, nor the truth of this experience.

Hornblow's assessment is instructive for another reason: the narrative he created to summarize the plot. Whenever a witness to a performance—either critic or patron—relates the story of a show, he or she ordinarily identifies the basic subject of the play, then supplies enough elements of the story to explain how it unfolded. The details serve to clarify the point of the drama, as the witness saw it.

Consider, for example, Walton's discussion of *Granny Maumee*. He began with a survey of background details that he thought were essential to understanding the drama as it unfolded onstage. The tragedy told the story of an old woman who "practices the black art," hates all whites because a white mob burned her son at the stake many decades earlier for a crime he did not commit, and who has raised two granddaughters. Granny is blind because when she tried to rescue her son, the flames burned her eyes. As the story opens, Granny and one of her granddaughters, Pearl, prepare for the arrival of Sapphie who will visit for the first time since having gone to town to work for white people, having gotten married, and having borne a son. When Granny discovers that the baby is a mulatto—the first child to mar her "royal black" line—and that his father is a descendant of her son's murderers, Granny plans a horrible death for the white man using voodoo. In the end, however, she cannot go through with the evil deed. She tells the white man that "she and her dead son would show more kindliness toward him than he and his people did toward them." Then Granny Maumee drops dead.[13] Walton structured his narrative about the play to emphasize the injustices Granny had endured to justify her lapse into the "black art" and, perhaps, to make more remarkable her turning from it and embracing the ethos of Christian love.

Louis De Foe's narrative of *Granny Maumee* resembled Walton's in general outline but with a few significant differences. " 'Granny Maumee' is woven around the tragic discovery of a blind old negro mammy that her great-grandson, the man-child in whom are centered her ambition and her pride, has the blood of the Caucasian in his veins," he wrote. "Her own son had been burned at the stake by a mob. She has sworn eternal hatred to the white race. She has prepared a welcome for her granddaughter and the infant son. Then ensues the tragedy of the discovery, which stirs the latent voodooism in her nature. She performs her incantations, but before she dies the compassion and religious impulses of her nature overcome her hatred and she forgives the child's white father." De Foe praised Jackson-Stuart's portrayal of the "mingled passions" and "pathos" of the character. Structured with the same essential background details as Walton's review—except for failing to note that Granny lost her sight trying to save her innocent son—De Foe's version of *Granny Maumee* also emphasized the victory of compassion over revenge. But it is interesting to note that the old woman's "religious impulses" are never identified specifically as Christian, and elsewhere in the essay, De Foe called "the negro's pride of race" the chief theme of the play and "the superstitious impulse" the "predominant characteristic" of the race.[14]

The review in the *New York Sun* similarly placed a different spin on the same details of the story.

> Granny is one of those ebony mummies of great but uncertain age and blind, who cherishes a bitter hatred of the whites who lynched her only son. She hopes for two things. One is a male heir and the other is vengeance. There is a certain lofty pride in her respect for her pure royal black strain. Occasionally she reverts to Congo voodooism and works herself into a frenzy of rage. The scene takes place on the day of the return of her daughter with the first male issue in the family. Granny's faltering sight returns to her sufficiently to discover that the baby is a mulatto. Her anger is terrible and she plans the destruction of the white father. But in her visions over her incantations she is taught forgiveness then dies.

Like De Foe, this reviewer failed to see that the lynched son had been innocent and that Granny had lost her sight trying to save him. Granny's Christianity receives no emphasis; indeed, her decision to forgive the white father is expressed in passive terms. And the author observed in conclusion that "there is nothing essentially characteristic about the negro race in 'Granny Maumee.'"[15]

The last sentence in the *New York Sun*'s critique alerts us to the subtle way reviews like these raised questions even as they conveyed their own messages. Seeing "nothing essentially characteristic about the negro race" in the play, did the writer mean that Granny's pride of race was idiosyncratic, or that forgiveness was not typical of African Americans, or that lynching rarely touched black families in America, or that mulatto children were normally welcomed rather than reviled? The review offers no more information on which to base an answer to this question. But clearly the reviewer *expected* the plays to capture the essence of a unified African American character—that unlike whites, of whom many types existed, all African Americans shared the same experience and responded in the same ways.

Black and white reviewers in New York drew very different meanings from this play. Walton saw race pride, Negro heroes and Caucasian villains, and Christian forgiveness. His colleague on the *New York Age,* James Weldon Johnson, no less decisive, argued that this "stark tragedy of Negro life" went directly to the "roots of the race problem," and he ultimately concluded that *Granny Maumee* contained "powerful propaganda against lynching."[16] None of the white reviewers highlighted Granny's Christian spirit, the race problem, white villains, or lynching as important themes. Instead, like Francis Hackett, they saw the play as an example of race hate in reverse, or like Rennold Wolf, they saw it as a "fascinating study of . . . an old voodoo woman."[17] But taken together, the essays written by white witnesses to the drama, whose publications reached a far larger audience than their black counterparts, gave prejudice against African Americans a wide variety of escape hatches. The language used to describe the main character in and the dramatic action of *Granny Maumee* did little to challenge the dominant view of black Americans—they were primitive, guided by superstition, prone to use voodoo, and posed a potential menace to whites.

One of Torrence's friends wrote to him after the three plays closed at the Garrick Theatre to say that *Granny Maumee* had put the "poor remnants of [his] sensibility . . . dreadfully to the test." Although he believed the play contained "a real touch of greatness," the correspondent chided the playwright: "[Y]ou must have known the play would be painful in the process & that the reactions at the end would not quite restore the balance. . . . [O]ne ought to bring extraordinary nerves to Torrence plays." By contrast, Torrence's friend thought *The Rider of Dreams* a "clear joy" and a "delight."[18] The playwright's wife, Olivia Torrence, informed family members back in Xenia that the audience "applauded all throughout the *Rider of Dreams*," and she thought that when the Broadway run came to an end, the play might be continued on the vaudeville stage.[19] What these writers expressed privately, the critical community underscored publicly in their uncontained enthusiasm for *The Rider of Dreams*. As Heywood Broun put it, " 'Granny Maumee' aroused great attention when it was played by the stage society a few years ago, but it was another play which made the deep impression last night. 'The Rider of Dreams,' " he declared, "is a capital one-act comedy."[20]

Part of the exuberance for the play stemmed from the performance by Opal Cooper, a genial cabaret singer who brought Madison Sparrow to life. "A huge negro delighting in the name of Opal Cooper," wrote Broun, "played the dreamer with fine fervor and humor." The actor "smiled so broadly after the sixth or seventh encore that it was easy to see he had been having the best sort of a time even when he was called upon to sulk."[21] Apparently, Cooper's amiable personality and open smile drew people to him both on and off the stage, for near the end of the run the *New York Morning Telegraph* sent Djuna Barnes to the Garrick Theatre to interview the cast of *Three Plays for a Negro Theater*, and well over half of the column that appeared was devoted to Cooper.[22]

The part Cooper played in *The Rider of Dreams*, Madison Sparrow, an unemployed laborer who dreams of making a fortune in business, also seemed to strike a chord with the audience because he was familiar. Although Blanche Deas portrayed a hard-working, devout African American washerwoman, whose labor and savings has held the family together for more than a decade, her performance inspired very little commentary. Likewise, the kindly Dr. Williams, who restores the lost savings, employs Madison as a music teacher, and lectures him on the necessity of providing for his family, attracts little attention. But Madison Sparrow's profligacy and irresponsibility—his childlike joy and his sulky dejection—seemed to fulfill the audience's expectations for black manhood. The story of *The Rider of Dreams* also provided many critics with a chance to reinforce the usual unflattering view of black Americans.

Torrence set the one-act play in the kitchen of a "colored family," where Lucy Sparrow was to be at work on baskets of laundry she took in to provide for her family. In his opening description, Torrence noted that Lucy and her son, Booker, "as well as the room show a painstaking neatness despite the disorder necessary in the process of a professional 'wash.' " Lucy drills Booker in a catechism while they wait for Madison to arrive for the evening meal.[23] Torrence imagined a scene of poor but striving people for whom manual labor,

Christian piety, and constant struggle were facts of life. Madison descends on the room with his dreams for comfort, his secret plan to get rich quick, and his jovial opposition to his wife's piety and hard, poorly remunerated toil.

Both Lester Walton and James Weldon Johnson hailed the comedy as a study in African American types. Walton found the "natural and faithfully portrayed types of Negro life" quite satisfying because they were "familiar and real."[24] Johnson reported that "the principal character of the 'Rider of Dreams' is neither an overdressed, strutting dandy, nor is he a big, stupid slob with his face corked black and his mouth painted red. He is a real human being and a real Negro, . . . and the type of colored man that may be found in every Negro community." But so, too, were the other characters. Together, Johnson believed, they recreated a "slice of life."[25] For these two African American writers, it was not just Madison Sparrow who struck the right note—all the characters represented types well-known in African American neighborhoods.

White reviewers described Madison Sparrow somewhat differently. Charles Wood called him a "nigger ne'er-do-well with a most amiable disposition, unhampered by practicality, efficiency, systematic morality and the other well-known vices of civilization."[26] Both Alexander Woollcott and Clayton Hamilton saw the main character as "a playboy of the southern world" who, Hamilton continued, "drifted all too easily through life along the lines of impulses both lyrical and lovely and every now and then was dashed to disaster because of the inexplicable incongruity between the world of actuality and his more alluring world of dreams."[27] A reviewer for the *New York American* described Cooper's part as "a happy-go-lucky fellow who had been a dreamer," and Francis Hackett called him a "light-fingered" "negro thief."[28] Torrence replied to Hackett in the following issue of *The New Republic*, saying "It is a misconstruction of the individual character and of the type to assume, as does this review, that [Madison Sparrow] is 'light-fingered.' "[29]

More than these descriptions, however, the narratives of the drama reveal what, precisely, the writers in the crowd saw. Walton saw Sparrow "duped by a white man" into withdrawing his family's savings of eight hundred dollars for a business venture. The white man forged Lucy's name so the transaction could be completed without the wife knowing of it. Although clearly misled by this treacherous white man, Sparrow confesses his evil deed to his wife— a moment Walton considered a "highlight" of the play—and Dr. Williams saves the day when he returns the lost money, wrenches a promise from Sparrow to be a better husband, and gives Madison a job and his wife a deed to the house. As in *Granny Maumee*, Walton emphasized a version of the story that reversed the typical racial identity of villain and hero, and highlighted Sparrow's essential honesty.[30] Louis De Foe's review in the *World* similarly reported this chain of events and praised its "exceedingly human appeal."[31] Charles Wood, another white reviewer who reported essentially the same details as Walton, emphasized two points that Walton did not. As a critic for the *Masses*, Wood first identified the man who led Sparrow astray as a "white capitalist" who also steals a guitar as a down payment on the future profits they will reap. Second, Wood noted that Torrence wrote an ending that went way beyond the typical Broadway show. The happy ending—money returned, house purchased, job offered—he argued, was not so happy, for Sparrow "must work. He must never drink again. He must teach music and the landlord's children will be his first pupils." Sparrow's "contrite" agreeability to these terms demonstrated further for readers of the *Masses* the oppressive nature of the capitalist system. The story, as Wood saw it, was more a class drama than a race drama.[32]

More typically reviewers failed to see the white figure and his role in leading Sparrow down the wrong path, so the onus for the family's troubles rests squarely on the shoulders of Madison Sparrow. Consider, for example, Alexander Woollcott's brief summary of *The Rider of Dreams*: "An amused and friendly study of a playboy of the Southern world who dreams great dreams, but gets into all manner of trouble when he tries to obey them in an alien and fiercely practical world. He has no 'honin' fo' honesty,' and while he's no drunkard, he admits he's not 'a frantic' on the subject. You leave him at last hugging a guitar which a wise and understanding friend has given him as a means of expressing what is astir within him."[33] A "playboy," a "dreamer," impractical, dishonest, and an occasional drinker, Madison Sparrow falls into trouble, it would seem from this report, because he has asked for it. Similarly the *New York Evening Post* cited Sparrow as the "lazy happy-go-lucky husband," and "the alleged head of the household," "whose dreams and general shiftlessness involve him in theft and forgery."[34] Arthur Hornblow noted the bad influence but refused to identify the person's race. "A shiftless husband falls in with a slick person who induces him to get from the bank the eight hundred dollars which his hardworking wife has saved up in order to buy the house in which they live. The shiftless husband has always dreamed of living without work and having plenty of money. He is to form a partnership with the slick person which will realize this dream." Moreover, the husband "had stolen or taken a guitar" so he could amuse himself while the money rolled in. Madison Sparrow and the "slick person" together created the crisis, but the evil action is done by Sparrow alone.[35]

In a couple of instances the plays provided an excuse to offer racial commentary more or less unrelated to the dramas themselves. James Metcalfe, for example, published a comment on *Three Plays for a Negro Theater* in the

April 19 edition of *Life*. The first word in the review—"Under"—provided a graphic artist an opportunity to draw a caricature that cued the magazine's readers to take a particular point of view on the race dramas. At the artist's touch, the "U" became an enormous, curved piece of watermelon whose center had been gobbled away by a thick-lipped, buck-toothed African American who grasped the piece with both hands and appeared to be about to take another big bite. The caricature runs counter to Metcalfe's opening remarks that complimented the "colored players" at the Garden Theatre, but perhaps it captured the spirit of his conclusion that the "melting-pot metaphor" applied to the American theater made for "strange possibilities for the stage of the future."[36]

In *The Rider of Dreams*, the part of Booker Sparrow, the impish child who appears in the first scene with his mother, drew some intriguing comments. Hailed by black and white writers alike as a "perfect pickaninny," Joseph Burt had become something like a tiny mascot for the black cast and a favorite subject of many writers. Djuna Barnes, for example, highlighted his popularity with the playwright, director, and members of the cast and commented on his naturalness on stage and the spontaneity of his portrayal of the pert little Booker Sparrow.[37] Heywood Broun launched into an unexpected soliloquy on the virtues of black children as personified by Burt. "It is difficult to understand the prejudice in some families in favor of white children since the small blacks seem so much more interesting," Broun wrote after cheering Burt as a "perfect pickaninny." He continued: "Perhaps the best arrangement would be to have them black up to ten years old, and then exchange them for white children." Perhaps the idea of adult black men in the family was too much for Broun.[38]

The two plays about modern times with their central characters—Granny Maumee and Madison Sparrow—made recognizable as primitive and vengeful or irresponsible and child-like types—contained themes and details that *could* have produced a fair amount of soul-searching on the part of white critics, audiences, and readers as they contemplated race relations in twentieth-century America. But generally they did not. As we have seen, it was possible to contain the critique of American race relations implicit in the plays and to fit them instead into more familiar patterns of thought in which blacks alone caused their own trouble, represented the threat of violence in society, and were generally primitive, poorly educated, and deservedly cast on the margins of American life.

The third play, *Simon, the Cyrenian*, elicited the least commentary. Perhaps the obscurity of the two biblical references—to Simon's carrying of the cross of Jesus and to the wife of Pilate pleading with her husband to have nothing to do with the trial of the Nazarene—took critics in the audience by surprise. When they cited St. Luke as the source of Simon's story, they probably were relying on Torrence's inclusion of a brief passage from that book on the program, for none cited the other gospel accounts of Simon or the sources for the story about Pilate's wife. Descriptions of the play in both black and white columns tended to be brief and direct. Arthur Hornblow's summary was typical: " 'Simon the Cyrenian,' entitled a passion interlude, concerns the cross-bearer of Jesus as he was about to be led to death. Historically, it seems, this follower was black. He, in the acting, suffers his indignities with dignity; is reviled and slapped and beaten and has a crown of thorns thrust on his head by a vile jester."[39] Frequently, the drama critics commented more on the set and costumes by Robert Edmond Jones than on the content of the drama. Alexander Woollcott thought the play "brilliantly staged" by Jones, and H. B. Frissell exclaimed in the *Southern Workman,* "The costumes are splendid, and the dark skins of the actors are set off by primary colors in rich combinations."[40] Heywood Broun went further by arguing the play "would amount to little" were it not for the opportunity it afforded Jones "to present one of the finest stage pictures of the year."[41] Walton used the space set aside for *Simon, the Cyrenian* in his lengthy review in the *New York Age* to praise Jones "for this perfect blending of colors and various negroid types," a point missed by Arthur Hornblow, who ended his commentary with the observation that "whites were used in the minor numerous [*sic*] parts."[42]

In another respect, the final play of the evening exacted less commentary than the others, because the main point was harder to obscure. Not surprisingly, James Weldon Johnson asserted that "Simon stands out symbolical of all that the Negro race has suffered and endured for centuries," and he was echoed by Clayton Hamilton in *Vogue,* who wrote that Simon's story symbolized the burden "laid upon the shoulder of the negro race."[43] Alexander Woollcott quoted Torrence's words from the program: "That Jesus' cross bearer was a black man is a fact that holds a certain suggestion bearing upon a phase of modern society," but he thought the program only called attention to "a rather obvious symbolism."[44] Only the critic for the *New York Evening Post* made the racial significance of the story explicit. "Mr. Torrence, by a somewhat bold interpretation of the quoted text, makes Simon a noted warrior and rebel, the object of the mockery of the Roman soldiers, and thus presents him as an object lesson of the cruelties suffered in the past, by the negro at the hands of the white race. The scene is not without its sting or its appeal."[45]

This last sentence—"The scene is not without its sting or its appeal"—is curious. Why did the play cause a "sting"? Was the sting felt by the writer for the *Evening Post* related to Torrence's friend's complaint that *Granny Maumee* was "painful" and that without "extraordinary nerves" one could barely endure it? The sting and the pain of these witnesses affected Charles Wood as well, who wrote of *Granny Maumee,* "It isn't altogether pleasant to think of, but it is a situation which, we must all admit, is true to life in these United States." These scattered confessions amid the more frequent efforts to neutralize the radical implications of the three plays ultimately reveal another kind of reception that helps explain how the talk of the town was followed by silence and cultural amnesia. Just as the language used to discuss characters and themes in *Granny Maumee, The Rider of Dreams,* and *Simon, the Cyrenian* made the African American recognizable in stereotypical terms and thus softened the impact Torrence's plays might have had on prevailing views on race in America, these expressions of discomfort suggest a kind of "uncanny" experience that resulted in a collective averting of the eyes from a scene too painful to confront. The sting arose from the recognition that injustice persisted in a nation devoted to "liberty and justice for all," and the "appeal" lay, perhaps, in the hope that this injustice could be rectified. Together these linguistic and psychological responses to the first black actors on the Great White Way show how race dramas in 1917 exposed the drama of race relations in the United States.[46]

"A BUNCH OF NEGRO PLAYERS —A GATHERING OF NEGRO ARTISTS"

In a review of *Three Plays for a Negro Theater* that appeared in the *New York Evening Journal* after the production had moved to the Garrick Theatre, the drama critic, self-styled as "Zit," urged *everyone* to see the plays before they closed. Responding to oft-expressed reservations by white theatergoers about attending a performance by black actors, Zit tried to reassure readers that if they were "looking for novelties" they would find them at the Garrick. According to the critic, white people kept asking "Why would I want to see a bunch of negro players?" Zit's answer, essentially, was—you won't. Instead you'll see "a gathering of negro artists."[47] Zit's article captured important aspects of the popular and critical response to the pioneers on the cast of Torrence's dramas: Who were these actors, how should their performances be evaluated, and if the names were unfamiliar why would one waste time and money on a company of untrained and unskilled amateurs? Almost all the city's influential critics had something to say about the actors and their style and ability. And like their comments on the plays, what they said about the actors—whether they saw "a bunch of Negro players" or a "gathering of Negro artists"—reveals a great deal about race relations in early twentieth-century America.

Though opinions on the acting varied wildly, the white critical community shared one perspective—almost total ignorance of the stars on the African American Stage in New York and around the country. Advance notices for the three plays that appeared in influential white dailies reported the date and place of the opening performance, identified the playwright, producer, and director/stage artist but mentioned none of the actors scheduled to appear. The *New York Times* and *New York Tribune,* for example, included biographical information on the three white sponsors of the play but mentioned none of the actors.[48] Some, like the brief announcements that appeared in *Variety* and the *New York Evening Post,* did not even mention the playwright by name, noting instead the fact that "a company of colored performers" would appear on a Broadway stage.[49] But even Robert Benchley, invited to a rehearsal just days before the premiere of the plays, named none of the stars in the show. Instead, he insisted that few of the performers "have been acting in negro stock companies, for it was found that long association with melodrama and comedy written for white actors had made them less natural in their speech, more stagy in their gesture and not so well adapted to the expression of the pure African as those who have not imitated themselves away from it."[50] By contrast, the *New York Age* began announcing the premiere in early March—even before a full cast had been assembled—and in the final announcement, Walton identified Hapgood as the producer, Robert Edmond Jones, "the well-known stage artist," as director, Ridgely Torrence as the playwright, and "Blanche Deas, Lottie Grady, Inez Clough, Mme. Marie Jackson-Stuart, Alex Rogers, Jesse A. Shipp, Andrew Bishop and other actors of ability and promise" as members of the cast.[51] But interestingly enough, even Walton did not include brief resumes of the leading actors in the show, as one could expect to find in white reviews of white Broadway shows.

After seeing a performance, however, drama critics almost always commented on the quality of the acting, and some singled out specific players for particular praise. By far the most popular performer in the company—especially among white critics—was Opal Cooper. Louis Sherwin identified Cooper as a "cabaret entertainer in Harlem who had never been on stage before in his life," and insisted that his portrayal was "something I shall never forget," for "no white actor could have even remotely approached the robust, exuberant vitality of his performance."[52] Clayton Hamilton, likewise unaware of Cooper's professional experience, praised the "gigantic and amiable negro hitherto unknown to fame, named Opal Cooper."[53] Heywood Broun, too, raved about Cooper's performance, which he believed would have been "impossible" for a "white player" to match. "We do not think that anyone but a negro could carry the scene in which the black man triumphantly chants of the dream which has shown him the way to fortune. Here the actor was at his best. He revelled in his lines. We can remember hardly any other performer who conveyed the sense of ecstasy as this negro actor did last night."[54] Two other reviewers, however, so completely unfamiliar with the black performers, confused Opal Cooper with Joseph Burt, who played Booker Sparrow.[55] At the end of the season, George Jean Nathan placed both Cooper and Inez Clough on his top ten lists for male and female Broadway actors.

If Opal Cooper elicited nearly unanimous praise, Marie Jackson-Stuart drew the most uneven commentary. Heywood Broun devoted one of his "In Wigs and Wings" columns in the *New York Tribune* to Jackson-Stuart. Her tour-de-force performance did much "to convince us of our ignorance on the matter of acting." Jackson-Stuart, Broun insisted, "had one of the most stirring voices we had heard in a season. She had dignity, authority and fire, and she played with blessed restraint."[56] Francis Hackett noted "real limitations" in Jackson-Stuart's portrayal of Granny Maumee, but, he confessed, "I found myself curiously thrilled whenever she raised her empty gaze and declared 'My eyes will yit behold!' "[57] Arthur Hornblow, certainly less enthusiastic than Broun and Hackett, noted only that "Marie Jackson-Stuart had several speeches of a length that would tax any memory," and that she had not forgotten any of her lines.[58] Torrence, however, considered Jackson-Stuart the weak link in the company. In response to his lament, Torrence's mother wrote, "I am sorry you could not acquire a good actress to take the part of Granny Maumee—it is a thrilling play when it is acted right."[59] And Mary Burrill of Washington, D. C., suggested that Torrence audition Emma Lee Williams as a replacement for Jackson-Stuart, as she had "considerable dramatic talent" and a "rich musical voice."[60]

On the whole, the critical community divided into two camps on the matter of acting, and the assessments, whether positive or negative, were laden with racial assumptions. The first camp, convinced that none of the players had any training or experience, praised the naturalness of the performances. The review that appeared in the *New York American,* for example, touted the "company of non-professional and largely untrained negro actors" as having "a natural dramatic expression."[61] Louis Sherwin, berated the "curious" and "despicable" snobbishness of fellow whites who had heretofore kept black actors off the stages of Broadway. "[T]here is in the race a lack of the self-consciousness that gives them a greater natural aptitude for acting and various forms of song," he argued. "They have a peculiar idiom in their speech and their music."[62] Francis Hackett believed the actors displayed "unusual power and charm" in spite of "much amateurishness." Had they been "Puritans," he wrote, "perhaps they would not speak so musically. Thank the Lord they were not Puritans.

Besides their speech there is . . . a real capacity for creating illusion."[63] And in a rather backhanded compliment, the critic for the *New York Evening Post* highlighted the actors' "feeling," "humor," "genuine emotion" and "intuition," which shone through in spite of "insufficient training and experience" and the "appearance of woodenness." The explanation this writer offered for the "angularity, stiffness, and hesitancy" of the performance rested on the assumption that African Americans lacked the intelligence needed to move from thought to action. "The whole secret of what is known as spontaneity in acting lies in the facility and rapidity with which the mental design is translated into outward expression," a lesson that amateurs—"the majority of these players are yet in this category"—have to learn.[64] These tributes to the actors reflected certain ideas the critics held about appropriate expression by African Americans—it was "natural," "instinctive," "unself-conscious," and "intuitive." As good qualities in a performance, they conveyed the natural condition of the characters in the plays—primitive and uneducated.

The second camp of critics found little to praise in the performance of the actors, because they felt that the acting was not up to the white standard on Broadway. The *New York Evening Post* critic prefaced his evaluations of the black actors with the remark that "nothing, of course, could be more ridiculous or unjust" than to judge "the actors by the established high standards of the professional white theater." Many, of course, *did* compare black acting to white and found it hopelessly deficient. Burns Mantle did not expect the "colored players to equal in any particular the performance of the white actors," so he was not especially disappointed by their inferior histrionic abilities. Instead of investing large sums of money "to prove them good imitators," however, Mantle thought they should have been given money to develop a "dramatic literature for their stage."[65] Alexander Woollcott, by far the most savage in his criticism of the blacks' performances, saw the decision to use African American actors to play "various and exacting roles" as one that led "perhaps inevitably— to a disturbingly and needlessly inadequate performance. Mr. Torrence's plays are badly acted at the Garden—quite too badly acted. . . . Now and then the presence of a genuine negro in the cast illumines one of Mr. Torrence's touches splendidly, but these rewards are few and the price is high. For the most part a Broadway cast of average competence could have served the plays far, far better."[66] Heywood Broun tried to neutralize Woollcott's caustic remarks a month later by noting that if the flamboyant critic of the *New York Times* had been in charge of the production, he would "first get a burnt cork and then Mrs. Fiske."[67]

Between these two camps, the African American actors could find little room to lay a foundation for a tradition of praiseworthy acting in America.

Implicit in the praise lay the idea that gaining experience and training would spoil their naturalness, and at bottom this view carried the notion that African Americans were uncultivated people, therefore only uncultivated actors could portray them. James Weldon Johnson conveyed this idea in an article for the *New York Evening Post* in which he attempted to explain why blacks had been barred from white stages until 1917. "The Negro's place on the American stage, has always been limited and circumscribed. The idea that a colored performer could do anything else besides making an audience laugh seems rarely to have entered a manager's head. This attitude," he explained, "has been due largely to the popular national conception of the Negro as a happy-go-lucky, laughing, shuffling, banjo-picking being; a conception which ignores the other side of the truth—that the life of every thinking Negro in the United States is part of a great tragedy."[68]

The lack of training, opportunity, breadth, and experience that was rued by Johnson but lauded by the black actors' defenders, came in for scorn when it was applied to the white theatrical community. At the turn of the century, critics like Norman Hapgood had blasted commercial theaters for restricting the range of roles actors could perform. Actors who worked for the likes of Charles Frohman, he argued, "cannot then have a repertory, but at best one part a year." The result was that actors lacked versatility, depth, range, and general acting ability.[69] A decade and a half later, with the emergence of various stock companies and Little Theaters in New York, critics hailed the new opportunities for actors to gain experience and to broaden their acting range. The *New York Times* quoted David Bispham, a prominent figure in the city's theater circles: "If we are to have more virile things we must have actors who are equipped to do them properly. The only way we are going to develop our actors and equip them properly is to give them a chance to establish their versatility." The audience's enthusiasm for "type actors," he went on, should not obscure the fact that actors forced to play the same "type" over and over again became "dispirited and imitative."[70] Thus, training or experience (and preferably both) were necessary for white actors whose work had established the "high standards of the professional white theater."

On the other side, those who saw the black performance as "imitative" of, but inferior to, white performance offered no alternative to which the African American thespians could aspire. They were not supposed to try to be like white actors, but they were bound to be judged by the terms set for white performance. What is perhaps hidden in the double standard is the fact that most critics found few *white* actors who matched their histrionic ideal. White actors—no less than the Negro Players—lacked range and versatility; too many women won roles because of their beauty rather than talent; white actors received little training for the stage; and far too many actors paid little "regard to elocution" and were thus products of "the slipshod methods prevalent in the American theatre to-day."[71]

The white performers who were regarded as exemplary for the profession, however, had prepared for stage work in ways remarkably similar to those of the African American stars of Torrence's dramas and of the African American Stage in general. Most had some formal education in the public schools and some, like the stars of the black musical comedy companies, had either attended college or had earned a college degree. They eschewed acting schools, even though such schools appeared in ever growing numbers from the 1880s through the early 1900s. White actors generally developed their talent by working in stock companies and repertory theaters, where they could play a variety of roles—just as many in the cast of *Three Plays for a Negro Theater* had done. Like Leigh Whipper and Aida Overton Walker, white performers observed and copied the styles of successful, more experienced players. And many white actors were, like Alex Rogers, avid readers. In short, except for the fact that their skin tone gave them access to Broadway stages, where critics came to know the actors' looks, voices, styles, and movements, white actors gained experience and a reputation in the same ways that black actors had developed.[72]

But starring on Broadway proved to be a critical advantage for white actors. In the end it is doubtful that many more than a handful of critics agreed with Zit's assertion that *Three Plays for a Negro Theater* were interpreted by a "gathering of negro artists," for artistry demands preparation, training, skill, and self-consciousness. The more generous of the critics offered words of praise undoubtedly meant to encourage these pioneers on the Broadway stage but nevertheless betraying their limited expectations for black expression and their even more limited understanding of the diversity of American Negroes. The harshest critics suggested that "negro artists" was oxymoronic at best. More than three months after the plays closed at the Garrick Theatre, the *New York Sun* ran a lengthy article called "The Negro and the Stage," which offered a final assessment of the place and ability of African American actors on the American Stage. In its brutal conclusion, the essay suggests another layer of meaning in the production:

> Of course, more experienced observers of the theatre know there is no Negro drama in the American theatre, never was and never will be. The Negro as an actor has limitations which would always interfere with his larger influence in the drama. Mrs. Hapgood's experiment was a highly interesting bric-a-brac but nothing more. It was unfortunate for the proclamations of the belated discovery of the Negro Theatre that they

did not appear in the amiable monthly magazines until the men had taken up their careers in the necessary art of white-washing and the women had gone back to the washtub. . . . What the Negro can do for the theatre was well-established long ago. When the famous "Jim Crow" impersonation made the humor of the race immortal its creator copied the gait and manner of a Negro he had seen and studied. The American Negro in later years inspired many comedians, but there were few of the genuine Negroes who really were capable in themselves of any deliberate comedy.

They appeared in Negro minstrelsy a score of years ago; they have been recently seen in musical plays and they occasionally act in the varieties. But as entertainers consciously striving to create laughter by their artistic efforts or even to appeal to more serious emotions they are not successful, there spontaneity and naturalness disappear.[73]

There was no ambivalence in his assessment: African Americans would never succeed as actors; their place was on the working end of a paintbrush or washboard. They could inspire white performers and entertain white audiences but there would be no Negro drama in America. It was clear that blacks were not and never would be white. The essential question raised by much of the critical commentary—and by this piece in particular—dealt with an arena wider than any stage: Can Negroes be American?

CITIZENSHIP AND ART ON THE GREAT WHITE WAY

When asked by an interviewer for the *New York Times* to explain why he had chosen to write plays about Negro Americans, Torrence responded that he had been inspired by the example of the Irish Players. He believed he could do for Negro Americans what Lady Gregory and John Millington Synge had done for the similarly neglected Irish—he could present their lives as novel dramatic material that would help build up a distinctive national theater. "In the Irish Theatre he saw the qualities of a whole race used as dramatic material, and the peculiar talents of that race utilized to give the productions a flavor of their own," the *Times* reported. "Knowing from his experience that the negro race had its qualities quite as distinctive he longed to make the first experiment in the new field."[74] The comparison of Torrence to Synge, Emilie Hapgood to Lady Gregory, and the Negro Players to the Dublin Players found expression in any number of critical reviews of *Three Plays for a Negro Theater*. Indeed, Torrence's motive, as expressed in this interview and elsewhere, struck a responsive chord with drama critics because it coincided with the urgent quest for a distinctive national theatrical tradition.

By the time Torrence and Hapgood produced the three plays, the Irish Theatre had attained international fame and respectability. In addition to Synge, Padraic Colum had become both a representative and enthusiastic spokesman for the movement. And rising as the movement did in the midst of a renewed struggle to obtain home rule, if not complete independence from England, it represented an effort to create a form of national art that arose from the lives of a people struggling to maintain and assert a unique national character. Thus, the theater in Ireland, as imagined by champions of the Irish people, spoke directly to questions of politics and citizenship.

Three Plays for a Negro Theater and the more extensive effort to establish a National Negro Theatre, like the Irish Theatre to which they were compared, brought to the surface important matters of political consequence. Whereas writers like W. E. B. Du Bois reminded fellow citizens that African ancestors had been in North America from the beginning of the seventeenth century and that through the centuries their descendants had tilled the soil, cleared the land, and contributed skill, strength, and loyalty to a developing nation, white artists and writers had imagined an America made up only of Anglo-Saxon people. In 1917, more than fifty years after the end of the Civil War, African Americans, by law, enjoyed the status of citizens, but they were only beginning to find a place in the art of the nation. The commentary surrounding the first appearance in a national drama of any significance shows as well that many white writers still considered the idea of black citizenship problematic. Broadway, like the national theater it hosted, was a Great White Way in more than one sense.

Some writers seemed to have been jarred into an awareness of a dark presence in the United States to which they had given little thought before this historic production. Francis Hackett referred to the production as "an artistic Cinderella"—a sooty, smudged serving girl forced to work while her step-sisters lived in comfort—and the lives they portrayed as "one undiscovered country in emotional America . . . Negro country."[75] The *Drama League Monthly* called the plays "native dramatic works" that showed, "at last, appreciation of one of America's richest dramatic resources." The phrase, "at last," indicated that up to that time this rich resource had been untapped.[76] *Current Opinion* quoted Louis Sherwin as saying that the plays "opened up that sadly neglected storehouse of dramatic material—the life of the American Negro."[77] Elsewhere, Sherwin praised Torrence for showing Americans that "our conception" of African American life was "cheap, narrow, snobbish, and vulgar, and that in ignoring such a fertile source of drama and poetry for so long we had been cheating ourselves out of genuine artistic enjoyment."[78] Clayton Hamilton, discussing the music provided by the Clef Club between the plays, noted that "immortal songs" had come from the musical imagination of "millions of our fellow citizens but thus far, we have not hearkened and, in consequence, we have not heard." Of the plays, Hamilton wrote, "The great thing—the really great thing—about Mrs. Hapgood's project was the opportunity which it afforded to the public of New York to appreciate and realize the magnificence of the negro race. The richest folklore in America is the folklore of the negroes. They have made for us our finest melodies, our most imaginative legends, and they have given us our deepest and most delightful humor. Yet this rich mine of material has, thus far, remained unworked, and scarcely even touched, by our American theatre."[79]

Several themes unite these remarks. One is the recognition that black Americans had been hidden in America, recognition evident in such words as "undiscovered," "neglected," "ignoring," "not hearkened," "unworked," and "scarcely even touched." African Americans lived in the United States, but it was as if they had been invisible until 1917. Another theme involved the intrinsic value of African Americans—a "Cinderella" or soon-to-be-discovered princess, a "rich" and "fertile" resource, a "storehouse" of drama, and a "rich mine." So, in theory, this new discovery promised to be a national asset that would enrich the country and its art. Perhaps most telling of all were the phrases that distinguished "them" from "us." Whose conception was "our conception," and who had been cheating "ourselves" out of artistic pleasure? Who had failed to discover, neglected, ignored, and not hearkened to the emotions, lives, and music of black Americans? "They" had made melodies and legends for "us"; "they" had given "us" humor, according to Clayton Hamilton. But one wonders to whom "our American theater" belonged.

This critical difference between us and them, white and black, crept into many of the reviews. The *New York Evening Journal*'s Zit urged readers to "waive nationality and race" as they considered going to see the three plays, by noticing in part that the Negro Players "do not pretend to talk as the white men. They talk in their own tongue. They act in their own way. The scenery is just what would be expected where they live. . . . They are great in their line of work."[80] In his interview with Djuna Barnes, Opal Cooper claimed to speak for "us colored folks" who hoped "our plays would be given der chance—we are just a little sceptical [*sic*] yet—we comes forth with fear and much tremblin', sir. We're like the mole, sir, hidin' low and keeping powerful quiet—but our hide is valuable." African Americans, according to Cooper, were valuable but vulnerable, hopeful but fearful, and just beginning to emerge from behind the veil. He went on to insist that black actors should not try "to be white" because it "makes a race poor when it does not keep its character clean and pure of other people's." To this lengthy discourse, Barnes volunteered the following observation: "Then you don't want to become Americanized, or like the whites."[81] Where Cooper made a distinction based on race, Barnes linked race and nationality. To become Americanized was to be like whites.

Some critics used the comparison between Torrence's three plays and the Irish Theatre to comment on this fundamental dissimilarity as well. The *New York Sun*'s drama critic noted that Torrence and Jones had "allowed it to become known" that they hoped "to accomplish for the negro" what playwrights in Ireland had done for the Irishmen. "It is not easy to see both situations in just the same light," the critic continued, "although the evident object of the movement launched last night is to develop the negro as a figure in the drama." The two situations in Ireland and the United States were not the same, according to this writer, but how did they differ? The critic did not address this implied question but did go on to proclaim the production of the three plays as "epochal for negro plays and players, as it represented their emancipation from the inertia and prejudice which has heretofore kept them from a general hearing."[82] Three words had slipped out—"emancipation," "inertia," and "prejudice." Slavery, a half-century in the past, continued to haunt African Americans, and the inability to move as well as the willingness to prejudge kept that nightmare alive.

The critic for the *New York Evening Post* offered another perspective on the question. He saw in Torrence's three plays "something like a folk theatre, entirely domestic—if not altogether national—and of an indisputable—if as yet incalculable—racial significance." This writer made a telling distinction in a sentence full of hesitation. "Domestic" versus "national" suggests something within the boundaries of the country but not entirely of the nation. The critic could not argue with the "racial significance" of the plays, but he also could not measure it. Perhaps he did not wish to confront the possibility of racial equality.[83] Clayton Hamilton also hesitated when comparing the three plays of Torrence to those of the Irish Theatre. "The negroes imagined and recorded so sympathetically by Ridgely Torrence," he wrote, "are related just as nearly to ourselves as the Irishmen imagined and recorded by John M. Synge are related to the theatre-going public of London."[84] By seeing Negro Americans in relation to "ourselves" as something akin to the relationship between the Irish and the English amounted to a view of African Americans as a separate people occupying a distinct region and desirous of a separate nation. But few black Americans in 1917, and none of those who took part in this historic production, saw their situation in such separate terms. They were Americans. They did not want anything more than their rightful place as American citizens.

Ridgely Torrence's friend and one-time lover, Zona Gale, touched on these issues in a laudatory essay for *Theatre Arts Magazine*. "To do for the negro theatrically what has been done for the Irish by the Irish Theatre movement is magnificently worth while," she began. "This is to interpret to the public—and perhaps to itself—a race never yet understood in a land which is not of its own choosing." By drawing on African American experience for dramatic material, American playwrights could "develop a new medium for artistic expression, with new graces, new freedom, an atmosphere indefinably other. We look into hearts where we are not accustomed to look. We find here dignities and withdrawals and a something walled in beyond the power of any ruling race to dominate." This passage, while unquestionably sympathetic to her old friend's artistic endeavor, reflects a number of subtle distinctions worth noting. "The public" and the race "itself" are presented as two separate entities, which means, at bottom, that the former exists without the latter; the public is white. Black American life as raw material for artistic expression remains "indefinably other," which states the difference more directly. In proclaiming the indomitability of black character, Gale nevertheless says without equivocation that black Americans have been subject to a "ruling race" that has tried to dominate them.

The most curious phrase of all, however, is near the beginning—"a race never yet understood in a land which is not of its own choosing." Obviously, Gale is here acknowledging the forced migration to America of Africans aboard slave ships in the seventeenth, eighteenth, and nineteenth centuries. But the lives portrayed in Torrence's plays either predated slavery in North America by more than a millennium or occurred after the end of the Civil War. The Granny Maumees and Madison Sparrows of the country had not chosen the United States as the nation of their birth, but for that matter, neither had Zona Gale. In short, Gale's essay betrayed doubts about the nationality of African Americans in the twentieth century. Later in the essay, in her plot summaries of the two modern plays, Gale remarked that *Granny Maumee* and *The Rider of Dreams* "both make one gasp—as does the revelation, say, about 'some disturbance of the Indians by drunken whites.' " She goes on to discuss Granny's pride in her "royal black" lineage and Madison Sparrow being "led into temptation and put upon by the white men." Of these bizarre situations Gale wrote, "One is not accustomed to see either one's race or one's nation regarded impersonally. Only other races, other nations." In other words, this writer "gasped" at the thought that her race and her nation—a white race and a white nation—could be viewed in something other than flattering terms. But what Gale saw was not a biracial nation in which unfortunate, deplorable incidents happened, but her white nation exposed to shame.[85]

Critics and commentators who wrote of the plays and African American actors in terms that distinguished "them" from "us," "their" art from

"American" art, and "domestic" from "national" provide important clues as to how the production and the idea it represented were received. The hesitation, the gasping, and the outright denial of African American participation in national art—responses prevalent in reviews written by white writers—points to a conclusion of enormous political significance. Even writers supportive of Torrence's plays and Hapgood's production could not bring themselves to embrace Negro Americans as fellow citizens or to revise their view of national art to include the lives, talents, and perspectives of nonwhite people. Moreover the narratives they wove out of the various elements in the plays and the assessments they included in their published commentary provided their readers with ways of considering the novelty of black actors on Broadway without challenging their opinions on the "race question."

By contrast, African American commentators linked the fortunes of African Americans on stage with the national drama of the United States. W. E. B. Du Bois believed that the *Three Plays for a Negro Theater* was the first effort to give "the American stage a drama that will lift it above silly songs and leg shows." As he saw it, the "American world" was not a "white world," but one that included every skin tone from "white" to "dark brown." With the Torrence plays and the Negro Players, Du Bois hoped that audiences would finally get some picture of Negro Americans other than "startling caricatures."[86] James Weldon Johnson noted that "some white people" would not like the plays "because they prefer the so-called 'Negro Comedy' which generally centers around a colored man and a chicken." Torrence's plays called upon actors to perform with artistic seriousness, and their success, Johnson insisted, "will mean a permanent place for the Negro in the dramatic world, and the beginning of a future for great Negro actors and Negro dramatists."[87] Lester Walton concluded his lengthy review of the three plays with the prophecy that "Negro plays, acted by Negroes, will furnish the stage with a wealth of romantic material. The drama, America and the negro will greatly profit by this daring and unique move in the interest of 'Art for art's sake.' "[88]

Even these brief excerpts from black reviews of the three plays, however, reveal important distinctions. Like the white reviewers, who seemed to assume that their readers would be white, black reviewers assumed their readers would be black. They wondered aloud what white Americans would think and say about the Negro performances. They did so not to invalidate white citizenship, but to point out the contradiction between the American ideal of democracy and racial discrimination. Walton put the matter most eloquently in a comment on the "mission of the stage." The "Negro play can play a most important part in the solving of one of America's most vexatious problems, made so in large measure because of the average white American's misconstruction of and indifference to what the Negro is really thinking and doing," he wrote. " 'Getting the Negro right' without 'getting the Caucasian right' will never bring about the desired racial amity in this country. The white man must be emancipated from some of the foolish notions he entertains about all colored peoples. As he does not visit our homes, our schools, or our churches in large numbers, the stage must be employed to visualize Negro life and point out to the white American the inconsistencies of color prejudice." *Three Plays for a Negro Theater,* he believed, were "one-hundred per cent American."[89]

Du Bois, Johnson, and Walton recognized that white opinions of the dramas mattered because racial inequality rested on ideas and misperceptions. If those ideas, which held that African Americans were only provisional citizens, could be changed and if those misperceptions, based on ignorance and separation, could be corrected, then one of America's "most vexatious problems," as Walton put it, could be solved. Solving the problem of racism meant much more than permitting blacks to perform on Broadway, although the stage played an important part in the solution. For these African American writers a black presence in America's theaters—"the regular theater going public," as Johnson called Broadway audiences—securely tied the world of entertainment to the world of politics. When American dramas reflected the rich variety of American complexions—"White shading into every beautiful color from cream to dark brown," in Du Bois's words—then the Great White Way would describe only the bright lights in the theater district of New York and art and citizenship would be shared in America.

The division in the critical commentary on *Three Plays for a Negro Theater* along racial lines, however, suggests that Negro actors and black dramas had not altered prevailing ideas about African Americans or race relations in the United States in 1917. The plays themselves—as literature, as performances, and as a production—contained many crosscurrents and contradictions. But of all of the messages that could have been derived from them, reviewers tended to pick up on only a few. African American critics saw the plays in opposition to conditions prevailing in the United States. The white majority, whose reviews and essays in the New York dailies and in periodicals devoted to the theater made the Negro Players, Torrence's dramas, and Hapgood's production the talk of the town, picked up on the least flattering, least challenging interpretations of the dramas. They found language to discuss the events at the Garden and Garrick Theatres that made it possible to avoid fundamental rethinking of race relations in the country. They could praise the plays because they saw in characters like Granny Maumee and Madison Sparrow figures they expected to find in the black community. Many did not recognize the "inconsistencies of color prejudice," because they did not see any white villains. And when they commented on the performances of black actors or on the deep significance of Negro plays they managed to weave into their critical assessments their doubts about including dark-skinned people in a national "we." Thus, the production of these dramas about Negro American life, on which the black theatrical community pinned hopes for greater racial understanding, were rather quickly forgotten. White critics saw this dramatic "first" in familiar light that reinforced their ideas about blacks as "natural" comedians, superstitious and menacing, and inferior in ability to whites. With little that was new, there was little to remember.

But looked at another way, the fact that the plays appeared and that prominent critics commented on them suggests that something was happening. A subject of profound social significance occupied New York critics in the spring of 1917—race relations and national art were considered together. The "discovery" of a hidden "resource," the "rich vein" of black experience, and even the painful awareness of an American legacy of injustice against black citizens, all point to a new wrinkle in the cultural fabric of the nation. If critics evaded some issues, recast the basic elements of Torrence's plots, or trotted out the tired, racist language of the day, they nevertheless also recognized race dramas as legitimate subjects for debate. At worst, they tried to shore up the barrier separating blacks and whites even as they saw the possibilities in race as a dramatic theme. At best, they felt the pain, the embarrassment, and the unpleasantness of the drama of race relations in America.

Thus, the critical reception alone does not completely explain the cultural amnesia that set in after *Three Plays for a Negro Theater* closed at the Garrick Theatre. The decision of the United States to enter the Great War in Europe was made and announced the day after the opening performance of the three dramas. The coming of war meant calling upon citizens to fight in a foreign war in the name of democracy. It is not merely that war eclipsed the theater, but rather that war talk—of citizenship, fitness for service, loyalty to the nation, willingness to serve—conditioned discussions about race. As Americans prepared for war, the plays and the people whose lives they presented faded once more into obscurity.

6

TIMING IS EVERYTHING

"All who hear the Clef Club Band sing the negro folksongs [*sic*] in connection with the negro plays at the Garrick will earnestly believe that among this people are several songs that alone have the reality of suffering and longing and hope, that simple appeal of earth and toil, together with the necessary marching qualities to move men.

And what could be more appropriate than to have the negro, virtual slaves now as before, in the lead and supplying the keynote for those who have now for their purpose the thrusting of freedom and democracy upon Germany!"

J. J. L., New York Tribune, April 30, 1917

O N APRIL 2, 1917, Woodrow Wilson presented a resolution to a special session of Congress, calling for the United States to declare war on Germany. The country would be fighting, he argued, "for the ultimate peace of the world and for the liberation of its people, the German peoples included: for the rights of nations great and small and the privilege of men everywhere to choose their way of life and obedience. The world must be made safe for democracy. Its peace must be planted upon the tested foundations of political liberty."[1] Two days later, the Senate overwhelmingly endorsed the president's resolution, and two days after that, the House of Representatives approved it as well. The United States, though still months away from sending troops to Europe, considered itself at war with Germany. On the night that the Senate passed Wilson's war resolution, the president attended the Belasco Theatre in the nation's capital to see *Very Good Eddie,* a show that only recently had left Broadway. A press release sent to the most influential metropolitan dailies reported, "The orchestra played 'The Star Spangled Banner' and as the President was recognized the audience rose for a tumultuous demonstration."[2] The theater served as a site for a patriotic display.

The next day another historic event took place in a theater—*Three Plays for a Negro Theater* opened at the Garden Theatre in New York. They, too, were greeted with enthusiastic applause. The evening's entertainment also featured music—African American folk songs and instrumental pieces. Here the comparison ends. In the weeks and months that followed, Americans increasingly became absorbed in the European conflict while the memory of the glorious opening night at the Garden Theatre faded and eventually all but disappeared.

Chroniclers who kept alive the memory of the historic production of the three one-act race dramas insisted in later years that the coincidence of war with the Broadway run of *Three Plays for a Negro Theater* resulted in the upstaging of the theater by the weightier matter of impending conflict. James Weldon Johnson remembered in *Black Manhattan* that the "increasing stress of the war . . . crushed" the innovative production, and W. E. B. Du Bois in *The Gift of the Black Folk* saw the play as part of a movement to "initiate a Negro Theatre" in America, a movement "interrupted by the war."[3] Torrence's chief biographer, John Clum, writing in the early 1970s, picked up on these themes, arguing that "an important factor in the failure of the plays at the box office may well have been the United States' declaration of war on the day after the plays' opening. With such momentous front-page news, few people probably bothered to read the reviews."[4] A little over a decade later, Freda L. Scott repeated the oft-told tale in an article on race dramas and the Harlem Renaissance by noting: "Unfortunately, the show opened the day before the United States entered World War I and its potential run was stunted."[5]

This interpretation of the aborted beginning of African American performance in legitimate theaters on Broadway promotes the idea that the production, because it was a form of entertainment, could not compete with the more serious matter of war. The war "crushed" interest in the plays, "interrupted" the movement to advance race dramas, accounts for their "failure" at the box office, "stunted" the run, and diverted attention away from the critical raves. The war no doubt did affect the success of Torrence's three dramas, but not for the reasons these writers have offered. It was not the impending conflict itself that doomed the production, but the national self-consciousness that accompanied preparations for battle that made the implicit critique of race relations in America unpalatable and troubling.

More than three weeks after the United States decided to enter the Great War in Europe on the side of England and France, a writer identified only by the initials "J. J. L." wrote a letter to the editor of the *New York Tribune*. In typical fashion, the letter had a title—"Our War Song from the Negro"—and the gist of the writer's message was that the country needed a war song as inspiring as the famous Irish song *Tipperary*. Unmistakably tongue-in-cheek, if not openly a statement against America's involvement in the war across the Atlantic, J. J. L.'s letter proposed deriving a U.S. war song from African American folk songs currently being performed at the Garrick Theatre by the Clef Club Orchestra between the one-act plays presented by the Negro Players. The songs, this writer observed, struck just the right note of "suffering and longing and hope," and they contained the "marching qualities" needed to "move men." In the final paragraph of the letter, J. J. L. cut to the heart of the hypocrisy of the United States' entry into the war. "And what could be more appropriate than to have the negro, virtual slaves now as before, in the lead and supplying the keynote for those who have now for their purpose the thrusting of freedom and democracy upon Germany!"[6] J. J. L., inspired by the Clef Club's performance between Torrence's three one-act plays, pointed out the inconsistency of a nation, still divided between free and slave, setting out to make the world safe for democracy.

J. J. L.'s letter to the *New York Tribune* suggests that in spite of what critics had written about them, the plays conveyed a clear message that was not lost on those who witnessed them. If the plays in part reinforced the writer's view that Negro Americans remained as unfree in 1917 as they had been before the Civil War, then something of the intentions of the cast and the playwright might have gotten through to the audience. If white lynch mobs burned innocent black men at hitching posts, if white confidence men preyed upon black hopes for economic security, and if white employers "des would have their way" with black servants, then how could the United States justifiably carry the banner of justice and liberty into a world at war? This letter, though only one among the hundreds on other subjects that appeared in dailies in New York and across the country, suggests that some Americans in 1917—unlike the majority of drama critics—were prepared to face the challenge posed by the pioneering race dramas on Broadway.

The letter also anticipated a problem confronting the Wilson adminis-tration, the solution of which would ultimately work against the general acceptance of *Three Plays for a Negro Theater* and their incorporation into American culture. The problem involved explaining the nation's war aims to a population who had reelected Wilson *because* "He Kept Us Out of War." The solution included a barrage of "patriotic" images, slogans, and campaigns that defined the point of going to war, that discussed the principles for which the nation stood, and that were overwhelmingly "white" in their orientation.[7] Unlike other wars in which the country's leaders could point to a clear and present danger to the sovereignty of the nation or in which the declaration of war followed close on the heels of a direct attack on U.S. citizens, property, or military installations, the Great War had not posed the same kind of immediate threat. Although U.S. citizens had died aboard the *Lusitania,* which was sunk by German submarines, the attack had taken place in 1915, two years before Congress voted to support a declaration of war. In his study of Missouri in these years, Christopher C. Gibbs has shown that the First World War represented an extremely unpopular conflict among the men and women of the "Show Me" state, and he speculates that their opposition was not singular.[8] Americans across the country demanded that their government show them the necessity of war before they sent their sons across the sea armed and in uniform, before they bought Liberty Bonds or planted Liberty Gardens, and before they rescinded their support for Senator Robert La Follette's War Referendum.

In the end, Americans did follow their leaders' call to arms, and before the war ended, more than one hundred thousand citizens—including blacks and whites—gave their lives in the Allied cause. In the course of mobilizing the nation to fight in the "war to end all war," various cultural figures enlisted in the cause of creating self-consciousness about the nation's essential character, and they gave expression in posters, newsreels, song lyrics, speeches, and advertisements to an America for which they believed the majority of Americans would be willing to fight. They flooded the media with their ideas and imagery, thus creating a highly charged atmosphere in which any discussion pertaining to American culture would take place. It was in this context of hoary, gaunt-faced Uncle Sams, rosy-cheeked cherubs harvesting the fruits of their Liberty Gardens, and white goddesses of Liberty bravely fending off the monstrous Huns that the critical discussion of the Negro Players, *The Rider of Dreams,* *Granny Maumee,* and *Simon, the Cyrenian* took place. Given the unflattering image of race relations implicit in the plays, their cultural substance cut against the grain of the war-inspired debate about the meaning of America heating up in the spring and summer of 1917. Talk of the war conditioned talk of the plays, upsetting the timing of actors delivering such controversial lines about the country. And as veterans of the stage well know, timing is everything.

The coming of war did not present bad timing for all those involved in the theater and in the field of entertainment. Two days after the passage of the war resolution, George S. Kaufman voiced the concerns of many theater people that the war would bring show business to a crashing halt, but he predicted that after a slight slump in the first shock of war, "interest in the theatre" would "revert to normal soon."[9] Others saw the war as a grand opportunity for American playwrights. Lawrence Southerland proclaimed in May 1917, "To-day when America's international relations were never more critical, and when the eyes of every American are turned eagerly to Washington, the time is ripe for a big patriotic play voicing the sentiments of our people. The native dramatist," he believed, "never had a more splendid opportunity."[10] A few months later Clayton Hamilton echoed Southerland's call, arguing, "The conditions are so ripe that the opportunity has become an obligation. Our public desires and demands a certain number of serious dramas every season; and for the first time in the history of our theatre, conditions require manifestly that these serious plays should be written about American life by American authors."[11]

For some theater people, those with the right kind of play about "American life," the war proved propitious. While *Three Plays for a Negro Theater* were playing at the Garden Theatre, the Globe Theatre featured a play by Hartley Manners called *Out There*. James Metcalfe, normally caustic in the face of substandard drama and performance, called the play "an inspiration" and "a stimulant to patriotism for Americans men and women both" even though he conceded that "it would not be hard to point out flaws in the dramatic construction of Mr. Manners's play" or to show how the leading lady "failed to reach the possibilities of her role." Metcalfe explained that the troubled times required a different kind of criticism. "The theatre is more than scenes, speeches and impersonations," he began. "An institution so close to the hearts and minds of the public may be profitably considered on grounds broader, particularly in times like these, than whether what it does is well or badly done." The basic message of the play, he thought, must be considered as well. And *Out There*, "coming just at the moment when it does, when America needs an incentive to the putting aside of individual gain and individual comfort for the country's good . . . seems to have a special mission and to accomplish it well."[12] Alexander Woollcott of the *New York Times* agreed with Metcalfe. *Out There*, he proclaimed, "is a play of the moment and for the moment. It has been brought forward in New York at a time so psychologically right as to be the envy of every counting house on the Rialto." As an "uncomplicated, unperplexed study of patriotism," *Out There* "strikes a hundred chords strung tight by the great events to which we march."[13]

The problem for Torrence's three dramas and the cast who performed them was not that they clashed with a world war. Rather, some of the messages they carried clashed with the desired self-image of a nation in the process of convincing itself to go to war. The actors and the themes they developed were black; the desired self-image was white. The dramas exposed a national legacy of injustice, but Americans wanted to fight for what was right. And the call for patriotic plays of, by, and for America was a call to citizen dramatists and performers. As the national crisis deepened, African Americans found themselves in a steep, uphill battle to claim their birthright as Americans on the field of battle as well as on the stages of the Great White Way.

WAR FOR BLACK CITIZENSHIP

If some Americans questioned the "Americanness" of plays about African American life acted by Negro American performers, it was because many questioned the "Americanness" of Negroes. Although half a century separated the nation preparing to face a European enemy in 1917 from the nation divided against itself in civil war in the 1860s, the intervening decades had done little to establish the validity of Negro citizenship inscribed in the Thirteenth, Fourteenth, and Fifteenth Amendments to the Constitution. Between Jim Crow, lynching, poll taxes, and the threat of terrorism by white supremacists, the rights guaranteed by the Constitution were not always enjoyed by African American citizens of the United States. Eloquent editorials by such journalists as Lester Walton, W. E. B. Du Bois, and James Weldon Johnson, as well as such grassroots campaigns as the effort to stamp out racial discrimination in the theaters, went largely unheeded on the other side of the color line.

If the quotidian struggle for dignity and the occasional victories against Jim Crow gave African Americans hope for improving their status and the opportunities available to them, the wartime rhetoric of their white countrymen reminded them of their exclusion from the American mainstream. Even before Wilson's war resolution passed the House of Representatives, the debate over Negro loyalty and Negro qualifications as soldiers had begun. The Universal Service Bill prepared by Republican representatives included African American troops in the plan for military training, a provision that elicited a howl from white southerners. The *New York Evening Post* reported on April 5, 1917, that "the negro question" was going to "cause controversy in the present session of Congress" as it considered the matter of "universal military service." While ranking Republicans vowed to fight to include blacks in the armed services, their southern colleagues on the other side of the aisle fumed vehemently against the idea. " 'We of the South cannot stand for the inclusion of negroes in the universal service plan,' " the report quoted a South Carolinian as saying. " 'It would bring down upon the districts where negroes far exceed the whites in number a danger far greater than any foreign foe.' " The image of " 'placing . . . arms in the hands of a large number of negroes and . . . training them to work together in organized units,' " represented " 'the very thing which the South has always fought against.' " The old antebellum fear of armed insurrection by slaves had not dissipated in the fifty-five years since

Emancipation. Revealing, too, was the observation that black citizen soldiers were more dangerous than a "foreign foe."[14]

As Congressional debate over whether or not Negro Americans could serve in their country's military raged, another concern arose. In early 1917 reports began to circulate in the media that Germans planned to destabilize the United States by planting propaganda among African Americans to urge disloyalty. A federal investigation into the charge revealed no evidence to support it. A trustee of the Hampton Institute, Dr. William J. Schieffelin, was quoted as saying that blacks' " 'record in every national crisis ought to be held sufficient to give us every confidence that they will be loyal and true Americans.' "[15]

Apparently that record did not suffice. A flood of statements affirming their loyalty issued forth from African Americans across the country. A typical response was that of William Holtzclaw, an African American educator in Utica, New York, who sent an exasperated letter to the editor of the *New York Evening Post*. "I cannot understand how anyone familiar with the history of the negro can question his loyalty," he wrote. "The negro has proved his patriotism from the Boston Massacre to Corrizal. He has suffered much at the hands of his countrymen, but still this is his country, and in my opinion he will stand with Decatur in the feeling that: 'My Country; may she ever be right, but right or wrong, My Country.' "[16] Students and faculty members at Wilberforce University organized a patriotic rally at the African American institution in Ohio. After speeches by Dr. Scarborough and Hallie Q. Brown, the assemblage "repudiated strongly" the report about Germans trying to stir up revolts among African Americans. The students then passed "patriotic resolutions" and "declared themselves ready to defend the flag."[17] A few days later, in nearby Xenia, portions of Robert Russa Moton's letter to Woodrow Wilson pledging blacks' loyalty, appeared in the local newspaper. The journalist who prepared the essay concluded that the Negro "will do as he always has done—prove loyal to the American Flag."[18] Even the *New York World* concluded an editorial on "Negro Patriotism" with the resounding assertion: "There is not the least question about the quality of their Americanism."[19]

Up to the summer of 1917, the conflict over black loyalty to and black citizenship in the United States had been principally a war of words—words that shaped the conversation about such matters as race dramas in American culture. In July, however, the war of words gave way to shooting, burning, murder, and riot in East St. Louis. For more than a year, local manufacturers in East St. Louis had recruited African Americans from Mississippi and western Tennessee as well as recently arrived immigrants to work in their businesses in the hope of breaking the power of unions over their labor force. In the aftermath of a strike in late 1916, for example, managers of the Aluminum

Ore Company began hiring African American workers in large numbers, as had the Missouri Malleable Iron Works and other industrial concerns in the area. The unions refused to offer membership to the black workers and considered them instead to be strikebreakers. Throughout the month of June, spasmodic violence by disgruntled white union men against what they saw as African American intruders set the tone for the race war that exploded on July 2, 1917.[20]

By the time order had been restored, thousands of African Americans had lost their homes, hundreds had been killed, and hundreds of thousands of dollars in property had been destroyed. According to Congressman L. C. Dyer of Missouri, one witness "saw members of the militia of Illinois shoot Negroes. He saw policemen of East St. Louis shoot Negroes. He saw this mob go to the homes of these Negroes and nail boards up over the doors and windows and then set fire and burn them up. He saw them take little children out of the arms of their mothers and throw them into the fires and burn them up." Dyer estimated that altogether more than five hundred people had been killed.[21] An Illinois Congressman concurred that "conditions there at the time beggar description." A ten-year-old boy whose mother had been shot was gunned down as he ran about sobbing for her, and before he was dead, someone threw his body into the flames. Another woman and her two-year-old baby were shot, then burned. "The most sickening things I ever heard of were described in the letters that I received from home giving details of the attack."[22]

The National Association for the Advancement of Colored People hired lawyers to defend the African Americans who were blamed for the riot. They met to discuss ways of protesting against the outrages perpetrated in East St. Louis. Within about three weeks of the riot, they had organized a massive, silent march down Fifth Avenue in New York City. The banners carried by the ten thousand men, women, and children who proceeded wordlessly down Fifth Avenue from Fifty-seventh Street to Twenty-third Street articulated the issues at stake in this war between the races. "Make America Safe for Democracy," read one; "We are Maligned as Lazy and Murdered When We Work," read another. Other banners reminded onlookers of African American participation in past wars—"The First Blood for American Independence Was Shed by a Negro— Crispus Attucks," "12,000 of Us Fought with Jackson at New Orleans," "3,000 Negroes Fought for Independence Under George Washington," and "200,000 Black Men Fought for Your Liberty in the Civil War." Perceiving themselves as genuine patriots, the marchers carried American flags, and according to one observer did nothing "which smacked of outlawry, bitterness, disloyalty, or radicalism"—nothing "anarchistic" or "un-American."[23]

Recognizing the inconsistencies in a nation fighting a war overseas in the name of democracy and Christianity but treating its citizens of color in undemocratic and unchristian ways did not prevent African Americans from responding to the call to arms. Leaders like W. E. B. Du Bois urged black Americans to "close ranks," set aside the battle for fair treatment at home in the interest of a greater battle abroad.[24] Black institutions like Fisk University also urged young African American men not to "rock the boat," because the nation is at war. "This is the war of the people of the United States," wrote an editorialist in October 1917, "for all of them are being asked in one way or another to carry some of its burdens. All of us are together in the same boat on the sea of war."[25] War songs written by African Americans also reflected their determination to support the war effort. The Reverend J. H. Hubbard of the Ebenezer Methodist Episcopal Church in Jacksonville, Florida, penned lyrics to *The Soul Cry of the Colored Soldier* (1917) that promised:

> You may count me ever loyal to the call of Uncle Sam,
> I'm a gallant colored soldier; yes, a fighting Son of Ham.

Lester Walton made unity the centerpiece of a song, *All for One, One for All*, he wrote in 1918.[26] Even African American radicals like A. Philip Randolph acknowledged black support for the war. The *Messenger* blasted the NAACP for forfeiting a golden opportunity to point out that the United States was "fighting *to make the world safe for democracy* . . . while the Negro at home, though bearing the burden in every way, is denied economic, political, educational and civil democracy. And this despite his loyalty and patriotism in the land of the free and the home of the brave!"[27]

Like their white counterparts, young black men came to military camps through selective service or voluntary enlistment, hoping to defend their country's interests. As war approached, some African Americans saw the military as a site where meritorious effort would be rewarded—where able black leaders could assume the rank of officer, for example. In 1915, Captain Richard P. Roots wrote an impassioned letter to Lindley Garrison, secretary of war, asking that the War Department consider creating Negro regiments. He recalled the experience of the black Forty-eighth and Forty-ninth Regiments in the Spanish-American War, noting that the white field and staff officers treated the black line officers "very little better than enlisted men or with no more courtesy." The African American, he argued, is a citizen regardless of all laws to the contrary, and identifies himself as a "new Negro," not one of the " 'Uncle Tom' class, the passing of whom so many white citizens regret." As an American citizen and a new Negro, the African American "wants the same chance as the white man."[28]

Captain Roots's letter raised a subject that would prove to be a touchy one for the duration of the war—a subject that sparked much controversy, conflict, and debate. The doubts displayed in the political arena, socially, culturally, and economically as to the legitimacy of black citizenship in the twentieth century found expression in the military as well. Had there been no question, then the housing, training, and location of as well as opportunities available to black soldiers would have presented no difficulty. But in 1917 and 1918, these matters generated reams of tortured memoranda, daily insults and friction between white and black Americans, occasional outbursts of violence, and an ongoing skirmish on the home front that created ill will between the races and absorbed resources better used in waging war against the foreign enemy.

In August and September 1917, prominent, high-ranking officers considered at least six different plans for black soldiers. One plan called for one black regiment in each of the sixteen projected cantonments across the country, a plan General Bliss considered "dangerous" because "white and colored troops would be organized and armed in the same way." Another plan would locate black soldiers in camps near the main cantonments but "detached" by about a mile, an arrangement that would cost nearly sixteen million dollars. Others proposed concentrating all black soldiers in two cantonments in the South, but "the presence of such very large bodies of colored troops, organized and armed, would meet with great opposition." General Bliss favored plan six, which would suspend the call for black soldiers "for a little while" until the number of white troops had been seriously reduced. Then after only a short stay in stateside camps, the black troops would be trained "under arms" in France.[29]

At the end of his memorandum to the secretary of war, General Bliss conceded that once black troops arrived in France, he anticipated few problems "arising from racial differences. Experience has shown that when troops are once in the field these differences disappear."[30] So a biracial army posed no military threat; rather, the problems sprang from prejudice against blacks on the home front. The sentiments on the domestic scene conditioned the experience of black soldiers. Their assignments depended on the prevailing beliefs about African Americans.

Brigadier General Lytle Brown thought black soldiers were best suited to "lower grades in the supply and ammunition trains," while white troops could be used for "higher grades" including duty at the front. The use of black troops would "release a large number of white men for combatant duty, whose services in that capacity would be more valuable than the services of a corresponding number of colored men."[31] Black soldiers so assigned found themselves under the command of "white men experienced in handling colored labor," not officers of the same race.[32] Moreover, as stevedores, black soldiers were issued blue overalls and brogans rather than regular army uniforms. Black soldiers at Camp Lee objected to being clad in the garb of "servants" and engaged in "involuntary" service while the "white draftees at the camp" were "all excused from service in the stevedore section."[33]

The chief reason given for different treatment of black soldiers was that they were "much inferior" to white soldiers. They came largely from "the ignorant, illiterate, day labor classes," suffered "inferior physical stamina," could not stand up to "strenuous field service" or the "rigors of the damp, cold winter in France," and carried "venereal disease." In short, "the combatant value of colored draft troops" was "considerably lower than that of white draft troops."[34] Given this prevailing view, it is no wonder that high-ranking officers doubted the ability of African Americans to qualify as officers. Brigadier General Henry Jervey, for example, penned a memorandum in July 1918 explaining why so few blacks were officers; they simply were not intelligent in the same proportion, he insisted. Standards at "the white training schools" were established for "white men and if the colored men did not come up to white men's standards they did not receive a commission." The army sought those with "greatest mentality, natural intelligence, initiative and qualities of leadership"—characteristics that for Jervey a priori excluded blacks.[35]

A report issued by the chief of the training and instruction branch of the Army War College, however, casts some doubt on the standards to which those training to be officers were held. The report, which not too surprisingly featured photographs of white officers candidates, noted that "it was impossible to establish conclusively either the fitness or the unfitness" of the students who passed through the course. Although instructors at the Army War College asked soldiers to take part in a series of exercises to test leadership qualities, self-sufficiency, map-reading skills, and creative analysis, and although they rated each soldier's performance, they had established no set standard that would differentiate unqualified candidates from those likely to succeed as officers. Regardless of this admission, the instructors *did* assign a rating to each student who took part in the College. Their decision to label black candidates as "unfit" officer material, thus, may not have reflected their performance on specific tests.[36]

Those African Americans who managed to get the endorsement of their instructors and who made it into the ranks of the officers learned quickly that their rank did not protect them from race prejudice, disrespect, and disobedience. When the commanding officer at Camp Meade, for example, instituted a policy whereby any soldier, white or black, failing to salute a black officer would be subject to court-martial, he came under attack by leaders all across the South. A Congressman from South Carolina lectured the secretary of war that this policy flew in the face of "common sense," because it subjected "young men of southern birth" to "wanton humiliation" and made "southern renunciation of 'prejudice' an army test." The policy, he believed, would interfere with the training of "patriotic and enthusiastic boys for battle."[37]

These attitudes held and actions taken by some of the most powerful men in the United States armed forces set the tone for troubled relations between the races on the home front. In 1917, abuse heaped upon black soldiers and officers in Houston, Texas, prompted a bloody race riot involving black soldiers and white policemen and citizens. Two Negroes and seventeen whites died in the melee; by the end of the year, thirteen black soldiers had died at the gallows, sixteen more awaited execution, and several dozen others faced life in prison.[38] In the nation's capital, laws against "loafing," imposed by the military, targeted black soldiers found in Negro neighborhoods and suspected of visiting prostitutes. White citizens groups organized to oppose the use of black troops to guard the highways leading into and out of Washington. Black coast artillery units were banned because, it was argued, sufficient white units already existed.[39] From location to assignment to training to treatment by civilians, African American soldiers in 1917 and 1918 found themselves reviled in a white military and in a white country.

The three race dramas appeared at a moment when the United States was about to engage in a two-front war—one abroad and one at home. The war atmosphere with its clouds of doubt about Negro American citizenship, loyalty, and patriotism served as a filter through which the theatrical performances were viewed and evaluated. The view expressed by military and political leaders that blacks were mentally, physically, and morally deficient by nature may help explain why Madison Sparrow emerged as the star of the show. He, too, displayed character weaknesses that coincided with the portrait of African Americans with which many Americans were already comfortable and which justified their assignment to the "lower grades" of service. Likewise, Granny Maumee, with her simmering rage against whites, posed a threat no less horrific than large numbers of Negro soldiers organized and armed. And Simon's willingness to bear the cross of Jesus might have reminded audiences of the potency of Christian belief among African Americans, but it was the legacy of servitude and suppression he represented that made the deeper impression. That message, too, cut against the grain of a nation constructing a self-righteous platform from which to denounce oppression and inequality abroad. But perhaps most importantly the plays were about Negroes, and those involved in the production claimed to be shaping American theater. Theater in America in 1917—no less than the armed forces—was a "white organization," and the encroachment of black performers and black themes on the Great White Way was as unwelcome as black combat troops, black officers, and black regiments. The race dramas on Broadway paled in comparison with the drama of race relations in wartime America.

In some respects, however, the struggle over American culture that the appearance of race dramas on Broadway provoked was as serious as the riots, violence, court martials, unequal military assignments, and denial of officers commissions. For culture served as the intellectual bulwark on which the unfair actions rested. The war did not divert attention away from the frivolous land of make-believe. Rather, entertainment itself became serious business, and controlling the content of and participation in this field represented the power to determine what Americans would offer up their lives for and whose America they would defend. In 1917 and 1918, the two fronts of war met on the battlefield of entertainment, and the outcome of that battle made America safe for two-tiered democracy.

CULTURAL SKIRMISHES

In late April, the *New York Herald* ran an article on *Three Plays for a Negro Theater* entitled "Mrs. Emilie Hapgood's Theatrical Negro Novelty an Experiment that Puzzles and Interests Broadway." According to this piece, the Broadway world was "stunned" by Hapgood's decision to produce Negro plays. "Everybody was astonished at this new kink in the progress of the drama. The newspaper reviews on the following morning were found deployed in skirmish order, some many miles from their bases." The battle metaphor, perhaps a result of the preparations for war now underway, signalled a new summary of the commentary on the dramas that had appeared by that time. Instead of noting the general agreement among critics that the plays and players were impressive, this article presented the premiere and the critical response to it as a clash, a "skirmish" that "stunned," "astonished," "interested," and "puzzled" the world of the theater. "Broadway hasn't entirely got its bearings on the production yet," the writer concluded.[40] In early May, W. E. B. Du Bois penned a brief note to Torrence expressing both his gratitude for and encouragement of the playwright's efforts on behalf of African Americans. He, too, employed a wartime metaphor, writing, "Now that the skirmish is over I want to express to you again my deep appreciation of your work and perseverance in beginning the Negro Theatre despite all discouragements. I hope the matter will not stop here."[41] What the *New York Herald* had called "three plays, all worthily done" on April 6, and what Du Bois had hailed, on April 22, as the first plays to elevate the American stage, they now discussed as a "skirmish."[42] The conversation about the plays had begun to be colored by war.

Torrence's three dramas, intended, of course, for civilian audiences, were not the only form of entertainment that caused a cultural skirmish. Those involved in providing entertainment for the troops found themselves in pitched battles over music and drama to be performed in the cantonments at home and behind the lines overseas. They also wrestled with one another over how to present American doughboys to the public in film and newsreels. Moreover, they disagreed over who should be in charge of organizing and providing entertainment. Embedded in all these struggles lay ideas and attitudes about race and citizenship that further explains the role of culture in the wielding of power and in the praising and forgetting of the first African American dramatic performers on Broadway.

Within a month of the passage of the war resolution, Secretary of War Newton Baker began organizing the Commission on Training Camp Activities. He named Raymond B. Fosdick, the brother of the Reverend Harry Emerson Fosdick of New York's Riverside Church, as chair of the commission. Initially, the charge of the Fosdick organization was to arrange for good relations between the towns near the sixteen cantonments and to provide healthy amusements for the soldiers. But as Fosdick took control of the commission, he defined the mission in more explicitly moral terms. Recognizing that European allies had waited until after the fact to deal with such matters as disease and drunkenness among their soldiers, Fosdick determined to prevent them in the United States Army by offering healthful alternatives to vice. Because men were being drafted into service, the chairman believed that the "Government itself must assume responsibility for eliminating these evils." The state owed that much to the "families from which they come and to the men themselves."[43]

Beginning in late April 1917, the members of the Commission on Training Camp Activities met once a week, and as the months passed, the original group of five commissioners grew steadily to include more experienced theater managers, musicians, and entertainers. By late July, the commission had worked out details for erecting an amusement hall in each army camp and had planned a program of plays, vaudeville shows, and miscellaneous attractions. The search began in earnest for "a competent manager" to be "in charge of each camp theatre."[44] Before long, Raymond B. Fosdick appointed Marc Klaw, of the famous Klaw & Erlanger production team, to be on the commission, and later familiar figures on Broadway—David Belasco, Lee Shubert, A. L. Erlanger, Edward F. Albee, George M. Cohan, Irving Berlin, and Arthur Hammerstein—appeared on commission stationery as "Committee Heads."[45] Two groups were conspicuous by their absence from this commission—advocates of the New Movement in the Theater and African Americans.

The absence of the artistic avant garde no doubt reflected Marc Klaw's connections and preferences. Since he had been invited to join the commission to attract other experienced theater managers, he understandably turned to people he knew and who shared his sympathies. These people naturally did not include the "new arters" and theatrical "revolutionaries," who had disparaged his work and who had attacked his syndicate in the previous two decades. Moreover, the programs demanded by soldiers included "light amusement"— minstrel shows, musical farce, musical comedy, vaudeville routines, and short dramatic sketches—the very kinds of stage entertainment in which Klaw and his associates specialized.[46] When the *Drama League Monthly* asked what the boys in camp most enjoyed for diversion, Lieutenant R. C. W. answered, "Good concerts by orchestras, bands, coon quartets—pretty nearly anything, but by all means it must be good. Don't try to pass off any second hand amusements on us. Give us vaudeville, boxing and that sort of stuff, too. Nothing highbrow, but things that stir up a fighting spirit."[47] In practice, the selection of Klaw gave an edge to commercial theater interests over the New Movement in the Theater, and wedged in the popular mind became the idea that "highbrow" entertainment lacked patriotism.

The exclusion of African Americans from the commission reflected a general lack of interest in Negro Americans and Negro soldiers, even though black cultural expression appeared in the lieutenant's list of popular attractions. The reports of the weekly meetings of the commission make no mention of the entertainment of black troops until April 4, 1918, nearly a year after the commission had been founded. At this meeting, the representative from the military, General Pierce, agreed to find out and report on the "disposition of colored troops." Two and a half months later, the commissioners discussed at length "the importance of the work among colored soldiers." Up to then, they agreed, "it had been the custom to attend to the white men first, but that hereafter the white and black must be attended to at the same time, so as to put a stop to the growing feeling among negroes that they were being neglected." One member reported that the YMCA recently had decided to treat white and black soldiers alike, and another conceded that black soldiers undoubtedly "felt slighted" when they entered a camp "where everything had been done for the white men" and nothing existed for them. But even after the decision was made officially to address the needs of black soldiers, the treasurer asked that his itemized budget, which listed expenditures for white soldiers' entertainment separately from those for black soldiers' entertainment, be omitted from the public statement because "it might result in a good deal of ill-feeling." The commission agreed, and the budget was excised from the official report.[48] One can only speculate as to the source of the "ill feeling." Would it have come from African Americans who would learn how little money had been appropriated for their activities or from whites angry that any public funds had been devoted to the entertainment of black troops?

These reports, while reflective of the attitudes of the men officially in charge of entertaining troops encamped in the United States, however, are somewhat misleading in that they assume an air of innocent unawareness that black troops desired entertainment in camp. Fosdick had known at least since November 1917 that black troops had fewer recreational options available to them in the cantonments than did their white counterparts. Emmett Scott, a special assistant to the secretary of war on African American issues, had urged Fosdick in mid-November to investigate the need for recreational activities at Camps Ayer and Framingham in Massachusetts, where black troops were stationed. White troops were encouraged to take part in sports and physical training, and white officers had been commissioned to organize such programs, but no such recreation existed for black soldiers. Scott recommended that Fosdick put someone like Charles A. Newman, president of the Gladiator Athletic Association in Boston and an experienced, successful track, football, and basketball coach, in charge of such activities for black troops.[49]

If Fosdick knew in November 1917 that little provision had been made for black soldiers' recreation and entertainment, he also might have known a month later that Marc Klaw, on advice from Emmett Scott, had appointed Lester A. Walton, drama critic of the *New York Age,* "to organize minstrel and dramatic companies among the colored draftees stationed at the various cantonments throughout the country." When Klaw and Walton had met on December 3, 1917, to discuss the appointee's duties, the commissioner had noted that he had already begun organizing minstrel and dramatic companies. Indeed, a month earlier, the *New York Times* had reported that George Cohan, Sam Harris, Irving Berlin, and two unnamed "professional minstrel men" had begun scouting local talent for use in programs for soldiers. When he spoke with Walton, Klaw insisted that he had "no intention to discriminate on account of color," and that he wanted the programs performed before mixed audiences. He also promised that the commission would back "at least one colored attraction" for the "cantonment circuit."[50]

In the weeks following his appointment, Walton sprang into action. He used the pages of the *New York Age* to urge parents of soldiers to purchase "smileage booklets," the commission's package of coupons that served as tickets to the shows in the camp. Most shows cost only ten cents, but Walton urged families with boys in the military to buy either five-dollar or one-dollar booklets so their sons, husbands, or brothers could take advantage of "Liberty Theatres."[51] He published an enthusiastic article on "racial amity" at Camp Upton, located in nearby Long Island.[52] Walton also began scanning newspaper reports on programs across the country to be able to tap talent outside of New York for the shows he would help produce. In January 1918, he reported to J. J. Mayer that he had discovered an exceptionally talented regiment in Rockford, Illinois, and asked for permission to recruit there for "organizing a first class dramatic company for our Liberty Theatres." In reply, Mayer informed Walton that he would send an assistant to help get "the buffalo theatre in operation."[53] By March, with a cast of performers and rehearsals underway, Walton prepared for a premiere performance of his Minstrel Show in Camp Upton, a show to which Klaw looked forward "with anticipation of real pleasure."[54]

From the beginning, however, Walton's relationship to the Commission on Training Camp Activities was murky. Shortly after his appointment, Walton asked Klaw why his name had not been added to the official stationery. Klaw reassured him that it soon would be added with an indication, as well, that "the organization of entertainment of the colored draftees is in your charge."[55] Later, in March, when Klaw had not covered Walton's expenses for the show at Camp Upton, the African American drama critic received a letter from Joseph Roycroft, Director of the Liberty Theatres and one of the charter members of the commission, promising to reimburse Walton. Roycroft asked Walton to correspond with him on matters concerning shows and expenses; Marc Klaw, it turned out, had resigned from the commission.[56] With Marc Klaw out of the picture members of the commission refused to acknowledge Walton's position as one of the Committee Heads, even though his name now appeared on the group's official stationery.[57] They politely received copies of New York Age articles he forwarded, noting only that they had heard that he "would like to cooperate in this way in reassuring your readers concerning social conditions that obtain in camp."[58] When Walton asked if he could "obtain the half rate on the Long Island Railroad the same as the Colored Government employees" to reduce travel expenses between Manhattan and Camp Upton, the commission stonewalled, sending him to military officials.[59] And in June, when Walton asked once more about the commission's commitment to organizing a "colored show," an issue he had "been bringing up . . . for several months," the acting chairman of the commission referred him to J. Howard Reber, the representative in charge of the Liberty Theatre Circuit, who, he believed, "would be most pleased . . . to have any suggestions or ideas" from Walton.[60]

In September 1918, after months of courteous but firm dismissals, and with no sign of support for an African American show, Walton exploded in a letter to Malcolm McBride. "I am writing to ascertain my status with the Commission," he began, "as I am unable to exactly state to my friends and the public whether I am in or out. It has been impossible for me to carry out the comprehensive program originally outlined by Mr. Marc Klaw and myself; in fact, I have not been able to do very much for the colored soldiers." Walton had learned secondhand that his plan for getting up "wholesome entertainment for the colored troopers" had been discarded. He resented the implication that he was a mere "job-seeker" and asked only that he be told where he stood.[61] Within days, Walton learned that the Military Entertainment Service had disbanded, and that the commissioners resented his "being too insistent" on the matter of black entertainment. As a parting shot, Walton expressed "regret" for having been involved in "this unpleasant incident" and reminded the commission that thanks to his "insistence" African Americans had bought millions of dollars of Liberty Bonds, thousands of dollars of War Savings Stamps, and "smileage" booklets that helped defray the costs of the Liberty Theatre. He believed that only "by giving the Negro proper representation" could the interests of black soldiers be served. While "doing the right thing might clash" with prevailing attitudes toward African Americans, he concluded sarcastically, "I am sure it will be consistent with the ideas of right and in tune with the song of 'Democracy' now sweeping this country."[62] If he ever really had been a "Committee Head" on the Commission on Training Camp Activities, Walton now had left.

Walton's experience shows how stubbornly members of the Commission on Training Camp Activities resisted the idea that African American theater people should have a hand in entertaining American troops and the principle that black troops deserved the same consideration as white troops. Their determination to limit the participation of people like Walton in the commission's activities and their belief that white troops took precedence over black troops had the effect of drawing fairly narrow boundaries around the desired American self-image and the content of American culture. In this respect commission members reflected attitudes held by others in the government working feverishly to concoct patriotic images and slogans and by white America in general. The neglect of other races, however benign it may have been, did not prevent negative images of nonwhites from creeping into entertainment for white soldiers and the general public. But without a valued nonwhite voice on committees, commissions, and production staffs, those offensive portrayals simply went unchecked.

Of course, the content of amusements for soldiers differed little from that served up in commercial theaters and playhouses for civilians, and nonwhites typically fared none too well in mass culture. Well before the war, *Birth of a Nation* had won great acclaim in the cultural mainstream. It featured black Americans as vicious, monstrous animals bent on violence, revenge, and the deflowering of white maidens. *Theatre Magazine* hailed it as the "biggest thing in moving pictures produced . . . by American brains," even though it also acknowledged that the film stirred up "racial bitterness" and rehashed the "blunders that marked the Reconstruction period." Nevertheless, *Birth of a Nation* represented for *Theatre Magazine* a "remarkable achievement," one that "compels the highest praise."[63] Shortly after the First World War, D. W. Griffith argued that the American motion picture industry had begun to "Americanize" the world and that American men and women on film represented the "highest type on earth." Walton, however, responded to Griffith's claim by noting that the great filmmaker did "not have in mind the colored American. Only white Americans are depicted on the screen as heroes and in dignified roles to command respect and admiration." While the Griffiths of Hollywood made the public believe that "all heroes and heroines are of white complexion," they also advanced the idea that "the Negro has a corner on ignorance and buffoonery."[64]

African Americans were shown as not only murderous, ignorant, or clownish, but also as lazy and thieving. Shortly after the United States entered the Great War, Walton reviewed a stage show called *Pals First,* in which one of the characters announces, "I never saw a nigger in my life that wouldn't steal!" Such a show demonstrated that producers "[did] not regard the Negro seriously, believing him to be a happy-go-lucky inoffensive sort of a human being who does not possess the temerity to command respect."[65] Walton also found a Nora Bayes show with Native Americans, Hawaiians, and African Americans to be both encouraging and disheartening. On the one hand, he argued, the cast of Bayes's show made "quite a democratic gathering, a sort of congress of races." On the other hand, terms like "nigger" and "coon" were sprinkled liberally through the lyrics and dialogue, while ethnic epithets like "sheeny," "kike," "dago," and "harp" were avoided.[66] Documentaries often were little better than the lighter diversions. In 1913, a Pathe newsreel pictured Woodrow Wilson throwing out a baseball at a professional game, a story on German peasants dressed in their Sunday best, and then a story about African American refugees flooded out of their homes near Memphis. To make light of their plight, the filmmakers had placed bowls of mush and bread in front of three "little black, half-starved pickaninnies," and rolled the film as they greedily gobbled down the food.[67] Thus, various forms of popular culture, whether produced for diversion and amusement or for education and a "realistic" look through the camera's eye, purveyed a steady flow of distorted, stereotypical pictures of blacks in America.

Other races came off little better than blacks. Indians typically appeared in plays and films as butchers of white homesteaders and as foils for the advancing civilization of ranchers, railroads, and small towns. Asians, frequently portrayed as a "yellow peril" in the nation's popular press or as opium dealers and white slave traders in novels by Frank Norris, evoked fears based on their racial distinctiveness. Films like *The Cheat* (1915) and *The Silent Menace* (1917) featured Japanese characters as dangerous influences in American life. In *The Cheat* a Japanese man barely escapes a lynch mob after being accused of raping a white woman. *The Silent Menace* revolves around Japanese who are suspected of spying on the United States. They are presented as "sneaking, snake-like creature[s]."[68] Such racial caricatures presented serious obstacles for Americans to move in the direction of accepting, if not celebrating, a nation made up of many races—of acknowledging a multiracial and multicultural reality.

In the middle of 1918, Walton reported in the *New York Age* that America's Over There League, a group responsible for sending performers to France to entertain the troops, had circulated an announcement of their plan to organize "nigger minstrels." When he saw the announcement, Walton immediately fired off a letter of protest to one of the league's members. In his reply, the member could not understand why Walton objected to the term; after all, the memorandum also contained references to "dago," "rube," "squaw," and "English dude." Surely, "nigger" was not any worse.[69] Had Walton gained access to the regular reports by music directors at the nation's army camps, he no doubt would have been dismayed to learn that the term was, in fact, in common use. The Camp Grant report for December 1918, for example, listed two upcoming events for the soldiers—"Burlesque, Scotch High Ball, Pharce [*sic*] of Judge for a Day," and "Nigger scetch [*sic*], Dr. Skumton's New Discovery."[70] Kenneth Westerman from Camp MacArthur near Waco, Texas, said he had searched for Negro songs, but found that none existed in print. Waxing enthusiastic in his own way, Westerman wrote, "No one but a 'nigger' can sing them. I can't describe it so you can get the atmosphere, but 1200 black men stretched out in the sun, with their eyes half shut, droning away on these songs are something that only the heat of the South can produce; and still 'droning' doesn't express it for they have more volume and tone color than a whole regiment of white men."[71] Westerman routinely called the black soldiers under his direction "niggers," and he frequently threw in asides that revealed his attitude toward them. "When you start a bunch of niggers off on their daily work with an hours [*sic*] singing they sure can work the rest of the day," he reported.[72] Max Weinstein, music director at Camp Meade in Maryland, praised the band of the 368th Infantry as a "corker." The band, transferred to Camp Meade from Camp Upton on Long Island, featured a drum major— the "only one in captivity," Weinstein noted, who had made President Wilson laugh until he cried—who strutted "in real cake-walk fashion," and the band became popular in Baltimore. Weinstein ended his report by noting the "good spirit" created by music in the camps. " 'Lawde me, we'se jes' chock full o' dat down dis 'away.' "[73]

Other official reports reaching Washington from the various camps often contained passages by white officers trying to imitate black dialect. In fact, *all* references to black speech appeared in mangled English. Westerman, of course, led the way. Writing from Texas, he believed "every nigger in the Battalion" hated to leave for France without their beloved music director. " 'Mah Lo'd we-all hate to leave you he'e,' 'Ah'll show miss you,' 'Whah doan dey let you-all come along,' " they supposedly said as they bid him farewell.[74] William McEwan, stationed in Camp Johnson, South Carolina, believed that the black soldiers were so grateful to him for teaching them the fundamentals of music that they did little favors for him. One man stopped him to say he was a " 'first-class bah bah' " and would cut McEwan's hair " 'good 'nuf so you'h not ashamed to take off you'h hat in New York, suh.' "[75] Max Weinstein from Camp Meade told of a trip he made to Alabama, "to a place located three miles from no place and four miles from no place else," accompanied by local leaders to a black church. He reproduced the black elder's speech for his superiors in Washington: "Bredern and Sistern, we have wid us today Jedge Brewer. You all knows de Jedge an' Mista Roberts fo' who ye all works. An' den we have Mista—ah—wot's yo name, please? Thank you. Mista Weinstein. Mista Weinstein is workin' wid de COLORED soldiers. He learns 'em how to sing. Bredern and Sistern, dere ain't no white man wot can teach us to sing fo' dey all has to use de books. Chillun, where de books leave off—dat's where we begins."[76]

After reading the regular reports from music directors across the country, it is hard to escape the conclusion that despite the language and mimicking of black dialect, many of these white officers felt deep, genuine affection for the black men who took part in their bands, choirs, and camp "sings." And given the fact that many of the officers were located in southern camps, the dialect they attempted to reproduce may well have reflected some of the pronunciations and locutions they heard in everyday conversations. But what remains troubling is the fact that African American commentary found expression *only* in dialect and that the images of African Americans perpetuated the stereotype with which most whites were familiar: "Twelve hundred black men stretched out in the sun," music as a prerequisite for black labor, imprecise use and pronunciation of standard English, and natural rather than cultivated musical ability. Regardless of whatever evidence may have existed to the contrary, narratives like these drew heavily on preconceived notions about black character, traits, and abilities, thus reinforcing a uniform, and not particularly flattering, view of black Americans.

Despite the affection some white military leaders may have developed for African American soldiers, that warmth did not translate into a desire to include African Americans in the successful execution of war in Europe. The oft-expressed view in the white media that African Americans lacked the fortitude and courage to wage war was seldom contradicted even when ample evidence of black bravery existed. In August 1918, a film produced by Hearst-Pathe, designed to apprise Americans at home of life in the trenches of France, focused almost exclusively on white soldiers. Two scenes stood out, because they featured African Americans. The first scene involved a black soldier fumbling with French, a language obviously beyond his ability to master; the second scene featured two black men debating whether the army or the navy would be the safer branch in which to serve. Inept and cowardly, these three blacks offered the only glimpses of African Americans in uniform.[77] Two months later, the motion picture service of the French Army released a film that pictured American soldiers of both races. Walton called the showing "truly a novel experience to see those dusky Americans portrayed with becoming dignity and respect."[78] Walton did not mention in his review of the film the fact that black troops sent to France—like the Fifteenth Infantry Regiment, known as the "Hellfighters"—had to serve under French command if they wanted to see combat. As Reid Badger explained in his biography of James Reese Europe, one of the soldiers in this regiment, "Still unwilling to break with army tradition and order the New York regiment to join an American combat division, the American high command gave [Colonel] Hayward a choice. He could return with his men to the United States and await the formation of one of the proposed black divisions, or be transferred immediately to the French Army." Hayward's decision to fight with the French placed his regiment in the thick of battle and produced numerous black soldiers decorated for bravery.[79]

According to Badger, sympathetic and laudatory reports by influential white journalists on three prominent New York dailies told of Henry Johnson's and Needham Roberts's heroic stand against a German attacking party in June 1918. Their stories were "spread by the Associated Press to papers all across the country."[80] But like the three race dramas that took Broadway by storm in April 1917 only to be largely forgotten by the end of the summer, the black soldiers' heroism faded from public memory by the time the Armistice ended the war in November 1918. A film called *America's Answer,* released about the time the war ended, showed American soldiers awarded for valor. None of them were African American, and Henry Johnson, a hero in June and the first American to be presented a *Croix de Guerre* by the French, was nowhere to be seen in November. Walton, ever vigilant when it came to the mistreatment of members of his race, laid the blame for this inexcusable neglect squarely on the shoulders of George Creel's Committee on Public Information. "The consistent manner in which the colored soldier has been completely blotted out has not been due to an oversight. Far from it. The moving picture camera has failed to gaze momentarily on the faces of brave, black Americans because a tacit understanding exists . . . to keep the colored soldier in the background as much as possible." The Committee on Public Information had been charged with the task of "keeping the American public educated about our soldiers," but in the case of African American soldiers and their families back home, the committee had "failed miserably." Indeed, the failure was so great as to be "nothing short of criminal." Walton went on to reveal that George Creel had agreed to show films of African Americans in France but only to African American audiences—a form of "Jim Crow" policy at the highest level of government. And the general absence of black Americans from materials generated by the Creel Committee, Walton argued, amounted to a form of "suppression."[81]

Walton had a point. While it is debatable whether the committee could have succeeded in overturning decades of prejudice, stereotype, and mistreatment by featuring African American soldiers in the natural course of promoting national pride, the power of the committee to shape public opinion should not be underestimated. In the space of a few months, Creel and his collaborators had succeeded in making a bitter enemy, "the Huns," out of one of America's best-loved immigrant groups. Butchers, thugs, and ape-like destroyers of civilization, the Huns of the Creel Committee's imagination sparked fear, suspicion, and action on the part of an American public persuaded by the propaganda. Many communities banned German language in the public schools, in some places American citizens burned books by German authors, and generally speaking, music by German composers was banned from public performance. Threats and acts of violence against German Americans— including prominent Christian pacifists like Walter Rauschenbusch—followed in the wake of Creel's work. Even in remote areas like rural southwest Iowa, the impact of the Hun image inspired fear. There, a little boy, worried lest his father hire a German American farm laborer, explained that the foreigner was " 'iable to cut off our hands and feets"—a concern that reflected the pervasiveness of stories about the vicious deeds of Kaiser Bill's hosts against the children of Belgium.[82]

The decisions by the Creel Committee to exclude African American war heroes from films celebrating the bravery of American soldiers, to include insulting cameos of black soldiers at their worst in newsreels, and to refuse to use the crisis of war as an opportunity to imagine a more inclusive portrait of American society, citizenship, and patriotism, all represented choices— deliberate choices that demonstrated the continuing doubts about the genuine Americanness of blacks in the United States. Those doubts about African Americans as U.S. citizens colored all of the cultural conversations going on in 1917 and 1918, whether they took place between military officers, between Music Directors and their superiors in Washington, or between the Committee on Public Information and the public at large. These conversations interrupted and redirected the discussion about the Negro Players and the race dramas they interpreted in April 1917. As the weeks passed and the fervor for a more narrowly defined "America" grew, the positive comments about the plays and the hopeful claim for an American dramatic tradition they made sounded more and more like an unwelcome comment at a polite dinner party. It was best, it would seem, just to ignore it.

Add to the overlapping conversations about race and war in 1917 the affiliation of the white principals with the New Movement in the Theater, a movement temporarily out of favor, and the evaporation of the enthusiasm for *Three Plays for a Negro Theater* begins to make more sense. It served the best interests of none of the white participants in the dramatic conversation to bring up the subject if it could be avoided. Moreover, after Torrence proclaimed to the world what *he* thought the dramas signified, the plays and players became even more taboo as subjects for a nation going to war. The man who had done so much to inaugurate an African American Theater also uttered the words that drove the nails into the coffin of this progressive effort in the theater.

AIN'T GONNA STUDY WAR NO MORE

A little more than a week after *Three Plays for a Negro Theater* opened in the Garden Theatre and after the war resolution had passed both houses of Congress, a full-page article on Torrence appeared in the Sunday Magazine of the *New York Times*. Based on an interview with the playwright, the article focused mainly on Torrence's view of the impact of war on American literature. Although the interviewer wanted to talk about war, Torrence made it clear that he was a pacifist. "My dream," he told the journalist, "is that our nation may stand for non-resistance as a heroic example to humanity." In fact, Torrence went further than many pacifists in America by urging non-resistance even if the United States itself were invaded by a foreign army. The playwright believed that the war would help make American literature—dramatic and otherwise—more cosmopolitan, "less localized" and less concerned "with purely American scenes and themes." The "rhythmic crisis" of impending war, he argued, would produce an artistic "renaissance"; after the war the arts would flower, beautifully, once more.

The reason Torrence had been selected for an exclusive *New York Times* interview, of course, was that his three plays about African Americans had caused such a stir on Broadway and in the drama columns of New York's dailies. Perhaps the interviewer thought that Torrence would have a position on the war as daring as the themes of his dramas. If so, he or she must not have been too disappointed. For in this interview, Torrence boldly spoke out against U.S. involvement in the Great War. Instead of linking his dramatic efforts to the creation of an America as democratic in its art as in its political life—an America worth defending—Torrence offered another position on his plays. *Granny Maumee* and *Simon, the Cyrenian*, he asserted, were plays about non-resistance. In one stroke, Torrence linked the admirable forgiveness of Granny Maumee and the Christ-like humility of the bold African rebel to the dangerous, potentially un-American creed of pacifism.[83]

A few days before Torrence's interview appeared in the *New York Times*, Randolph Bourne, an outspoken leftist and antiwar writer, had made the same claim for the plays. Readers of the *New York Tribune* may have noticed Bourne's letter to the editor in which he recounted his experience at the Garden on the evening of the second performance by the Negro Players. "It was good Friday," he began. "And it was the day of the proclamation of war as the solemn tones pealed out in the last play *Simon, the Cyrenian*, with its setting of the Crucifixion—'They that take the sword shall perish by the sword'—you could hear the audience catch its breath as it realized the piercing meaning of this heroic little drama of non-resistance played before a Christian nation that was going into a world war on the very day that its churches celebrated devoutly the anniversary of this very warning."[84] Promoters for the plays excerpted the end of Bourne's letter—"It seems imperative that no person with imagination miss this"—to plug the production in an advertisement that appeared in the *New York Times* the following Sunday, but some readers undoubtedly noticed that Bourne's longer, acid attack on American hypocrisy was missing.[85] Between Torrence's interview in the *New York Times* and Bourne's letter to the editor of the *New York Tribune*, the race dramas, and perhaps unintentionally, the African American performers who brought them to life on the stage, were tarred with the brush of nonresistance. And before long, in wartime America, nonresistance smelled a great deal like cowardice.

Both Torrence and Bourne were committed pacifists before the opening of the three plays. Indeed, Bourne had been part of a party organized in honor of Olivia Torrence's birthday in February 1917, a party described by Torrence as a "Pacifist Party, all of us being strong Pacifists."[86] After the interview in the *Times* appeared, Torrence's friend Zona Gale praised the playwright for his courageous stand and asked that he send at least one hundred copies of the article along with Bourne's letter to the editor of the *Tribune* to a Miss Joy Young of the Union Against Militarism so she could forward them to members of that group as well as to New York Woman's Peace Party members.[87]

Bourne's antiwar sentiments were well known, and, according to Robert Westbrook, they led to his having a complete falling out with John Dewey, whom up to that time Bourne had admired as America's most trenchant and democratic philosopher.[88] But Torrence's proclamation of his pacifist position was something of a dramatic and unexpected revelation. Close friends and family members, of course, knew of his convictions. In the midst of the run, Torrence took time out to advise his younger brother, Findley Torrence, to "join the Quaker church in Xenia and so have a better chance of escaping conscription when they begin it."[89] Once the plays closed at the Garrick Theatre, Torrence's mother tried to console him with the observation that the plays were "too beautiful and peaceful to suit the masses in these stirring war times," and she worried about Torrence and his wife: "I do hope you dear ones will not get into trouble with your peace sentiments."[90] But aside from these private and semipublic assertions, Torrence's belief in nonresistance had not been the topic of much open discussion. Until the war came, Torrence *never* referred to his three dramas as the "non-resistance plays," but always as the "darky" plays or as plays to initiate a Negro theater in America. And in later years, when he reminisced about them, he never spoke of them as plays for pacifism.[91]

Torrence's decision to use the publicity generated by the novel dramatic experiment to further the cause of peace was deliberate, principled, and undoubtedly fatal for the long run of his plays. And the playwright knew at the time that this was not a popular position. The day Torrence wrote his brother to encourage him to take steps that would help him later avoid being drafted was the same day his *New York Times* interview appeared on newsstands. He sent his brother a copy of the piece, describing it as an "interview in which I managed to insert as much Pacifist talk as possible. A little later that much of that kind of talk will be a hanging matter."[92] A few days later, Torrence informed his family that the plays had left the Garden and were now playing at the Garrick Theatre. It had not been a profitable show, but it was "a great artistic success." The critics, he noted, were "unanimous in their approval and praise," but the "audiences are slim." The reason for this mixed reception, he believed, was that "the time may not be ripe for it just now while the war is at this stage."[93]

"A little later" and "the time may not be ripe"—these were admissions that the timing for pacifism was bad in 1917. Torrence was right. Even one of his friends wrote him two days after she read the *New York Times* interview to try to shame him into recanting. "[S]ilence before outrage, subservience to oppression, failure to defend the heritage of others as well as our own," surely these were unforgivable sins of omission. This generation, if they followed the advice of Torrence and his pacifist friends, would be the "first Americans—the very first—to deny our duty and to refuse to fulfil [*sic*] our mission so nobly made clear in our past."[94] At least Grace Ellery Channing-Stetson felt sufficient concern and affection for Torrence to express her concern and to try to persuade him not to side against the war. Not everyone was so kindly disposed toward people like Torrence. In a brief notice of an attack by a "militant pacifist" against Senator Henry Cabot Lodge, the *New York World* pointed out the unbecoming aggressiveness of many antiwar activists. They expected to interrupt preparedness meetings and physically attack respected government leaders without being punished, but they themselves bodily removed any hecklers from their peace meetings and made fun of guardsmen as "tin soldiers." "Most of them will probably calm down in time and escape the insane asylum," the editorialist concluded.[95] James Metcalfe similarly discussed peace advocates in loaded language. He predicted that the war undoubtedly would inspire "a lot of on-the-spot dramatists" to write "war plays galore." Some might look to Teddy Roosevelt for good, farcical material, while others might find themes in "the perverted Pacifist and in the Professional Prohibitionist" who took advantage of the conflict to push their particular agendas.[96] Shameful, insane, or perverted, pacifists provoked negative responses ranging from disappointment to utter dismissal. But all of these examples suggest that pacifists would have to populate the margins, not the center, of American life.

Torrence knew the seriousness of taking an antiwar stance in wartime America. He tried to convince his family in Xenia that antiwar rallies attracted thousands of enthusiastic supporters in spite of what they might read to the contrary in the newspaper. The antiwar fervor grew apace, he believed. But in other letters he reported evidence that should have shaken this faith in America's tolerance for pacifism or in the swelling numbers of nonresistants. Friends were arrested, jailed, and tried for antiwar activities as the legislature cracked down on all potentially seditious and subversive citizens and as the Creel Committee fired the nation for battle.[97] As far as I know, Torrence himself escaped persecution for his beliefs—that is, he did not serve time in jail, was not arrested at the peace rallies he attended, and did not find himself as the defendant in a sedition suit brought by the federal government. At the same time that he made himself a prime target for persecution, the machinery was not fully in place to go after relatively harmless artists like himself, and by the time the hunt for subversives was on, Torrence's plays were largely yesterday's news and mostly forgotten.

So the decision to take a pacifist stand through an interview about his three race dramas cost Torrence personally very little. But the timing of his comments—unprecedented and never again repeated in public—could not have been worse for the subjects of and actors in his three dramas. In spite of his disdain for violence and armed conflict, Torrence handed fervent patriots ammunition to fuel their campaign against black citizens, and for all of his pacifist ardor, Torrence could not protect the black citizens he wanted to advance from the attacks already being made against their character and claim to American citizenship. If *Granny Maumee* ultimately was about nonresistance, then innate pacifism might explain why blacks had not risen up against the injustice of their oppressors. If *Simon, the Cyrenian* was a pacifist text, then the black embrace of Christianity served, perhaps, as a mask and a shield for latent cowardice. And if two of the three plays were somehow about pacifists and the third, as we have seen, was about an irresponsible, happy-go-lucky, petty thief too lazy to work for an honest living, then perhaps that helps explain why *Three Plays for a Negro Theater* were so quickly dismissed from the nation's cultural debate in 1917. For Americans who spent the summer preparing for war sought the confidence to go "over there" with the conviction that American character as well as American democracy would triumph. Pacifists and slackers, the Creel Committee soon would make clear, were not essentially American.

The critical responses to the Negro Players' performances and the three race dramas—especially those that appeared in the first few days after the initial showing—demonstrate the preconceptions, ignorance, and partial sight that many in the critical community brought to the race plays. They found language that limited the radical implications of these experimental plays with their unusual perspective on race relations in the United States and with their cast of admirable black performers. Even without the additional burden of war, the plays likely would have won only limited support. But it is clear, nevertheless, that the "cultural skirmish" generated by the three race dramas meant that critics were at least predisposed to grapple with some of the issues that confronted them on stage. The war, however, generated its own kind of cultural skirmishes—over who qualified to bear arms in defense of the nation, what constituted a genuine American culture, and how to construct a narrative of America's victorious campaign after the war came to an end. These cultural conflicts in an age of anxiety left little space for American citizens of color and none whatsoever for pacifists and slackers. When war talk interrupted and eventually drowned out race talk, American culture absorbed very little of the *Three Plays for a Negro Theater*—on the grounds of race and politics.

7

FORGETTING TO REMEMBER

"You promised that you'd
Forget me not,
But you forget to remember."

Irving Berlin, Remember, *1925*

TEN YEARS AFTER *Three Plays for a Negro Theater* enjoyed its brief run on Broadway, Alain Locke edited a volume of dramas about African American life that he called a "source book of native American drama." Among the plays included in this collection were three by Ridgely Torrence, *Granny Maumee, The Rider of Dreams,* and *Danse Calinda,* and Locke hailed Torrence as one of the pioneers who had recognized "the dramatically undeveloped potentialities of Negro life and folkways as a promising province of native idioms and source materials in which a developing national drama can find distinctive new themes, characteristic and typical situations, authentic atmosphere." At the end of the collection of plays, Locke included an essay by Montgomery Gregory, a professor of drama at Howard University, that offered a chronology of African American involvement in the theatrical life of the United States. Gregory identified April 5, 1917, as the date that marked "the first important movement in the development of an authentic drama of Negro life," and like others who would write about the production of Torrence's three plays, the Howard professor regretted that "such a significant project" began "at such a tragic hour," the entry of the United States into the European war. Despite its "untimeliness," Gregory believed the production had made an indelible impression on the New York stage, and for evidence of the new enthusiasm for the legitimacy of Negro drama, he cited Arthur Hornblow's initial review of the plays in *Theatre Magazine.* By 1927, Gregory concluded, the work of the Negro Players had yielded an abundant dramatic harvest, because black drama was no longer considered a "novelty" but had become a staple of the American stage.[1]

Writing in 1927, the high watermark of what Ann Douglas calls Aframerican culture, Gregory, perhaps, decided to overlook the fact that Arthur Hornblow had long since forgotten the three one-act plays; perhaps he did not notice. If he identified with other Harlem Renaissance artists and intellectuals, Gregory may well have assumed that his version of American theater history would be read widely and generally absorbed by Americans of all races at a moment when black cultural expression surged into the center of the popular arts of the nation. But in spite of periodic reminders—Du Bois in 1924, Locke in 1927, Johnson in 1930, Frederick Bond in 1940, Isaacs in 1947, and Gerald Bradley in 1964—*Three Plays for a Negro Theater* has not stuck in the collective memory of the American people. Moreover, when it has been dredged to the surface, it appears as an episode in *black* theater history but not as a momentous event in *American* theater history.[2]

Like others who remembered Torrence's plays and the Negro Players, Gregory also noted the bad timing of their opening as a reason for explaining the relatively short run. But this oft-repeated excuse rings hollow when we consider that the preparation for war supposedly required the mobilization of the entire body politic and that Americans were called to pull together for the campaign across the ocean. Then, at a moment of profound self-consciousness and self-definition, cultural leaders in the United States circled the wagons around only a part of the citizenry—its white constituency—and turned a blind eye to the people of color whose labor and ingenuity had contributed to the capacity of the nation to assume a role in international affairs and whose music and art had lent the most important elements to whatever was distinctive in American entertainment. They pursued national unity and strength in democracy, but they created a climate that perpetuated division along the color line and denied democratic participation to at least one-tenth of its citizens. The fact that the moment proved to be bad for the debut of African American drama in the nation's theater capital only reveals the thick encrustation of race prejudice and inegalitarianism on national consciousness.

Talk of the plays got lost in the talk of war. But it is not the demise of the three plays that should concern us as much as this pattern of forgetting. When an event is forgotten, the effect is the same as if the event never had occurred. Thus every step toward racial integration, cultural collaboration, or erasing the color line becomes a first step, wobbly and uncertain. Each clumsy step, unconnected to those that have gone before, belies the American devotion to an ideal of progress, because without a past or a precedent, we have no standard against which to measure movement either forward or backward. Forgetting and remembering are both acts of will; both are serious matters for collective cultural identity and national history. What we remember reflects what we consider important and what we believe has made us the people and nation we are today. What we forget we exclude from the narratives we make up about our collective experience.

The three race dramas of 1917, however, were not entirely forgotten. They had a traceable past, and they were followed by other acts and actors more clearly and generally remembered. The story of the first black actors on the Great White Way is not complete until we examine briefly what difference they made in the evolution of twentieth-century American culture and social life. When the curtain fell for the last time in the Garrick Theatre, the actors removed their costumes and makeup and left the theater. They, the stagehands, the theater manager, and the white sponsors all went on with their lives. The question that remains is: How did that magic moment in 1917 alter the world of make-believe and the American society that regularly entered its enchanted realm for clues as to who they were?

OPAL COOPER: A RIDER OF DREAMS

Shortly after the three race dramas closed at the Garrick Theatre, the *New York Times* announced that Emilie Hapgood had decided to continue sponsoring the African American actors and that in the following season they would appear on Broadway "in a new program of plays." The *Times* also reported that Hapgood was planning a tour of the black thespians and hoped to present them in Torrence's plays in London and Paris.[3] Olivia Torrence wrote her in-laws in Xenia the day after the plays closed that "the hope" of those connected with the production was "to keep the company together and to get enough money soon to take them to Chicago and elsewhere." She also mentioned that there was some talk of staging *The Rider of Dreams* on vaudeville.[4] The tours to London, Paris, and Chicago never materialized, but the players did perform "elsewhere." By the middle of May, the playwright had informed his family that the comedy starring Opal Cooper had, indeed, made it to a vaudeville stage. "It is being played at the Harlem Opera House three times a day and I am now on my way up there to attend to a lot of business connected with it," he wrote.[5] So at least a part of the cast continued to represent the Negro Players before the footlights after the dramas left Broadway.

Opal Cooper, Blanche Deas, Alex Rogers, and Joseph Burt left the glamour of Broadway for a three-performances-a-day show in Harlem. Others also found work in Harlem, and some joined stock companies that presented shows at the Lafayette Theatre. Andrew Bishop, for example, starred in the Lafayette Theatre's production of William Vaughn Moody's *The Great Divide* in late May. Jesse Shipp returned to stage managing, and in connection with the Quality Amusement Corporation, he staged *My Friend from Kentucky* at the Attucks Theatre in Norfolk, Virginia, in October 1920. A decade later he returned to Broadway as "Abraham" in *The Green Pastures* by Marc Connelly, which opened at the Mansfield Theatre in early 1930. Inez Clough appeared in Em Jo Basshe's *Earth*, which opened at the Fifty-second Street Theatre in March 1927, and two years later starred in *Harlem* by Wallace Thurman and William Jourdan at the Apollo Theatre.[6] As a dramatic organization, the Negro Players, however, disbanded, and many of the original cast of *Three Plays for a Negro Theater*—if they continued performing—attracted no further notice from New York's black or white critics.

For Opal Cooper, the heady days of the Broadway run followed by the demanding performance schedule at the Harlem Opera House gave him reason to hope for better opportunities to come. He had wanted a part in *Simon, the Cyrenian* "to play something tragic and serious" instead of the comic role he played in *The Rider of Dreams*.[7] But he had succeeded in the part of Madison Sparrow, generally winning praise from audiences and critics and earning a spot on George Jean Nathan's list of ten best actors. George Cram Crook of the Provincetown Players had been so taken with his performance in Torrence's comedy that he wrote to the playwright looking for Cooper. "There is a wonderful part in Eugene O'Neill's new 50 minute play for that gifted negro actor—Cooper I think who said in your play 'Ah wants to make my own music,'" Cook wrote, and he asked whether the performer was in the city and available to audition.[8] Perhaps the "rider of dreams" could have become O'Neill's "dreamy kid," but Cooper probably never knew that Cook had searched for him. In September 1918, Opal Cooper was in an entirely different kind of theater, in military costume.

In May 1919, when Cooper wrote his third letter to Torrence, the actor appeared to be optimistic about his future and expressed a "very strong desire to get back to the civil life" while he still enjoyed good health. His experience in France, though marked by numerous "hardships" including service at the front, had been—and continued to be—positive. Like other African Americans, Cooper believed the French people were "*very good* for a man (of the color I happen to be) to come in contact with." They accepted black soldiers "at face value," and when they used the term "friendship" it was with "much more sincerity than is generally understood at home." He had made many friends, had entertained the troops as a sergeant in the 807 Pioneer

Infantry Band, and had become somewhat famous for his rendition of *I'm Sorry, Dear.* Within about a month of his arrival in France, his commanding officer had rushed Cooper's unit to the front, "where the big guns of 'jerry' just wouldn't let us sleep, and we kept on moving forward until the armistice was signed." Cooper told his friend that he was "glad we had the opportunity to *complete* our *bit*," confiding that he could now "return home with a clear conscience." Cooper's unit was decorated for distinguished service under fire, an honor of which the actor-cum-soldier was "very proud." At the end of this friendly letter, Cooper extended warm greetings to "Mrs. Hapgood" and "Mr. Jones" and indicated that he would like to meet with Torrence when he returned to the United States. Having maintained contact with the playwright who had given him a chance on Broadway, the sergeant hoped to exchange his role in the military for a part in another Torrence play.[9]

The next letter Cooper sent to the playwright, unfortunately undated, suggests that Cooper's postwar career had not taken off as he had hoped it would. Indeed, the formal tone of his writing leaves the impression that Cooper's wartime letters to Torrence had gone unanswered and that Cook's interest in the black actor had not been passed on. "Several years ago I appeared in 'The Rider of Dreams,' written by you," Cooper began by way of reintroducing himself to the playwright. "Since that time, I have been working and studying abroad." Now that he was back in New York, the singer/actor had begun looking for opportunities to appear on either the stage or screen, and he thought, perhaps, the playwright could help him. He asked to make an appointment with Torrence some afternoon; Cooper worked all night every night, he reported, at the Salon Royal at 310 West Fifty-eighth Street. By this time, probably sometime in the late 1920s or early 1930s (he indicated an interest in appearing in a "talkie"), Charles Gilpin had won fame for his portrayal of the Emperor Jones in O'Neill's highly acclaimed drama, other black actors had appeared on Broadway, and the time must have seemed ripe for a seasoned veteran of the stage to land a part in one of the new race dramas. No letter survives to confirm whether Torrence answered the letter or made an appointment with Cooper. Eventually, Cooper looked elsewhere for work.[10]

More than two decades after starring in *The Rider of Dreams,* a desperate and disappointed Opal Cooper turned once again to Ridgely Torrence for assistance. After struggling to get work in the United States for several years in the 1920s and 1930s, Cooper had gone back overseas. In the 1930s he had returned to cabaret singing in Paris, had landed a part in a play at the Theatre de Paris, and had acted in a 1938 French film called *Le Revolte.* Cooper also had traveled to Asia, working as a soloist for the Bombay Symphonic Orchestra. Recently he had done a benefit performance for an influential society woman in the hope of being noticed. But now in 1939, with another war in Europe having erupted, Cooper was back in the United States and unemployed for the first time in six years. And to his dismay, the entertainment world was vastly different from the one he had left behind. Now, an entertainer—even a seasoned entertainer like Cooper—needed an agent just to book a nightclub act. Cooper had been able to make all his own arrangements in Europe and the Far East, he assured Torrence, but no New York agent was willing to take him as a client. He had auditioned to be the understudy for Paul Robeson, but without an agent and without any standing in the New York entertainment market, he had been turned down. "I am as energetic as ever," he insisted, "and making an effort to become known and thus overcome the handicap of being a 'stranger or refugee' in my own country."[11] Six months later, Cooper wrote Torrence, probably for the last time. He still had not found work and had been forced to move from Manhattan to a less expensive apartment on Edgecombe Avenue. "[P]lease keep me in mind in case you hear of anything for me," he pleaded.[12]

By the time he wrote Torrence for the last time in 1940, Cooper in some respects bore a striking resemblance to Madison Sparrow. He just wanted to make music, and he had counted on the help of a white playwright to realize his dream. Torrence, however, had let him down, even though in 1939 he might have been able to help. Notes from his travels to various black theaters in the United States indicate that Torrence knew most of the influential black playwrights, managers, actors, and companies performing in the country, but he did not introduce Cooper to any of his professional contacts. Unlike the imaginary "Rider of Dreams," however, Cooper had worked hard at his profession for twenty-five years. He had shouldered the responsibility of citizenship when his country had called in 1918, and he had made the most of the opportunities that had come his way in Europe and Asia. Perhaps Cooper simply had bet on the wrong horse—the playwright, who never wrote another play and gradually lost touch with the most influential figures on Broadway, instead of the stage designer, Robert Edmond Jones, who had become dean of American stage artists by the eve of the Second World War. Others who might have helped him—Lottie Grady, Jesse Shipp, Alex Rogers, Inez Clough, and Emilie Hapgood—were all long since dead, and no one else connected with the plays had won sufficient success in the world of theater to help Cooper realize his dream of returning to the New York Stage. Even Lester Walton, the producer of *Darkydom* in which Cooper had first enjoyed fame, had left show business and the *New York Age* to serve as United States Minister to Liberia. Opal Cooper, like the others, eventually disappeared from the scene.

Cooper's disappointing postwar career should not be seen exclusively as evidence of the failure of *Three Plays for a Negro Theater* to affect the color line on the stage. In the years he spent overseas as a soldier, as a student, and later as a professional entertainer, cultural life in the United States had been transformed. It had become tougher than ever for performers to break into the entertainment industry, which relied heavily on novelty and innovation. Popularity one year did not guarantee it for the next. No longer taking its cues from Europe, the American world of entertainment valued experience and exposure in the American media and put less stock in popularity overseas. Perhaps Cooper and the other interpreters of the three plays were latter-day Moses figures. They helped lead others to the promised land of Broadway even though they themselves were not permitted to make it their home. In the years following the pioneer performance in 1917, African Americans began making appearances in New York's famed theater district.

In some ways, the spell of the color line was broken by the appearance of the Negro Players on Broadway in 1917. In the next couple of years, no longer having to be the "first" to dare, stage managers began casting African American performers in black roles. In 1918, for example, Edward E. Rose staged Booth Tarkington's *Penrod* at the Globe Theatre and cast two black actors in the roles of two black boys, who "romp about and play detective with their playmates as white and colored boys are wont until the demon race prejudice asserts itself." Walton congratulated Rose for using black actors to play the parts and for refusing to force them to speak in black dialect. They spoke "plain 'United States,' " he wrote, and were "readily understood by all."[13] The following year, Nora Bayes convinced her manager to hire a black actor to play the part of "Washington," her butler, in a show called *Ladies First*. The manager approached "Happy" Rhone, a musician performing with the Clef Club Orchestra, with an offer that persuaded him to give up "gigging" for a time, and according to Walton, he made a "big hit." Rhone's selection convinced the black critic that "Broadway producers" had begun to realize that "race actors play Negro parts more acceptably than white thespians."[14] Eugene O'Neill used an all-black cast for *The Dreamy Kid* in 1919, as did Octavius Roy Cohen for the production of *Come Seven* in 1920. While Kenneth Macgowan charged some of the actors in *Come Seven* with performing with "hokum," he praised Arthur Aylsworth, Earle Fox, Lucille LaVerne, and Henry Hamlin for their "legitimately effective" work.[15] Perhaps as surprising was a notice in the *New York Age* in late 1920 that "a cast composed of colored and white artists" in a "play dealing with [the] Negro problem drew large audiences to the Lafayette."[16]

These minor breakthroughs or second and third steps after Torrence's plays prompted a kind of restlessness among African Americans regarding the limits placed on their work in the theater. They wanted more than the occasional bit part and were reluctant to wait until a white playwright decided to address the race question or create another minor black character. In 1923, for example, Professor Gregory received a letter from Anne Wolter, who had been working with a group of black actors in New York since 1918, asking for the titles of race dramas the group could perform. She explained to Gregory that she had had "great difficulty in finding the kinds of plays they would like to give."[17] Some companies contented themselves with interpreting dramas by whites typically performed by white actors. To celebrate the second anniversary of its founding, for example, the Lafayette Stock Company tackled Charles Gounod's operatic version of *Faust* in March 1918.[18] But others wanted to present race dramas written by blacks, and in the next few years more such dramas began to appear.

Salem Tutt Whitney and J. Homer Tutt, for instance, set their Smart Set Company to the task of interpreting a play called *The Children of the Sun* in 1919. In this drama the characters travel from Japan to India to Persia to Egypt to Abyssinia only to discover that these "children of the sun" and the civilizations they created all sprang from Africa. Another Negro company presented *The Problem*, written as a dramatic response to *Birth of a Nation*, in theaters in Philadelphia and Baltimore, and Alex Rogers's *Jasper Lee's Revenge* appeared at the Lafayette Theatre in 1920.[19] Black playwrights like Willis Richardson and Eulalie Spence began writing dramas that would gain fame later in the decade. They shared with struggling black writers like James William Henderson a desire to create race dramas "dealing seriously with the Negro as a man: not as a mere happy-go-lucky, irresponsible, good-natured, grinning, superstition-haunted type of individual, nor as a passive, pathetic, meek, pitiful creature dependent upon the powers and initiative of others, but as a normal human being struggling grimly against terrific odds—hoping, fearing, doubting, loving, hating, laughing, and weeping as other men."[20]

By 1919 opportunities for studying the art of acting had expanded, too. Franklin H. Sargent, head of the American Academy of Dramatic Arts in New York, began accepting black students.[21] Howard University began offering courses in drama with the arrival of Thomas Montgomery Gregory. The Howard Players and the Krigwa Players in Cleveland, along with other stock companies across the country, offered African Americans more venues for refining their histrionic talents. As time passed, it became more difficult for critics to charge black actors with lack of training, and in fact, shortly after the first black cast appeared on Broadway, the Drama League declared Charles Gilpin, the original "Emperor Jones," to be one of the ten people who had done the most for American theater in 1920.

Opal Cooper may well have missed the furor surrounding Gilpin's award; he was still studying and performing in France. If news of the unprecedented honor reached him, it probably only fortified his belief that when he returned to the United States he could pick up where he had left off and ride his dreams by singing, acting, and entertaining racially mixed audiences as he had in 1917. Instead, he returned to a nation that already had largely suppressed any memory it had of him. Other black entertainers crowded to the front of audition lines; some won parts, and others even won fame. In the two decades following his success, Cooper did indeed become a "stranger or refugee" in his own country. But he was not alone. Black actors could perform, black musicians could make music, black singers could sing, and black dancers could dance, but as long as collective memory failed, they would always be struggling for the rights, the fair play, and the recognition requisite for first-class citizenship.

TERRIBLE HONESTY

In the 1920s, Aframerican culture began to blossom in New York and elsewhere. Jazz became synonymous with the decade. Writers of the Harlem Renaissance produced books, articles, poetry, plays, and stories that appeared in pages once reserved for white writers. Racially mixed casts appeared on New York stages, and Charles Gilpin, Paul Robeson, Bessie Smith, and Louis Armstrong became household names. The cultural expressions of this era that were unmistakably American were also unmistakably the product of biracial collaboration. Especially in the field of music, the African American elements won widespread recognition.

No one to date has captured the vibrancy and richness of this cultural moment more brilliantly than Ann Douglas in *Terrible Honesty: Mongrel Manhattan in the 1920s.* She not only describes in fascinating detail the unprecedented collaboration between black and white artists, she also links the emergence of "Aframerica" with the dawning of the "American century," the arrival of the United States as a modern, self-sufficient world power. Art and culture in the Jazz Age, she demonstrates, did battle with the remaining vestiges of Victorianism, the power of the prim and moral matriarch, and the nineteenth-century ethos of restraint, and cleared the way for—indeed, embodied—the modern corporate, consumerist America that took a prominent place in the postwar international order. America's modern mentality, Douglas asserts, can be seen in the "terrible honesty" of its cultural movers and shakers. Nothing, no matter how grim, distasteful, sordid, or heathen, should be exempted from scrutiny and discussion, they believed. Only exposure of false hypocrisy could undo the power of Victorianism and liberate men and women in urban America.

The desire for utter frankness—terrible honesty—sprang in part from disillusionment about progress in the aftermath of the Great War, in which business interests cloaked in democratic idealism sent thousands of American boys to their deaths in the trenches of France. An age in which the media flourished by making disillusionment the stuff of its appeal gave postwar art a sharper edge than it had had before. And if people had lost faith in progress and idealism, truisms of Victorian America, then why not go all the way and be "bad" with gusto? In order to negate all the "truths" Victorians had taken for granted, cultural rebels scaled the walls of taboo to explore all the forbidden earthly delights. In 1920s America the taboo against racial mingling went down with the rest in the name of "terrible honesty." Of course other historical factors played their parts in this cultural revolution as well. An industrial economy in gestation for several decades reached the point of take off and matured at an accelerated rate during, after, and because of the war. The lure of jobs and greater freedom in northern cities drew thousands of African Americans from the rural South to create a biracial reality in which cultural collaboration could take place. Moreover, Victorianism had already sustained several severe body blows—the 1890s economic depression, the rise of ragtime music and cakewalk dancing, the arrival of millions of immigrants, and progressive legislation that took some of the pressure off individuals to take full responsibility for all that befell them—that left it reeling and shaken by the eve of war in the 1910s.

The story of the first black actors on the Great White Way testifies to the cultural skirmishes of the early twentieth century that prepared the ground for the "terrible honesty" and the "mongrel" culture of the 1920s. Earlier black migrations to places like Xenia, Ohio, fired the imagination of writers like Torrence. The debate over what constituted authentic Americanness raged at the turn of the century. Black entertainers pressed into the music business, onto the musical comedy and vaudeville stages, and onto Broadway before the nation went to war. And conflicts between those in the New Movement in the Theater and upholders of traditional commercial theater already had chipped away at the barriers separating Victorian propriety from the darker side of American life. Unhappy marriages, infidelity, class divisions in the mecca of democracy, and the reality of racial miscegenation all found expression on the American stage in the two decades preceding the Jazz Age.

As the memory of this debut of black actors on Broadway began to fade from the consciousness of America's cultural leaders, "Aframerica" began to thrive. But it, too, would eventually fade from the collective American memory.

Amid the myriad examples of black expression in the American mainstream, fruitful collaboration between blacks and whites, and the absorption of black culture by white Americans, Douglas offers a couple of keen observations that should make us pause. "White consciousness of the Negro's rights and gifts (however severe the limitations of that consciousness) and black confidence that Negroes could use white models and channels of power to achieve their own ends (however mistaken time would prove that confidence to be) reached a peak of intensity in the 1920s never seen in American history before or since," she writes in the opening pages.[22] The terrible honesty of the 1920s that made every issue free game in the search for truth eventually gave way to the more typical desire to hide, evade, gloss over, and suppress that which made Americans uncomfortable or lay them open to criticism. Forgetting took many forms. Douglas later notes that works like Zora Neale Hurston's *Their Eyes Were Watching God*, Nella Larsen's *Quicksand* and *Passing*, Wallace Thurman's *The Blacker the Berry*, and Jean Toomer's *Cane*, "among the best literature to come out of New York in the modern era," were not reissued or recognized until after World War Two. Many works of the Harlem Renaissance still have not been reprinted by commercial publishers, and it was not until Arnold Rampersad edited a collection of Langston Hughes's poetry in 1994 that an adequate edition existed.[23] "To date," she continues, "there are no full-length reliable biographies of most of the important writers, organizers, and performers of the Harlem Renaissance—[Nella] Larsen, [Countee] Cullen, [Rudolph] Fisher, [Jessie] Fauset, Walter White, [Wallace] Thurman, [Alain] Locke, Charles Gilpin, Charles Johnson, James P. Johnson, and [Ethel] Waters still await full biographical treatment."[24] By contrast nearly all of her white protagonists have been the subject of biographies, and several—Hemingway, Fitzgerald, and O'Neill—spawned a veritable cottage industry of scholarship and biographical writing.

Douglas's *Terrible Honesty* helps put the story of Torrence and the Negro Players into perspective. It was as easy to forget the celebrated figures of 1920s Aframerica, the height of black and white cultural cooperation, as the spectacular debut of black actors on Broadway in 1917. As her own story makes clear, white America placed limits on its acceptance of black art and artists just as it did on the civil rights, economic opportunities, residential possibilities, schooling, and movement of black citizens. Lynching, discrimination, and exclusion coexisted with jazz, the Charleston, and O'Neill plays. Even in its heyday, Aframerican culture elicited commentary similar to the reviews of *Three Plays for a Negro Theater*.

The limits of Aframerican culture are nowhere more clearly seen than in the critical conversation about Eugene O'Neill's *The Emperor Jones*, which opened in Greenwich Village in November 1920 and quickly found its way to Broadway.

The star of the drama was Charles Gilpin, an African American actor who had endured more than two decades of disappointment in black touring groups, on vaudeville, and as a member of various black stock companies. In late 1920 and early 1921, Gilpin became *the* topic of conversation in New York and around the country, because critics and audiences agreed that he displayed profound powers of interpretation in the role of Brutus Jones. In 1921, the Drama League selected both O'Neill and Gilpin as two of the ten people who had had the most significant impact on theater in America in the past season. And in the years that followed, O'Neill emerged as America's most gifted national playwright, and *The Emperor Jones* represented the most important breakthrough for African Americans on the American Stage.[25] Perhaps, indeed, Americans had come to embrace Aframerican culture in the postwar era.

Because of the interest in this play and its place of importance in the nation's dramatic literature, it is worthwhile to take a closer look at it and at its reception. The "terrible honesty" that made it a must-see drama for fashionable New Yorkers contained residue of a less honest and undeniably terrible bygone era. The widespread belief that the play was in fact the Great American Play for which the nation long had been waiting seems rather curious. The drama is not set in the United States; the cast of characters includes only one American—Brutus Jones, an African American, at that; and no white Americans appear on stage. The only white character, a despicable petty criminal named Smithers, hails from England. Moreover, *The Emperor Jones* is not a drama about the race question as such; it does not deal with the color line in America or with the social, economic, and political chasm that separated the races in 1920. Rather, the spotlight remains on the title character, a former Pullman porter convicted of murdering a black gambler who escapes from a convict labor gang by bashing in the skull of a white guard. Jones makes his way successfully to an island of black people, probably somewhere in the Caribbean, where within two years he establishes himself as emperor and uses his power to extract tribute and taxes from the dark-skinned people—"dem fool bush niggers," as he contemptuously calls them—who live on the island.[26]

The drama opens on the eve of revolution. Oppressed long enough by this domineering emperor, the people have begun to gather in the hills to amass a force sufficient to overthrow the tyrant. Jones, informed by the English scoundrel Smithers of the plot to end his reign, sets off to leave the island with the great wealth he has accumulated. Always conscious that this "emperor job" would not last forever, Jones has made plans for his escape, charting a path and leaving deposits of food along the way. Confidently, he sets out to make his getaway.

As the play unfolds, Jones finds that fatigue and nightfall have thwarted his plans. As the darkness enfolds him and the native drums beat a tattoo in the distance, Jones's fear of his past and of ghosts ("ha'nts") undermines his progress. He gets lost in the forest and imagines seeing the ghosts of the gambler and of the white guard whom he murdered; he also believes that he himself has been auctioned as a slave to haughty white men. With each vision, he fires a shot from the gun he carries for protection, then plunges headlong into the darkness. In the end, he returns barefoot, his clothing in tatters, to the village, his point of departure, where he is captured and killed by the revolutionaries. The natives, believing Jones's fabulous story on his arrival that only a silver bullet could destroy him, have gathered all the bits of silver they can find to mold one bullet. With that bullet, they end the reign of the Emperor Jones.

O'Neill crafted a dramatic story that rested firmly on many of the traditional beliefs white Americans held about their black neighbors. Indeed, the emperor's character is conveyed rather transparently by his given name, Brutus. Jones wanted power and wealth without having to work for it; he was homicidal and dangerous; and his belief in spirits and "ha'nts" brings about his demise. In fact, O'Neill gave the white character, Smithers, the final word. As the lifeless body of Brutus Jones is carried offstage by the soldiers, Smithers tells Lem, their leader, "And I s'pose you think it's yer bleedin' charms and yer silly beatin' the drum that made 'im run in a circle when 'e'd lost 'imself, don't yer? Stupid as 'ogs, the lot of 'em! Blarsted niggers!"[27] Perhaps that is why Margaret Mayorga concluded that O'Neill's drama explored the "fundamentals of Negro characteristics" and shows "how the development of the Negro from the days of his bushman ancestors, and through his slave experiences, has resulted in a type of mind which finds it impossible to escape from its inheritance even when given its freedom."[28]

Gilpin, no doubt, threw himself into the characterization of an increasingly terrified man, running for his very life. But in time, he found it impossible to continue in the role. He could not bring himself to recite some of O'Neill's lines. No wonder—the script called on Jones to characterize his subjects as lazy, irresponsible liars. "When I sleeps, dey sneaks a sleep, too, and I pretends I never suspicions it. All I got to do is ring de bell an' dey come flyin', makin' a bluff dey was wukin' all de time," he insists near the beginning of the drama.[29] Jones refers to his subjects variously as "low-flung woods' niggers," "black trash," and "bush niggers."[30] He partly credits their ignorance and cowardice for his success as emperor, and he believes he will escape when the time comes for the same reason. "Think dese ig'nerent bush niggers dat don't got brains enuff to know deir own names even can catch Brutus Jones? Huh, I s'pects not!"[31]

Gilpin began drowning himself in alcohol and changing some of O'Neill's precious script. Gilpin found himself out of the cast when *The Emperor Jones* played in London and out of the acting profession by 1927.[32]

Most white critics who reviewed O'Neill's drama agreed that the universal theme the playwright developed in *The Emperor Jones* was fear escalating into panic. The *Theatre Magazine* critic noted, "When we watch Gilpin in this play we do not stop at feeling what a negro in these circumstances feels and does and says—we are partakers of the experience of man in the grip of terror." As he saw it, the play invited the audience to imagine and to share in the experience of "gradual fear, mounting by almost imperceptible degrees to stark panic."[33] Alexander Woollcott of the *New York Times,* who disliked the production—which he described as a series of "long, unventilated intermissions interspersed with fragmentary scenes"—nevertheless saw it as an "extraordinarily striking and dramatic study of panic fear." While the "indescribable foreboding" represented the "secret" of the play's success as great drama, Woollcott viewed it in somewhat less universal terms. Like many others, the *Times* critic saw the play as a study in race. It was, he argued the "race memory of old Congo fears" that brings the "burly darky" to his death at the hands of the "natives."[34] In the pages of *Theatre Arts Magazine,* Kenneth Macgowan called *The Emperor Jones* "a study of personal and racial psychology of real imaginative truth."[35]

Not everyone saw *The Emperor Jones* as a play about human fear; some writers cast it specifically in racial terms. The *Outlook,* for example, reported that in Jones's night of terror, the "brittle armor of the theology of his childhood" gives way and "leaves him at heart a primitive savage, as superstitious as the wild pursuers whose drums continually throb through the forest aisles."[36] Likewise *Current Opinion* identified the central idea of *The Emperor Jones* as "the fact that the exemplar of an inferior race will succumb to weaknesses against which even a weak member of a superior race may be proof."[37] The descent into terror for these writers could be explained on the grounds of race. The vicious Pullman-porter-turned-emperor gets his come-uppance through his own inherent weakness and his racial susceptibility to fear.

Critics concurred principally on their estimation of Charles Gilpin. Heywood Broun of the *New York Tribune* called his performance one "of heroic stature," and Alexander Woollcott called it "an uncommonly powerful and imaginative performance."[38] *Theatre Magazine* graced its review of the play with a photograph of Gilpin in his Emperor's regalia. The caption read: "Charles S. Gilpin, The first negro actor to gain the front rank of his profession."[39] Even their praise could not prevent their ignorance of the African American Theater from being exposed. *Theatre Magazine* apparently had forgotten the honors bestowed by George Jean Nathan on Opal Cooper and Inez Clough for their performances in *The Rider of Dreams* and *Simon, the Cyrenian,* honors that technically made Gilpin the third African American actor to reach the "front rank" of the acting profession. The magazine's pronouncement also overlooked the brilliant and enormously popular entertainers like Bert Williams ("the funniest man in America") and George Walker of the black musical comedies who had captivated Broadway at the dawn of the century. Kenneth Macgowan incorrectly identified Gilpin as the actor who "had played a wise old negro in one of Ridgeley [*sic*] Torrence's plays produced some years ago by Robert E. Jones."[40] Macgowan confused Gilpin with Alex Rogers, who played "Dr. Williams" in *The Rider of Dreams*; Gilpin did not have even a minor role in any of Torrence's three plays.

So, embedded in the white critics' enthusiasm for *The Emperor Jones* are comments that betray the limits of Aframerican culture's reach, even in Mongrel Manhattan. The drama did not challenge basic attitudes toward African American character. While the drama demanded virtuoso acting and imaginative sets, the message conveyed by a fair number of white critics was that Gilpin had played well the part of a typical Negro—brutish, susceptible to superstition, and doomed to failure. The chief breakthrough seemed to be that, in the 1920s, black vices could be viewed as art.

Oddly enough, black critics, who in the 1910s had summarized plots in great detail to persuade African Americans to visit productions like *Pride of Race* or *The Nigger,* published not a word about the essence of the drama. James Weldon Johnson, W. E. B. Du Bois, and Lester Walton all devoted at least one column or article to the play being lavishly praised by the white critical community, but none of them encapsulated the story line, and none commented on the implication of this view of blacks for race relations in the United States. Instead, they showed solidarity with Charles Gilpin, an African American actor who was making a hit on Broadway. They crowed about the future of black actors on the American stage and predicted that Gilpin's success would pave the way for others. Of these three critical writers, Johnson alone noted the difference between the reception for Gilpin and that accorded the Negro Players on the Great White Way. He quoted passages from reviews by Broun and Woollcott, the latter a southerner who "does not go into ecstasies over colored artists simply because they are colored. It was he," Johnson recalled sourly, "who could see very little in the 'Negro Players,' who produced the Ridgely Torrence plays several years ago."[41] For these African American critics, *The Emperor Jones* was neither a play about the descent into terror nor a study in race psychology. O'Neill's drama represented for them a play starring a fellow African American.

In the absence of critical reviews written by black critics and essayists, it is difficult to know for certain how African American audiences saw this revolutionary drama. As long as Gilpin won fame and recognition, African American critics seemed to clench their teeth, reluctant to critique the story line and the upshot of *The Emperor Jones*. In fact, in the middle of the show's relatively long run on Broadway, another incident eventually captured the interest of writers—both black and white. In February 1921 the Drama League polled its members for the names of ten people who had most influenced the American stage in the season just coming to a close; Charles Gilpin received enough votes to make the final list. Rumors spread that Drama League leaders did not want to ignore the wishes of the members but also did not want the black actor at the banquet organized to honor the winners. Some members reported that the Drama League asked the restaurant if it would object to a black guest, hoping that the color line in the restaurant would provide an excuse not to extend Gilpin an invitation. When the restaurant managers replied that Gilpin was welcome, the league planned to notify the star of his honor but to neglect extending an invitation to the banquet. The *New York Age* reported that the league's board had decided to "send him a nice letter assuring him of the high esteem in which he was held" but to withhold the invitation.[42] Others believed that Gilpin had been asked to accept the honor but to excuse himself from the banquet. At last, the Drama League relented and sent Gilpin an invitation. On March 8, 1921, Charles Gilpin took his place between Gilda Varesi, a fellow honoree, and Mrs. Rollin Kirby of the Drama League, dined at the banquet, and graciously accepted the honor and applause of his professional peers and friends of the theater. He was the only African American in attendance.[43]

In one sense the response of the theater people who attended the banquet and of the critics who covered the gala event provide evidence of the changed times. Many prominent figures went out of their way to protest the threatened exclusion of Gilpin. A petition signed by other honorees protested the decision to exclude the African American actor. Robert Edmond Jones announced angrily, "If this report is true, I think it is outrageous and I shall refuse to attend the dinner."[44] And when they found themselves as part of the first "mixed" banquet, they applauded noisily and enthusiastically and, according to the *New York Tribune*, "stood up and cheered him."[45] Instead of averting their faces, wishing to avoid the prospect of unpleasantness, they leapt forward to show their willingness to tolerate and accept a dark-skinned actor.

Likewise, the black press, which had failed to provide a single summary of the play, covered the scandal surrounding the banquet. Lester Walton and James Weldon Johnson, in particular, reveled in the idea of whites honoring a black star and saw his inclusion as a signal event. Nothing less than an equal invitation to and full participation in the Drama League banquet would mollify them after the initial snub. Johnson argued that Gilpin had "done a great service to his race and to his country by impressing upon the American people the principle that a man should be judged, and judged only on his individual merit."[46] Walton also used Gilpin's fame on Broadway to encourage Harlemites to patronize the Lafayette Theatre. After all, he reminded readers, had not Gilpin gotten a start on the boards of the venerable Harlem stage?[47] Not all African American writers, however, hailed Gilpin as a champion of the race. The *Messenger,* for example, blasted the celebrated actor for his failure to stand up for his manhood and his race and for displaying docility and servility.[48]

Their silence about the play, however, cannot be overlooked. Those who desired to support Gilpin had to praise him, and even those who denounced him as a coward failed to comment on the plot of the drama in which he performed. Unlike *Granny Maumee,* which had prompted Johnson to proclaim that the drama had been about lynching, *The Emperor Jones* was difficult to discuss in the terms of race uplift or progress in U.S. race relations. The character of Jones had come to the island as a murderer, an escaped convict, and a petty confidence man, scornful of fellow people of color, and he had brought about his own demise. How could anyone find hope or comfort—or even a terribly honest perspective on relations between the races in the United States—in such a play?

Once Gilpin accepted the honor bestowed on him by the Drama League, enjoyed being wined and dined by admirers in white as well as black theater circles, and eventually moved on, *The Emperor Jones* found a number of other interpreters. Without Gilpin's success hanging in the balance, African Americans were freer to engage the substance of the play. Langston Hughes witnessed a performance of *The Emperor Jones* in a Harlem theater in the 1920s, and he recalled that the "audience didn't know what to make" of it.

> And when the Emperor started running naked through the forest, hearing the Little Frightened Fears, naturally they howled with laughter.
> "Them ain't no ghosts, fool!" the spectators cried from the orchestra,
> "Why don't you come on out o' that jungle back to Harlem where you belong?"
> In the manner of Stokowski hearing a cough at the Academy of Music, Jules Bledsoe stopped dead in his tracks, advanced to the footlights, and proceeded to lecture his audience on manners in the theatre. But the audience wanted none of *The Emperor Jones.* And their manners had been all right at all the other shows. . . . So when Brutus continued his flight, the audience again howled with laughter. And that was the end of *The Emperor Jones* on 135th Street.[49]

The black audience's glee offended Jules Bledsoe; O'Neill's portrayal of blacks obviously offended Negro audiences. As Aframerican culture took shape in the 1920s, the crosscurrents, the misunderstandings across the color line, and the limitations of cross-race collaboration continued as before.

In some respects the so-called culture wars of the 1990s represent echoes of the cultural skirmishes of 1917. Americans continue to struggle with the question of who qualifies as a genuine citizen and which values and expressions constitute the core of the culture. With mountains of popular and academic studies of black history at our disposal and a bloody civil rights struggle behind us, we proceed as if we have come to terms with our past. But returning to this one episode—the performance by black actors of race dramas on Broadway—should remind us that storing and pigeonholing information is not the same as confronting our collective experience. A confrontation that restores our memory—that shakes us out of our collective cultural amnesia—requires new narratives, new structures, new protagonists, and new denouements. The old story with a few dark faces tucked in here and there no longer suffices, and a segregated history leaves unfinished the task of putting all of the pieces together. Blacks and whites together made possible the debut of black actors on Broadway in 1917. They acted on behalf of a protean American culture. Let us not forget.

NOTES

1. OPENING NIGHT AND THE MORNING AFTER

1. For accounts of who attended opening night, see "Mrs. Hapgood Presents Negro Players at Garden," *New York Herald,* April 6, 1917; and "The Theatre," *New York Evening Sun,* April 6, 1917. Clippings appear in Ridgely Torrence Papers, Manuscript Division, Firestone Library, Princeton University (hereinafter RTPA), box 11, folder 5. For character sketches of the critics, see H. L. Kleinfield, "Alexander Humphreys Woollcott," *Dictionary of American Biography* (New York: C. Scribner's Sons, 1928–1958), supplement 3, 842–43; E. J. Kahn, Jr., *The World of Swope* (New York: Simon & Schuster, 1965), 260–61; and "The Men Who Roast the Plays—New York Critics as Seen by John Held," *Theatre Magazine* 25 (March 1917): 138–39.

2. Jones first attracted attention in 1915 as a contributor to an exhibit on the "new stagecraft" sponsored by the New York Stage Society and as the designer for a production of Granville Barker's *The Man Who Married a Dumb Wife.* For a sampling of this early notice, see K. Macgowan, "America's First Exhibition of the New Stagecraft," *Theatre Magazine* 21 (January 1915): 28; Alexander Woollcott, "Second Thoughts on First Nights," *New York Times,* February 7, 1915, sec. 7, p. 4, col. 1–3; and "The Gentleman of the Decoration," *New York Times,* February 14, 1915, sec. 7, p. 4, col. 4–5. In 1916 and 1917, Jones himself became the subject of essays and was invited to write about his artistry in the days following the production of *Three Plays for a Negro Theater.* See "With the Theatre Artists," *Theatre Arts Magazine* 1 (November 1916): 37; Hiram K. Moderwell, "Scenery That Helps the Actor," *Theatre Magazine* 24 (September 1916): 128; Hiram Kelly Moderwell, "The Art of Robert Edmond Jones," *Theatre Arts Magazine* 1 (February 1917): 51–61; and Robert Edmond Jones, "The Future Decorative Art of the Theatre," *Theatre Magazine* 25 (May 1917): 266.

3. "Three Playlets—Thursday Night at the Garden," *New York Times,* April 1, 1917, sec. 8, p. 6, col. 1; and Elizabeth Hiatt Gregory, "What Society Is Doing for the Stage," *Theatre Magazine* 25 (June 1917): 338–39.

4. Torrence's intimate friendships with contemporary artists are best discussed in Percy MacKaye, ed., *Letters to Harriet by William Vaughn Moody*; Hermann Hagedorn, *Edwin Arlington Robinson, A Biography*; and John M. Clum, *Ridgely Torrence*.

5. "Music and Drama," *New York Evening Post,* April 3, 1917, p. 11, col. 4. See also Robert C. Benchley, "Can This Be the Native American Drama?" *New York Tribune,* April 1, 1917, part 5, p. 6, col. 1–6; "The Week's Grist," *New York Tribune,* April 1, 1917, part 4, p. 3, col. 3–4; "News of the Week," *New York Times,* March 25, 1917, sec. 8, p. 6, col. 4–5; and "Three Playlets—Thursday Night at the Garden," *New York Times,* April 1, 1917, sec. 8, p. 6, col. 1. In the weekly African American newspaper, the *New York Age,* advance notice of the debut of black actors on Broadway was given nearly a month before opening night. See "Negroes to Be Seen on Broadway," *New York Age,* March 8, 1917, p. 6, col. 2; Lester A. Walton, "Art for Art's Sake," *New York Age,* March 15, 1917, p. 6, col. 1; and "Theatrical Jottings," *New York Age,* March 29, 1917, p. 6, col. 2.

6. No writer made this point more clearly than James Weldon Johnson in *Black Manhattan.* "April 5, 1917, is the date of the most important single event in the entire history of the Negro in the American theatre; for it marks the beginning of a new era," he wrote. "On that date a performance of three dramatic plays was given by the Coloured Players at the Garden Theatre in Madison Square Garden, New York and the stereotyped traditions regarding the Negro's histrionic limitations were smashed." See Johnson, *Black Manhattan,* 175. For overviews of turn-of-the-century black musical comedy, see Paul Carter Harrison and Bert Andrews, *In the Shadow of the Great White Way: Images from the Black Theatre*; Frederick W. Bond, *The Negro and the Drama*; Allen Woll, *Black Musical Theatre: From Coontown to Dreamgirls*; Thomas L. Riis, *Just before Jazz: Black Musical Theatre in New York, 1890–1915*; and Henry T. Sampson, *Blacks in Blackface: A Source Book on Early Black Musical Shows.*

7. Ridgely Torrence to Jean Cavinee, May 20, 1936, in RTPA, box 34, folder 8. He repeated essentially the same story in his manuscript "Notes on the Negro Theatre" in 1939. See RTPA, box 9, folder 8. Oddly enough, however, Torrence did little to urge his own family to attend the plays.

8. Torrence originally entitled this play *The Nest Egg.* The main characters and the white forger, Wilson Byrd, were given names that made the title a play on words. *The Nest Egg* also gives a much better idea of the play's focus than does *The Rider of Dreams.* It is not clear when or why the play's name was changed, but I would speculate that the decision to do so resulted from Torrence's desire to be identified with John Millington Synge, the Irish playwright who authored *Riders to the Sea* as part of his appropriation of Irish folk life for the Dublin Theatre. Synge's play, a very short tragedy, and Torrence's play bear no resemblance to one another except for their titles. See Mrs. W. V. Moody to Ridgely Torrence, February 1, 1915, RTPA, box 47, folder 4, for an early reference to "The Nest Egg," and compare John Millington Synge's *Riders to the Sea* (Boston: J. W. Luce & Co., 1911) with Torrence's second play in *Granny Maumee, The Rider of Dreams, Simon, the Cyrenian: Plays for a Negro Theater.*

9. A program from later in the run includes the names of carpenters, electricians, stage manager, and others associated with the play. That these people were African American is indicated in a letter written nearly two decades later by Torrence. He wrote that "every person connected with the production, including even the stage hands," were of "the colored race." See Ridgely Torrence to Jean Cavinee, May 20, 1936, RTPA, box 34, file 8.

10. See Matthew 27:32; Mark 15:21; and Luke 32:26. John contains no reference to a crossbearer named Simon.

11. See Matthew 27:19.

12. Torrence, *Granny Maumee, The Rider of Dreams, Simon, the Cyrenian: Plays for a Negro Theater,* 94.

13. Ibid., 111.

14. Although not in attendance until the next night, Randolph Bourne commented on the effect of the play on the audience. In a letter to the editor of the *New York Tribune,* he wrote: "It was Good Friday. And it was the day of the proclamation of war as the solemn tones pealed out in the last play, *Simon, the Cyrenian,* with its setting for the Crucifixion—'They that take the sword shall perish by the sword'—you could hear the audience catch its breath as it realized the piercing meaning of this heroic little drama of non-resistance played before a Christian nation that was going into a world war on the very day that its churches celebrated devoutly the anniversary of this very warning." The letter appeared on the editorial page on April 10, 1917; it is quoted in part in Clum, *Ridgely Torrence,* 111.

15. Merlin J. Clusium to Ridgely Torrence, April 5, 1917, in RTPA, box 25, folder 2.

16. " 'Colored Players' at Garden Theatre," *New York Sun,* April 6, 1917, p. 7, col. 1; Heywood Broun, "Negro Players Score Success in Interesting Bill of Short Plays," *New York Tribune,* April 6, 1917, p. 11, col. 6; "Dramas of Negro Life at Garden," *New York World,* April 6, 1917, p. 11, col. 1; "Three Negro Plays Played by Negroes," *New York Times,* April 6, 1917, p. 11, col. 1.

17. "Mrs. Hapgood's Colored Players," *New York Evening Post,* April 6, 1917, p. 6, col. 3; and "The Theatre," *New York Evening Sun,* April 6, 1917; and Burns Mantle, "Negro Actors Present Unique Programme of Negro Plays at Garden Theatre," *New York Evening Mail,* April 6, 1917, 8, clippings of the latter two articles in RTPA, box 11, folder 5.

18. Torrence was fairly compulsive about saving letters and newspaper clippings about the three plays. Since his mother, now a widow, was unable to make the trip from Xenia, Ohio, to New York to see the plays, he bundled up these tokens of his success and sent them out to her so she could share his triumph. In the first few heady days after opening night, he and his wife wrote letters home, enclosing cards, notes, and clippings and asking that his mother eventually return them. The bulk of these letters can be found in RTPA, box 25, folder 2. The clippings appear in RTPA, box 11, folder 5.

19. Lester A. Walton, "Negro Actors Make Debut in Drama at Garden Theatre," *New York Age,* April 12, 1917, p. 1, col. 1.

20. James Weldon Johnson, "The Negro and the Drama," *New York Age,* April 19, 1917, p. 4, col. 3; "Music and Art," *Crisis* 14 (May 1917): 84; and "The Negro Players," *Southern Workman* 46 (June 1917): 323.

21. "Mr. Hornblow Goes to the Play," *Theatre Magazine* 25 (May 1917): 280.

22. "The Negro in American Drama," *Theatre Magazine* 25 (June 1917): 350.

23. "Mr. Hornblow Goes to the Play," *Theatre Magazine* 25 (July 1917): 21; and Arthur Hornblow, *A History of the Theatre in America: From Its Beginnings to the Present Time.*

24. James Metcalfe, "Some Things That Bloom in the Spring," *Life* 69 (April 19, 1917): 685; "Confidential Guide," *Life* 69 (May 3, 1917): 773; and James Metcalfe, "The Season Gets the Hook," *Life* 69 (May 31, 1917): 950–51.

25. Louis V. De Foe, "The Drama's False Friends," *Theatre Magazine* 26 (August 1917): 63.

26. Charlton Andrews, "Theatrical History in America," *Drama* 13 (February 1914): 153.

27. See Hornblow, *History of the Theatre in America;* Margaret G. Mayorga, *A Short History of the American Theatre: Commentaries on Plays Prior to 1920*; Mary Caroline Crawford, *The Romance of the American Theatre*; and Brander Matthews, *Rip Van Winkle Goes to the Play and Other Essays on Plays and Players.* Hornblow's history was reviewed in *Theatre Arts Magazine* as the "first complete record covering with anything like thoroughness the two centuries of the theatre in America." See "Theatre Arts Bookshelf," *Theatre Arts Magazine* 4 (April 1920): 174. For a comment on Crawford's book, see Charlton Andrews, "Theatrical History in America," *Drama* 13 (February 1914): 151–53.

28. See for example *The American Theatre: A Sum of Its Parts* (New York: Samuel French, 1971); C. W. E. Bigsby, *A Critical Introduction to Twentieth Century American Drama*; Jane F. Bonin, *Major Themes in Prize-Winning American Drama*; Alan S. Downes, ed., *American Drama*; and Howard Taubman, *The Making of the American Theatre.* One work from this period stands out for its attempt to be inclusive of the artistry of black Americans: Garff B. Wilson, *Three Hundred Years of American Drama and Theatre.*

29. Johnson, *Black Manhattan;* Bond, *The Negro and the Drama;* W. E. B. Du Bois, *Gift of the Black Folk: The Negroes in the Making of America*; and Edith J. R. Isaacs, *The Negro in the American Theatre.*

30. Johnson, *Black Manhattan,* 179.

31. Lary May, *Screening Out the Past: The Birth of Mass Culture and the Motion Picture Industry.*

32. For an excellent study of both these phenomena, as seen through the lives of James Reese Europe and Vernon and Irene Castle, see Reid Badger, *James Reese Europe: A Life in Ragtime.*

33. For an example of the discussion of the possible effect of the war on American theaters, see George S. Kaufman, "Broadway and Elsewhere," *New York Tribune,* April 8, 1917, part 4, p. 1, col. 4–5.

34. Lawrence Southerland, "Patriotism on the American Stage," *Theatre Magazine* 25 (May 1917): 286–88.

35. Ever since Thomas Bender's clarion call for a new synthesis more than a decade ago, scholars have wrestled mightily with the difficult task of fashioning a narrative from a mountain of disparate monographs and studies of particular communities. Indeed, as Shelley Fisher Fishkin has noted, a spate of new work in the past five years alone has begun to "remap" American cultural life. See Bender, "Wholes and Parts: The Need for Synthesis in American History," *Journal of American History* 73 (June 1986): 120–36; and Fishkin, "Interrogating 'Whiteness,' Complicating 'Blackness': Remapping American Culture," *American Quarterly* 47 (September 1995): 428–66. For examples of very recent attempts to create a new synthesis, see Edward Countryman, *Americans: A Collision of Histories* (New York: Hill & Wang, 1996); Ronald Takaki, *A Different Mirror: A History of Multicultural America*; and Priscilla Wald, *Constituting Americans: Cultural Anxiety and Narrative Form.* I am borrowing the mirror imagery from both Takaki and Wald. Takaki notes that until we construct a "different mirror," countless Americans will continue to stand before the looking glass of American history and see no trace of themselves. In a slightly different way, Wald employs a discussion of mirrors and culture. Drawing an analogy between what Sigmund Freud called the "uncanny" and cultural anxiety, Wald suggests that racial exclusion occurs in the body politic when, as a group, Americans have had the uncanny experience of seeing a reflection of themselves that they found repulsive. Creating a different mirror and recognizing that not all Americans will like it (especially those satisfied with the old, warped model) are important insights that inform this project.

36. Loren Kruger, *The National Stage: Theatre and Cultural Legitimation in England, France, and America,* esp. chap. 1. The points made by Kruger parallel some of the ideas presented by Jackson Lears in his influential discussion of Antonio Gramsci's theory of cultural hegemony. See Lears, "The Concept of Cultural Hegemony: Problems and Possibilities," *American Historical Review* 90 (June 1985): 567–93. Kruger also explicitly draws on the work of Victor Turner for his ideas about liminality, "social drama," and the process of cultural legitimation. See Turner, *The Anthropology of Performance* (New York: PAJ Publications, 1988).

37. Lears, "The Concept of Cultural Hegemony"; and Susan Curtis, *Dancing to a Black Man's Tune: A Life of Scott Joplin,* preface.

38. The following represents a small sample of articles that appeared in the United States around the turn of the century, discussing distinctive American cultural forms and character traits: Richard Aldrich, "American Composers," *Etude* 17 (May 1899): 135–37; "Americans in the Rough," *Outlook* 81 (December 23, 1905): 956–57; Helen Campbell, "Is American Domesticity Decreasing, and If So, Why?" *Arena* 19 (January 1898): 86–96; Arthur Farwell, "The Struggle toward a National Music," *North American Review* 186 (December 1907): 565–70; H. E. Kriehbiel, "The Distinctive Note in American Music," *Etude* 24 (March 1906): 108; William O. Partridge, "The American School of Sculpture," *Forum* 29 (June 1900): 493–500; John Clark Ridpath, "Shall the United States Be Europeanized," *Arena* 18 (December 1897): 827–33; Jessie

Trimble, "The Founder of an American School of Art," *Outlook* 85 (February 23, 1907): 453–60; and "What Is the American Spirit?" *Independent* 53 (August 8, 1901): 1873–74. In another context, I have discussed the significance of this quest for a distinctive American culture. See Curtis, *Dancing to a Black Man's Tune,* 11–18, 162–71.

39. Robert Benchley, "Can This Be the Native American Drama?" *New York Tribune,* April 1, 1917, part 5, p. 6, col. 1–6; Lester A. Walton, "Negro Actors Make Debut in Drama at Garden Theatre," *New York Age,* April 12, 1917, p. 1, col. 1; p. 6, col. 1–2.

40. I first became aware of this approach through conversations with and books by David Roediger. As he and others who have followed his lead have shown, the race problem as it typically is defined unfairly places the burden for interracial conflict on African Americans. Without recognizing "whiteness" as well as "blackness," it is easy to slip into a mode of thinking that essentializes a white perspective. See David R. Roediger, *The Wages of Whiteness: Race and the Making of the American Working Class*; and *Towards the Abolition of Whiteness.* For an excellent discussion of this new impulse in American historical research, see Shelley Fisher Fishkin, "Interrogating 'Whiteness,' Complicating 'Blackness.'" For an essay on the privileges that accrue to people claiming whiteness, see George Lipsitz, "The Possessive Investment in Whiteness: Racialized Social Democracy and the 'White' Problem in American Studies," *American Quarterly* 47 (September 1995): 369–87. For an insightful essay that reflects on the seeming "naturalness" of whiteness in film, see Richard Dyer, *The Matter of Images: Essays on Representation,* 141–63.

41. One of the most insightful studies of African American theater includes a discussion of the tension that exists between black playwrights and American audiences. The author, Helene Keyssar, argues that the nature of American drama has been shaped most decisively by American audiences that expect to see themselves represented onstage as white, middle-class, and in a family. Given those requirements, she insists, black playwrights face a fundamental challenge unless they try to write black experience as close as possible to these specifications. See Keyssar, *The Curtain and the Veil: Strategies in Black Drama,* chap. 1.

42. "Eugene Walter—The Insurgent Dramatist," *Theatre Magazine* 8 (October 1908): 272.

43. Randolph Hartley, "New Dramatists Who Have Captured Broadway," *Theatre Magazine* 12 (September 1910): 81. In addition to being white, the American dramatist portrayed by Hartley also unquestionably was a man.

44. Burns Mantle, "Negro Actors Present Unique Programme of Negro Plays at Garden Theatre," *New York Evening Mail,* April 6, 1917, 8, in RTPA, box 11, folder 5. In Mantle's article, the word *negro* was not capitalized, a matter deserving explanation. I have chosen to leave the word as it first appeared, because at the time of writing, Mantle's refusal to capitalize Negro represented the convention on white dailies. Four years earlier, Lester A. Walton had begun a campaign to convince newspaper editors to change this practice. He met with little success until 1918, when the *New York World* changed its policy (and a few years later hired Walton to write a column on African

Americans in New York). It would not be until the 1930s that a majority of newspapers agreed to capitalize Negro.

45. Louis Sherwin, "The Beginnings of the Negro Theatre," *Vanity Fair* 8 (June 1917): 54, 96. The quote appears on page 54.

46. Curtis, *Dancing to a Black Man's Tune*; Badger, *James Reese Europe*.

47. Carl Van Vechten, "The Great American Composer: His Grandfathers Are the Present Writers of Our Popular Ragtime Songs," *Vanity Fair* 8 (April 1917): 75, 140; Badger, *James Reese Europe*; Ethel Waters, *His Eye Is on the Sparrow* (Garden City, New York: Doubleday, 1951); and Ann Douglas, *Terrible Honesty: Mongrel Manhattan in the 1920s.*

48. Curtis, *Dancing to a Black Man's Tune,* esp. chap. 6. The title of a recent book on minstrelsy reflects its author's recognition of the coexistence of cultural collaboration and continued social segregation and racial inequality; see Eric Lott, *Love and Theft: Blackface Minstrelsy and the American Working Class.*

49. Van Vechten, "The Great American Composer."

50. "More about Negro Music," *New York Sun,* April 18, 1917, sec. 3, p. 5, col. 2–3;

51. Woollcott, "Three Negro Plays Played by Negroes," *New York Times,* April 6, 1917, p. 11, col. 1.

52. W. E. B. Du Bois, "The New Negro Theatre," *New York Call,* April 22, 1917. Clipping in RTPA, box 11, folder 5.

53. Walton, "Negro Actors Make Debut in Drama at Garden Theatre," *New York Age,* April 12, 1917, p. 6, col. 1.

54. Susan Gubar, *Racechanges: White Skin, Black Face in American Culture*; Douglas, *Terrible Honesty.*

55. Interest in American cultural history has grown steadily since the 1980s and has come, in the opinion of some scholars, to occupy a central place in current historiography. The following two collections of essays edited by Richard Wightman Fox and T. J. Jackson Lears offer excellent examples of the kinds of cultural inquiries undertaken in the past couple of decades: *The Culture of Consumption: Critical Essays in American History, 1880–1980*; *The Power of Culture: Critical Essays in American History.* See also Paul Conkin and John Higham, eds., *New Directions in American Intellectual History*; John Toews, "Intellectual History after the Linguistic Turn," *American Historical Review* 92 (October 1987): 879–907; James Henretta, "Social History as Lived and Written," *American Historical Review* (1979): 1293–1321; and Lears, "The Concept of Cultural Hegemony."

56. Fishkin, "Interrogating 'Whiteness,' Complicating 'Blackness,'" 456.

2. THE ROAD TO BROADWAY

1. Torrence to Jean Cavinee, May 20, 1936, RTPA, box 34, folder 8; see also Torrence, "Notes on the Negro Theatre," c. 1939 in RTPA, box 9, folder 8; and Olivia Torrence to Torrence Family, n.d. (April 1917), in RTPA, box 25, folder 2.

2. Lester A. Walton, "The Future of the Negro on the Stage," *Colored American Magazine* 6 (May and June 1903): 442.

3. Miss Bryant to Ridgely Torrence, n.d.; Kathryn Hunt to Torrence, April 24, 1917; Philip M. Brisbane to Torrence, April 17, 1917; and Hallie E. Queen to Torrence, April 14, 1917, all of which can be found in RTPA, box 25, folder 2.

4. Johnson, *Black Manhattan,* 78–86; Du Bois, *The Gift of Black Folk,* 309, 10; and Isaacs, *The Negro in the American Theatre,* 19–21.

5. James H. Dormon, "Shaping the Popular Image of Post-Reconstruction American Blacks: The 'Coon Song' Phenomenon of the Gilded Age," *American Quarterly* 40 (December 1988): 450–71. For fascinating new interpretations of minstrelsy, see Lott, *Love and Theft*; and Roediger, *The Wages of Whiteness.*

6. Bond, *The Negro and the Drama,* 44–45; Bart Kennett, *Colored Actors' Union Theatrical Guide* (Washington, D.C.: n.p., 1925), 41; and Harrison and Andrews, *In the Shadow of the Great White Way,* 7.

7. Johnson, *Black Manhattan,* 104–5.

8. " 'Mr. Lode of Koal,' A Broadway Show," *New York Age,* September 16, 1909, p. 6, col. 1–2; "Better Accommodations for Colored Performers," *New York Age,* September 30, 1909, p. 6, col. 1–2.

9. Lester A. Walton, "Bert Williams in Vaudeville," *New York Age,* April 21, 1910, p. 6, col. 1–2.

10. Carl Van Vechten, "The Negro Theatre," *In the Garret* (New York: Knopf, 1920), 312–13. For other work on Williams, see Eric Lidell Smith, *Bert Williams: A Biography of the Pioneer Black Comedian*; and Ann Charters, *Nobody: The Story of Bert Williams.*

11. "The Negro on the Stage," *Theatre Magazine* (April 1903), quoted in Bond, *The Negro and the Drama,* 49.

12. Isaacs, *The Negro in the American Theatre,* 41.

13. Lester A. Walton, "Bert Williams Feature of the Follies of 1910," *New York Age,* June 23, 1910, p. 6, col. 1–2. Walton, playing the role of booster as well as critic, quoted passages from reviews of the Follies that appeared in other New York dailies. See also "Plays and Players," *Theatre Magazine* 12 (August 1910): 34–35.

14. Quote is from Isaacs, *The Negro in the American Theatre,* 40. See "What News of the Rialto?" *New York Times,* sec. 2, p. 9, col. 1–3; Bond, *The Negro and the Drama,* 49; and Mabel Rowland, *Bert Williams, Son of Laughter; A Symposium Tribute to the Man and to His Work.*

15. "Bert Williams in Vaudeville," *New York Age,* April 21, 1910, p. 6, col. 1.

16. "Bert Williams Turns Philosopher," *New York Age,* December 1, 1910, p. 6, col. 1.

17. Mrs. Evelyn C. Davis to Walton, February 25, 1953, in Lester A. Walton Papers, Schomburg Center for Research in Black Culture, New York (hereinafter LAWPA), box 17, file 14. Davis wrote, "In discussing Bert Williams, the great Negro comedian, we discovered that no one knew much about him personally," and she asked Walton to supply as much information about Williams as possible. Doris E. Saunders to Walton, May 13, 1953, in LAWPA, box 18, file 20. Saunders, too, hoped "to do something in the way of a biography of Bert Williams" and told Walton she would appreciate any

information or anecdotes he could offer. Lester A. Walton to Louis Sobol, February 7, 1956, in LAWPA, box 18, file 14. In response to Sobol's request for Walton's input into a Broadway Hall of Fame, Walton wrote a letter to add the names of Bert Williams, Ernest Hogan, Bob Cole, and Rosamond Johnson to Sobol's list. For a brief discussion of the limits placed on Williams, see Robert W. Snyder, *The Voice of the City: Vaudeville and Popular Culture in New York,* 120–21.

18. "Red Moon's Rays," *New York Age,* March 25, 1909, p. 6, col. 3; "Smart Set Opens Big," *New York Age,* September 8, 1910, p. 6, col. 2; "New Act Pleases Managers," *New York Age,* February 9, 1911, p. 6, col. 3–4; "Theatrical Jottings," *New York Age,* July 18, 1912, p. 6, col. 2; Lester A. Walton, "Amathesp Club Show," *New York Age,* December 19, 1912, p. 6, col. 1–2; "Will Give Big Bill," *New York Age,* January 23, 1913, p. 6, col. 2–3; "Lafayette Theatre," *New York Age,* April 24, 1913, p. 6, col. 3; "Lafayette Theatre," *New York Age,* November 20, 1913, p. 6, col. 3; "Children Admitted Free at Lafayette Theatre," *New York Age,* June 25, 1914, p. 6, col. 3–4; James Reese Europe to Ridgely Torrence, March 4, 1914, in RTPA, box 36, folder 1; and "Lincoln Returns to Vaudeville," *New York Age,* June 8, 1916, p. 6, col. 3.

19. Lester A. Walton, "In Quest of Egyptian Princess," *New York Age,* March 22, 1917, p. 6, col. 1.

20. Henry T. Sampson, *The Ghost Walks: A Chronological History of Blacks in Show Business, 1865–1910,* 191, 390, 393, 400, 402, 413, 425, 450, 460–63, and 468.

21. The reviews in *Indianapolis Freeman,* October 16, 1909, and November 20, 1909, are quoted in full in Sampson, *The Ghost Walks,* 481 and 488.

22. Lester A. Walton, "Plans for the Coming Season," *New York Age,* July 15, 1909, p. 6, col. 1–2; and "Mr. Lode of Koal," *New York Age,* November 18, 1909, p. 6, col. 2–3.

23. "Smart Set Drawing Crowds," *New York Age,* May 12, 1910, p. 6, col. 2; "Theatrical Jottings," *New York Age,* June 16, 1910, p. 6, col. 3; "Theatrical Jottings," *New York Age,* June 23, 1910, p. 6, col. 3, where the *Chicago Evening American* of June 18, 1910, is quoted.

24. "Pekinites en [*sic*] Tour," *New York Age,* May 4, 1911, p. 6, col. 3; "Theatrical Jottings," *New York Age,* May 23, 1912, p. 6, col. 4; Photo of Lottie Grady with caption in *New York Age,* June 20, 1912, p. 6, col. 2–3; "Theatrical Comment," *New York Age,* May 8, 1913, p. 6, col. 1–2.

25. "Negro Motion Pictures," *New York Age,* July 31, 1913, p. 6, col. 3; "Colored Pictures a Hit," *New York Age,* September 25, 1913, p. 6, col. 4.

26. "Theatrical Jottings," *New York Age,* April 20, 1916, p. 6, col. 3.

27. Sampson, *Blacks in Blackface,* 354; Harrison and Andrews, *In the Shadow of the Great White Way,* 7; and Sampson, *The Ghost Walks,* 108. See also Isaacs, *The Negro in the American Theatre,* 31.

28. Sampson, *The Ghost Walks,* 370, 454, and 483; "Theatrical Jottings," *New York Age,* November 16, 1911, p. 6, col. 2; and "News from Bandanna Land," *New York Age,* March 4, 1909, p. 6, col. 2–3.

29. Robert J. Douglass, "Inez Clough, Dramatic Actress, Dies in Chicago," *New York*

Age, December 9, 1933, p. 6, col. 3; "At the Lafayette," *New York Age,* May 18, 1916, p. 6, col. 4; "Lafayette Theatre," *New York Age,* October 19, 1916, p. 6, col. 2; "Lafayette Theatre," *New York Age,* November 16, 1916, p. 6, col. 3; and playbills for *The Hebrew,* Beaux Art Entertainment Bureau, Schomburg Center for Research in Black Culture, New York.

30. Douglass, "Inez Clough, Dramatic Actress, Dies in Chicago," *New York Age,* December 9, 1933, p. 6, col. 3.

31. Riis, *Just before Jazz,* 28, 44, 81–82, 91, 105, 117, and 120; Kennett, *Colored Actors' Union Theatrical Guide,* 50; and Joseph W. Reed, "A Tribute to the Black Thespian," *Colored American Magazine* 10 (January 1906): 753–55.

32. "News from Bandanna Land," *New York Age,* March 4, 1909, p. 6, col. 2–3.

33. "Jesse Shipp Laid to Rest after 50 Years in the Show Business," *New York Age,* May 12, 1934, p. 5, col. 2; Kennett, *Colored Actors' Union Theatrical Guide,* 50; Robert Mott to Jesse Ship [*sic*], September 29, 1910, in the Anne Cooke Collection of Theater Materials, Moorland-Spingarn Research Center, Howard University, Washington, D.C. (hereinafter ACC-MSRC), box 22–1, file 1; "Davis-Shipp Wedding," *New York Age,* September 8, 1910, p. 6, col. 3–4; Walton, "Amathesp Club Show," *New York Age,* December 19, 1912, p. 6, col. 1–2; "Lafayette Theatre," *New York Age,* May 15, 1913, p. 6, col. 5.

34. "Alex Rogers, Song Writer, Playwright, Dies Suddenly following a Heart Attack," *New York Age,* September 20, 1930, p. 1, col. 1–3; Riis, *Just before Jazz,* 44, 55, 94, 100, 117, and 119; and "News from Bandanna Land," *New York Age,* March 4, 1909, p. 6, col. 3.

35. Riis, *Just before Jazz,* 123, 147; Lester A. Walton, "Johnson and Rogers Form Vaudeville Team," *New York Age,* February 2, 1911, p. 6, col. 1; and "Theatrical Jottings," *New York Age,* October 19, 1911, p. 6, col. 4.

36. Riis, *Just before Jazz,* 105, 120; Flyer for "Alex Rogers and Henry S. Creamer's Big Musical Comedy Company," in the Leigh Whipper Papers, Moorland-Spingarn Research Center, Howard University, Washington, D.C. (hereinafter LWPA-MSRC), box 114–4, file 112.

37. "Bush Stock Company to Open at Lafayette," *New York Age,* December 23, 1915, p. 6, col. 3–4; "Over the Footlights," *New York Age,* December 23, 1915, p. 6, col. 1–3; Lester A. Walton, "Passing for White," *New York Age,* January 6, 1916, p. 6, col. 1–2; "At the Lafayette," *New York Age,* October 19, 1916, p. 6, col. 2; "Lafayette Theatre," *New York Age,* November 16, 1916, p. 6, col. 3.

38. Johnson, *Black Manhattan,* 178; Lester A. Walton, "The Pre-Lenten Recital," *New York Age,* February 22, 1912, p. 6, col. 1–2; and "Soap box Minstrels' Show," *New York Age,* May 9, 1912, p. 6, col. 2–3.

39. Johnson, *Black Manhattan,* 178; "At the Lafayette," *New York Age,* September 10, 1914, p. 6, col. 1–2; "Society Vaudeville Show," *New York Age,* May 12, 1910, p. 6, col. 1–2.

40. Johnson, *Black Manhattan,* 178; "The Lure of the Cabaret," *New York Age,* September 12, 1912, p. 6, col. 1–2; " 'Way Down South,' " *New York Age,* September 16,

1915, p. 6, col. 2; Uno, "Miller and Lyles Score a Big Hit," *New York Age*, October 28, 1915, p. 6, col. 1–3; "At the Lafayette," *New York Age*, May 18, 1916, p. 6, col. 4; "Theatrical Jottings," *New York Age*, December 7, 1916, p. 6, col. 5; and James Haskins, *Black Theatre in America*, 50.

41. Torrence's autobiographical statement is in RTPA, box 9, folder 1; Zona Gale, "The Colored Players and Their Plays," *Theatre Arts Magazine* 1 (May 1917): 140; and Robert C. Benchley, "Can This Be the Native American Drama?" *New York Tribune*, April 1, 1917, part 5, p. 6, col. 5–6.

42. Benchley, "Can This Be the Native American Drama?," *New York Tribune*, April 1, 1917, part 5, p. 6, col. 5; Gale, "The Colored Players and Their Plays," 140.

43. Benchley, "Can This Be the Native American Drama?" *New York Tribune*, April 1, 1917, part 5, p. 6, col. 6.

44. Sampson, *Blacks in Blackface*, 354.

45. Louis Calta, "Character Actor, 91, Is Honored at the St. Regis," *New York Times*, January 8, 1968, in LWPA-MSRC, box 114–1, file 1.

46. Curtis, *Dancing to a Black Man's Tune*, 158–59; Eileen Southern, ed., *Biographical Dictionary of Afro-American and African Musicians* (Westport, Conn.: Greenwood Press, 1982), 81–82, 76–77, and 128–29.

47. Lester A. Walton, "The Need of Preparation," *New York Age*, July 18, 1912, p. 6, col. 1–2.

48. Louis Calta, "Character Actor, 91, Is Honored at the St. Regis," *New York Times*, January 8, 1968, in LWPA-MSRC, box 114–1, file 1.

49. "Red Moon's Rays," *New York Age*, March 25, 1909, p. 6, col. 3.

50. Eugene Levy, *James Weldon Johnson, Black Leader, Black Voice*, 302; and Clum, *Ridgely Torrence*, 106–7.

51. For a general discussion of these plays, see Johnson, *Black Manhattan*, 185–86; and for reviews of individual shows (except *The Clansman*) see Lester A. Walton, " 'The Nigger,' A Great Play," *New York Age*, December 9, 1909, p. 6, col. 1–3; "At the Playhouses," *Theatre Magazine* 11 (January 1910): 2–8; Lester A. Walton, " 'Pride of Race' Powerful Play," *New York Age*, January 20, 1916, p. 1, col. 7; "The New Plays," *Theatre Magazine* 23 (February 1916): 116; "Harris to Stage Play of Negro Life," *New York Times*, May 25, 1916, p. 11, col. 3; and "Theatrical Notes," *New York Times*, June 15, 1916, p. 9, col. 4.

52. "Art," *Crisis* 2 (July 1911): 100–101; and an editorial by Lester A. Walton on the Hippodrome show, "Using the Real Thing," *New York Age*, October 5, 1911, p. 6, col. 1–2.

53. Lester A. Walton, "Charlie Case," *New York Age*, November 30, 1916, p. 6, col. 1.

54. Walton, "Passing for White," *New York Age*, January 6, 1916, p. 6, col. 1.

55. Haskins, *Black Theatre in America*, 48; and Kennett, *Colored Actors' Union Theatrical Guide*, 43–44. For Charles Gilpin's firsthand account of the origin and development of the Pekin Players, see Mary B. Mullett, " 'Where Do I Go from Here?' " *American Magazine* 91 (June 1921): 55, 133. It should be noted that other stock companies predated the Pekin Players, the best example being Worth's All-Star Stock

Company. Worth's was established in New York in 1896, but most of the participants specialized in musical comedy sketches and variety acts. Founded by Bob Cole and Billy Johnson, this stock company did play an important role in the formal training of black actors in the United States, but it probably differed considerably from the stock companies at the Pekin, Lafayette, and Lincoln Theaters formed in the first decade and a half of the new century. For a discussion of Worth's All-Star Stock Company, see Artee F. Young, "Lester A. Walton: Black Theatre Critic," 26, 33.

56. Lucie France Pierce, "The Only Colored Stock Theatre in America," *Theatre Magazine* 8 (January 1908): 27–28.

57. The quotes are from *New York Age,* March 13, 1913, 6, and March 20, 1913, 6, and are quoted in Riis, *Just before Jazz,* 164. See also a critic's comment on the coming of the group in Lester A. Walton, "Theatrical Comment," *New York Age,* March 6, 1913, p. 6, col. 1.

58. Lester A. Walton, "The Negro Players," *New York Age,* May 15, 1913, p. 6, col. 1–2.

59. Kennett, *Colored Actors' Union Theatrical Guide,* 48–49.

60. Sister M. Francesa Thompson, O.S.F., "The Lafayette Players, 1917–1932," in *The Theatre of Black Americans,* vol. 2, ed. Errol Hill, 15–19; Haskins, *Black Theatre in America,* 50; and Johnson, *Black Manhattan,* 172–73.

61. Young, "Lester A. Walton," 57–62; Loften Mitchell, "The History of the Negro in the American Theatre: Lester Walton and the Lafayette," *New York Amsterdam News,* May 29, 1965, p. 22, col. 1–2; Thompson, "The Lafayette Players, 1917–1932," 17–20; and Romeo L. Dougherty, "Lafayette Theatre, New York, A Negro Institution Whether They Want It That Way or Not," an article prepared for the Associated Negro Press, n.d., in LAWPA, box 6, file 2. For an account of traveling shows organized by Walton, see Ethel Waters and Charles Samuels, *His Eye Is on the Sparrow, An Autobiography by Ethel Waters* (New York: Da Capo Press, 1992), 141–63.

62. Haskins, *Black Theatre in America,* 52–53.

63. Riis, *Just before Jazz,* 141–46; Kennett, *Colored Actors' Union Theatrical Guide,* 35; and for oral accounts of T.O.B.A., see *Wild Women Don't Have the Blues.* Produced by Carol Doyle Van Valkenburgh and Christine Dale in association with WTTW, Chicago, PBS. Directed by Christine Dale. Production Company: Calliope Film Resources, 1989.

64. Kennett, *Colored Actors' Union Theatrical Guide,* 35.

65. "Well Known Performers Organize the 'Frogs,' " *New York Age,* July 9, 1908, p. 6, col. 2.

66. Lester A. Walton, "The Frogs," *New York Age,* August 6, 1908, p. 6, col. 2.

67. Lester A. Walton, "Judge Goff Heard From," *New York Age,* August 13, 1908, p. 6, col. 1–2; and "Frogs Are Incorporated," *New York Age,* August 20, 1908, p. 6, col. 3. In the late 1930s, Lester A. Walton reported to an acquaintance, Judge F. C. Fisher, about the sad demise of the Frogs. In 1928 and 1929, as one of the group's officers, Walton signed a third mortgage on the Frog's club meeting rooms. Because of the hard times that followed in the wake of the stock market crash, the association could not keep up payments. The holder of the mortgage took legal action against the signers,

and in 1938, Walton, on leave from the diplomatic post in Liberia that he had held since 1935, was served with papers to make a settlement. With Arthur B. Spingarn as his legal counsel, Walton negotiated a settlement for two thousand dollars, which Walton and one of the other signers paid from personal funds. See Walton to Judge F. C. Fisher, March 25, 1939, LAWPA, box 9, file—correspondence, 3/1939.

68. Lester A. Walton, "Colored Vaudevillans [sic] Organize," New York Age, June 10, 1909, p. 6, col. 1–3.

69. For a longer discussion of C.V.B.A., see Curtis, Dancing to a Black Man's Tune, 150–54, 58.

70. Filmscript, "Tenth Citizen, U.S.A.," n.d., in LAWPA, box 6, file 12; and Lester A. Walton to Walter M. Furlow, Pepsi Cola Company, March 26, 1953, in LAWPA, box 17, file 17.

71. Lester A. Walton to Stockton Hellfrich, NBC, June 8, 1953, in LAWPA, box 17, file 20.

72. Lester A. Walton, "What I Have Lived to See," an editorial that appeared in the St. Louis Post-Dispatch, n.d., clipping in LAWPA, box 23, file 4. For general biographical information, see Young, "Lester A. Walton," 38–41; "Lester A. Walton, Ex-Envoy, Is Dead: Crusader for Negro Rights Was 84—On City Board," New York Times, October 19, 1965, p. 43, col. 1; an autobiographical letter from Walton to Will Foster, November 21, 1937, in LAWPA, box 8, file 10. In spite of Walton's influence, long life, and many careers, he has largely escaped serious scholarly attention. For information on his education, see "St. Louis Negro Named U.S. Minister to Liberia," St. Louis Post-Dispatch, July 6, 1935, in LAWPA, box 15, Green Scrapbook, p. 5.

73. Curtis, Dancing to a Black Man's Tune, 131–45; for Walton's friendship with the Turpin family, see Walton to Nannie Turpin, July 22, 1939, in LAWPA, box 10, file 1; Walton's other friends are enumerated in a letter from J. Finley Wilson to Lester Walton, September 28, 1946, in LAWPA, box 16, file 26.

74. Young, "Lester A. Walton," 41–44; Lester A. Walton, "Death of Ernest Hogan," New York Age, May 27, 1909, p. 6, col. 1–2; Lester A. Walton, "Theatrical Profession Sustains Big Loss in Death of John Leubrie Hill," New York Age, September 7, 1916, p. 6, col. 1–2; for his collaboration with Sam Patterson, see Lester Walton to Harold Hoffman, March 8, 1952, LAWPA, box 17, file 20; Walton's papers show that his collaboration with Ernest Hogan began several years before 1906. The two collaborated on four songs in 1903, the contracts for which can be found in LAWPA, box 6, file 1.

75. Lester A. Walton, "Bandanna Land," New York Age, February 6, 1908, supplement, p. 10, col. 1–2.

76. Ibid., col. 1.

77. Lester A. Walton, "Morris Letter Causes Comment," New York Age, February 13, 1908, p. 6, col. 1.

78. Lester A. Walton, " 'The Black Politician,' " New York Age, April 2, 1908, p. 6, col. 1–2; Lester A. Walton, " 'Salome,' " New York Age, August 27, 1908, p. 6, col. 1–2; "Theatrical Comment," New York Age, January 14, 1909, p. 6, col. 1; and Lester A. Walton, " 'My Friend from Dixie,' " New York Age, February 16, 1911, p. 6, col. 1–2.

79. Lester A. Walton, "The Return of Cole and Johnson," *New York Age,* October 6, 1910, p. 6, col. 1–2.

80. Lester A. Walton, "McIntyre and Heath in Black Face," *New York Age,* October 21, 1909, p. 6, col. 1–2.

81. Lester A. Walton, "The Two Stage Forces," *New York Age,* December 24, 1908, p. 6, col. 1–2. For an earlier statement along the same lines, see Walton, "The Future of the Negro on the Stage," 439–42; and Lester A. Walton, "Judge Goff Heard From," *New York Age,* August 13, 1908, p. 6, col. 1.

82. Lester A. Walton, "The Awakening," *New York Age,* May 6, 1909, p. 6, col. 1–2.

83. Lester A. Walton, "Conspiracy of the White Press," *New York Age,* May 13, 1909, p. 6, col. 1–2.

84. See Walton's obituaries for these two entertainers: Walton, "The Death of 'Bob' Cole," *New York Age,* August 10, 1911, p. 6, col. 1–2—quote is from col. 1; and "Death of George W. Walker," *New York Age,* January 12, 1911, p. 6, col. 1–4.

85. Lester A. Walton, "Prejudice vs. Art," *New York Age,* February 12, 1914, p. 6, col. 1–2.

86. Lester A. Walton, "Negroes in New York Theatres," *New York Age,* November 18, 1909, p. 6, col. 1–2.

87. Lester A. Walton, "Is the Broadway Theatre Drawing Color Line?" *New York Age,* March 10, 1910, p. 6, col. 4.

88. Lester A. Walton, "Another Charge of Theatre Discrimination," *New York Age,* March 10, 1910, p. 6, col. 5.

89. Lester A. Walton, "Trouble at Victoria Theatre," *New York Age,* March 17, 1910, p. 6, col. 1; Lester A. Walton, "Sues under the Malby Act," *New York Age,* March 24, 1910, p. 6, col. 1; and Lester A. Walton, "Discrimination Cases in Court," *New York Age,* May 5, 1910, p. 6, col. 1.

90. Lester A. Walton, "Another Theatre Manager Fined," *New York Age,* November 23, 1911, p. 6, col. 1–2.

91. "Drawing Color Line Is Resented," *New York Age,* November 14, 1912, p. 1, col. 1–2. See also Jervis Anderson, *This Was Harlem 1900–1950,* 110–11.

92. Lester Walton appears as a minor figure in studies of the African American Stage like Riis, *Just before Jazz.* As the author of a weekly drama column in the *New York Age,* Walton had the ear of Harlem for more than a decade, shaping aesthetic standards, helping to make some careers, and no doubt contributing to the demise of others. But those who know Walton only from this column have no way of knowing his later involvement in politics, diplomacy, and civil rights activism, because no biography of him exists. Walton became active in Democratic Party politics in the 1920s, activity that can best be charted through correspondence with Claude A. Barnett in the Claude A. Barnett Papers, Chicago Historical Society (hereinafter CABPA) and in LAWPA. His interest in Liberia, dating from the late 1920s, launched his career as minister to Liberia, a position he held from 1935 to 1946. For details on this career, see Walter Christmas, *Negroes in Public Affairs* (Chicago: Educational Heritage, 1966), 190–91; Jake C. Miller, *The Black Presence in American Foreign Affairs* (Washington, D.C.:

University Press of America, 1978); and Ibrahim Sundiata, *Black Scandal: America and the Liberian Labor Crisis, 1929–1936* (Philadelphia: Institute for the Study of Human Issues, 1980). Files in the National Archives, in LAWPA, and in CABPA fill in additional details of his diplomatic career. To my knowledge, no study of his civil rights activism exists. His papers at the Schomburg, however, show him to be an active force on both the Commission on Intergroup Relations and the City Commission on Human Rights. For a brief introduction to Walton at this stage of his life, see Marguerite Cartwright, "Lester A. Walton—Distinguished Diplomat," *Negro History Bulletin* 19 (October 1955): 12–13.

93. Lester A. Walton, "Negro Actors Make Debut in Drama at Garden Theatre," *New York Age,* April 12, 1917, p. 1, col. 1–2.

94. Frank Ferguson to Ridgely Torrence, n.d., in RTPA, box 25, folder 2.

95. For discussions of the Stage Negro, see Laurence Hutton, *Curiosities of the American Stage,* 89–144; Young, "Lester A. Walton," 18–22; Bond, *The Negro and the Drama,* 20–21; and Isaacs, *The Negro in the American Theatre,* 20–27.

96. "Theatrical Comment," *New York Age,* March 30, 1911, p. 6, col. 1.

97. Lester A. Walton, "Negro Stage Types," *New York Age,* February 20, 1908, p. 6, col. 1–2. The *Dramatic Mirror* review is quoted in part in Walton's article.

98. Walton, "Conspiracy of the White Press," *New York Age,* May 13, 1909, p. 6, col. 1–2.

99. "Lafayette Theatre," *New York Age,* January 18, 1917, p. 6, col. 1–2.

100. Torrence, *Granny Maumee, The Rider of Dreams, Simon, the Cyrenian,* 11. The line is repeated later in the same scene on page 13.

101. Lester A. Walton, "Negro Life, Subject for Drama," *New York Age,* June 25, 1908, p. 6, col. 1–2.

3. WHITE ARTISTS BEHIND THE SCENES

1. Flyer can be found in RTPA, box 25, folder 2. MacKaye's comments are dated April 7, 1917.

2. Zona Gale, "The Colored Players and Their Plays," *Theatre Arts Magazine* 1 (May 1917): 139.

3. "Mr. Torrence's Story," *New York Times,* April 15, 1917, sec. 8, p. 6, col. 2–3.

4. Hagedorn, *Edwin Arlington Robinson,* 240.

5. Scott Donaldson, "Frederick Ridgely Torrence," *Dictionary of American Biography,* supplement 4 (New York: Charles Scribner's Sons, 1928–1958), 840; Clum, *Ridgely Torrence,* 82–99; and MacKaye, ed., *Letters to Harriet,* 24–32.

6. The letter is quoted in Hagedorn, *Edwin Arlington Robinson,* 282. See also MacKaye, *Letters to Harriet,* 32.

7. Hagedorn, *Edwin Arlington Robinson,* 243–46.

8. Clum, *Ridgely Torrence,* 80–81; for a description of Torrence's plays, see 59–64 and 75–81.

9. Torrence's letter to his family is quoted in Clum, *Ridgely Torrence,* 75; Hagedorn, *Edwin Arlington Robinson,* 164.

10. Clum, *Ridgely Torrence,* 24–25.

11. Ibid., 16.

12. R. S. Dills, *History of Greene County* (Dayton: Odell & Mayer, 1881), 464.

13. *Wiggins & McKillop's Directory of Greene County for 1878* (Columbus, Ohio: Wiggins and McKillop, 1878), 9; and *Edmondson's Xenia City Directory, For 1875 and 1876* (Xenia, Ohio: Edmondson Bros. & Gray, n.d.), 18 and 102.

14. Hagedorn, *Edwin Arlington Robinson,* 243; MacKaye, ed., *Letters to Harriet,* 319–20.

15. Clum, *Ridgely Torrence,* 85–90.

16. Ibid., 90–93.

17. For a good discussion of the important foundations laid by Torrence's generation, see Walter J. Meserve, *An Outline of American Drama,* 124–220. For a more concise linking of the efforts before World War I and social drama in the 1920s, see Walter J. Meserve, "Sidney Howard and the Social Drama of the Twenties," *Modern Drama* 6 (December 1963): 256–66.

18. "Mr. Torrence's Story," *New York Times,* April 15, 1917, sec. 8, p. 6, col. 2.

19. " 'We Have Rich, Dramatic Peasantry in Negroes,' " *The Purple Parrott* (Rockford College) 8 (November 22, 1934): 1.

20. See, for example, Clayton Hamilton, "Negro Plays," *Vogue* (May 15, 1917), in RTPA, box 11, folder 5; "Mrs. Hapgood's Colored Players," *New York Evening Post,* April 6, 1917, p. 6, col. 3; and " 'Colored Players' at Garden Theatre," *New York Sun,* April 6, 1917, p. 7, col. 1.

21. Autobiographical statement in RTPA, box 9, folder 1; see also Torrence to Jean Cavinee, May 20, 1936, in RTPA, box 34, folder 8. By the time Torrence wrote of the effect of Irish Theater on his thinking, that movement had gained acceptance in the United States. But in the 1910s, Torrence would have been exceptional as an ardent fan of their work. At the popular level, many Americans rebuffed the Irish experimental dramatists and performers. Lady Gregory included a chapter entitled " 'The Playboy' in America" in her reminiscences about the Irish Theater. When the Dublin Theatre company made its first tour in the United States in 1911, it was met with attacks in the press, moral diatribes against the themes of some of the plays to be performed, citizen protests calling for censorship, and several run-ins with the police. Many artists like Torrence found much to praise in their dramas, but the general public was not prepared for the "revolution" Irish Theater represented. See Lady Gregory, *Our Irish Theatre: A Chapter of Autobiography* (New York, London: G. P. Putnam's Sons, 1913), 169–252.

22. "Mr. Torrence's Story," *New York Times,* April 15, 1917, sec. 8, p. 6, col. 2.

23. "The Negro in American Drama," *Theatre Magazine* 25 (June 1917): 350.

24. Lester A. Walton, "Knowing the Negro," *New York Age,* April 19, 1917, p. 6, col. 1.

25. For these examples, see Clum, *Ridgely Torrence,* 104–5; see also RTPA, box 9,

folders 1 and 2. This last phrase casts doubt on the reliability of Torrence's memory. None of these men could have had "owners" in post-Reconstruction America, and it seems unlikely that former owners would have lived in Greene County, Ohio, as Torrence indicated.

26. Torrence to William Vaughn Moody, August 31, 1907, quoted in Clum, *Ridgely Torrence,* 96.

27. Thomas Lawrence King, "Black Settlement in Xenia, Ohio, 1850–1880: A Historical Geography" (M.A. Thesis, University of Colorado, 1981), 256–59; and William A. Joiner, *A Half-Century of the Negro in Ohio.*

28. Richard R. Wright, Jr., "The Negroes of Xenia, Ohio: A Social Study," *Bulletin of the Bureau of Labor* 48 (September 1903): 1006, 1014–15.

29. King, "Black Settlement," 242.

30. Wright, "The Negroes of Xenia, Ohio," 1008.

31. Ibid., 1023, 1028.

32. Frederick A. McGinnis, *A History and an Interpretation of Wilberforce University,* 166–68. For a slightly different view of both Xenia and Wilberforce, as seen through the eyes of a young professor who joined the Wilberforce faculty in 1894, see David Levering Lewis, *W. E. B. Du Bois: Biography of a Race, 1868–1919,* 150–78.

33. "Among Our Colored Citizens," *Xenia Daily Gazette,* October 10, 1885, p. 1, col. 5; "Colored Society," *Xenia Torchlight,* August 30, 1882, p. 3, col. 5; *Xenia Democrat-News,* May 1, 1886, p. 3, col. 2; *Xenia Daily Gazette,* October 16, 1885, p. 3, col. 1; and "Among Our Colored Citizens," *Xenia Daily Gazette,* September 30, 1885, p. 1, col. 5.

34. *Xenia Torchlight,* February 9, 1881, p. 3, col. 3; "Amusements," *Xenia Torchlight,* February 23, 1881, p. 3, col. 5; and "Opera House Xenia," *Xenia Torchlight,* February 28, 1883, p. 3, col. 8.

35. King, "Black Settlement," 218–20.

36. McGinnis, *History and Interpretation,* 179–80.

37. "Vote for Dr. Arnett," *Xenia Daily Gazette,* October 8, 1885, p. 1, col. 4.

38. McGinnis, *History and Interpretation,* 57.

39. Dills, *History of Greene County,* 479–80.

40. *Xenia Daily Gazette,* October 21, 1885, p. 3, col. 3.

41. Joiner, *A Half-Century of the Negro in Ohio,* 11, 53.

42. Wright, "The Negroes of Xenia, Ohio," 1013.

43. "Among Our Colored Citizens," *Xenia Daily Gazette and Torchlight,* May 24, 1890, p. 2, col. 3.

44. "Among Our Colored Citizens," *Xenia Daily Gazette and Torchlight,* April 30, 1890, p. 1, col. 4.

45. Helen Hooven Santmyer, *Ohio Town* (New York: Berkeley Books, 1956), esp. chap. 4, "The East End."

46. Torrence's Reminiscences, 1938, in RTPA, box 9, folder 2, quote is on p. 9, but see the entire passage, pp. 5–9.

47. See, for example, a letter from Torrence to his family, February 9, 1917, in RTPA, box 25, folder 1.

48. Torrence to his mother, January 5, 1916, in RTPA, box 25, folder 1.

49. Reminiscences in RTPA, box 9, folder 2; Clum, *Ridgely Torrence,* 104.

50. Quoted in Isaacs, *The Negro in the American Theatre,* 57.

51. James Reese Europe to Torrence, March 4, 1914, in RTPA, box 36, folder 1.

52. Torrence to his family, February 23, 1917, in RTPA, box 25, folder 1; and Torrence to his family, March 2, 1917, RTPA, box 25, folder 1.

53. Torrence to his mother, March 23 or 28, 1917, RTPA, box 25, folder 1.

54. Hallie Q. Brown to Torrence, April 27, 1917, RTPA, box 25, folder 2.

55. Algernon Brashear Jackson to Torrence, April 26, 1917, in RTPA, box 25, folder 2. Jackson had corresponded with Torrence a few years earlier when *Granny Maumee* was put on by the Stage Society. He wrote then that he believed the stage would serve as an important medium for promoting "mutual understanding between your race and mine" and encouraged Torrence to continue his work because "your high ideals in regard to the people of my race are bound to have their reward." See Jackson to Torrence, May 2, 1914, RTPA, box 42, folder 1.

56. James Weldon Johnson, "The Negro and the Drama," *New York Age,* April 19, 1917, p. 4, col. 3–4.

57. "A Poet and a Play-wright," *Crisis* (September 1917) in RTPA, box 11, folder 5.

58. Lester A. Walton, "Negro Actors Make Debut in Drama at Garden Theatre," *New York Age,* April 12, 1917, p. 1, col. 1–2.

59. See letters in Thomas M. Gregory Papers, Moorland-Spingarn Research Center, Howard University (hereinafter TMGPA-MSRC), box 37–2, file 64. Woodrow Wilson, by the way, thanked the Howard Players for the invitation, but not too surprisingly, he stayed away.

60. Walter White to Thomas Montgomery Gregory, February 27, 1922, and Torrence to Thomas Montgomery Gregory, May 6, 1922, both in TMGPA-MSRC, box 37–2, file 53.

61. George Streator, " 'A Nigger Did It' about a Play Called *Stevedore,*" *Crisis* 41 (July 1934): 216–17. The comment about *The Rider of Dreams* appeared at the end of the article and actually was something of a backhanded acknowledgment of the frequency with which Torrence's play was performed. "[*Stevedore*] is likewise recommended for colored dramatic clubs, which burden themselves annually with 'Lady Windermere's Fan' and 'The Rider of Dreams.' " For a brief notice of the Virginia Union Players, see "Little Theater Tournament," *Crisis* 41 (June 1934): 168.

62. Geraid G. Marans to Torrence, August 12, 1949, in RTPA, box 45, folder 1.

63. Djuna Barnes, "Interview with Negro Players," *New York Morning Telegraph,* April 22, 1917, in RTPA, box 11, folder 5.

64. Thomas M. Gregory to Torrence, February 24, 1922, in RTPA, box 30, folder 2.

65. Robert Edmond Jones to Torrence, September 1918, RTPA, box 42, folder 6.

66. The handwritten notes on his experience and contacts with those in the African American theater world and the final report submitted to the Rockefeller Foundation appear in RTPA, box 9, folder 8.

67. "The New Negro Theatre," *Crisis* 14 (June 1917): 80.

68. Mrs. Hapgood's Colored Players," *New York Evening Post,* April 6, 1917, p. 6, col. 3–4; "Mrs. Emilie Hapgood's Theatrical Negro Novelty," *New York Herald,* April 22, 1917, in RTPA, box 113, microfilm of scrapbook.

69. Flyer in RTPA, box 25, folder 2.

70. Walton, "Negro Actors Make Debut in Drama at Garden Theatre," *New York Age,* April 12, 1917, p. 6, col. 1.

71. Elizabeth Hiatt Gregory, "What Society Is Doing for the Stage," *Theatre Magazine* 25 (June 1917): 338.

72. "Emilie Hapgood Dies of a Stroke," *New York Times,* February 17, 1930, p. 21, col. 5; "Norman Hapgood," *Dictionary of American Biography,* supplement 2 (New York: Charles Scribner's Sons, 1928–1958), 280–82; and Lincoln Steffens, *The Autobiography of Lincoln Steffens* (New York: Harcourt, Brace & World, 1931), 311–26.

73. Norman Hapgood, *The Stage in America, 1897–1900.*

74. Michael D. Marcaccio, *The Hapgoods: Three Earnest Brothers,* 43.

75. Hutchins Hapgood, *A Victorian in the Modern World,* 147.

76. Marcaccio, *The Hapgoods,* 20–24.

77. Hapgood, *The Stage in America,* 51; Hapgood, "The Upbuilding of the American Theatre," *Atlantic Monthly* 83 (March 1899): 424; and Hapgood, "Theatrical Syndicate," *International Quarterly* 1 (January 1900): 99–122.

78. Marcaccio, *The Hapgoods,* 74–79; William Hapgood, "The House of Mr. Norman Hapgood," *Architectural Record* 18 (1905): 8–13. To underscore their prominence and privilege, I would note also a brief report from 1913. The Hapgoods installed an electric burglar alarm, and when it went off in early June 1913, while the family was away for the summer, representatives of the Holmes Protective Agency, accompanied by four policemen, hurried to the residence to investigate. See "Search Hapgood House," *New York Times,* June 7, 1913, p. 5, col. 6.

79. Hapgood, *A Victorian in the Modern World,* 146–47.

80. "Heads Stage Society," *New York Times,* April 1, 1914, p. 13, col. 2; and "Mrs. Hapgood Resigns," *New York Times,* March 30, 1915, p. 11, col. 2.

81. "Show New Stage Effects," *New York Times,* November 16, 1914, p. 8, col. 6; and Clayton Hamilton, "The Arts and Crafts Theatre," *Theatre Magazine* 25 (June 1917): 332.

82. Van Vechten's comments originally appeared in the *New York Press,* March 31, 1914, and are quoted in Clum, *Ridgely Torrence,* 106–7.

83. Torrence explained the Stage Society's policy in a letter to Harriet Moody, February 1914, quoted in Clum, *Ridgely Torrence,* 106.

84. Emilie Hapgood to Torrence, n.d., in RTPA, box 39, folder 4.

85. Ibid.; and Emilie Hapgood to Torrence, May 20, 1914, in RTPA, box 39, folder 4.

86. See two undated letters by Emilie Hapgood to Torrence and three others, dated, respectively, May 7, 1914; May 14, 1914; and October 22, 1915, all in RTPA, box 39, folder 4.

87. Gregory, "What Society Is Doing for the Stage," 338; Emilie Hapgood to Torrence, October 22, 1915, in RTPA, box 39, folder 4, where Hapgood tells Torrence of having

bought the rights to Galsworthy's play; and "Three Playlets—Thursday Night at the Garden," *New York Times,* April 1, 1917, sec. 8, p. 6, col. 1, for a brief resume of Emilie Hapgood's career to 1917.

88. Marcaccio, *The Hapgoods,* 83–84; "Mrs. Hapgood Gets Divorce," *New York Times,* July 24, 1915, p. 9, col. 4; Norman Hapgood, *The Changing Years*; Hapgood, *A Victorian in the Modern World,* 126, 128, 146–47. Emilie and Ruth remained close after the divorce. Ruth was with her mother when she died in Italy in 1930. See "Emilie Hapgood Dies of a Stroke," *New York Times,* February 17, 1930, p. 21, col. 5.

89. Emilie Hapgood to Torrence, n.d., RTPA, box 39, folder 4.

90. Torrence to his family, March 17, 1917, in RTPA, box 25, folder 1.

91. Olivia Torrence to the Torrence Family, n.d., RTPA, box 25, folder 2.

92. Olivia Torrence to the Torrence Family, n.d., RTPA, box 25, folder 2.

93. Marcaccio, *The Hapgoods,* 85.

94. "The New Philanthropy," *Crisis* 15 (March 1918): 232. An advertisement that appeared in an earlier issue of *Crisis* called for contributions to be made to the Circle for Negro War Relief, Inc., in care of Harrison Rhodes or Mrs. Hapgood. See *Crisis* 15 (February 1918): 201.

95. Lester A. Walton, "Caruso's Non-Appearance," *New York Age,* February 16, 1918, p. 6, col. 2; and "Emilie Hapgood Dies of a Stroke," *New York Times,* February 17, 1930, p. 21, col. 5. Notice of the successful concert appears in *Crisis* 15 (January 1918): 141.

96. Olivia Torrence to Ridgely Torrence, September 29, 1917, RTPA, box 54, folder 6.

97. Emilie Hapgood to Torrence, n.d., and Emilie Hapgood to Torrence, May 7, 1914, in RTPA, box 39, folder 4.

98. Robert Benchley, "Can This Be the Native American Drama?" *New York Tribune,* April 1, 1917, part 5, p. 6, col. 1.

99. Robert Edmond Jones, "The Future Decorative Art of the Theatre," *Theatre Magazine* 25 (May 1917): 266.

100. Ibid.

101. Percy MacKaye, *Robert Edmond Jones: A Comment on His Work in the Theatre,* see first page of text, entitled "Chronological Notes."

102. Ibid., 1. According to the 1880 census, Strafford County, New Hampshire, where Milton is located, was home to only 47 African Americans. The county's total white population was 35,511, about three thousand of whom were foreign-born. So Milton was homogeneous in both ethnic and racial terms. See *1880 Census: Statistics of the Population of the United States,* vol. 1 (Washington: Government Printing Office, 1883), 401, 421.

103. Hiram K. Moderwell, "The Art of Robert Edmond Jones," *Theatre Arts Magazine* 1 (February 1917): 51–52.

104. Ibid., 52–53; and Ruth Gottholdt, "New Scenic Art of the Theatre," *Theatre Magazine* 21 (May 1915): 248.

105. "Max Reinhardt and His Famous Players," *Theatre Magazine* 14 (August 1911): 56–60, vi.

106. Moderwell, "The Art of Robert Edmond Jones," 53; and Gottholdt, "New Scenic Art of the Theatre," 248.

107. Gottholdt, "New Scenic Art of the Theatre," 248; Moderwell, "The Art of Robert Edmond Jones," 54; and MacKaye, *Robert Edmond Jones,* chronological notes.

108. "Exhibition of Stage Decoration," *New York Times,* February 17, 1915, p. 11, col. 4; and Kenneth Macgowan, "America's First Exhibition of the New Stagecraft," *Theatre Magazine* 21 (January 1915): 28.

109. MacKaye, *Robert Edmond Jones,* 3.

110. Moderwell, "The Art of Robert Edmond Jones," 57; and MacKaye, *Robert Edmond Jones, passim.*

111. Moderwell, "The Art of Robert Edmond Jones," 54.

112. Alexander Woollcott, "Second Thoughts on First Nights," *New York Times,* February 7, 1915, sec. 7, p. 4, col. 1.

113. "The Gentleman of the Decoration," *New York Times,* February 14, 1915, sec. 7, p. 4, col. 4.

114. Moderwell, "The Art of Robert Edmond Jones," 56.

115. "Mr. Hornblow Goes to the Play," *Theatre Magazine* 24 (October 1916): 204a; James Metcalfe, "The New Season Struggling Hard," *Life* 68 (September 7, 1916): 404.

116. Moderwell, "The Art of Robert Edmond Jones," 57; "Notes on the Costumes in 'Caliban of the Yellow Sands,'" *Theatre Arts Magazine* 1 (November 1916): 28–29.

117. Frank Cheney Hersey, "Caliban at Boston," *Theatre Arts Magazine* 1 (August 1917): 196.

118. Moderwell, "The Art of Robert Edmond Jones," 58.

119. Jones, "The Future Decorative Art of the Theatre," 266; also a notice, "With the Theatre Artists," *Theatre Arts Magazine* 1 (November 1916): 37, for a recap of Jones's activities in the 1916–1917 theater season.

120. Sheldon Cheney, "New York's Best Season," *Theatre Arts Magazine* 1 (February 1917): 70.

121. *Theatre Magazine* 25 (April 1917): 198.

122. Robert Edmond Jones to Torrence, May 7, 1915, in RTPA, box 42, folder 6. For evidence of their mutual friendship with Emilie Hapgood, and for the quoted material, see MacKaye, *Robert Edmond Jones,* 5.

123. Johnson, *Black Manhattan,* 219–21.

124. Robert Edmond Jones to Thomas Montgomery Gregory, n.d., TMGPA-MSRC, box 37–2, file 50.

125. "The New Philanthropy," *Crisis* 15 (March 1918): 232.

126. "Art," *Crisis* 5 (February 1913): 167–69.

4. NEW MOVEMENT, OLD PREJUDICES

1. Constance D'Arcy Mackay, *The Little Theatre in the United States,* 1.

2. Ibid., 69–70. Mackay referred to the cast as the Negro Players, a term that will appear in the pages to follow, and one the actors themselves preferred. While many journalists called the group the Colored Players, the actors believed "colored" could refer to any nonwhite people. Some black critics endorsed the actors' decision.

3. For a general introduction to the New Movement in the Theater, see Edmond McAdoo Gagey, *Revolution in American Drama*; and for a good, brief summary of this moment in theater history, see Walter Meserve, *An Outline of American Drama*, 124–212.

4. MacKaye, ed., *Letters to Harriet*, 40.

5. The scholarship on this late-nineteenth-century adjustment to social and cultural change is extensive. Much of it, such as Robert Wiebe's *The Search for Order, 1877–1920* and David Thelen's *The New Citizenship: Origins of Progressivism in Wisconsin, 1885–1900*, offers explanations of the dramatic political reorientation that produced progressivism in the early twentieth century. Others have focused more exclusively on the cultural dimension of this transformation of American life. For an introduction to some of the salient issues in the cultural changes in America at the turn of the century, see T. J. Jackson Lears, *No Place of Grace: Antimodernism and the Transformation of American Culture, 1880–1920*; John F. Kasson, *Amusing the Million: Coney Island at the Turn of the Century*; Lewis Erenberg, *Steppin' Out: New York Night Life and the Transformation of American Culture, 1890–1930*; Alan Trachtenberg, *The Incorporation of America: Culture and Society in the Gilded Age*; Herbert Gutman, *Work, Culture and Society in Industrializing America*; Nell Irvin Painter, *Standing at Armageddon: The United States, 1877–1919*; Lawrence W. Levine, *Highbrow/Lowbrow: The Emergence of Cultural Hierarchy in America*; and Curtis, *Dancing to a Black Man's Tune*. For a fresh and insightful examination of the troubling question of identity in an age of anxiety, see Robert Cousins, "Citizenship and Selfhood: Negotiating Narratives of National and Personal Identity, 1900–1920."

6. Alfred Kuttner, "Dramatic Issues," *New Republic* 1 (December 12, 1914): 22.

7. Curtis, *Dancing to a Black Man's Tune*, 11–18, 161–79.

8. Laurence Hutton, *Curiosities of the American Stage*, 36–44; quoted material is from p. 40 and pp. 42–43.

9. John Corbin, "The American Drama," *Form* 34 (July 1902): 63.

10. Hamlin Garland, "Ibsen as a Dramatist," *Arena* 2 (June 1890): 82. Garland's article echoed an article that appeared in the previous issue of *Arena* and that concluded that American writers must "find here on native soil the spring whose waters fill us with immortal thirst." See Alfred Hennequinn, "Characteristics of the American Drama," *Arena* 1 (May 1890): 700–709.

11. MacKaye, ed., *Letters to Harriet*, 38–39.

12. Clum, *Ridgely Torrence*, 85.

13. Robert Edmond Jones, "The Future Decorative Art of the Theatre," *Theatre Magazine* 25 (May 1917): 266.

14. "What We Stand For," *Theatre Arts Magazine* 1 (May 1917): 149.

15. Mary Caroline Crawford, *The Romance of the American Theatre*, 389–90, 400.

16. "Eugene Walter—The Insurgent Dramatist," *Theatre Magazine* 8 (October 1908): 272.

17. Franklin Fyles, *The Theatre and Its People* (New York: Doubleday, Page & Company, 1900), 3–13, 99–103.

18. T. R. Sullivan, "A Standard Theatre," *Atlantic Monthly* 75 (May 1895): 686–89.

19. Norman Hapgood, "The Upbuilding of the Theatre," *Atlantic Monthly* 83 (March 1899): 421.

20. Winthrop Ames, "The Ills of the Theatre," *New York Times,* May 7, 1916, sec. 2, p. 8, col. 2.

21. "Struggle of the American Theater with the American Audience," *Current Opinion* 62 (January 1917): 28.

22. W. S. Lockwood, "Shakespeare in the Slums," *Theatre Magazine* 12 (October 1910): 122–26.

23. The most complete study of the syndicate by a contemporaneous investigative journalist is Norman Hapgood, "Theatrical Syndicate," *International Quarterly* 1 (January 1900): 99–122. See also Charles Henry Meltzer, "The Ideal and the Real 'New Theatre,'" *Theatre Magazine* 8 (April 1908): 92–95; and "Break in Truce of Theatre Factions," *New York Times,* February 6, 1915, p. 11, col. 1. For a positive view of the syndicate see John Corbin, "The American Drama," *Form* 34 (July 1902): 63–76, esp. pp. 65–67. For an insightful recent discussion of the syndicate and responses to the syndicate by turn-of-the-century actors, see Benjamin McArthur, *Actors and American Culture, 1880–1920,* 214–20.

24. Hapgood, *The Stage in America,* 6.

25. "The New Theatre," *Theatre Magazine* 4 (December 1908): 144–46; and "The Results of the New Theatre's First Season," *Theatre Magazine* 12 (July 1910): 26–29.

26. "The New Theatre and Some of Its Problems," *Theatre Magazine* 13 (February 1911): 38–40.

27. Mackay, *Little Theatres,* 2–15; "On Little Theatres," *Theatre Magazine* 22 (July 1915): 64–65; and Walter Prichard Eaton, "The Amateur Spirit in the Theatre," *Theatre Magazine* 25 (May 1917): 292, 314.

28. Zona Gale, "The Wisconsin Players," *Theatre Arts Magazine* 1 (May 1917): 128–30; "New Books about the Theatre," *Theatre Arts Magazine* 2 (December 1917): 63–64, a review of Thomas Dickinson's *The Insurgent Theatre* (1917); and B. Russell Herts, "Dramatic Insurgency in Wisconsin," *Theatre Magazine* 17 (January 1913): 27, viii.

29. Mackay, *Little Theatres,* 27–33, 46–53, and 61–63; for two interesting reviews of the Washington Square Players, see James Metcalfe, "Running the Dramatic Gamut," *Life* 68 (October 19, 1916): 626–27; and James Metcalfe, "Of Making Plays There Is No End," *Life* 68 (November 30, 1916): 948–49.

30. Percy MacKaye, *The Playhouse and the Play*; Percy MacKaye, *The Civic Theatre in Relation to the Redemption of Leisure.*

31. "Play Society Is Formed," *New York Times,* May 4, 1916, p. 9, col. 5.

32. Archie Bell, "David Belasco Attacks Stage Tradition," *Theatre Magazine* 13 (May 1911): 164; and MacKaye, *Robert Edmond Jones,* 3.

33. MacKaye, *Robert Edmond Jones,* 4; John Mason Brown, *Upstage: The American Theatre in Performance,* 136–60; and Jacques Copeau, "The New School of Stage Scenery," *Vanity Fair* 8 (June 1917): 36–114.

34. Edgar Lee Masters to Ridgely Torrence, April 1, 1915, RTPA, box 45, folder 8.

35. James Metcalfe, "A Pause for Retrospection," *Life* 68 (October 26, 1916): 721.

36. Wald, *Constituting Americans*. Another recent study that employs the imagery of the mirror and that seeks a different way of thinking about the narrative of American history is Takaki, *A Different Mirror*.

37. Hutchins Hapgood, "Realism of the Ghetto Stage," *Atlantic Monthly* 85 (June 1900): 839–40; Hutchins Hapgood, *Spirit of the Ghetto* (New York: Funk & Wagnalls, 1902).

38. Gregory Mason, "The Theatre of the Ghetto," *Theatre Magazine* 21 (February 1915): 81–83, 91–92; quote is from 81.

39. Ibid., 92.

40. Norman Hapgood, "Upbuilding the Theatre," 419.

41. Mayorga, *Short History*, 200.

42. Richard Burton, *The New American Drama*, 222–23.

43. Theopolis Lewis and Leigh Whipper, "These Are They," in LWPA-MSRC, box 114–1, file 1; and Riis, *Just before Jazz*, 75–79.

44. Walton's public announcement of his appointment and his report of the early conferences with Marc Klaw appeared in "Negro Member of Military Entertainment Service," *New York Age*, December 8, 1917, p. 1, col. 1–2. For a more detailed discussion of the relationship between Klaw and Walton during World War I, see below, chap. 6.

45. James Metcalfe, "A Little Bit of All Sorts," *Life* 68 (September 21, 1916): 495.

46. "The Results of the New Theatre's First Season," *Theatre Magazine* 12 (July 1910): 26–29.

47. Lester A. Walton, " 'The Nigger,' A Great Play," *New York Age*, December 9, 1909, p. 6, col. 1–3.

48. "At the Playhouse," *Theatre Magazine* 11 (January 1910): 2–8.

49. Walton, " 'The Nigger,' A Great Play," *New York Age*, December 9, 1909, p. 6, col. 1–3.

50. "At the Playhouse," *Theatre Magazine* 11 (January 1910): 2–8.

51. "Sheldon and Ames on 'The Age's' Review of 'The Nigger,' " *New York Age*, December 16, 1909, p. 6, col. 2.

52. Johnson, *Black Manhattan*, 205–6. It should also be added that Edward Sheldon served on the board of directors of the Circle for Negro War Relief, Inc., a biracial organization founded during World War I "To help the colored soldier before he goes to the front," "To help the colored soldier at the front," and "To help the family which the colored soldier leaves behind." See an advertisement in *Crisis* 15 (February 1918): 201.

53. Burton, *The New American Drama*, 99–102, 201.

54. Montrose Moses, *The American Dramatist*, 353–56; quoted material is on p. 356.

55. Mayorga, *Short History*, 284–85.

56. Francis Hackett, "After the Play," *New Republic* 10 (April 14, 1917): 325.

57. Ridgely Torrence to Jean Cavinee, May 20, 1936, in RTPA, box 34, folder 8.

58. Lester A. Walton, " 'Pride of Race' Powerful Play," *New York Age*, January 20,

1916, p. 1, col. 7; and p. 6, col. 1–3. Walton included excerpts from the *New York Press, New York Sun, New York World,* and *New York Evening Sun* in his review, from which quoted material is taken.

59. "The New Plays," *Theatre Magazine* 23 (February 1916): 116.

60. Heywood Broun, "Negro Players Score Success in Interesting Bill of Short Plays," *New York Tribune,* April 6, 1917, p. 11, col. 6.

61. "The Negro in American Drama," *Theatre Magazine* 25 (June 1917): 350.

62. Louis Sherwin as quoted in "First Steps Toward a National Negro Theatre," *Current Opinion* 62 (May 1917): 328.

63. Carl Van Vechten, *In the Garret* (New York: Knopf, 1920), 312, 316.

64. Daniel Gregory Mason to Ridgely Torrence, July 25, 1910, RTPA, box 45, folder 6.

65. Daniel Gregory Mason to Ridgely Torrence, June 15, 1914, RTPA, box 45, folder 6. These private comments are echoed by modern-day private expressions that appropriate black language and culture. For an insightful comment on this phenomenon, see Gubar, *Racechanges,* xiii-xxiii.

66. Zona Gale to Mrs. Torrence, August 21, 1914, RTPA, box 38, folder 6.

67. Alfred Grunberg, "Geo. M. Cohan and Percy MacKaye Collaborators," *Theatre Magazine* 22 (December 1915): 298.

68. Burton, *New American Drama,* 61–62; Crawford, *Romance of the Theatre,* 399; and Mayorga, *Short History,* 177–78.

69. Percy MacKaye, *Percy MacKaye: A Sketch of His Life,* 3.

70. Ibid., 3–6.

71. MacKaye, ed., *Letters to Harriet,* 30–31.

72. Ibid., 32; Crawford, *Romance of the American Theatre,* 398.

73. "In the Bandbox," *New York Times,* December 27, 1914, sec. 8, p. 2, col. 7–8.

74. MacKaye, *The Civic Theatre,* 15.

75. Percy MacKaye, *The New Citizenship: A Civic Ritual Devised for Places of Public Meeting in America,* 5.

76. Ibid., 14.

77. Ibid., 6, 89–91.

78. Ibid., 69.

79. Werner Sollors, *Beyond Ethnicity: Consent and Descent in American Culture,* 89–91; Cousins, "Citizenship and Selfhood," 130–39.

80. Cousins, "Citizenship and Selfhood," 66–71.

81. MacKaye, *The New Citizenship,* 8–9.

82. Percy MacKaye, *Caliban, By the Yellow Sands,* xv.

83. "Scenes and Characters in 'Caliban,' the Great Shakespeare Masque," *Theatre Magazine* 24 (July 1916): 9.

84. Levine's *Highbrow/Lowbrow: The Emergence of Cultural Hierarchy in America* introduces this idea of a division between serious and popular art in America at the turn of the century. Quote by MacKaye is from *Caliban,* xviii.

85. MacKaye, *Caliban,* xix-xxi.

86. MacKaye, *Percy MacKaye,* 9.

87. "Plan American Drama Year," *New York Times,* May 25, 1916, p. 11, col. 3; "American Drama Year Is Now Planned for 1917," *New York Times,* May 28, 1916, sec. 2, p. 5, col. 7–8; and "For Community Drama," *New York Times,* June 14, 1916, p. 11, col. 5. The Arthur Hopkins production called *The Happy Ending* received few, if any, positive notices.

88. Quoted in MacKaye, *Community Drama,* 51, 53, 58.

89. "At the Theatre," *Theatre Magazine* 24 (July 1916): 8.

90. Joyce Kilmer, "Percy MacKaye Predicts Communal Theatre," *New York Times,* May 14, 1916, Sunday magazine, pp. 13–14, col. 1–4.

91. "The Follies of 1916," *Life* 68 (July 1916): 69.

92. Seymour Barnard, "Education: A Community Masque," *Masses* 8 (September 1916): 14–15. The *Masses's* attack on MacKaye's masque also questioned the democratic character of the form. "Education" contains the following preface: "The spoken word being essential, according to the authors of masques recently produced, lines are herewith provided. But it is understood that nobody in the audience can hear what is said. Only the few having the price to buy a libretto beforehand and the time to read it, know what is going on. During the performance, late-comers pass between the audience and the scene, and by the time every one is seated, those who have had enough begin to file out. This furnishes the action of the masque." Olivia Torrence to Ridgely Torrence, August 14, 1916, RTPA, box 54, folder 6, tells of having read the parody in *Masses.*

93. "Burlesque Masque with a 'Caliban, Jr.'" *New York Times,* June 1, 1916, p. 9, col. 3.

5. The Talk of the Town

1. Findley Torrence to Ridgely Torrence, April 10, 1917, in RTPA, box 58, folder 3.

2. Lester A. Walton, "Negro Actors Make Debut in Drama at Garden Theatre," *New York Age,* April 12, 1917, p. 1, col. 1–2; 6, col, 1–2. Quoted material is from p. 6, col. 1.

3. Torrence, *Granny Maumee,* 3–7.

4. "Mrs. Hapgood's Colored Players," *New York Evening Post,* April 6, 1917, p. 6, col. 4; " 'Colored Players' at Garden Theatre," *New York Sun,* April 6, 1917, p. 7, col. 1; "Mr. Hornblow Goes to the Play," *Theatre Magazine* 25 (May 1917): 280; Walton, "Negro Actors Make Debut in Drama at Garden Theatre," *New York Age,* April 12, 1917, p. 1, col. 2; and Heywood Broun, "Negro Players Score Success in Interesting Bill of Short Plays," *New York Tribune,* April 6, 1917, p. 11, col. 6.

5. Walton, "Negro Actors Make Debut in Drama at Garden Theatre," *New York Age,* April 12, 1917, p. 1, col. 2.

6. "Mrs. Hapgood's Colored Players," *New York Evening Post,* April 6, 1917, p. 6, col. 3–4.

7. "The Theatre," *New York Evening Sun,* April 6, 1917, in RTPA, box 11, folder 5.

8. Burns Mantle, "Negro Actors Present Unique Programme of Negro Plays at Garden Theatre," *New York Evening Mail,* April 6, 1917, 8, in RTPA, box 11, folder 5.

9. "Mrs. Hapgood's Colored Players," *New York Evening Post,* April 6, 1917; and Rennold Wolf, "Negro Players at the Garden Theatre," *New York Morning Telegraph,* April 1, 1917, sec. 4, p. 1, in RTPA, box 11, folder 5.

10. "Three Negro Plays Played by Negroes," *New York Times,* April 6, 1917, p. 11, col. 1; and "Dramas of Negro Life at Garden," *World,* April 6, 1917, p. 11, col. 1.

11. Broun, "Negro Players Score Success in Interesting Bill of Short Plays," *New York Tribune,* April 6, 1917, p. 11, col. 6.

12. Hornblow, "Mr. Hornblow Goes to the Play," *Theatre Magazine* 25 (May 1917): 280.

13. Walton, "Negro Actors Make Debut in Drama at Garden Theatre," *New York Age,* April 12, 1917, p. 1, col. 2.

14. Louis De Foe, "Dramas of Negro Life at the Garden," *New York World,* April 6, 1917, p. 11, col. 1.

15. " 'Colored Players' at Garden Theatre," *New York Sun,* April 6, 1917, p. 7, col. 1.

16. Johnson, "The Negro and the Drama," *New York Age,* April 19, 1917, p. 4, col. 3.

17. Francis Hackett, "After the Play," *New Republic* 10 (April 14, 1917): 325; Wolf, "Negro Players at the Garden Theatre," *New York Morning Telegraph,* April 1, 1917, sec. 4, p. 1.

18. Hale to Ridgely Torrence, April 29, 1917, in RTPA, box 25, folder 2. The writer of this letter identifies himself by a first name as well as by the last name of "Hale," but the handwriting is impossible to decipher.

19. Olivia Torrence to Torrence Family, n.d., RTPA, box 25, folder 2.

20. Broun, "Negro Players Score Success," *New York Tribune,* April 6, 1917, p. 11, col. 6.

21. Ibid.

22. Djuna Barnes, Interview with the Colored Players, *New York Morning Telegraph,* April 22, 1917, sec. 2, p. 1, in RTPA, box 11, folder 5.

23. Torrence, *Granny Maumee,* 35–38.

24. Walton, "Negro Actors Make Debut in Drama at Garden Theatre," *New York Age,* April 12, 1917, p. 1, col. 1.

25. Johnson, "The Negro and the Drama," *New York Age,* April 19, 1917, p. 4, col. 3.

26. Charles Wood, review of *Three Plays for a Negro Theater* in *Masses* 9 (June 1917), in RTPA, box 11, folder 5.

27. Clayton Hamilton, "Negro Plays," *Vogue* (May 15, 1917); and "Three Negro Plays Played by Negroes," *New York Times,* April 6, 1917, p. 11, col. 1. The use of the same phrase, "a playboy of the southern world," may have been the result of the fact that Woollcott's review predated Hamilton's by about a month. But the appeal of the phrase probably arises from its play on the title of one of John Millington Synge's works—*Playboy of the Western World.* Many critics compared Torrence to this Irish playwright, and as I speculated in an earlier chapter, Torrence's decision to rename his play *The Nest Egg The Rider of Dreams* seems to have been a gesture toward Synge.

28. "Negro Drama Capably Played," *New York American,* April 6, 1917, in RTPA, box 11, folder 5; and Hackett, "After the Play," *New Republic* 10 (April 14, 1917): 325.

29. "Defense by a Dramatist," *New Republic* 10 (April 21, 1917): 356.

30. Walton, "Negro Actors Make Debut in Drama at Garden Theatre," *New York Age,* April 12, 1917, p. 1, col. 1.

31. De Foe, "Dramas of Negro Life," *New York World,* April 6, 1917, p. 11, col. 1.

32. Wood, review of *Three Plays for a Negro Theater,* in *Masses,* 9 (June 1917).

33. "Three Negro Plays Played by Negroes," *New York Times,* April 6, 1917, p. 11, col. 1.

34. "Mrs. Hapgood's Colored Players," *New York Evening Post,* April 6, 1917, p. 6, col. 4.

35. Hornblow, "Mr. Hornblow Goes to the Play," *Theatre Magazine* 25 (May 1917): 280.

36. James Metcalfe, "Some Things That Bloom in the Spring," *Life* 69 (April 19, 1917): 684–85.

37. See H. B. Frissell, "The Negro Players," *Southern Workman* 46 (June 1917): 323; "Negro Dramas Capably Played," *New York American,* April 6, 1917, in RTPA, box 11, folder 5; and Barnes, "Interview with the Colored Players," *New York Morning Telegraph,* April 22, 1917, sec. 2, p. 1, in RTPA, box 11, folder 5.

38. Broun, "Negro Players Score Success," *New York Tribune,* April 6, 1917, p. 11, col. 1.

39. Hornblow, "Mr. Hornblow Goes to the Play," *Theatre Magazine* 25 (May 1917): 280.

40. "Three Negro Plays Played by Negroes," *New York Times,* April 6, 1917, p. 11, col. 1; and Frissell, "The Negro Plays," 324.

41. Broun, "Negro Players Score Success," *New York Tribune,* April 6, 1917, p. 11, col. 6.

42. Walton, "Negro Actors Make Debut in Drama at Garden Theatre," *New York Age,* April 12, 1917, p. 1, col. 2; and Hornblow, "Mr. Hornblow Goes to the Play," *Theatre Magazine* 25 (May 1917): 280.

43. Johnson, "The Negro and the Drama," *New York Age,* April 19, 1917, p. 4, col. 3; Hamilton, "Negro Plays Seen on Stage," *Vogue* (May 15, 1917).

44. "Three Negro Plays Played by Negroes," *New York Times,* April 6, 1917, p. 11, col. 1; " 'Colored Players' at Garden Theatre," *New York Sun,* April 6, 1917, p. 7, col. 1, also quotes Torrence but does not give the author credit.

45. "Mrs. Hapgood's Colored Players," *New York Evening Post,* April 6, 1917, p. 6, col. 3.

46. Keyssar, *The Curtain and the Veil;* Wald, *Constituting Americans.*

47. Zit, "Zit Lauds Work of Negro Players," *New York Evening Journal,* April 25, 1917, in RTPA, box 11, folder 5.

48. "Three Playlets—Thursday Night at the Garden," *New York Times,* April 1, 1917, sec. 8, p. 6, col. 1; and "The Week's Grist," *New York Tribune,* April 1, 1917, part 4, p. 3, col. 3–4.

49. "Music and Drama," *New York Evening Post,* April 3, 1917, 11, col. 4; and "Colored Stock in Garden," *Variety,* March 30, 1917, p. 1, col. 2.

50. Robert C. Benchley, "Can This Be the Native America Drama?" *New York Tribune,* April 1, 1917, part 5, p. 6, col. 5.

51. Quote is from Lester A. Walton, "Things Theatrical," *New York Age,* April 5, 1917, p. 6, col. 1. For earlier announcements and editorials see, "Negroes to Be Seen on Broadway," *New York Age,* March 8, 1917, p. 6, col. 2; Lester A. Walton, "Art for Art's Sake," *New York Age,* March 15, 1917, p. 6, col. 1; and "Theatrical Jottings," *New York Age,* March 29, 1917, p. 6, col. 2.

52. Louis Sherwin, "The Beginnings of the Negro Theatre," *Vanity Fair* (June 1917): 96.

53. Hamilton, "Negro Plays Seen on Stage."

54. Broun, "Negro Players Score Success," *New York Tribune,* April 6, 1917, p. 11, col. 6.

55. "Dramas of Negro Life at Garden," *New York World,* April 6, 1917, p. 11, col. 1; and "Mrs. Hapgood's Colored Players," *New York Evening Post,* April 6, 1917, p. 6, col. 4.

56. Broun, "In Wigs and Wings," *New York Tribune,* May 6, 1917, in RTPA, box 11, folder 5.

57. Hackett, "After the Play," *New Republic* 10 (April 14, 1917): 325.

58. Hornblow, "Mr. Hornblow Goes to the Play," *Theatre Magazine* 25 (May 1917): 280.

59. Mama to "My Dear Children," May 7, 1917, in RTPA, box 58, folder 3.

60. Mary Burrill to Ridgely Torrence, n.d., in RTPA, box 25, file 2.

61. "Negro Drama Capably Played," *New York American,* April 6, 1917, in RTPA, box 11, folder 5.

62. Louis Sherwin, "The Colored Players at the Garden," *New York Globe and Commercial Advertiser,* April 6, 1917, in RTPA, box 11, folder 5.

63. Hackett, "After the Play," *New Republic* 10 (April 14, 1917): 325.

64. "Mrs. Hapgood's Colored Players," *New York Evening Post,* April 6, 1917, p. 6, col. 3.

65. Mantle, "Negro Actors Present Unique Programme," *New York Evening Mail,* April 6, 1917, 8, in RTPA, box 11, folder 5.

66. "Three Negro Plays Played by Negroes," *New York Times,* April 6, 1917, p. 11, col. 1.

67. Broun, "In Wigs and Wings," *New York Tribune,* May 6, 1917, in RTPA, box 11, folder 5.

68. Johnson, "The Colored Players," *New York Evening Post,* Saturday magazine, April 14, 1917, in RTPA, box 11, folder 5.

69. Hapgood, *The Stage in America,* 32.

70. "Bispham on the Bandbox," *New York Times,* January 10, 1915, sec. 7, p. 7, col. 5.

71. Quote is James Metcalfe, "The New Season Struggling Hard," *Life* 68 (September 7, 1916): 404–5; Judson D. Stuart, "The High Cost of Stage Beauty," *Theatre*

Magazine 21 (May 1915): 238–40; "Bispham on the Bandbox," *New York Times,* January 10, 1915, sec. 7, p. 7, col. 5; Norman Hapgood, "The Upbuilding of the Theatre," *Atlantic Monthly* 83 (March 1899): 419–25.

72. McArthur, *Actors and American Culture,* 33–34, 103–4.

73. This passage is quoted in full in Walton, "A Hot-Weather Victim," *New York Age,* August 16, 1917, p. 6, col. 1–2.

74. "Mr. Torrence's Story," *New York Times,* April 15, 1917, sec. 8, p. 6, col. 2–3.

75. Hackett, "After the Play," *New Republic* 10 (April 14, 1917): 325.

76. "The Negro Plays," *Drama League Monthly* 2 (September 1917): 448.

77. "First Step toward a National Negro Theater," *Current Opinion* 62 (May 1917): 328.

78. Sherwin, "The Beginning of the Negro Theatre," *Vanity Fair* (June 1917): 54.

79. Hamilton, "Negro Plays Seen on Stage," *Vogue* (May 15, 1917), in RTPA, box 11, folder 5.

80. Zit, "Zit Lauds Work of Negro Players," *New York Evening Journal,* April 25, 1917, in RTPA, box 11, folder 5.

81. Barnes, "Interview with Colored Players," *New York Morning Telegraph,* April 22, 1917, sec. 2, p. 1, in RTPA, box 11, folder 5.

82. " 'Colored Players' at Garden Theatre," *New York Sun,* April 6, 1917, p. 7, col. 1.

83. "Mrs. Hapgood's Colored Players," *New York Evening Post,* April 6, 1917, p. 6, col. 3.

84. Hamilton, "Negro Plays Seen on Stage," *Vogue* (May 15, 1917), in RTPA, box 11, folder 5.

85. Zona Gale, "The Colored Players and Their Plays," *Theatre Arts Magazine* 1 (May 1917): 139–40.

86. Du Bois, "The New Negro Theatre," *New York Call,* April 22, 1917, RTPA, box 11, folder 5.

87. Johnson, "The Negro and the Drama," *New York Age,* April 19, 1917, p. 4, col. 3–4.

88. Walton, "Negro Actors Make Debut in Drama in Garden Theatre," *New York Age,* April 12, 1917, p. 6, col. 2.

89. Ibid., p. 1, col. 1; and p. 6, col. 1–2.

6. TIMING IS EVERYTHING

1. Arthur S. Link, ed., *The Papers of Woodrow Wilson,* vol. 41 (Princeton: Princeton University Press, 1966), 525.

2. "Wilson at Theatre Cheered by Audience," *New York Tribune,* April 5, 1917, p. 2, col. 5; "President at Theatre Greeted with Cheers," *New York World,* April 5, 1917, p. 1, col. 6; "Society," *Washington Evening Star,* April 5, 1917, p. 8, col. 2, and p. 26, col. 8, for advertisement of *Very Good Eddie* at the Belasco Theatre. Despite the *Evening*

Star's puffery of the play as "the season's greatest hit," the play had not merited a single review in the *New York Times* during its run at the Princess Theatre in New York.

3. Johnson, *Black Manhattan,* 179; and Du Bois, *Gift of the Black Folk,* 310–11.

4. Clum, *Ridgely Torrence,* 111.

5. Freda L. Scott, "Black Drama and the Harlem Renaissance," *Theatre Journal* 37 (December 1985): 429.

6. "Our War Song from the Negro," J. J. L. to the Editor, *New York Tribune,* April 30, 1917, in RTPA, box 11, folder 5.

7. For a good, thorough study of the origins, strategies, and products of the Committee on Public Information, see Stewart Halsey Ross, *Propaganda for War: How the United States Was Conditioned to Fight the Great War of 1914–1918.*

8. Christopher C. Gibbs, *The Great Silent Majority: Missouri's Resistance to World War I*; David P. Thelen, *Robert M. La Follette and the Insurgent Spirit.*

9. George S. Kaufman, "Broadway and Elsewhere," *New York Tribune,* April 8, 1917, part 4, p. 1, col. 4.

10. Lawrence Southerland, "Patriotism on the American Stage," *Theatre Magazine* 25 (May 1917): 288.

11. Clayton Hamilton, "A Demand for Serious Drama," *Theatre Magazine* 26 (October 1917): 191.

12. James Metcalfe, "A Play Suited to the Minute," *Life* 69 (April 12, 1917): 640.

13. Alexander Woollcott, "Out There," *New York Times,* April 8, 1917, sec. 8, p. 5, col. 1, and for information on its appearing at the Globe Theatre, see " 'Out There' Proves Most Appealing," *New York Times,* March 28, 1917, p. 11, col. 1.

14. "Opposition to Negroes in Service Plan," *New York Evening Post,* April 5, 1917, p. 8, col. 1.

15. "Doubt Alleged German Plots among Negroes," *New York Evening Post,* April 5, 1917, p. 9, col. 3.

16. "Negroes Loyal," W. H. Holtzclaw to the Editor, *New York Evening Post,* April 8, 1917, p. 8, col. 6.

17. "Colored Students Hold a Patriotic Rally Wednesday," *Xenia Daily Gazette,* April 5, 1917, p. 4, col. 4–5.

18. Oscar Price, "The Negro Part in the National Crisis," *Xenia Daily Gazette,* April 10, 1917, p. 2, col. 4.

19. "Negro Patriotism," *New York World,* April 8, 1917, editorial sec., p. 2, col. 2–3.

20. David M. Kennedy, *Over Here: The First World War and American Society,* 281–82; Elliott Rudwick, *Race Riot at East St. Louis, July 2, 1917.*

21. James Weldon Johnson, *Along This Way: The Autobiography of James Weldon Johnson,* 320.

22. Ibid. Toni Morrison offers a literary account of the riot and the silent march that followed it in *Jazz* (New York: Penguin Books, 1992), 53–59.

23. Johnson, *Along This Way,* 319–21; Lester A. Walton, "Nearly Ten Thousand Take Part in Big Silent Protest Parade Down Fifth Avenue," *New York Age,* August 2, 1917, p. 1, col. 1–3.

24. Du Bois's position on the war has been the subject of serious scholarly debate. See Mark Ellis, "'Closing Ranks' and 'Seeking Honors': W. E. B. Du Bois in World War I," *Journal of American History* 79 (June 1992): 96–124; David Levering Lewis, *W. E. B. Du Bois: Biography of a Race, 1868–1919,* 553–60; and William Jordan, "'The Damnable Dilemma': African-American Accommodation and Protest during World War I," *Journal of American History* 81 (March 1995): 1562–83.

25. Isaac Fisher, "Do Not Rock the Boat," *Fisk University News* 8 (October 1917): 1–8.

26. A copy of Hubbard's song can be found in the Emmett Scott Papers, National Archives (hereinafter ESPA, NA), Record Group (RG) 107, E96, box 1, file W; and an undated manuscript of Walton's song appears in LAWPA, box 6, file 3. In a letter from Albion Holsey to Emmett Scott, a Walton song is the subject of discussion. Walton had asked Holsey to show the song to Scott and if he approved of it, to have Scott forward the piece to Mr. Weinstein, one of the Army's Camp music directors. No additional correspondence survives to indicate the fate of Walton's song. See Holsey to Scott, September 7, 1918, in ESPA, NA, RG107, E96, box 1, file H.

27. "Pro-Germanism among Negroes," *Messenger* 2 (July 1918): 13.

28. Richard P. Roots to Lindley Garrison, August 26, 1915, NA, RG165, E296, file 8142–2.

29. Memorandum from Brigadier General Joseph Kuhn to Chief of Staff, September 21, 1917, and General Bliss to Secretary of War, August 24, 1917, in NA, RG165, E296, file 8142–17.

30. Ibid.

31. Brigadier General Lytle Brown to Chief of Staff, June 4, 1918, NA, RG165, E296, file 8142–146.

32. Brigadier General Henry Jervey to the Adjutant General, May 6, 1918, NA, RG165, E296, file 8142–145.

33. William H. Davis to Emmett Scott, November 8, 1917, in ESPA, NA, RG107, E96, box 2, file D.

34. Brigadier General Lytle Brown to Chief of Staff, June 4, 1918, NA, RG165, E296, file 8142–146.

35. Brigadier General Henry Jervey to Chief of Staff, July 13, 1918, NA, RG165, E296, file 8142–177.

36. Reports by Chief, Training and Instruction Branch, n.d., NA, RG165, E296, file 10876–217.

37. J. W. Ragsdale to Newton D. Baker, November 15, 1917, ESPA, NA, RG107, E96, box 2, file R.

38. Johnson, *Along This Way,* 321–23.

39. For commentary on Anti-Loafing Law and a copy of H.R. 12567, which was presented on June 26, 1918, see NA, RG165, E296, files 8082–135 and 8082–143; on coast artillery see Colonel William R. Smith to Adjutant General, August 9, 1917, NA, RG165, E296, file 8142–5; and for the white opposition to black guards, see Emmett Scott to Secretary of War, October 30, 1917, in ESPA, NA, RG107, E96, box 2, file— Memos for Secretary of War.

40. "Mrs. Emilie Hapgood's Theatrical Negro Novelty an Experiment That Puzzles and Interests Broadway," *New York Herald,* April 22, 1917, in RTPA, box 11, folder 5.

41. W. E. B. Du Bois to Ridgely Torrence, May 9, 1917, in RTPA, box 25, folder 2.

42. "Mrs. Hapgood Presents Negro Players at Garden," *New York Herald,* April 6, 1917; and Du Bois, "The New Negro Theatre," *New York Call,* April 22, 1917, both in RTPA, box 11, folder 5.

43. "Fosdick Heads Board on Camp Life Morals," *New York Times,* May 6, 1917, sec. 1, p. 3, col. 2; and "Making Vice Unattractive in Soldier's Camps," *New York Times,* May 20, 1917, sec. 6, p. 6, col. 1–4.

44. Minutes of Meeting of Commission on Training Camp Activities, April 27, 1917–February 19, 1919, NA, RG165, E403; quote is from meeting on July 26, 1917.

45. Ibid., meeting of August 24, 1917, and for an example of stationery, see Marc Klaw to Lester Walton, March 5, 1918, in LAWPA, box 6, file 2.

46. See Bulletins of the Department of Dramatic Activities, esp. nos. 3, 4, and 13, in NA, RG165, E405, for commentary on popular shows in the camps.

47. Lieutenant R. C. W., O. R. C., "Let 'George' Do the Entertaining," *Drama League Monthly* 2 (December 1917): 541.

48. Minutes, April 4, 1918, June 18, 1918, and August 21, 1918, NA, RG165, E403.

49. Emmett Scott to Raymond Fosdick, November 14, 1917, NA, RG165, E393, no. 17298. This file also includes a letter from Charles A. Newman to Scott, October 27, 1917, which reports on the neglect of black recreation and to which Scott referred in his letter to Fosdick.

50. "Negro Member of Military Entertainment Service," *New York Age,* December 8, 1917, p. 1, col. 1–2; and "Real Theatres in Every National Army Camp," *New York Times,* November 4, 1917, sec. 7, p. 4, col. 1–4.

51. Lester A. Walton, " 'Smileage,' " *New York Age,* December 22, 1917, p. 6, col. 1–2.

52. Lester A. Walton, "Racial Amity at Camp Upton," *New York Age,* January 19, 1918, 1, col. 1–3.

53. Lester A. Walton to J. J. Mayer, January 22, 1918, NA, RG165, E393, no. 17253.

54. Marc Klaw to Lester A. Walton, March 5, 1918, in LAWPA, box 6, file 2.

55. Marc Klaw to Lester A. Walton, December 24, 1917, in LAWPA, box 16, file 5.

56. Joseph Roycroft to Lester A. Walton, March 9, 1918, in LAWPA, box 6, file 2. Klaw's resignation came about at least in part because of Fosdick's disappointment in his organizing entertainment. In an article in the *New York Review,* it was hinted that Klaw was forced to quit because the National Association of Motion Picture Producers refused to cooperate with him in distributing films to the camps. Fosdick denied the validity of the claim, but after Klaw stepped down from the commission, William Brady of the NAMPP suddenly became involved in the commission's activity. Once Klaw left, Walton had no personal affiliation with any of the commissioners. See Raymond Fosdick to Marc Klaw, March 9, 1918, NA, RG165, E393, no. 26619; "Marc Klaw Was Forced to Resign as Chairman of Army Amusement Board," *New York Review,* March 9, 1918, p. 1, col. 1, in NA, RG165, no. 26626; Hollis Cooley to Raymond Fosdick, March 27, 1918, NA, RG165, E393, no. 28893; and Marc Klaw to Raymond Fosdick, March 11, 1918, NA, RG165, E393, no. 26632.

57. See, for example, Hollis Cooley to Raymond Fosdick, March 27, 1918, NA, RG165, E393, no. 28893.

58. Quote is from Sadie V. Perlman to Lester A. Walton, March 29, 1918, NA, RG165, E393, no. 28918. For Walton's other correspondence regarding articles he published in the *New York Age,* see Lester A. Walton to Sadie V. Perlman, April 4, 1918; and Special Assistant Director of Publicity to Lester A. Walton, April 8, 1918, both in NA, RG165, E393, no. 28892.

59. Hollis Cooley to Malcolm L. McBride, March 14, 1918, NA, RG165, E393, no. 26630.

60. Lester A. Walton to Malcolm L. McBride, June 26, 1918, and McBride to Walton, June 28, 1918, NA, RG165, E393, no. 33502.

61. Lester A. Walton to Malcolm L. McBride, September 12, 1918, NA, RG165, E393, no. 38771.

62. Lester A. Walton to Malcolm McBride, September 21, 1918, NA, RG165, E393, no. 39561.

63. "'The Birth of a Nation,'" *Theatre Magazine* 21 (April 1915): 212. For a fresh interpretation of *Birth of a Nation* in the context of conflict over households in America, see Cousins, "Citizenship and Selfhood," 157–72.

64. Lester A. Walton, "World to Be 'Americanized' by Such Films as 'Birth of a Nation,'" *New York Age,* June 7, 1919, p. 6, col. 1.

65. Lester A. Walton, "Commanding Respect," *New York Age,* May 24, 1917, p. 6, col. 1–2.

66. Lester A. Walton, "Nora Bayes in Song," *New York Age,* May 17, 1917, p. 6, col. 1–2. Bayes redeemed herself in Walton's eyes a year later, when she refused to perform at a cantonment in Spartanburg, South Carolina, because her black maid was refused accommodations there. See Lester A. Walton, "Democracy at Spartanburg, S.C.," *New York Age,* August 10, 1918, p. 6, col. 1–2.

67. Lester A. Walton, "The Flood Refugees," *New York Age,* June 5, 1913, p. 6, col. 1.

68. *The Cheat* is the subject of considerable film criticism. For a good overview of this criticism, see Gina Marchetti, *Romance and the 'Yellow Peril': Race, Sex, and Discursive Strategies in Hollywood Fiction,* 10–32. For a good study of the portrayal of various immigrant groups in early American films, see Kevin Brownlow, *Behind the Mask of Innocence.* For *Silent Menace,* see Lester A. Walton, "The Silent Menace," *New York Age,* March 29, 1917, p. 6, col. 1.

69. Lester A. Walton, "Theatrical Chit-Chat," *New York Age,* July 6, 1918, p. 6, col. 1.

70. Weekly Reports of Camp Dramatic Directors, Camp Grant, December 14, 1918, NA, RG165, E401.

71. *Music in the Camps* 1 (July 6, 1918): 2, Westerman, Camp McArthur [*sic*], NA, RG165, E405.

72. *Music in the Camps,* 1 (August 17, 1917): 9, Westerman, Camp MacArthur, NA, RG165, E405.

73. *Music in the Camps* 1 (June 15, 1918): 4–6, Weinstein, Camp Meade, NA, RG165, E405.

74. *Music in the Camps* 1 (July 27, 1918): 2–3, Westerman, Camp MacArthur, NA, RG165, E405.

75. *Music in the Camps* 1 (July 15, 1918): 2–3, McEwan, Camp Johnson, NA, RG165, E405.

76. *Music in the Camps* 1 (August 10, 1918): 8–9, Weinstein, Camp Meade, NA, RG165, E405.

77. Lester A. Walton, "The Colored Soldier on Screen," *New York Age,* August 24, 1918, p. 6, col. 1–3.

78. Lester A. Walton, "French War Pictures," *New York Age,* October 19, 1918, p. 6, col. 1–2.

79. Badger, *A Life in Ragtime,* 171, and chaps. 12, 13.

80. Ibid., 186.

81. Lester A. Walton, "Our Colored Heroes in the Movies," *New York Age,* November 30, 1918, p. 6, col. 1–2.

82. For the experience of German Americans during World War I, see Frederick C. Luebke, *Bonds of Loyalty: German-Americans and World War I*; Don H. Tolzman, ed., *German-Americans in the World Wars*; Phyllis Keller, *States of Belonging: German-American Intellectuals and the First World War*; Nell Painter, *Standing at Armageddon,* 334–35. For information about Walter Rauschenbusch, a German American theologian who became a target of anti-Germanism, see Susan Curtis, *A Consuming Faith: The Social Gospel and Modern American Culture,* 113. The little boy was one of my uncles. The story was told to me by my grandmother, not for the perspective of a child on German Americans, but because she thought it was cute that he said " 'iable" instead of "liable."

83. " 'Rhythmic Crisis' Now Sweeping over World," *New York Times,* April 15, 1917, Sunday magazine, p. 14.

84. Bourne to editor of *New York Tribune,* April 10, 1917, cited in Clum, *Ridgely Torrence,* 111. Perhaps the Negro Players ad-libbed the line quoted by Bourne, but it does not appear in the published text of *Simon, the Cyrenian.*

85. Advertisement in *New York Times,* April 15, 1917, sec. 8, p. 6, col. 7.

86. Ridgely Torrence to his family, February 23, 1917, RTPA, box 25, folder 1.

87. Zona Gale to Ridgely Torrence, April 1917, RTPA, box 38, folder 6.

88. Robert Westbrook, *John Dewey and American Democracy* (Ithaca: Cornell University Press, 1991), chap. 7.

89. Ridgely Torrence to Findley Torrence, April 15, 1917, RTPA, box 25, folder 2.

90. Mama to "My Dear Children," May 7, 1917, RTPA, box 58, folder 3.

91. See Torrence's autobiographical statement in RTPA, box 9, folder 1; Ridgely Torrence to Jean Cavinee, May 20, 1936, RTPA, box 34, folder 8; and "Notes on the Negro Theatre," RTPA, box 9, folder 8.

92. Ridgely Torrence to Findley Torrence, April 15, 1917, RTPA, box 25, folder 2.

93. Ridgely Torrence to his family, April 20, 1917, RTPA, box 25, folder 2.

94. Grace Ellery Channing-Stetson to Ridgely Torrence, April 17, 1917 (?), RTPA, box 34, folder 8. Although the date is difficult to read, the timing of the letter and internal evidence suggest that it was written in 1917.

95. "Militant Pacifists," *New York World,* April 3, 1917, p. 10, col. 3.

96. James Metcalfe, "Another Dramatization of DuMaurier," *Life* 69 (May 3, 1917): 773.

97. Ridgely Torrence to his family, June 1, 1917, RTPA, box 25, folder 2. Other letters in this particular file contain information about friends of Torrence harassed for their pacifist sentiments and activism.

7. FORGETTING TO REMEMBER

1. Alain Locke, ed., *Plays of Negro Life: A Source Book of Native American Drama,* introduction, 409–23.

2. Even the most recent study of the American stage, Ronald H. Wainscott's *The Emergence of the Modern American Theater, 1914–1929,* makes only passing reference to Torrence without noting the significance of the production of the three plays. Similarly, Ann Douglas calls Eugene O'Neill's decision to use black actors for his race plays in the 1920s "revolutionary," downplaying the fact that the "revolution" had begun several years earlier. See Douglas, *Terrible Honesty,* 80.

3. "Theatrical Notes," *New York Times,* May 7, 1917, RTPA, box 11, folder 5. A similar announcement appeared later in the year in a newly established radical African American periodical. See Lovett Fort-Whiteman, "Announcement," *Messenger* 1 (November 1917): 29.

4. Olivia Torrence to Torrence family, n.d., RTPA, box 25, folder 2.

5. Ridgely Torrence to his family, May 18, 1917, RTPA, box 25, folder 2.

6. "Lafayette Theatre," *New York Age,* May 24, 1917, p. 6, col. 3–4; Lester A. Walton to Jesse Shipp, October 5, 1920, ACC-MSRC, box 22–1, file 1; Johnson, *Black Manhattan,* 219–22, 209, 217.

7. Barnes, "Interview with the Colored Players," *New York Morning Telegraph,* April 22, 1917, sec. 2, p. 1, in RTPA, box 11, folder 5.

8. George Cram Cook to Ridgely Torrence, n.d., RTPA, box 35, folder 2.

9. Opal Cooper to Ridgely Torrence, May 15, 1919, RTPA, box 35, folder 2. Cooper mentions in this letter that he had written two other letters to the playwright, but they do not appear in Torrence's correspondence file.

10. Opal Cooper to Ridgely Torrence, n.d., RTPA, box 35, folder 2.

11. Opal Cooper to Ridgely Torrence, November 15, 1939, RTPA, box 35, folder 2.

12. Opal Cooper to Ridgely Torrence, May 5, 1940, RTPA, box 35, folder 2.

13. Lester A. Walton, "Juvenile Actors Captivate Broadway," *New York Age,* September 28, 1918, p. 6, col. 1.

14. Lester A. Walton, " 'Happy' Rhone in Broadway Cast," *New York Age,* March 22, 1919, p. 6, col. 1–2.

15. Douglas, *Terrible Honesty,* 80; and Kenneth Macgowan, "The New Season," *Theatre Arts Magazine* 4 (October 1920): 267–73, quote is from pp. 271–72.

16. Lester A. Walton, "Inconsistencies of Race Prejudice Are Pointed Out in 'Justice,'" *New York Age,* December 11, 1920, p. 6, col. 1.

17. Anne Wolter to Thomas Montgomery Gregory, June 25, 1923, TMGPA-MSRC, box 37–2, file 53.

18. Lester A. Walton, "Gala Week at the Lafayette Theatre," *New York Age,* March 2, 1918, p. 6, col. 2.

19. Lester A. Walton, " 'The Children of the Sun' Most Pretentious of All Smarter Set Offerings," *New York Age,* September 27, 1919, p. 6, col. 1; Lester A. Walton, " 'Jasper Lee's Revenge' Is a Negro Classic," *New York Age,* March 20, 1920, p. 6, col. 1.

20. Johnson, *Black Manhattan,* 181–91; Thomas Montgomery Gregory, "Significant and Historic Programs of Plays in the History of the American Theatre," TMGPA-MSRC, box 37–4, file 128; and James William Henderson to Thomas Montgomery Gregory, January 4, 1923, TMGPA-MSRC, box 37–2, file 50.

21. Lester A. Walton, "Dramatic Students Appear in Private Rehearsal with Success," *New York Age,* May 10, 1919, p. 6, col. 1–2.

22. Douglas, *Terrible Honesty,* 5.

23. Ibid., 85.

24. Ibid., 87.

25. One need only consider the typical chronology of the history of American drama to appreciate O'Neill's importance. Historical studies of theater before O'Neill focus on theaters, actors, particular productions of importance and their sociological (not artistic) significance. From O'Neill's day to the present, so the standard argument goes, one can begin to discuss artistic merit and a national drama. For an excellent discussion of the rapid consolidation of that chronology, see Susan Harris Smith, *American Drama: The Bastard Art,* esp. chap. 3.

26. My summary of O'Neill's play is based on a version published during the run on Broadway. Eugene G. O'Neill, "The Emperor Jones," *Theatre Arts Magazine* 5 (January 1921): 29–59, quote on p. 34.

27. Ibid., 59.

28. Mayorga, *Short History,* 324.

29. O'Neill, "The Emperor Jones," 36.

30. Ibid., 36, 37, 41.

31. Ibid., 37.

32. Douglas, *Terrible Honesty,* 86–87. According to Douglas, by 1926 Gilpin was running an elevator, a job he left to portray Jones. A year later he lost a Hollywood job because he "refused to play Tom (of *Uncle Tom's Cabin*) as a sentimental and harmless darky." Gilpin died in obscurity in 1930.

33. W. A. L., "A Negro Genius in Greenwich Village," *Theatre Magazine* 33 (January 1921): 8.

34. Alexander Woollcott, "The New O'Neill Play," *New York Times,* November 7, 1920, sec. 7, p. 1, col. 1.

35. Kenneth Macgowan, "The New Season," *Theatre Arts Magazine* 5 (January 1921): 5–7. This issue also published O'Neill's drama in its entirety.

36. "Not as Others Are, but Still Worth While," *Outlook* 126 (December 22, 1920): 711.

37. " 'The Emperor Jones' Is Hailed as a Great Play," *Current Opinion* 70 (January 1921): 55.

38. Broun is quoted by James Weldon Johnson, "A Great Play and a Great Actor," *New York Age*, November 13, 1920, p. 4, col. 4; and Woollcott, "The New O'Neill Play," *New York Times*, November 7, 1920, sec. 7, p. 1, col. 1.

39. W. A. L., "A Negro Genius in Greenwich Village," 8.

40. Macgowan, "The New Season," 7. Macgowan also misidentified Robert Edmond Jones as the producer rather than the director.

41. James Weldon Johnson, "A Great Play and a Great Actor," *New York Age*, November 13, 1920, p. 4, col. 4.

42. "Drama League Dinner Causes Discussion of the Color Line," *New York Age*, February 26, 1921, p. 1, col. 3.

43. James Weldon Johnson, "The Close of the Gilpin Incident," *New York Age*, March 12, 1921, p. 4, col. 3–4.

44. "Drama League Dinner Causes Discussion of the Color Line," *New York Age*, February 26, 1921, p. 6, col. 1. Jones's comment is attributed to a quote from the *New York World*, February 23, 1921.

45. Johnson, "The Close of the Gilpin Incident, *New York Age*, March 12, 1921, p. 4, col. 4. Johnson quotes from the *New York Tribune*'s report.

46. Ibid.

47. Lester A. Walton, "Want Drama and Music at Lafayette; Reason Management Changed Policy," *New York Age*, February 12, 1921, p. 6, col. 1–2.

48. "Charles Gilpin and the Drama League," *Messenger* 3 (March 1921): 203–4. Nowhere in this attack on Gilpin did the author comment on the substance of the plays. The basis for his or her anger with Gilpin was the actor's readiness to avoid the banquet so as not to ruffle the feathers of racists.

49. This passage is quoted in Abiodun Jeyifous, "Black Critics on Black Theatre in America," in Errol Hill, ed., *The Theater of Black Americans*, 2:132. Hughes's portrayal of the crowd's reaction to the O'Neill drama should not obscure the fact that it did set a standard for African American performance. Paul Robeson later played Brutus Jones, and at least one critic saw this role as the single most important standard against which to judge black (male) histrionic talent. See Gwendolyn Bennett, "The Emperor Jones," *Opportunity* 8 (September 1930): 270–71.

Selected Bibliography

Primary Sources

THE ARGUMENT ADVANCED in this book rests largely on primary print and archival sources, for which citations are provided in the notes. Rather than listing newspaper and periodical titles and naming important repositories I visited, I offer this brief bibliographic essay to explain which sources proved most helpful for particular dimensions of the project and where those sources can be found.

The greatest challenge posed by this study of the 1917 production of Torrence's plays was to find out about the performers who brought them to life. While I could rely on a great deal of excellent scholarship on the world of African American entertainment in the first two decades of the twentieth century to get a handle on the development of theatrical institutions and companies, I was unable to learn much about the experience of these particular actors. To piece together their careers before 1917, I pursued three different strategies. The first was to read the drama page of the *New York Age* from Lester A. Walton's first appearance in 1908 until the early 1920s. He occasionally wrote on actors like Jesse Shipp and Alex Rogers in his feature column, but tucked away under such headings as "Theatrical Jottings" and "Theatrical Comment," I discovered bits of information on a majority of the actors in the show. In addition to this intensive reading of the newspaper, I consulted encyclopedic studies of black performers by Eileen Southern, Henry T. Sampson, and Paul Carter Harrison and Bert Andrews, as well as Bart Kennett's *Colored Actors' Union Theatrical Guide*, published in 1925, and James Weldon Johnson's *Black Manhattan*. The third main body of sources for black theater appears in several archival collections. The Lester A. Walton Papers, housed at the Schomburg Center for Research in Black Culture, contains a few documents from Walton's careers as a lyricist, songwriter, and theater manager, a fairly extensive collection of newspaper clippings pertaining to theater in Harlem, and a rich personal correspondence from the 1910s to the 1960s, which can be mined for specific information about the theater, early African American films, and Walton's efforts to tap into radio and television in the 1950s. The Moorland-Spingarn Research Center at Howard University in Washington, D. C., contains several collections rich in sources on black theater. The Leigh Whipper Papers focuses mostly on that actor's life and career, but it also includes artifacts from pre–1920s theater in Harlem and an essay written with Theopolis Lewis that looked back on conditions for black actors in the early 1900s. The Anne Cooke Collection of Theater Materials includes a few items of interest. The Thomas Montgomery Gregory Papers, which include the writings and correspondence of the noted Howard professor of drama, contain valuable correspondence between Gregory and various writers, performers, and artists associated with the New Movement. It was this collection more than the others at Howard that shaped my thinking, because it became apparent that no concerted effort before 1920 emerged to forge links between Gregory's activities in Washington and the theatrical avant garde, largely in New York. Five letters from Opal Cooper to Ridgely Torrence, included in the extensive Ridgely Torrence Papers in the Manuscript Division of the Firestone Library at Princeton University, offered important insight into the post–1917 career of one of the most celebrated members of the cast.

The Torrence papers, not unexpectedly, proved invaluable for learning more about the playwright and his circle of friends. Of equal value, however, was the large collection of reviews of the production clipped from newspapers and magazines in 1917. By the time I reached this collection, I already had encountered a great deal of the critical response from reading the *New York Times, Theatre Magazine, Theatre Arts Magazine, Crisis, New York Age, Current Opinion,* and the *New Republic* in Purdue's HSSE and Undergraduate Libraries, the *New York Sun, World, Evening Post,* and *Tribune* in the newspaper archive at Columbia University's Butler Library, and *Life* at the New York Public Library. The Torrence papers added reviews from newspapers to which I would not have had ready access. Moreover, reading them as a set helped recreate a sense of the time's ongoing debate and excitement. I rounded out the research on Torrence by visiting his hometown of Xenia, Ohio, whose public library has an extraordinary collection of local documents in the Greene County Room—newspapers, business directories, county histories, reminiscences, sociological surveys, and monographic literature—from the nineteenth and early twentieth centuries. After my visit to Xenia, I became even more convinced that there was a great deal about his boyhood home to which Torrence turned both a blind eye and a deaf ear.

The final major archival source for this project were papers relating to the Commission on Training Camp Activities during World War I, housed at the National Archives. Two record groups contained important sources: RG107, in which one finds the papers of Emmett J. Scott, special assistant to the secretary of war, and RG165, which is the umbrella collection of all material pertaining to the war. Because race mattered in 1917 and earlier, documents involving African Americans are clustered together within RG165, and this classification permits the researcher to eavesdrop on conversations about race, soldiering, and citizenship at the highest levels of the military. The Commission on Training Camp Activities left a rich body of correspondence as well as a bound copy of the minutes of their meetings and reports from the camp music and theater directors, who reported to them. At several important junctures, I filled in some missing pieces of the story of Lester A. Walton's involvement in the commission's activities by consulting Walton's correspondence in his papers at the Schomburg.

These constitute the bulk of the primary sources consulted for this project. Below I have listed the theses, dissertations, articles, and books as secondary sources on which this study draws. I have included published works by Percy MacKaye, Ridgely Torrence, Norman and Hutchins Hapgood, James Weldon Johnson, and W. E. B. Du Bois. While at certain points in the text these works were analyzed as primary sources, I think they stand on their own as important secondary works on the plays, players, sponsors, and the theatrical avant garde of the 1910s.

SECONDARY SOURCES

Dissertations and Theses

Cousins, Robert. "Citizenship and Selfhood: Negotiating Narratives of National and Personal Identity, 1900–1920." Ph.D. diss., Purdue University, 1997.

King, Thomas Lawrence. "Black Settlement in Xenia, Ohio, 1850–1880: A Historical Geography." M.A. thesis, University of Colorado, 1981.

Young, Artee F. "Lester A. Walton: Black Theatre Critic." Ph.D. diss., University of Michigan, 1980.

Articles

Bender, Thomas. "Wholes and Parts: The Need for Synthesis in American History." *Journal of American History* 73 (June 1986): 120–36.

Dormon, James H. "Shaping the Popular Image of Post-Reconstruction American Blacks: The 'Coon Song' Phenomenon of the Gilded Age." *American Quarterly* 40 (December 1988): 450–71.

Ellis, Mark. " 'Closing Ranks' and 'Seeking Honors': W. E. B. Du Bois in World War I." *Journal of American History* 79 (June 1992): 96–124.

Fishkin, Shelley Fisher. "Interrogating 'Whiteness,' Complicating 'Blackness': Remapping American Culture." *American Quarterly* 47 (September 1995): 428–66.

Henretta, James. "Social History as Lived and Written." *American Historical Review* 84 (December 1979): 1293–1321.

Jordan, William. " 'The Damnable Dilemma': African-American Accommodation and Protest during World War I." *Journal of American History* 81 (March 1995): 1562–83.

Lears, T. J. Jackson. "The Concept of Cultural Hegemony: Problems and Possibilities." *American Historical Review* 90 (June 1985): 567–93.

Lipsitz, George. "The Possessive Investment in Whiteness: Racialized Social Democracy and the 'White' Problem in American Studies." *American Quarterly* 47 (September 1995): 369–87.

Rogin, Michael. "Making America Home: Racial Masquerade and Ethnic Assimilation in the Transition to Talking Pictures." *Journal of American History* 79 (December 1992): 1050–77.

Stephens, Judith L. "Black Drama and the Harlem Renaissance." *Theatre Journal* 37 (December 1985): 426–39.

Toews, John. "Intellectual History after the Linguistic Turn." *American Historical Review* 92 (October 1987): 879–907.

Books

Anderson, Jervis. *This Was Harlem 1900–1950*. New York: Farrar, Straus & Giroux, 1981.

Andrews, Bert, and Paul Carter Harrison. *In the Shadow of the Great White Way: Images from the Black Theatre*. New York: Thunder's Mouth Press, 1989.

Badger, Reid. *James Reese Europe: A Life in Ragtime*. New York: Oxford University Press, 1995.

Bigsby, C. W. E. *A Critical Introduction to Twentieth Century American Drama*. New York: Cambridge University Press, 1982.

Bond, Frederick W. *The Negro and the Drama*. College Park, Md.: McGrath Publishing, 1969.

Bonin, Jane F. *Major Themes in Prize-Winning American Drama.* Metuchen, N.J.: Scarecrow Press, 1975.

Brown, John Mason. *Upstage: The American Theatre in Performance.* Port Washington, N.Y.: Kennikat Press, 1930.

Brownlow, Kevin. *Behind the Mask of Innocence.* New York: Alfred A. Knopf, 1990.

Burton, Richard. *The New American Drama.* New York: Thomas Y. Crowell, 1913.

Charters, Ann. *Nobody: The Story of Bert Williams.* New York: Macmillan, 1970.

Clum, John M. *Ridgely Torrence.* New York: Twayne Publishers, 1972.

Conkin, Paul, and John Higham, eds. *New Directions in American Intellectual History.* Baltimore: Johns Hopkins University Press, 1979.

Crawford, Mary Caroline. *The Romance of the American Theatre.* Boston: Little, Brown, 1913.

Curtis, Susan. *A Consuming Faith: The Social Gospel and Modern American Culture.* Baltimore: Johns Hopkins University Press, 1991.

————. *Dancing to a Black Man's Tune: A Life of Scott Joplin.* Columbia: University of Missouri Press, 1994.

Douglas, Ann. *Terrible Honesty: Mongrel Manhattan in the 1920s.* New York: Farrar, Straus & Giroux, 1995.

Downes, Alan S., ed. *American Drama.* New York: Thomas Y. Crowell, 1960.

Du Bois, W. E. B. *The Gift of Black Folk: The Negroes in the Making of America.* New York: AMS Press, 1971.

Dyer, Richard. *The Matter of Images: Essays on Representation.* London: Routledge, 1993.

Erenberg, Lewis. *Steppin' Out: New York Night Life and the Transformation of American Culture, 1890–1930.* Chicago: University of Chicago Press, 1981.

Gagey, Edmond McAdoo. *Revolution in American Drama.* New York: Columbia University Press, 1947.

Gibbs, Christopher C. *The Great Silent Majority: Missouri's Resistance to World War I.* Columbia: University of Missouri Press, 1988.

Gubar, Susan. *Racechanges: White Skin, Black Mask in American Culture.* New York: Oxford University Press, 1997.

Gutman, Herbert. *Work, Culture and Society in Industrializing America.* New York: Alfred A. Knopf, 1976.

Hagedorn, Hermann. *Edwin Arlington Robinson, A Biography.* New York: Macmillan, 1938.

Hapgood, Hutchins. *A Victorian in the Modern World.* New York: Harcourt, Brace, 1939.

Hapgood, Norman. *The Changing Years*. New York: Farrar & Rinehart, 1930.

————. *The Stage in America, 1897–1900*. New York: Macmillan, 1901.

Haskins, James. *Black Theatre in America*. New York: Thomas Y. Crowell, 1982.

Hill, Errol, ed. *The Theatre of Black Americans*. 2 vols. Englewood Cliffs, N.J.: Prentice-Hall, 1980.

Hornblow, Arthur. *A History of the Theatre in America: From Its Beginnings to the Present Time*. Philadelphia: J. B. Lippincott, 1919.

Hutton, Laurence. *Curiosities of the American Stage*. New York: Harper & Bros., 1891.

Isaacs, Edith J. R. *The Negro in the American Theatre*. College Park, Md.: McGrath Publishing, 1947.

Johnson, James Weldon. *Along This Way: The Autobiography of James Weldon Johnson*. New York: Penguin Books, 1990.

————. *Black Manhattan*. New York: Da Capo Press, 1991.

Joiner, William A. *A Half-Century of the Negro in Ohio*. Wilberforce, Ohio: Smith Advertising, 1915.

Kasson, John F. *Amusing the Million: Coney Island at the Turn of the Century*. New York: Hill & Wang, 1978.

Keller, Phyllis. *States of Belonging: German-American Intellectuals and the First World War*. Cambridge: Harvard University Press, 1979.

Kennedy, David M. *Over Here: The First World War and American Society*. New York: Oxford University Press, 1980.

Keyssar, Helene. *The Curtain and the Veil: Strategies in Black Drama*. New York: Burt Franklin, 1981.

Kruger, Loren. *The National Stage: Theatre and Cultural Legitimation in England, France, and America*. Chicago: University of Chicago Press, 1992.

Lears, T. J. Jackson. *No Place of Grace: Antimodernism and the Transformation of American Culture, 1880–1920*. New York: Pantheon Books, 1981.

Lears, T. J. Jackson, and Richard Wightman Fox, eds. *The Culture of Consumption: Critical Essays in American History, 1880–1980*. New York: Pantheon Books, 1983.

————. *The Power of Culture: Critical Essays in American History*. Chicago: University of Chicago Press, 1993.

Levine, Lawrence W. *Highbrow/Lowbrow: The Emergence of Cultural Hierarchy in America*. Cambridge: Harvard University Press, 1988.

Levy, Eugene. *James Weldon Johnson: Black Leader, Black Voice*. Chicago: University of Chicago Press, 1973.

Lewis, David Levering. *W. E. B. Du Bois: Biography of a Race, 1868–1919*. New York: Random House, 1993.

Locke, Alain, ed. *Plays of Negro Life: A Source Book of Native American Drama*. New York: Harper & Row, 1927.

Lott, Eric. *Love and Theft: Blackface Minstrelsy and the American Working Class*. New York: Oxford University Press, 1993.

Luebke, Frederick C. *Bonds of Loyalty: German-Americans and World War I*. Dekalb: Northern Illinois University Press, 1974.

McArthur, Benjamin. *Actors and American Culture, 1880–1920*. Philadelphia: Temple University Press, 1984.

McGinnis, Frederick A. *A History and an Interpretation of Wilberforce University*. Blanchester, Ohio: Brown Publishing, 1941.

Mackay, Constance D'Arcy. *The Little Theatre in the United States*. New York: Henry Holt, 1917.

MacKaye, Percy. *Caliban, By the Yellow Sands*. Garden City, N.Y.: Doubleday, Page, 1916.

———. *The Civic Theatre in Relation to the Redemption of Leisure*. New York: Mitchell Kennerley, 1912.

———. *The New Citizenship: A Civic Ritual Devised for Places of Public Meeting in America*. New York: Macmillan, 1915.

———. *Percy MacKaye: A Sketch of His Life*. Reprinted from the 25th Anniversary Report of the Class of 1897, Harvard College, 1922.

———. *The Playhouse and the Play*. New York: Macmillan, 1909.

———. *Robert Edmond Jones: A Comment on His Work in the Theatre*. N.p., 1920.

MacKaye, Percy, ed. *Letters to Harriet by William Vaughn Moody*. Boston: Houghton Mifflin, 1935.

Marcaccio, Michael D. *The Hapgoods: Three Earnest Brothers*. Charlottesville: University Press of Virginia, 1977.

Marchetti, Gina. *Romance and the 'Yellow Peril': Race, Sex, and Discursive Strategies in Hollywood Fiction*. Berkeley: University of California Press, 1993.

Matthews, Brander. *Rip Van Winkle Goes to the Play and Other Essays on Plays and Players*. New York: Charles Scribner's Sons, 1926.

May, Lary. *Screening Out the Past: The Birth of Mass Culture and the Motion Picture Industry*. New York: Oxford University Press, 1980.

Mayorga, Margaret. *A Short History of the American Theatre: Commentaries on Plays Prior to 1920*. New York: Dodd, Mead, 1932.

Meserve, Walter. *An Outline of American Drama*. Totowa, N.J.: Littlefield, Adams, 1965.

Moses, Montrose. *The American Dramatist*. Boston: Little, Brown, 1925.

Painter, Nell Irvin. *Standing at Armageddon: The United States, 1877–1919*. New York: W. W. Norton, 1989.

Riis, Thomas. *Just before Jazz: Black Musical Theatre in New York, 1890–1915.* Washington: Smithsonian Institution Press, 1989.

Roediger, David R. *Towards the Abolition of Whiteness.* London: Verso Press, 1994.

———. *The Wages of Whiteness: Race and the Making of the American Working Class.* London: Verso Press, 1991.

Ross, Stewart Halsey. *Propaganda for War: How the United States Was Conditioned to Fight the Great War of 1914–1918.* Jefferson, N.C.: McFarland, 1996.

Rowland, Mabel. *Bert Williams, Son of Laughter; A Symposium Tribute to the Man and to His Work.* New York: Negro Universities Press, 1969.

Rudwick, Elliott. *Race Riot at East St. Louis, July 2, 1917.* Carbondale: Southern Illinois University Press, 1964.

Sampson, Henry T. *Blacks in Blackface: A Source Book on Early Black Musical Shows.* Metuchen, N.J.: Scarecrow Press, 1980.

———. *The Ghost Walks: A Chronological History of Blacks in Show Business, 1865–1910.* Metuchen, N.J.: Scarecrow Press, 1988.

Smith, Eric Lidell. *Bert Williams: A Biography of the Pioneer Black Comedian.* Jefferson, N.C.: McFarland, 1992.

Smith, Susan Harris. *American Drama: The Bastard Art.* New York: Cambridge University Press, 1997.

Snyder, Robert W. *The Voice of the City: Vaudeville and Popular Culture in New York.* New York: Oxford University Press, 1989.

Sollors, Werner. *Beyond Ethnicity: Consent and Descent in American Culture.* New York: Oxford University Press, 1986.

Southern, Eileen, ed. *Biographical Dictionary of Afro-American and African Musicians.* Westport, Conn.: Greenwood Press, 1982.

Takaki, Ronald. *A Different Mirror: A History of Multicultural America.* Boston: Little, Brown, 1993.

Taubman, Howard. *The Making of the American Theatre.* New York: Howard McCann, 1965.

Thelen, David P. *The New Citizenship: Origins of Progressivism in Wisconsin, 1885–1900.* Columbia: University of Missouri Press, 1972.

———. *Robert M. La Follette and the Insurgent Spirit.* Boston: Little, Brown, 1977.

Tolzman, Don H., ed. *German-Americans in the World Wars.* Muenchen, Germany: K. G. Saur, 1995.

Torrence, Ridgely. *Granny Maumee, The Rider of Dreams, Simon, the Cyrenian: Plays for a Negro Theater.* New York: Macmillan, 1917.

Trachtenberg, Alan. *The Incorporation of America: Culture and Society in the Gilded Age.* New York: Hill & Wang, 1982.

Turner, Victor. *The Anthropology of Performance*. New York: PAJ Publications, 1988.

Wainscott, Ronald H. *The Emergence of the Modern American Theater, 1914–1929*. New Haven: Yale University Press, 1997.

Wald, Priscilla. *Constituting Americans: Cultural Anxiety and Narrative Form*. Durham, N.C.: Duke University Press, 1995.

Westbrook, Robert. *John Dewey and American Democracy*. Ithaca: Cornell University Press, 1991.

Wiebe, Robert. *The Search for Order, 1877–1920*. New York: Hill & Wang, 1967.

Wilson, Garff B. *Three Hundred Years of American Drama and Theatre*. Englewood Cliffs, N.J.: Prentice-Hall, 1965.

Woll, Allen. *Black Musical Theatre: From Coontown to Dreamgirls*. Baton Rouge: Louisiana State University Press, 1989.

INDEX